HUMAN SECURITY AND INTERNATIONAL LAW

The concept of 'human security' has influenced discourse and practice and has been the subject of vigorous debate. Despite its relevance to central questions of international law, human security has until recently received little attention from international lawyers. This book has two related goals: to evaluate human security as a concept that could be used in the analysis of international law, and to determine what insights about a human security approach might be gained by considering it from the perspective of international law. The first part of the book examines the evolution and meanings of the concept and its links with existing theories and principles of international law. The second part explores the ways in which human security has been and could be used in relation to the diverse topics of humanitarian intervention, internally displaced persons, small arms control, and global public health. The analysis sheds new light on debates about the concept's potential and limitations.

Studies in International Law: Volume 14

Studies in International Law

Human Security and International Law

Prospects and Problems

Barbara von Tigerstrom

·HART·
PUBLISHING

OXFORD AND PORTLAND, OREGON
2007

Published in North America (US and Canada) by
Hart Publishing
c/o International Specialized Book Services
920 NE 58th Avenue, Suite 300
Portland, OR 97213-3786
USA
Tel: +1-503-287-3093 or toll-free: (1)-800-944-6190
Fax: +1 503 280 8832
E-mail: orders@isbs.com
Website: www.isbs.com

Hart Publishing, 16C Worcester Place, Oxford, OX1 2JW
Telephone: +44 (0)1865 517530 Fax: +44(0)1865 510710
E-mail: mail@hartpub.co.uk
Website: http://www.hartpub.co.uk

British Library Cataloguing in Publication Data
Data Available

ISBN: 978-1-84113-610-3

Typeset by Hope Services Ltd, Abingdon
Printed and bound in Great Britain by
Lightning Source UK Ltd

Acknowledgements

This book began as my dissertation for my PhD at the University of Cambridge Faculty of Law, and I have accumulated many debts both during my doctoral work and since. I could not have hoped for a better supervisor for this project than Dr Susan Marks, to whom I am extremely grateful for her unfailing support and encouragement, as much as for her diligent and thoughtful critiques of my work.

I was also privileged to have as examiners for the PhD Professor James Crawford and Dr Matthew Craven, both of whom provided comments which have been invaluable in undertaking revisions for this publication.

It would not have been possible to undertake the PhD without the financial support provided by the following: Social Sciences and Humanities Research Council (Canada), Government of Alberta, Alberta Law Society, Government of Canada, Cambridge Commonwealth Trust, and British Federation of Women Graduates.

I would also like to thank the Academic Council on the United Nations System (ACUNS) for organising and making it possible for me to attend the 2004 ACUNS/ASIL Summer Workshop on Global Governance and Human Security, as well as the workshop organisers, directors, and other participants, especially Elizabeth Riddell-Dixon (University of Western Ontario), who provided useful feedback on a paper which was an early precursor of chapter seven of this book, and Kitty Arambulo (Office of the UN High Commissioner for Human Rights), whose discussions of the relationship between human security and human rights helped me to clarify my thinking on this difficult point. Thanks are also due to Christopher McDougall and Kumanan Wilson (University of Toronto) for useful exchanges about the International Health Regulations and for inviting me to their symposium (supported by the Public Health Agency of Canada) on 'The State of National Governance Relative to the New International Health Regulations', held in Ottawa in November 2006.

At every stage of this project, I have been fortunate to be surrounded by supportive friends and colleagues, to whom I am grateful for their patience and insight in discussing my work. Special thanks go to Caroline Foster (University of Auckland) and Linda Reif (University of Alberta) for reading and commenting on drafts of the dissertation, and the members of the International Law Group at the University of Canterbury (especially Alex Conte, Neil Boister, and Geoff Leane). The University of Canterbury School of Law and University of Saskatchewan College of Law have provided productive and pleasant working environments and support for research assistance. My student research assistants, Danie Beukman (University of Canterbury), Zoe Oxaal, Jennifer Souter, Jody Busch, and Erin Schroh (University of Saskatchewan), provided excellent research and editing assistance.

Finally, I would like to thank my family, and to dedicate this book to my parents, whose love and support have made anything seem possible and everything worthwhile.

Contents

Abbreviations

ACHR	American Convention on Human Rights
AJIL	*American Journal of International Law*
APEC	Asia-Pacific Economic Cooperation
BYBIL	*British Year Book of International Law*
CAT	Convention Against Torture
CHS	Commission on Human Security
CRC	Convention on the Rights of the Child
DDA	Department of Disarmament Affairs
DFAIT	Department of Foreign Affairs and Trade (Canada)
ECHR	European Convention for the Protection of Human Rights and Fundamental Freedoms
ECOSOC	Economic and Social Council
ECOWAS	Economic Community of West African States
EJIL	*European Journal of International Law*
ETS	European Treaty Series
EU	European Union
FRY	Federal Republic of Yugoslavia
G8	Group of Eight
HDI	human development index
IASC	Inter-Agency Standing Committee
ICCPR	International Covenant on Civil and Political Rights
ICESCR	International Covenant on Economic, Social and Cultural Rights
ICISS	International Commission on Intervention and State Sovereignty
ICJ	International Court of Justice
ICLQ	*International and Comparative Law Quarterly*
ICRC	International Committee of the Red Cross
IDP	internally displaced person
IHR	International Health Regulations
ILC	International Law Commission
IRRC	*International Review of the Red Cross*
MOFA	Ministry of Foreign Affairs (Japan)
NATO	North Atlantic Treaty Organization
NGO	non-governmental organisation
OAS	Organization of American States
OASTS	Organization of American States Treaty Series
OCHA	Office for the Coordination of Humanitarian Affairs

OECD	Organisation for Economic Co-operation and Development
OSCE	Organization for Security and Co-operation in Europe
PCIJ	Permanent Court of International Justice
PHEIC	public health emergency of international concern
RIAA	Reports of International Arbitral Awards
SADC	Southern African Development Community
SALW	small arms and light weapons
SARS	Severe Acute Respiratory Syndrome
SAS	Small Arms Survey
UN	United Nations
UNAIDS	Joint United Nations Programme on HIV/AIDS
UNCHR	United Nations Commission on Human Rights
UNDP	United Nations Development Programme
UNESCO	United Nations Educational, Scientific and Cultural Organization
UNGA	United Nations General Assembly
UNHCR	United Nations High Commissioner for Refugees
UNHRC	United Nations Human Rights Council
UNSC	United Nations Security Council
UNTS	United Nations Treaty Series
WHA	World Health Assembly
WHO	World Health Organization
WTO	World Trade Organization

Introduction

IN THE YEARS since the Cold War, there have been many attempts to reconceptualise security. Among the most prominent of these is the concept of human security. Since its introduction in the mid 1990s, this concept has been taken up and promoted by several national governments, most notably those of Canada and Japan, as a key part of their foreign policies. The concept has been proposed as a new 'paradigm' for foreign policy, a 'template' to assess policy and practice.[1] A dozen states from various regions are currently members of the Human Security Network, an informal coalition dedicated to advancing human security.[2] Human security has also found its way into the discourse and practice of some international organisations. In addition, a major international commission was formed in 2001 to study and promote human security, and other recent international commissions have also referred to the concept in their reports.[3] In the words of one scholar,

> by [the year] 2000 debate, advocacy, and thinking about human security had breached a significant threshold. It was well developed conceptually, was being advocated widely by policymakers and academics, and was feeding into some areas of defence and foreign policy.[4]

The *Human Development Report*'s prediction that the 'idea of human security . . . is likely to revolutionize society in the 21st century'[5] may be

---

[1] Canada, Department of Foreign Affairs and Trade (DFAIT), *Freedom from Fear: Canada's Foreign Policy for Human Security* (Ottawa, DFAIT, 2000) <http://www.humansecurity.gc.ca/pdf/freedom_from_fear-en.pdf> (accessed 27 February 2007), at 1; Canada, DFAIT, *Human Security: Safety for People in a Changing World* (Ottawa, DFAIT, 1999), at 8.

[2] Human Security Network, 'The Human Security Network' (2006) <http://www.humansecuritynetwork.org/network-e.php> (accessed 25 April 2007). See ch 1, n 94 and accompanying text.

[3] Commission on Human Security, *Human Security Now: Protecting and Empowering People* (New York, Commission on Human Security, 2003) <http://www.humansecurity-chs.org/finalreport/index.html> (accessed 26 February 2007); Commission on Global Governance, *Our Global Neighborhood: The Report of the Commission on Global Governance* (Oxford, Oxford University Press, 1995); International Commission on Intervention and State Sovereignty (ICISS), *Responsibility to Protect: Report of the International Commission on Intervention and State Sovereignty* (Ottawa, International Development Research Centre, 2001) <http://www.iciss.ca/pdf/Commission-Report.pdf> (accessed 26 February 2007). See ch 1, nn 109–20 and accompanying text.

[4] A Burke, 'Caught between National and Human Security: Knowledge and Power in Post-crisis Asia' (2001) 13 *Pacifica Review* 215, at 219.

[5] United Nations Development Programme (UNDP), *Human Development Report 1994* (Oxford, Oxford University Press, 1994), at 22.

somewhat exaggerated, but it has already had a significant impact that merits attention.

The concept of human security has been used in different ways, but some common distinctive features can be identified. At the core of the concept is the shift from states' security to the security of individuals as the primary concern. Security can be understood very generally to mean freedom from threats, including both the objective reality of protection and the subjective sense of feeling secure. From this starting point, different concepts of security can be distinguished by identifying the referent object, threats, and means with which we are most concerned. As we will see, the concept of human security was developed as a reaction to 'traditional' realist notions of national security that had been dominant throughout the Cold War. These conceptions of security emphasise the security of the nation-state from external military threats. Human security, in contrast, focuses on the security of the individual human beings who inhabit states, and their protection from a wide range of threats, from military and criminal violence to hunger and disease.

Human security is an integrative concept that is relevant to a wide range of areas. It has been invoked in a variety of contexts including development, peace-building, the International Criminal Court, anti-personnel mines, and assistance to displaced persons. A former Secretary-General of the United Nations referred to human security as the 'unifying concept' of the organisation, and called on scholars to generate knowledge about the concept and its application.[6] It is not clear whether the concept's popularity in political discourse will continue to rise or has already passed its peak, but it has already made a sufficient impact to suggest that it will have some lasting significance. During the period of research for this book, the quantity of secondary literature on the subject has increased exponentially, making the task of reviewing the relevant literature both challenging and exciting. One significant gap has existed in the literature and analysis, however, and to a large extent remains today. Despite the increasing breadth and depth of discussion in related disciplines, the concept of human security has received relatively little attention from legal scholars.[7] This book is intended to contribute to this dimension of the literature—or more precisely, to begin to forge links between international relations and foreign policy writings on the concept and the literature on various aspects of international law. Certainly, not everyone agrees that

---

[6] K Annan, 'The Quiet Revolution' (1998) 4 *Global Governance* 123, at 136–7.

[7] Notable exceptions include: G Oberleitner, 'Human Security: A Challenge to International Law?' (2005) 11 *Global Governance* 185; C Bruderlein, 'People's Security as a New Measure of Global Stability' (2001) 842 *IRRC* 353; BG Ramcharan, *Human Rights and Human Security* (The Hague, Martinus Nijhoff, 2002); D Newman, 'A Human Security Council? Applying a "Human Security" Agenda to Security Council Reform' (1999–2000) 31 *Ottawa Law Review* 213.

the concept of human security is a useful or positive addition, and the most significant concerns or objections will be considered in later chapters. However, its influence demands that we have a better understanding of the implications of using a 'human security approach'.

This book, then, is concerned with the significance of this new approach to security for international law. We might pause to ask, though: why should human security matter for international law? Why, indeed, should international law matter for human security? Whether, and in what ways, they matter will be explored through the chapters that follow, but a few points are worth noting at the outset. Security is an important human value—although of course not the only one—and the provision of security is one of the central purposes of legal systems.[8] The law is a major instrument and framework for the pursuit of security. Our understanding of what security means will determine what we demand from the law in this role, the kind of framework for action that we want it to provide, and what we want it to achieve. In international law, the UN Charter is perhaps the clearest example of the law giving expression to a particular concept of security (collective security), but the principles, rules, and institutions of international law provide the means and the environment for our pursuit of security in many other less obvious ways.

An attempt to reconceptualise security also raises questions about law because it inevitably has a normative dimension.[9] Since security is a social construction more than an objective fact, defining security amounts to making a normative claim about when we should consider ourselves to be secure. Even when the reformulation of security concepts is presented as a response to changing external conditions, it reflects judgements of value that are no less important for being unstated. Security is sometimes treated as a distinct area of study and practice, but the way security is defined reflects and has profound implications for our view of society, including law as part of society. As political theorist RBJ Walker reminds us, 'claims about security are a serious matter. They cannot be dissociated from even more basic claims about who we think we are and how we might act together.'[10] For example, as we will see, the shift from a state-centred to a human-centred approach to security is linked to a particular view of the relative moral value of states and individuals, and of the value of

---

[8] At least one legal philosopher has suggested that security is the essential foundation and purpose of law: see N Duxbury, 'Human Security and the Basic Norm' (1990) 76 *Archiv fur Rechts- und Sozialphilosophie* 184, discussing the work of Luis Recaséns Siches. One need not go this far to accept that security is one important purpose of the law, among others.

[9] See, eg, DA Baldwin, 'The Concept of Security' (1997) 23 *Review of International Studies* 5, at 5; RBJ Walker, 'The Subject of Security' in K Krause and MC Williams (eds), *Critical Security Studies: Concepts and Cases* (Minneapolis, University of Minnesota Press, 1997), at 62; B McSweeney, *Security, Identity and Interests: A Sociology of International Relations* (Cambridge, Cambridge University Press, 1999), at 84–8.

[10] Walker, above n 9, at 66.

individuals in relation to each other. Our preference for one security concept over another is based not only on assessments of their conceptual clarity and empirical soundness, but also on moral judgements about the policies they can be used to justify and the views of society they reflect.

Attempts to redefine security must therefore be understood to have potentially significant implications for how we see the law, and since human security is primarily a concept for use in foreign policy, it seems particularly important to understand what it means for international law. In addition to being a goal of foreign policy, human security is sometimes described as an approach or orientation, one that makes the security of individual human beings our central concern. This idea can be used as a perspective from which to examine international law. Put another way, studying human security provides us with an opportunity to explore how international law might be different if we thought differently about security. Especially considering the increasing influence of human rights, in many ways the concept of human security is not new to international law. It has been suggested that 'the political project represented by the human security agenda may be built on the already existing precedents within international law'.[11] Some of these precedents will be explored in later chapters. We will see that the conceptual framework of human security has many parallels in international law, and that in various respects the concept is also reminiscent of certain theoretical perspectives familiar to international lawyers.

The general question to be explored in this book, then, is how human security might be used to inform the analysis of international law. What functions or roles might the concept have in relation to international law? How can the concept be used to analyse particular areas of the law, and what insights does this analysis yield? Is the existing framework of international law compatible with this new concept of security? How does the law enable or resist the pursuit of human security as a goal or orientation of foreign policy? As these questions suggest, there are two interconnected levels of inquiry simultaneously operating throughout the book: the first seeks to determine what observations we can make about international law by examining it from the perspective of human security, while the second attempts to evaluate this analysis, asking whether and how the concept is useful in this context.

Chapter one will introduce the concept of human security, describing its origins and its use in international political discourse. Chapter two will then discuss debates in the literature relating to the definition of the concept, its utility, and its relationship to existing frameworks. The key aspects of the concept as understood and used in this book are also

---

[11] H Owens and B Arneil, 'Human Security Paradigm Shift: A New Lens on Canadian Foreign Policy?' (1999) 7(1) *Canadian Foreign Policy* 1, at 9.

outlined, including the implications of taking a 'human-centred' approach to security and acknowledging that human security is a common global concern. In chapter three, the relationship between human security and international law will be explored across a range of different areas. This chapter will review examples of international law being used as an instrument in the pursuit of human security and examine some views of the compatibility of human security with international law. It will also identify parallels between certain norms and principles of international law, on one hand, and the central elements of the human security concept, on the other.

The next four chapters will look at what the concept might contribute to discussions of particular topics within contemporary international law. Chapter four examines the debate on humanitarian intervention; chapter five focuses on the protection of internally displaced persons; chapter six deals with the proliferation of small arms and light weapons; and chapter seven discusses global disease surveillance and control. The four areas selected represent different kinds of concerns relevant to human security, and areas in which the concept of human security has been used in different ways. Each of them has already been the subject of considerable discussion and debate, but they present different types of problems in international law, including the development, interpretation, and application of legal norms. Together the four chapters will serve to illustrate and critique some of the ways in which the concept of human security may be used in analyses of international law. Finally, the Conclusion will offer some observations on these questions and draw together common themes that emerge from the preceding chapters.

1

Origins and Development of the Concept of Human Security

INTRODUCTION

HUMAN SECURITY IS a relatively new concept, and although it has become familiar to many in recent years, it is still not widely known or well understood outside certain academic and policy circles. Before beginning to explore its relationship with international law, it is important to have a sense of its origins, meanings, and uses. This chapter will trace the genesis of the concept, making note of some of its most important precursors, and provide a brief account of the ways in which human security has come to be used in international affairs.[1] Chapter two will then discuss the scholarly debate surrounding the definition and utility of human security.

HISTORY AND ANTECEDENTS OF THE CONCEPT

The concept of human security, as currently used in scholarship and policy discussions, is a product of the convergence of ideas from security studies and international development.[2] In both areas, there were calls for attention to the impact that policies were having on individuals. Debates about the meaning of security yielded new conceptual frameworks, while 'human development' introduced a 'people-centred' paradigm for designing and evaluating policy.

---

[1] For a recent extensive discussion of the concept's history, see SN MacFarlane and YF Khong, *Human Security and the UN: A Critical History* (Bloomington, Indiana University Press, 2006). See also K Bajpai, 'Human Security: Concept and Measurement' (Kroc Institute Occasional Paper 19:OP:1, August 2000).

[2] King and Murray call the publication of the *Human Development Report 1994* (see below nn 55 and 66*ff*), which is usually credited with introducing the concept into modern discourse, a 'unifying event' at the intersection of the development and security communities: G King and CJL Murray, 'Rethinking Human Security' (2001–2002) 116 *Political Science Quarterly* 585, at 589.

Rethinking Security

In very general terms, 'security' refers to freedom from danger or, in its subjective sense, from fear. It involves the protection of some referent object by reducing its vulnerability and by eliminating or lessening threats to its survival or well-being.[3] Efforts to define and redefine security have been 'something of a cottage industry' in recent decades, producing an enormous quantity of literature.[4] There are many ways of classifying concepts of security,[5] but three main dimensions can be used to organise a discussion: the referent object (who or what is being secured); the nature of the threat from which the object is being secured; and the means of seeking security. These dimensions are often indicated by modifiers to the term 'security' (for example, 'national security', 'environmental security' or 'collective security', respectively). Although the dimensions are distinct, common usage or accepted definitions of a term may import other aspects; for example, national security means security of the nation-state but has also traditionally meant security of the state from external military threats, protected by military means.

Human security seeks to reorient the pursuit of security by placing individual human beings at the centre of security concerns. This idea and its implications can best be understood in the context of larger debates about the meaning of security. These debates generally take as their starting point what is referred to as the 'traditional' conceptualisation of security, by which is meant a realist view of national security. Given its long-standing dominant position in international relations theory, realism has been the traditional or orthodox view against which others have been shaped and defined.[6] Unsurprisingly, it has also had an overriding influence on security studies and prevailing understandings of national and international security. Although there is considerable diversity within realism,[7] it is usually associated with a view that emphasises power poli-

---

[3] B Buzan, *People, States and Fear: An Agenda for International Security Studies in the Post-Cold War Era*, 2nd edn (New York, Harvester Wheatsheaf, 1991) [*People, States and Fear*], at 112*ff*.

[4] DA Baldwin, 'The Concept of Security' (1997) 23 *Review of International Studies* 5.

[5] See, eg, *ibid*, at 13–17; Buzan, *People, States and Fear*, above n 3, at 116*ff*; E Rothschild, 'What is Security?' (1995) 124(3) *Daedalus* 53, at 55; D Fischer, *Nonmilitary Aspects of Security: A Systems Approach* (Aldershot, Dartmouth, 1993), at 14–15.

[6] B Buzan, 'The Timeless Wisdom of Realism?' in S Smith, K Booth and M Zalewski (eds), *International Theory: Positivism and Beyond* (Cambridge, Cambridge University Press, 1996) ['Timeless Wisdom'], at 47–8; S Burchill, 'Realism and Neo-realism' in S Burchill and A Linklater (eds), *Theories of International Relations* (New York, St Martin's Press, 1995), at 67; J Steans, *Gender and International Relations: An Introduction* (Cambridge, Polity Press, 1998), at 38.

[7] J Donnelly, *Realism and International Relations* (Cambridge, Cambridge University Press, 2000), at 6. Donnelly suggests a typology of realist paradigms (at 11*ff*). The description here draws in particular from Donnelly, at ch 1; Buzan, 'Timeless Wisdom', above n 6; Burchill, above n 6; M Sheehan, *International Security: An Analytical Survey* (Boulder, Colorado, Lynne Rienner, 2005), at ch 2.

tics among states as the central feature of international relations. In this view, states are the dominant actors in the international system and they can be analysed as unitary actors within that system, largely without regard for their internal characteristics. Due to the egoistic and conflict-prone nature of human beings and the anarchical nature of the international system, states are driven to pursue power as their primary goal. The realist view is sceptical of moral constraints on states' behaviour and of the possibility of preventing war, so states must prepare for war and maximise their own power in order to ensure their survival.[8] The national interest is therefore defined in terms of strategic power, especially military power. The understanding of security that flows from this view takes the state as its primary or sole referent, and is chiefly concerned with defending the state from external military threats: 'a nation is secure to the extent to which it is not in danger of having to sacrifice core values, if it wishes to avoid war, and is able, if challenged, to maintain them by victory in such a war.'[9] The realist view emphasises both military threats and military power as the means to guard against these threats. In the anarchical system, self-help and the accumulation of military power are the keys to security. National security, defined in these terms as the 'preservation of state independence and autonomy' from external threats, has dominated analyses of security.[10]

Although some of the difficulties with this view of security were apparent much earlier,[11] it was primarily in the 1980s and 1990s that a large body of literature emerged seeking to question various aspects of it.[12] A number of reasons for this have been cited, among them dissatisfaction with the resulting security framework, including security dilemmas, the arms race, and nuclear deterrence as a policy of national security.[13] Increasing concern with economic and environmental issues led to calls for consideration of non-military threats.[14] With the end of the Cold War came the need to reformulate security policy in a way that

[8] JA Tickner, *Gender in International Relations: Feminist Perspectives on Achieving Global Security* (New York, Columbia University Press, 1992), at 32.

[9] A Wolfers, 'National Security as an Ambiguous Symbol' in A Wolfers, *Discord and Collaboration: Essays on International Politics* (Baltimore, Johns Hopkins Press, 1962), at 150, citing W Lippmann.

[10] Sheehan, above n 7, at 6.

[11] See, eg, Wolfers, above n 9, originally published in 1952.

[12] For an overview of critiques and the 'traditionalist counterattack', see B Buzan, 'Rethinking Security after the Cold War' (1997) 32 *Cooperation and Conflict* 5 ['Rethinking Security'], at 6–12. See also the discussion in MacFarlane and Khong, above n 1, at 127*ff*.

[13] K Booth, 'Security and Emancipation' (1991) 17 *Review of International Studies* 313, at 318. Tickner suggests that security policies in the nuclear age 'stretched the traditional concept of national security to its limit' by making state security dependent on the insecurity of citizens (above n 8, at 52). See also Buzan, *People, States and Fear*, above n 3, at 49: 'deterrence policy displays the divorce between individual and national security at the highest and most visible level.'

[14] Buzan, 'Rethinking Security', above n 12, at 6–7.

would be more appropriate in the new context. Realism had been presented as an objective and neutral framework, in opposition to 'idealist' approaches to international relations,[15] but as its critics have pointed out, the realist approach to security has both practical and normative implications of its own. Concerns about these implications sparked interest in rethinking the traditional concept of national security.[16] Some critiques focus primarily on one dimension of security, while more radical ones engage all of them.

Typically, at least in the early stages, critiques called for the 'broadening' of the concept of security, in particular expanding the range of threats that were considered relevant to national security.[17] In its most limited form, this means taking account of the role of environmental, resource, human rights and other issues in precipitating conflict.[18] In this approach, even if we are primarily concerned with military threats to national security, attention must be paid to problems that, left unaddressed, may lead or contribute to military conflict. Hence, it is legitimate to widen the ambit of security threats to include these causal factors. This approach can to some extent be accommodated even within a 'traditionalist' framework of national security, since it is concerned with issues that 'bear directly on the likelihood and character of war'.[19]

Taking this a step further, writers such as Jessica Tuchman Mathews and Richard Ullman argued that non-military threats including economic and environmental problems could be just as serious in their own right as military ones, and so should receive attention as security issues.[20] Ullman

---

[15] Burchill, above n 6, at 82; Sheehan, above n 7, at 7.

[16] Regarding practical and 'intellectual' concerns, see KR Nossal, 'Seeing Things? The Adornment of "Security" in Australia and Canada' (1995) 49 *Australian Journal of International Affairs* 33, at 45–6; on the normative or moral concerns, see B McSweeney, *Security, Identity and Interests: A Sociology of International Relations* (Cambridge, Cambridge University Press, 1999), at 91.

[17] See Sheehan, above n 7, at ch 4.

[18] On environmental change and conflict, see, eg, T Homer-Dixon, 'Environmental Scarcity and Intergroup Conflict' in MT Klare and DC Thomas (eds), *World Security: Challenges for a New Century*, 2nd edn (New York, St Martin's Press, 1994); D Deudney, 'The Case Against Linking Environmental Degradation and National Security' (1990) 19 *Millennium: Journal of International Studies* 461, at 469–74; MS Soroos, 'Global Change, Environmental Security, and the Prisoner's Dilemma' (1994) 31(3) *Journal of Peace Research* 317, at 318–19. On human rights, see, eg, V Wiebe, 'The Prevention of Civil War through the Use of the Human Rights System' (1995) 27 *New York University Journal of International Law and Politics* 409, at 410–12; Canada, Department of Foreign Affairs and Trade (DFAIT), *Freedom from Fear: Canada's Foreign Policy for Human Security* (Ottawa, DFAIT, 2000) <http://www.humansecurity.gc.ca/pdf/freedom_from_fear-en.pdf> (27 February 2007) [*Freedom from Fear*], at 5.

[19] SM Walt, 'The Renaissance of Security Studies' (1991) 35 *International Studies Quarterly* 211, at 213.

[20] RH Ullman, 'Redefining Security' (1983) 8(1) *International Security* 129; JT Mathews, 'Redefining Security' (1989) 68(2) *Foreign Affairs* 162; JT Mathews, 'The Environment and International Security' in MT Klare and DC Thomas (eds), *World Security: Challenges for a New Century*, 2nd edn (New York, St Martin's Press, 1994).

proposed defining a threat to national security as 'an action or sequence of events that (1) threatens drastically and over a relatively brief span of time to degrade the quality of life for the inhabitants of a state, or (2) threatens significantly to narrow the range of policy choices available to the government of a state or to private, nongovernmental entities (persons, groups, corporations) within the state'.[21] The first category includes war but also internal conflict, blockades, raw materials shortages, terrorist attacks, and natural disasters; the second a situation in which there are fewer opportunities for trade, investment, and cultural exchange, and in which important values are threatened.[22] In a leading work, Barry Buzan identified five areas of national security issues: military, political, economic, societal, and ecological.[23] The concept of 'comprehensive security', which has been influential especially in the Asia–Pacific context, includes reference to a broader range of non-military threats, and in that respect is considered an important precursor to human security.[24]

The well-known concepts of collective security and common security provide variations on the traditional model of state security in terms of the *means* of seeking security. Collective security, exemplified in the UN Charter, involves members of a group agreeing to renounce the use of force against each other and to defend any member of the group who is attacked.[25] It therefore remains situated in the military sphere in terms of both threats and means, and depends on military deterrence to enhance states' security, but emphasises cooperation among group members rather than individual self-help—a strategy viewed with scepticism by realist theorists. The later concept of common security is a more significant shift because it entails not only cooperation between states but also the reconsideration of military means of seeking security. The concept of common security as formulated by the Palme Commission is grounded in the recognition that in a nuclear age, nations cannot achieve security at

---

[21] Ullman, above n 20, at 133.

[22] *Ibid*, at 133–4.

[23] Buzan, *People, States and Fear*, above n 3, at 116–33.

[24] A Acharya and A Acharya, 'Human Security in Asia Pacific: Puzzle, Panacea or Peril?' (2000) 27 *CANCAPS Bulletin/Bulletin du CONCSAP* 1 <http://www.cancaps.ca/cbul27.pdf> (accessed 6 March 2007); W Kim and I Hyun, 'Toward a New Concept of Security: Human Security in World Politics' in WT Tow, R Thakur and I Hyun (eds), *Asia's Emerging Regional Order: Reconciling Traditional and Human Security* (Tokyo, United Nations University Press, 2000), at 39.

[25] See, eg, Commission on Global Governance, *Our Global Neighborhood: The Report of the Commission on Global Governance* (Oxford, Oxford University Press, 1995), at 80; R Väyryen, 'Multilateral Security: Common, Cooperative or Collective?' in MG Schechter (ed), *Future Multilateralism: The Political and Social Framework* (Tokyo, United Nations University Press, 1999), at 59. The notion of collective security is reflected in the UN Charter, arts 1(1), 2(4), and 2(5); note, however, that the Charter does not preclude individual self-defence in the event of an armed attack on a UN member, pending measures by the Security Council (art 51). On art 1(1) and collective security, see R Wolfrum, 'Article 1' in B Simma (ed), *The Charter of the United Nations: A Commentary*, 2nd edn, (Oxford, Oxford University Press, 2002), vol I, at 42–3.

others' expense, because of the threat of mutual destruction.[26] It therefore questions the utility of military deterrence[27] and exhorts states to consider the impact of their security decisions:[28] 'cooperative efforts and policies of interlocking national restraint' would serve everyone's best interests.[29]

Many attempts to reconceptualise security have remained within the framework of national security, in the sense that the state is the sole or primary referent object. However, some writings have suggested shifting the focus to other referent objects. The focus can be moved 'downwards' from the nation to individuals, or 'upwards' from the nation to the international system or biosphere.[30] In the realist view, the state is the primary referent object of security because it is the highest source of authority in an anarchic international system, and individual security is dependent on state security.[31] It would not be fair to say that the realist view is indifferent to the security of individuals, since the state's central purpose and the ultimate rationale for its pursuit of military power is the protection of its citizens, and its ability to exercise any of its other functions depends on being able to ensure its own security.[32] However, many have been troubled by the extent to which the state's security has tended to be pursued as an end in itself, and sometimes at the expense of its inhabitants' security. As a result, some have argued that the individual, rather than the state, should be the primary referent object of security. Although the state may have a crucial role in providing security for individuals, it should be considered an instrument of security rather than its central referent.[33] If the state often does not provide security for its citizens, some analysts question whether it should continue to be the focus of the study of security.[34] In this view, the human individual is the logical or moral centre of security concerns.[35] These arguments provide some conceptual foundations for the concept that has come to be labelled 'human security'.

Feminist critiques of the traditional approach to security have much in common with these 'people-centred' approaches to security,[36] although they are more complex and multidimensional. Feminist theorists have argued that the pursuit of national security as traditionally conceived does

---

[26] Independent Commission on Disarmament and Security Issues, *Common Security: A Programme for Disarmament* (London, Pan Books, 1982), at 6.

[27] *Ibid*, at 8.

[28] Väyryen, above n 25, at 56.

[29] Independent Commission on Disarmament and Security Issues, above n 26, at 6. See also *ibid*, at 8.

[30] Rothschild, above n 5, at 55; Commission on Global Governance, above n 25, at 82–84.

[31] Buzan, *People, States and Fear*, above n 3, at 22, 37–8.

[32] Sheehan, above n 7, at 11.

[33] Booth, above n 13, at 320; McSweeney, above n 16, at 58.

[34] SN MacFarlane and TG Weiss, 'The United Nations, Regional Organisations and Human Security: Building Theory in Central America' (1994) 15 *Third World Quarterly* 277, at 278–9.

[35] Booth, above n 13, at 320; McSweeney, above n 16, at 87.

[36] Steans, above n 6, at 122–8.

not necessarily make women more secure and in fact may contribute to their insecurity. Critiques of militarism by feminists using what has been called an 'impact-on approach' (examining impacts on women) have highlighted the detrimental effect that military spending has on society and disproportionately on women.[37] In addition, feminist analyses have sought to demonstrate links between militarism and sexism,[38] between different forms of violence,[39] and between unjust social relations and insecurity.[40] Increasing awareness of insecurities particular to women has also revealed the extent to which the realist focus on the state and national interest has obscured the diversity of identities and interests within states.[41] Drawing attention to the ways in which traditional approaches to security have perpetuated women's insecurity also provides the foundation for a more radical critique. As Peterson explains:

> The problem . . . is far deeper than our failure to take women's oppression seriously. My focus here on *gendered* states is not intended to mask but to illuminate other forms and expressions of structural violence. The problem—of and for world security—is that structural violence per se is not considered to be a matter of major importance . . . How has the systematic exploitation and degradation of human lives—and of our ecological support system—become so acceptable, so apolitical, so natural? How have the current 'rules of the game' been so effectively 'authorized' that we take them as 'givens'—inevitable, and therefore acceptable? How has our understanding of security been framed by sovereign state systems that themselves constitute profound and pervasive *in*securities?[42]

The implications of feminist analyses therefore reach beyond a concern with women's insecurity and open up possibilities for a 'fundamental rethink of our whole approach to understanding security'.[43]

This body of literature sets the stage for the reconceptualisation of security as human security, shifting the referent object of security to the individual, and simultaneously broadening the focus to include a broader range of threats and of means of providing security. These intellectual precursors continue to inform understandings of human security and its relationship to other types of security. The other important antecedent to human security, and its introduction as a distinct concept and term in international discourse, is to be found in development studies.

[37] *Ibid*, at 110–12.
[38] *Ibid*, at 116.
[39] *Ibid*, at 127.
[40] Tickner, above n 8, at 128–9.
[41] H Charlesworth and C Chinkin, *The Boundaries of International Law: A Feminist Analysis* (Manchester, Manchester University Press, 2000), at 93–4; VS Peterson, 'Security and Sovereign States: What Is at Stake in Taking Feminism Seriously?' in VS Peterson (ed), *Gendered States: Feminist (Re)Visions of International Relations Theory* (Boulder and London, Lynne Rienner, 1992), at 47.
[42] *Ibid*, at 49 (footnotes omitted).
[43] Steans, above n 6, at 116.

Human Development

The introduction of the concept of human security in the field of development occurred within the larger context of 'human development'.[44] The
latter concept has been explained and promoted most notably in the
United Nations Development Programme (UNDP) *Human Development
Report*, published annually beginning in 1990. Human development is
described as 'a process of enlarging people's choices' and capabilities.[45]
Proponents of human development were reacting to an approach to
development that concentrates exclusively on increasing income and
tends to equate economic growth with development. As one text on
development economics puts it, '[t]he terms "growth" and "development" are usually used to mean the same thing. A growth of per capita
income is supposed to contribute to a general rise in the standard of living
of the people in general.'[46] There has thus been a tendency to measure
development performance by emphasising growth of per capita gross
national product and other economic indicators.[47] However, many have
realised that the link between growth and development is complex:
growth without development may occur in a variety of circumstances, and
per capita income growth does not necessarily equate to an improvement
in the standard of living.[48] The *Human Development Report 1990* argued
that:

> Technical considerations of the means to achieve human development—and
> the use of statistical aggregates to measure national income and its growth—
> have at times obscured the fact that the primary objective of development is to
> benefit people.[49]

Human development treats economic growth as essential, but not
sufficient, requiring attention to the 'quality of growth and the equity of its
distribution'[50] and to the need for a link between economic growth and

[44] See generally MacFarlane and Khong, above n 1, at ch 4.
[45] UNDP, *Human Development Report 1990* (Oxford, Oxford University Press, 1990) [*HDR 1990*], at 10.
[46] S Ghatak, *Introduction to Development Economics*, 3rd edn (London, Routledge, 1995), at 34.
[47] It should be noted, however, that even a decade or more before the *Human Development Reports*, other reports such as the World Bank's *World Development Report* were using indicators such as life expectancy and literacy as well as economic indicators. For example, the table of basic indicators, Table 1 in World Bank, *World Development Report 1979* (Washington, DC, World Bank, 1979), includes life expectancy and adult literacy. Other tables show indicators relating to health and education (Tables 22 and 23).
[48] Ghatak, above n 46, at 34-35.
[49] UNDP, *HDR 1990*, above n 45, at 9. See also M ul Haq, *Reflections on Human Development*, 2nd edn (Delhi, Oxford University Press, 1999), at 4.
[50] UNDP, *Human Development Report 1995* (Oxford, Oxford University Press, 1995) [*HDR 1995*], at 122.

human lives to be consciously created rather than simply assumed.[51] The *Human Development Reports* introduced new indicators to measure development performance and evaluate the allocation of funds.[52] The human development index (HDI) includes indicators designed to measure life expectancy, level of education, food security, health, gender empowerment, and levels of violence and crime, for example, along with income.[53] Disaggregating the HDI by region, gender, income level, ethnic group or other classification allows countries to identify areas needing policy attention.[54] Figures and ratios in the tables on aid flows measure the amount of aid and its allocation to social priority sectors.[55] They provide 'a way of evaluating the allocation of funds . . . and of checking whether they really help to accomplish what are regarded as priority tasks'.[56]

According to the *Human Development Report 1995*, the 'real point of departure of human development strategies is to approach every issue in the traditional growth models from the vantage point of people'.[57] This 'people-centred' approach to formulating and evaluating policy is the key conceptual contribution of human development to human security. Generally speaking, this approach, transposed to the area of security, amounts to what we now know as 'human security'. In both contexts, using the label 'human' and calling the approach 'people-centred' may invite criticism because it seems to imply that other approaches ignore human beings: one might ask, 'Had development previously been "inhuman"?'.[58] The essence of both, however, is that they demand explicit and direct attention, and assign normative priority, to the impact of policies on the well-being and personal circumstances of people.

Human development and human security could therefore be described as parallel concepts, particular instances of a more general approach that is referred to, for lack of a better phrase, as 'people-centred' or 'human-centred'. When the concept of human security was first introduced in the *Human Development Report 1993*, it was as one of the 'five pillars of a people-centred world order'.[59] It still remains to be explained, however, why the proponents of human development became concerned with security in particular. The motivation for linking security concepts to

---

[51] ul Haq, above n 49, at 14–15.

[52] See the discussion in G Rist, *The History of Development: From Western Origins to Global Faith*, P Camiller (trans) (London, Zed Books, 1997), at 205–7.

[53] See UNDP, *HDR 1995*, above n 50, at 18 (as well as the HDI tables in each of the annual reports).

[54] *Ibid*, at 119.

[55] See, eg, UNDP, *Human Development Report 1993* (Oxford, Oxford University Press, 1993) [*HDR 1993*], Table 41; UNDP, *Human Development Report 1994* (Oxford, Oxford University Press, 1994) [*HDR 1994*], Table 19.

[56] Rist, above n 52, at 207.

[57] UNDP, *HDR 1995*, above n 50, at 123; ul Haq, above n 49, at 23.

[58] Rist, above n 52, at 205.

[59] UNDP, *HDR 1993*, above n 55, at 2.

human development apparently stemmed initially from concerns about financial resources: a desire to 'find a new motivation for development cooperation based on fighting the growing threat of global poverty rather than the receding threat of the cold war'.[60] The allocation of aid during the Cold War had been strongly influenced by strategic concerns.[61] It was hoped that forging a 'new' link between development and security—by redefining security—would influence public opinion and political will in rich countries towards a belief that cooperating for human development was (still) an investment in security.[62] In addition, talk of a 'peace dividend' from the end of the Cold War had raised hopes that resources could be shifted from military expenditures to finance development.[63] Redefining the concept of security to move away from military-focused state security and toward a holistic view of human security would reinforce the impetus to transfer resources from military to development spending.[64] Human security was therefore intended to be not only similar, but also complementary, to human development.

ARTICULATION AND USE OF THE CONCEPT

Introduction of the Concept

This interest in security from a development perspective prompted the convergence of ideas in the discussion of human security in the *Human Development Report*. The use of the concept and term 'human security' in current international discourse is usually traced back to the *Human Development Report 1994*, although the concept had been briefly introduced in the 1993 Report. According to this latter Report, the concept of security must change, from one focused on nations, arms, and territory to a greater concern with people, human development, food, employment, and the environment.[65] This suggests a shift in both the referent object of security and the means of achieving it. The discussion of human security in the 1994 Report makes this explicit, describing the concept of security as changing in two essential ways: a change in emphasis from territorial

---

[60] ul Haq, above n 49, at 136; see also UNDP, *HDR 1993*, above n 55, at 8. See also MacFarlane and Khong, above n 1, at 147–8.

[61] ul Haq, above n 49, at 120.

[62] *Ibid*, at 136; UNDP, *HDR 1993*, above n 55, at 8.

[63] See, eg, K Hartley, 'The Economics of the Peace Dividend' (1997) 24 *International Journal of Social Economics* 28.

[64] UNDP, *HDR 1993*, above n 55, at 2; ul Haq, above n 49, at 118. It is ironic, in light of this, that human security has been used to justify military spending in Canada: see J Jockel and J Sokolsky, 'Lloyd Axworthy's Legacy: Human Security and the Rescue of Canadian Defence Policy' (2000–2001) 56 *International Journal* 1, at 6.

[65] UNDP, *HDR 1993*, above n 55, at 2.

security to people's security, and a change in approach from security through armaments to security through sustainable human development.[66]

The *Human Development Report 1994* devotes a chapter to human security. It argues that we need to broaden our concept of security in the aftermath of the Cold War, to focus on the 'worries about daily life' of 'ordinary people' rather than the threat of a 'cataclysmic world event'.[67] The concept of human security as delineated in the Report has four basic characteristics: (1) it is a universal concern, relevant to everyone, everywhere; (2) its components are interdependent and threats to human security in one part of the world affect the whole world; (3) it is easier to ensure through early prevention than later intervention; and (4) it is 'people-centred'.[68] Human security is defined as 'safety from such chronic threats as hunger, disease and repression' and 'protection from sudden and hurtful disruptions in the patterns of daily life'.[69] The discussion outlines seven main categories of human security: economic, food, health, environmental, personal, community, and political.[70]

The Report proposed that the concept of human security be used at the Social Summit (1995 World Conference for Social Development)[71] as the basis for discussion and for a world social charter to be drawn up at the Summit.[72] In the event, the concept itself did not have a high profile at the Social Summit,[73] although similar ideas are expressed in the Declaration that was adopted, for example the need to focus on people, the need to reduce people's insecurity, and the relationship between peace and development.[74] In the period that followed, however, the concept gained in influence and popularity, making a limited but significant impact on foreign policy and the work of international organisations, and provoking debate among scholars and policy-makers, as we will see in the next chapter.

---

[66] UNDP, *HDR 1994*, above n 55, at 24.

[67] *Ibid*, at 22.

[68] *Ibid*, at 22–3.

[69] *Ibid*, at 23.

[70] *Ibid*, at 24*ff*.

[71] *Ibid*, at 5–6, 39.

[72] *Ibid*, at 6.

[73] A Canadian government document suggests that the concept was rejected during the Summit: Canada, DFAIT, *Human Security: Safety for People in a Changing World* (Ottawa, DFAIT, 1999) [*Human Security*], at 3. See also MacFarlane and Khong, above n 1, at 148–9.

[74] UN, 'Copenhagen Declaration on Social Development', 'Report of the World Summit for Social Development' (19 April 1995) UN Doc A/CONF.166/9, Resolution 1, Annex I, at paras 2, 5, 8, 20.

Why Now? Contextual Factors and the Search for a New Concept of Security

Both the development of the concept of human security and its adoption have been influenced by the historical context of the past decade. Perceptions about the changing international environment have encouraged the search for new concepts of security, and human security is seen by some as offering a valuable framework within which to understand and deal with this environment. Surrounding the concept of human security is a particular discourse—a way of articulating and discussing the pursuit of security—an important part of which is a narrative explaining the need for a new concept of security at this point in the world's history. The factual accuracy of some elements of this narrative may be open to question,[75] and it is debatable whether those elements necessarily point to human security as the only or even the best alternative framework. Nevertheless, they are important to understanding how and why people have used the concept.

The two key elements in this historical narrative are the end of the Cold War and the effects of globalisation.[76] In the post-Cold War environment, the prospect of large-scale interstate warfare ceased to be the international community's primary concern. Instead, the focus shifted to internal conflict as a central source of insecurity,[77] and concerns about the increasing proportion of civilian victims in those conflicts.[78] The result is a picture of a different sort of threat that apparently could not adequately be addressed using traditional security concepts. Fundamentally, the concern was that states were supposedly more secure than during the Cold War, but their citizens were not.[79] The end of the Cold War was also supposed to allow the international community, for so long preoccupied with superpower rivalries and the threat of nuclear war, to return to the 'true'

---

[75] See FO Hampson and DF Oliver, 'Pulpit Diplomacy: A Critical Assessment of the Axworthy Doctrine' (1998) 53 *International Journal* 383 for a critique of some of the assumptions surrounding the new human security discourse in Canada, for example the effect of the end of the Cold War.

[76] See also MacFarlane and Khong, above n 1, at 8–9. They also trace the historical context further back, tracing developments and precursors from the late nineteenth and early twentieth centuries, the interwar period, and during the Cold War (*ibid*, at 6–7, and chs 1, 2).

[77] See, eg, UNHCR, *The State of the World's Refugees: A Humanitarian Agenda* (Oxford, Oxford University Press, 1997) [*Humanitarian Agenda*], at 19–25; Canada, *Freedom from Fear*, above n 18, at 2.

[78] UNSC, 'Report of the Secretary-General to the Security Council on the Protection of Civilians in Armed Conflict' (8 September 1999) UN Doc S/1999/957; Canada, *Human Security*, above n 73, at 1; Canada, *Freedom from Fear*, above n 18, at 1, 2.

[79] Canada, *Human Security*, above n 73, at 1; Canada, *Freedom from Fear*, above n 18, at 2; S Ogata, 'International Security and Refugee Problems after the Cold War, Assuring the Security of People: the Humanitarian Challenge of the 21st Century' (Olof Palme Memorial Lecture, Stockholm, 14 June 1995) <http://www2.sipri.se/sipri/Lectures/Ogata.html> (accessed 26 February 2007).

purposes and principles of the United Nations. By some accounts, the adoption of human security reflected this return to foundational principles. Although human security represents a very different understanding of security from that emphasised in the UN Charter, some have sought to establish its continuity with the founding purposes and principles of the Charter.[80]

Globalisation has also played an important role in motivating the search for a new security concept, as the source of 'new' threats to security and of increasing interdependence of states and people. Many important threats to human security are portrayed as the 'dark side' or 'underside' of globalisation:[81] transnational organised crime; trafficking in illicit drugs, small arms, and human beings; environmental degradation; and terrorism. Since these threats are transnational in nature, they cannot be dealt with effectively by any one state alone, and so require international cooperation.[82] The interdependence of states and people in an increasingly globalised world means that threats in one part of the world are perceived to affect the security of people in other parts. One of the key assumptions in the adoption of a human security framework is that the people's security increasingly depends on distant actors rather than just the protection of their own state, and the security of even distant groups can be interdependent.[83] This idea of 'mutual vulnerability'[84] is an important element of one understanding of human security, as will be discussed further in chapter two.

It should be noted that, for Asian states, the experience of the economic crisis of the late 1990s also played a significant role in arousing interest in human security and in shaping thinking about the concept.[85] Human security provides a way of addressing the pervasive economic, social, and political effects of the crisis and the need for 'social safety nets' in the region.[86] This particular context may be one factor explaining the

[80] See, eg, UNDP, *HDR 1994*, above n 55, at 3; UNCHR, 'Summary Record of the 45th Meeting' 56th Sess (1 May 2000) UN Doc E/CN.4/2000/SR.45, Statement by the Minister for Foreign Affairs of Canada (Mr Axworthy), para 1; Australia, Department of Foreign Affairs and Trade, 'Future Directions for the United Nations,' (Inaugural Sir Kenneth Bailey Memorial Lecture, University of Melbourne, 29 April 1995) <http://www.dfat.gov.au/archive/speeches_old/minfor/gexi.html> (accessed 26 February 2007).

[81] See, eg, Canada, *Freedom from Fear*, above n 18, at 2.

[82] See, eg, Japan, Ministry of Foreign Affairs (MOFA), *Diplomatic Bluebook 2000: Toward the 21st Century—Foreign Policy for a Better Future* (Tokyo, MOFA, 2000), at ch II.3.A.

[83] See, eg, Commission on Human Security, *Human Security Now: Protecting and Empowering People* (New York, Commission on Human Security, 2003) <http://www.humansecurity-chs.org/finalreport/index.html> (26 February 2007) [CHS, *Human Security Now*], at 12. Interdependence is a recurring theme in the Commission's report.

[84] J Nef, *Human Security and Mutual Vulnerability*, 2nd edn (Ottawa, IDRC, 1999), at 2.

[85] A Acharya, 'Debating Human Security: East Versus West' (2001) 56 *International Journal* 442, at 448; Acharya and Acharya, above n 24. For an application of the human security concept to the crisis and its impacts, see X Furtado, 'Human security and Asia's financial crisis: A critique of Canadian policy' (2000) 55 *International Journal* 355.

[86] Acharya, *ibid*, citing the former Foreign Minister of Thailand.

divergent approaches to the concept, sometimes referred to as 'Asian' and 'Western' approaches, which will be explored in the next chapter.

Finally, the more recent historical context has been dominated by the terrorist attacks of September 11, 2001 and their aftermath, which have contributed to further rethinking of the ways in which we conceptualise and pursue security. The new emphasis on 'homeland security' represents a shift from earlier concepts of national security in that it redefines the threat to emphasise terrorist attacks rather than organised military attacks from other states.[87] It also 'calls for vast new intrusions of government, military, and intelligence forces, not just to secure the homeland from external threats, but to become an integral part of the workings of home, a home in a continual state of emergency'.[88] However, the official approach to security remains centred on the state (redefined as 'homeland') and militaristic responses, and a strong neorealist influence on US security policy has been noted.[89] The prevailing approach has been criticised as inadequate to deal with the new realities of globalisation and transnational terrorist networks.[90] At the same time, the extent to which counterterrorist measures create or increase insecurity for many individuals both within the United States and elsewhere has led to normative questioning of the dominant approach to security—analogous in many respects to the critical re-evaluations of security during and after the Cold War. Although human security has to some extent been marginalised by the resurgence of 'hard' security concerns post-September 11, many in government, non-governmental, and academic circles continue to advocate for its relevance. Some have explicitly called for the adoption of human security as an alternative approach better suited to the contemporary context.[91]

---

[87] The 2002 national strategy document defines homeland security as: 'a concerted national effort to prevent terrorist attacks within the United States, reduce America's vulnerability to terrorism, and minimize the damage and recover from attacks when they occur': Office of Homeland Security, *National Strategy for Homeland Security* (July 2002) <http://www.dhs.gov/xlibrary/assets/nat_strat_hls.pdf> (accessed 7 March 2007), at 2. The mandate of the Department of Homeland Security has more recently been expanded to include recovery from natural disasters or other catastrophic events, but terrorist attacks remain the key concern. See, eg, Department of Homeland Security, *Department Six-point Agenda* <http://www.dhs.gov/xabout/history/editorial_0646.shtm> (accessed 7 March 2007).

[88] A Kaplan, 'Homeland Insecurities: Reflections on Language and Space' (2003) 85 *Radical History Review* 82, at 90.

[89] M Beeson and AJ Bellamy, 'Globalisation, Security and International Order After 11 September' (2003) 49 *Australian Journal of Politics and History* 339, at 349.

[90] *Ibid.*

[91] See, eg, *ibid*; AM Agathangelou and LHM Ling, 'Power, Borders, Security, Wealth: Lessons of Violence and Desire from September 11' (2004) 48 *International Studies Quarterly* 517; D Bell and M Renner, 'A New Marshall Plan? Advancing Human Security and Controlling Terrorism' (8 October 2001) <http://www.worldwatch.org/node/1706> (accessed 26 February 2007); PH Liotta, 'Boomerang Effect: The Convergence of National and Human Security' (2002) 33 *Security Dialogue* 473.

Use of the Concept in Foreign Policy and International Organisations

In the late 1990s, the concept of human security began to be taken up and used by national governments, regional and international organisations, and some non-governmental organisations. Human security has been adopted as an important element in the foreign policy of a number of countries, the most prominent of which have been Canada and Japan. The Canadian Department of Foreign Affairs and International Trade (DFAIT) began using the concept in 1996 and pursued a 'human security agenda' over the following years,[92] using the concept as a framework for address-ing such issues as anti-personnel mines, the International Criminal Court, and protection of civilians in armed conflict.[93] The Canadian Foreign Affairs Department continues to administer funding and consultation programmes relating to human security. In 1998 Canada formed a partnership with Norway on human security (known as the 'Lysøen partnership'),[94] which subsequently evolved into the Human Security Network, an informal coalition of states committed to working together to strengthen human security. Austria, Canada, Chile, Costa Rica, Greece, Ireland, Jordan, Mali, the Netherlands, Norway, Slovenia, Switzerland, and Thailand are members of the Network, and South Africa participates as an observer. The Human Security Network holds annual ministerial meetings at which they have applied a human security approach to issues such as development, the role of non-state actors, small arms, peace support operations, HIV/AIDS, and food security.[95] Japan, the other most prominent advocate of human security in foreign policy, has been using and promoting the concept since the mid 1990s.[96] It has, for example,

[92] 'Timeline: Human Security in Canadian Foreign Policy' in R McRae and D Hubert (eds), *Human Security and the New Diplomacy: Protecting People, Promoting Peace* (Montreal and Kingston, McGill-Queen's University Press, 2001), at 267. The speech by then-foreign minister Lloyd Axworthy to the UN General Assembly in 1996 was the first of many to refer to human security: Canada, DFAIT, 'Notes for an Address by the Honourable Lloyd Axworthy Minister of Foreign Affairs to the 51st General Assembly of the United Nations', Statement 96/37 (24 September 1996) <http://w01.international.gc.ca/minpub> (accessed 26 February 2007).

[93] Canada, *Freedom from Fear*, above n 18; Canada, DFAIT, 'Axworthy Outlines Canada's United Nations Security Council Presidency Agenda', News Release No 64 (6 April 2000) <http://w01.international.gc.ca/minpub> (accessed 26 February 2007).

[94] Canada, DFAIT, 'Canada and Norway Form New Partnership on Human Security', News Release No 117 (11 May 1998) <http://w01.international.gc.ca/minpub> (accessed 26 February 2007).

[95] The relevant documents are collected in Human Security Network, 'Ministerial Meetings' <http://www.humansecuritynetwork.org/meeting-e.php> (accessed 26 February 2007).

[96] Japan, MOFA, *The Trust Fund for Human Security: For the 'Human-centered' 21st Century* (Tokyo, MOFA, 2006) <http://www.mofa.go.jp/mofaj/press/pr/pub/pamph/pdfs/t_fund21.pdf> (accessed 27 February 2007) [*Trust Fund*]; B Edström, 'Japan's Foreign Policy and Human Security' (2003) 15 *Japan Forum* 209.

incorporated human security into its Official Development Assistance policy.[97]

Both the UN Trust Fund for Human Security and the independent international Commission on Human Security were initiated and supported by the Japanese government.[98] Along with Japan, Thailand has been a promoter of the concept in Asia, where it has been used with increasing frequency but has had a mixed reception.[99] In part due to the efforts of Canada and Japan, human security has been referred to in the work of several intergovernmental organisations including the Group of Eight (G8), the Organization of American States, and the Asia-Pacific Economic Cooperation (APEC); it has also received some attention in the EU.[100]

Within the United Nations, in his role as Secretary-General, Kofi Annan was active in promoting a human security approach.[101] The concept has been used and referred to in various parts of the UN system, including, of course, the UNDP where it originated, as well as the United Nations High Commissioner for Refugees (UNHCR),[102] United Nations Educational, Scientific and Cultural Organization (UNESCO),[103] the UN Institute for Disarmament Research,[104] and the UN University.[105] There is, however, no common UN definition or position on human security, and some parts of the UN system have not embraced the concept.[106] Resistance on the part of some states has also limited its use in such key fora as the General

---

[97] Japan, *Trust Fund*, above n 96, at 7.

[98] *Ibid*, at 3, 9.

[99] See PM Evans, 'Human Security and East Asia: In the Beginning' (2004) 4 *Journal of East Asian Studies* 263.

[100] The report of an expert study group proposed making human security central to the EU's security policy: Study Group on Europe's Security, *A Human Security Doctrine for Europe: The Barcelona Report of the Study Group on Europe's Security Capabilities* (15 September 2004) <http://www.lse.ac.uk/Depts/global/Publications/HumanSecurityDoctrine.pdf> (accessed 7 March 2007). On human security in European security policy, see PH Liotta and T Owen, 'Sense and Symbolism: Europe Takes On Human Security' (2006) 36(3) *Parameters* 85.

[101] See, eg, K Annan, 'The Quiet Revolution' (1998) 4 *Global Governance* 123; UN, *Millennium Report of the Secretary-General of the United Nations: 'We the Peoples' The Role of the United Nations in the 21st Century*, by KA Annan (New York, United Nations, 2000), at 7, 43.

[102] See, eg, UNHCR, *Humanitarian Agenda*, above n 77, at ch 1.

[103] See, eg, UNESCO, 'SecuriPax Forum: The International Network for the Promotion of Human Security and Peace' <http://www.unesco.org/securipax> (accessed 26 February 2007); UNESCO, *What Agenda for Human Security in the Twenty-first Century?* (First International Meeting of Directors of Peace Research and Training Institutions, UNESCO, Paris, 27–28 November 2000) <http://unesdoc.unesco.org/images/0012/001238/123834e.pdf> (accessed 26 February 2007).

[104] UN Institute for Disarmament Research, 'Human Security' <http://www.unidir.ch/html/en/human_security.html> (accessed 26 February 2007).

[105] See, eg, UN University, 'Advancing Knowledge for Human Security and Development: UNU Strategic Directions 2005–2008' <http://www.unu.edu/strategicdirections05-08.pdf> (accessed 26 February 2007).

[106] MacFarlane and Khong, above n 1, at 10. On the inconsistent uptake within the UN see also K Timothy, 'Human Security Discourse at the United Nations' (2004) 16 *Peace Review* 19.

Assembly and the Security Council,[107] although it has quite often been invoked in the work of those bodies, and the 2005 World Summit Outcome expressed a commitment to 'discussing and defining the notion of human security in the General Assembly'.[108]

The concept of human security was adopted and used by the Commission on Global Governance and the more recent International Commission on Intervention and State Sovereignty (ICISS). The report of the Commission on Global Governance discussed various concepts of security, including human security, and emphasised the 'security of people and the planet' as its focus. The security of people, it said, 'must be regarded as a goal as important as the security of states'.[109] The ICISS report noted the increasing influence of the concept of human security in international relations and international law,[110] and cited its impact as part of the foundation for rethinking sovereignty as responsibility, a central idea of the report and its proposed shift in focus to the 'responsibility to protect'.[111] A few years later, the Secretary-General's High-Level Panel on Threats, Challenges and Change proposed a 'new and broader understanding' of collective security, addressing a broader range of threats and new collective strategies, institutions and responsibilities.[112] The report takes up the ICISS report's discussion of sovereignty as responsibility,[113] frequently refers to human security alongside state security, and stresses that the protection of states is important 'not because they are intrinsically good but because they are necessary to achieve the dignity, justice, worth and safety of their citizens'.[114]

In 2001, the Commission on Human Security, an independent international commission of experts, was established to pursue the following goals:

---

[107] MacFarlane and Khong, above n 1. They note that the term has never been used in a Security Council resolution, which remains true as of early 2007, although it has been used in other Security Council documents.

[108] UNGA Res 60/1 (24 October 2005) UN Doc A/RES/60/1, at para 143.

[109] Commission on Global Governance, *Our Global Neighborhood*, above n 25, at 80, 81.

[110] International Commission on Intervention and State Sovereignty, *Responsibility to Protect: Report of the International Commission on Intervention and State Sovereignty* (Ottawa, International Development Research Centre, 2001) <http://www.iciss.ca/pdf/ Commission-Report.pdf> (accessed 26 February 2007), at 6.

[111] *Ibid*, at 7, 13. This report will be further discussed below in chapter four, nn 68–9, 75 and accompanying text, and chapter five, nn 75–9, 91–3 and accompanying text.

[112] UN, *A More Secure World: Our Shared Responsibility* (Report of the Secretary-General's High-Level Panel on Threats, Challenges and Change) (New York, UN Department of Public Information, 2004) [*A More Secure World*], at 9–10.

[113] *Ibid*, at 17. As Odello notes, the High-Level Panel uses many ideas from the ICISS report, but without directly citing it: M Odello, 'Commentary on the United Nations' High-Level Panel on Threats, Challenges and Change' (2005) 10 *Journal of Conflict and Security Law* 231, at 235.

[114] UN, *A More Secure World*, above n 112, at 17.

1. to promote public understanding, engagement and support of human security and its underlying imperatives;
2. to develop the concept of human security as an operational tool for policy formulation and implementation; and
3. to propose a concrete programme of action to address critical and pervasive threats to human security.[115]

Co-chaired by former High Commissioner for Refugees Sadako Ogata and the eminent economist Amartya Sen, the Commission held a series of meetings and workshops, and produced its final report in 2003.[116] The report, entitled *Human Security Now*, sets out its approach to human security, defining the concept as 'protect[ing] the vital core of human lives in ways that enhance human freedoms and human fulfilment',[117] and emphasises both protection and empowerment in an integrated approach to address a range of insecurities including violent conflict and deprivation.[118] It then explores the human security approach in relation to issues of conflict (violent conflict, displaced persons, and post-conflict situations) and development (economic insecurity, health, and education),[119] before offering its conclusions and policy recommendations.[120] Following the publication of the report, an Advisory Board on Human Security was established to carry forward its recommendations. A Human Security Unit within the UN Office for the Coordination of Humanitarian Affairs (OCHA) now brings together the functions of the Advisory Board and the management of the UN Trust Fund for Human Security.[121]

The popularity of human security among governments and inter-governmental organisations has varied according to national political orientations and interests,[122] and in some cases the influence of individuals personally committed to a human security approach.[123] Some states have been quite resistant for various reasons, some of which will be explored in the next chapter, and even states that have advocated the

---

[115] Commission on Human Security, 'Plan for the Establishment of the Commission on Human Security', Press Release (24 January 2001) <http://www.humansecurity-chs.org/activities/outreach/pressrelease.pdf> (accessed 26 February 2007).

[116] CHS, *Human Security Now*, above n 83.

[117] *Ibid*, at 4.

[118] *Ibid*, at 2, 6–7, 10–12.

[119] The division between these two areas is made by the authors of the report: *ibid*, at 12.

[120] *Ibid*, at ch 8.

[121] Human Security Unit, 'Human Security Unit: Overview and Objectives' <http://ochaonline.un.org/DocView.asp?DocID=3293> (accessed 26 February 2007). For details see J Shusterman, 'An Interview with the Human Security Unit' (2006) 2 *Revue de sécurité humaine/Journal of Human Security* 97.

[122] See Timothy, above n 106, at 21–2, suggesting that human security is likely to appeal more to 'middle powers', and less to states with large military budgets or those reliant on the military–industrial complex.

[123] Two notable examples are Lloyd Axworthy (former Minister of Foreign Affairs for Canada) and Keizo Obuchi (former Prime Minister of Japan). On the latter see Edström, above n 96, at 214–19.

concept have been inconsistent in their commitment to it.[124] Although references to human security have become increasingly common in official documents, many of these references are merely in passing and without any apparent consideration of its implications—a common fate of newly popularised 'buzzwords', as Commission co-chair Amartya Sen has noted.[125] It would be fair to say that human security has remained on the margins of international discourse, and has not had the widespread impact that some of its advocates might have wished or predicted. However, its place is now established, even if that place is at the margins. It has taken on something of a 'life of its own', so that as its influence wanes in some quarters,[126] new interest and applications appear elsewhere.

A range of non-governmental organisations (NGOs) concerned with topics relevant to human security have used the concept to frame their work.[127] In the academic community, increasing interest has led to the formation of a number of groups, centres, and programmes focusing on the study of human security.[128] The body of academic literature on human security began to expand rapidly from about the year 2000 and continues to grow, now including several journal symposia, books, and a recently launched *Journal of Human Security*.[129] Scholars from several disciplines have contributed to a discussion of the meaning and utility of the concept, and its practical applications for policy. Recent efforts to gather empirical data on threats to human security have produced the *Human Security Report*, intended to be a regular publication paralleling the *Human Development Report*. The *Human Security Report 2005*, produced by the Human Security Centre at the University of British Columbia, seeks to

---

[124] See, eg, TS Hataley and KR Nossal, 'The Limits of the Human Security Agenda: The Case of Canada's Response to the Timor Crisis' (2004) 16 *Global Change, Peace & Security* 5.

[125] Quoted in Edström, above n 96, at 211.

[126] A Suhrke, 'A Stalled Initiative' (2004) 35 *Security Dialogue* 365.

[127] See, eg, African Human Security Initiative <http://www.africanreview.org/> (accessed 26 February 2007), a coalition of African NGOs; Project Ploughshares <http://www.ploughshares.ca/> (accessed 26 February 2007), a Canadian NGO focusing on arms.

[128] Eg, the Human Security Centre, based at the Liu Institute for Global Issues, University of British Columbia <http://www.humansecuritycentre.org/> (accessed 26 February 2007); the Institute for Human Security, an interdisciplinary research and education institute at the Fletcher School of Law & Diplomacy, <http://fletcher.tufts.edu/humansecurity/> (accessed 26 February 2007); the Harvard Program on Humanitarian Policy and Conflict Research, <http://www.hpcr.org/> (accessed 26 February 2007); and the European Training and Research Centre for Human Rights and Democracy in Graz, Austria <http://www.etc-graz.at/typo3/index.php?id=144> (accessed 7 March 2007); Center for Peace and Human Security at the Institut d'études politiques de Paris <http://www.peacecenter.sciences-po.fr/> (accessed 26 February 2007).

[129] *Revue de sécurité humaine/Journal of Human Security* <http://www.peacecenter.sciences-po.fr/journal/> (accessed 26 February 2007). The journal, the first issue of which was published in April 2006, is published by the Center for Peace and Human Security at the Institut d'études politiques de Paris.

identify and assess the incidence, causes, and consequences of 'global political violence'.[130] This initiative to improve the evidence base that informs policy making is of obvious importance, although the report's focus on political violence represents just one of several competing understandings of human security that have emerged from recent debates, as we will see in the next chapter.

The growing body of literature on human security has sought to address some of the important and difficult questions that continue to surround the concept. Human security can be—and has been—defined in many different ways, and scholars as well as political representatives have expressed a range of views on whether and how the concept is useful in analysis or policy making. Chapter two will discuss some of the most significant and contentious issues that have arisen in the literature.

---

[130] Human Security Centre, *Human Security Report 2005: War and Peace in the 21st Century* (New York, Oxford University Press, 2005), at viii, 1. An update was published in 2006: Human Security Centre, *Human Security Brief 2006* <http://www.humansecurity brief.info/> (accessed 7 March 2007).

2

Understanding Human Security

INTRODUCTION

HUMAN SECURITY HAS yet to enter the mainstream of security discourse, although references to it have proliferated in recent years. Although there are undoubtedly political and ideological reasons for this, it may also be attributable in part to ongoing uncertainty about the meaning and functions of the concept. In both official and academic discourse, debate about the definition of human security has been ongoing since the late 1990s. Opinions are also divided on the value of using human security in policy or analysis. Is human security really a new concept? Is it a useful concept, and if so, what exactly is its utility? What are the risks or 'opportunity costs' associated with adding human security to our discourse?

DEFINING HUMAN SECURITY

Despite (or perhaps because of) widespread use of the term 'human security', no universally accepted definition of the concept exists. In the words of one of its leading critics, 'everyone is for it, but few people have a clear idea of what it means'.[1] Even those who are generally sympathetic to use of the concept of human security acknowledge the challenge of adequately defining it. Many different definitions have been offered, and the proper scope and definition of human security have become a matter of some debate among governments and scholars. The difficulty of defining the concept and its broad scope have also led to concerns, discussed below, that it is too vague or broad to be practically or analytically useful.

As we saw in chapter one, the *Human Development Report* defined human security as having 'two main aspects. It means, first, safety from such chronic threats as hunger, disease and repression. And second, it means protection from sudden and hurtful disruptions in the patterns of

---

[1] R Paris, 'Human Security: Paradigm Shift or Hot Air?' (2001) 26 *International Security* 87 ['Paradigm Shift'], at 88.

daily life.'[2] Human security has two key dimensions, 'freedom from fear' and 'freedom from want', but can be threatened in any of seven inter-related areas: economic, food, health, environmental, personal, community, and political.[3] Economic security means having an 'assured basic income', either from work or 'in the last resort from some publicly financed safety net'.[4] Food security requires access to 'basic food', including both physical access and economic access, which is linked to economic security.[5] The report does not define health security, but reviews the most important and especially preventable causes of death in different populations, many of which are linked to economic or environmental insecurity.[6] Threats to environmental security include degradation of local eco-systems, water scarcity, lack of safe sanitation, desertification, severe air pollution, nuclear or chemical accidents, and natural disasters.[7] Personal security means security from physical violence of many forms, including torture, war, violent crime, or gender-based violence.[8] The community dimension is included because of the security that people derive from group membership, although it is noted that communities may also threaten people through oppressive group practices. Community security is threatened by 'modernization', ethnic conflict, and the treatment of indigenous populations.[9] Finally, political security or protection from state repression is identified as one of the most important aspects of human security.[10] The report emphasises that threats to one dimension of human security often spread to others, and that many threats cross national borders.[11]

The Canadian government, in taking up the concept, distanced itself from the United Nations Development Programme (UNDP) definition, criticising it as being too broad and ambitious, and therefore 'unwieldy as a policy instrument', and for 'emphasizing the threats associated with underdevelopment, . . . ignor[ing] the continuing human insecurity resulting from violent conflict'.[12] A key Canadian policy document on human security, significantly titled *Freedom from Fear*, defines human security as 'freedom from pervasive threats to people's rights, safety or

---

[2] UNDP, *Human Development Report 1994* (Oxford, Oxford University Press, 1994) [*HDR 1994*], at 23.

[3] *Ibid*, at 24–5.

[4] *Ibid*, at 25.

[5] *Ibid*, at 27.

[6] *Ibid*, at 27–8.

[7] *Ibid*, at 28–9.

[8] *Ibid*, at 30–1.

[9] *Ibid*, at 31–2.

[10] *Ibid*, at 32.

[11] *Ibid*, at 33–4.

[12] Canada, Department of Foreign Affairs and Trade (DFAIT), *Human Security: Safety for People in a Changing World* (Ottawa, DFAIT, 1999) [*Human Security*], at 3.

lives'.[13] Although this could be understood quite broadly, the Canadian position has focused on protection from violence—understood here as direct physical violence, rather than any broader notion of 'structural violence'.[14] The government has argued that 'Canada's contribution through its foreign policy has been to focus the concept of human security on protecting people from violence and to define an international agenda that follows from this objective'.[15] This approach has been followed by the Human Security Network[16] and in the *Human Security Report*, which justifies its use of the 'narrow' version of human security, focusing on political violence, on the grounds that first, other reports already analyse some of the threats to human security broadly defined, such as poverty, and second, that the broad concept has 'limited utility for policy analysis' because it 'lumps together' very diverse threats.[17]

Others have vigorously defended a broader definition of human security. Japan has criticised attempts to narrow the human security concept and agenda, arguing that 'freedom from want is no less critical than freedom from fear. So long as its objectives are to ensure the survival and dignity of individuals as human beings, it is necessary to go beyond thinking of human security solely in terms of protecting human life in conflict situations.'[18] Japan has defined human security as protection of the lives, livelihoods, and dignity of individuals,[19] and its use of the concept in foreign policy has emphasised development assistance. The Commission on Human Security used a broad definition in its report, defining human security as protection of:

[13] Canada, DFAIT, *Freedom from Fear: Canada's Foreign Policy for Human Security* (Ottawa, DFAIT, 2000) <http://www.humansecurity.gc.ca/pdf/freedom_from_fear-en.pdf> (accessed 27 February 2007) [*Freedom from Fear*], at 3.

[14] Structural violence refers to 'unintended harm done to human beings . . . a process, working slowly as the way misery in general, and hunger in particular, erode and finally kill human beings' as opposed to the intended, faster effect of 'direct violence': see J Galtung, 'Twenty-Five Years of Peace Research: Ten Challenges and Some Responses' (1985) 22 *Journal of Peace Research* 141, at 145–6.

[15] Canada, *Freedom from Fear*, above n 13, at 1.

[16] Human Security Network, 'The Vision of the Human Security Network' <http://www.humansecuritynetwork.org/menu-e.php> (accessed 27 February 2007).

[17] Human Security Centre, *Human Security Report 2005: War and Peace in the 21st Century* (New York, Oxford University Press, 2005) [*Human Security Report*], at viii.

[18] Japan, Ministry of Foreign Affairs (MOFA), 'Statement by Director-General Yukio Takasu at the International Conference on Human Security in a Globalized World' (Ulan-Bator, 8 May 2000) <http://www.mofa.go.jp/policy/human_secu/speech0005.html> (accessed 27 February 2007). See also Japan, MOFA, 'Toward Effective Cross-sectorial Partnership to Ensure Human Security in a Globalized World' (Statement by Mr Yukio Takasu, Director-General of Multilateral Cooperation Department, at the Third Intellectual Dialogue on Building Asia's Tomorrow, Bangkok, 19 June 2000) <http://www.mofa.go.jp/policy/human_secu/speech0006.html> (accessed 6 March 2007) and the official position of Thailand: Thailand, MOFA, 'Human Security' <http://www.mfa.go.th/web/23.php> (accessed 6 March 2007).

[19] See, eg, Japan, MOFA, *Diplomatic Bluebook 2002* (MOFA, Tokyo, 2002) <http://www.mofa.go.jp/policy/other/bluebook/2002/index.html> (accessed 6 March 2007), at 88.

the vital core of all human lives in ways that enhance human freedoms and human fulfilment . . . protecting people from critical (severe) and pervasive (widespread) threats and situations.[20]

The report deliberately avoids enumerating the content of human security, suggesting that the 'vital core' of life 'varies across individuals and societies'.[21] However, the Commission's discussion of human security encompasses threats such as disease, pollution, and deprivation, as well as physical violence.[22]

The two 'schools'[23] that have emerged are sometimes generally characterised as 'Western' and 'Asian' approaches, although these labels are too simplistic to be entirely accurate. As Acharya explains:

> It is tempting to see the divergent perspectives on human security, such as those held by Japan and Canada, as symptomatic of a familiar schism between Western liberalism and "Asian values." But this would be misleading. Disagreements about human security are as much West–West and East–East as East–West. They reflect genuine differences on philosophical and practical grounds.[24]

The difference also appears to have more to do with policy priorities than defining the concept of human security per se. For example, in narrowing its focus, Canada was attempting to set the limits of its 'human security agenda'.[25] The interests of particular countries are served in different ways by their respective approaches. A narrow definition allows governments to engage with a limited set of humanitarian and conflict issues while avoiding larger—and politically more difficult—questions about development and equitable distribution in the global economy. It has also been noted that Japan's development-focused approach has allowed it to maintain a more traditional position in its security policy and thereby avoid alienating its major security partner, the United States.[26]

There has also been a lively debate about the definition of human security amongst scholars. Advocates of a narrow definition have argued that the analytical clarity and utility of the concept depend on a more

---

[20] Commission on Human Security, *Human Security Now: Protecting and Empowering People* (New York, Commission on Human Security, 2003) <http://www.humansecurity-chs.org/finalreport/index.html> (accessed 27 February 2007) [CHS, *Human Security Now*], at 4.

[21] *Ibid.*

[22] *Ibid*, at 6 and chs 2–7.

[23] See K Bajpai, 'Human Security: Concept and Measurement' (Kroc Institute Occasional Paper 19:OP:1, August 2000), at 8. Bajpai discusses the Canadian and UNDP approaches and their similarities and differences at 9ff.

[24] See A Acharya, 'Debating Human Security: East Versus West' (2001) 56 *International Journal* 442, at 446–7.

[25] See Canada, *Freedom from Fear*, above n 13, at 1, 3.

[26] B Edström, 'Japan's Foreign Policy and Human Security' (2003) 15 *Japan Forum* 209, at 220. See also J Gilson and P Purvis, 'Japan's Pursuit of Human Security: Humanitarian Agenda or Political Pragmatism?' (2003) 15 *Japan Forum* 193, at 201, on the role that Japan's constitutional constraints have played in shaping its approach to human security.

focused definition. As seen above, the authors of the *Human Security Report* decided, partly on this basis, to limit its scope to 'political violence';[27] similarly, MacFarlane and Khong conclude that human security 'is about freedom from organized violence', suggesting this limited definition as a 'happy medium' between analytically weak inclusive approaches and an unduly narrow fixation on 'military-state security'.[28] A number of other scholars, such as Paris,[29] Lodgaard,[30] and Krause[31] have also rejected a broadly defined concept of human security on the basis that it is incoherent or unworkable. As we will see below, some have gone further to argue that *any* definition of human security lacks coherence, but broad definitions have been most strongly criticised. At the same time, however, others have argued just as strenuously that the inclusive and integrative nature of human security is one of its key strengths, and attempts to narrow it will undermine rather than increase its utility. Some scholars have proposed definitions that are at least as broad as those of the UNDP or Commission on Human Security. For example, Leaning's understanding of human security includes 'the social, psychological, political, and economic factors that promote and protect human well-being through time', encompassing not only 'minimum levels of food, water, and shelter' and 'a degree of protection from life threats' but also support for 'basic psychosocial needs for identity, recognition, participation, and autonomy'.[32] Defenders of a broad approach have argued that attempts to narrow our human security definition or policy agenda revert back to traditional understandings of national security, thus abandoning or subverting the transformative potential of the concept.[33] The narrow definition has also been criticised for excluding threats that are most relevant to many people, solely on the grounds that dealing with them would be too difficult.[34]

For some time the academic discussion of human security seemed to have 'foundered' on this problem of definition,[35] to the frustration of some

---

[27] Human Security Centre, *Human Security Report*, above n 17, at viii.

[28] SN MacFarlane and YF Khong, *Human Security and the UN: A Critical History* (Bloomington, Indiana University Press, 2006), at 245.

[29] Paris, 'Paradigm Shift', above n 1; R Paris, 'Still an Inscrutable Concept' (2004) 35 *Security Dialogue* 370, at 371.

[30] S Lodgaard, 'Human Security: Concept and Operationalisation' (Expert Seminar on Human Rights and Peace) (15 November 2000) UN Doc PD/HR/11.1 <http://www.upeace. org/documents/resources/report_lodgaard.doc> (accessed 7 March 2007).

[31] K Krause, 'The Key to a Powerful Agenda, if Properly Delimited' (2004) 35 *Security Dialogue* 367.

[32] J Leaning, 'Psychosocial Well-Being over Time' (2004) 35 *Security Dialogue* 354, at 354.

[33] AJ Bellamy and M McDonald, '"The Utility of Human Security": Which Humans? What Security? A Reply to Thomas and Tow' (2002) 33 *Security Dialogue* 373; D Roberts, 'Human Security or Human Insecurity? Moving the Debate Forward' (2006) 37 *Security Dialogue* 249, at 257.

[34] Roberts, above n 33, at 253.

[35] E Newman, 'A Normatively Attractive but Analytically Weak Concept' (2004) 35 *Security Dialogue* 358, at 358.

who thought the concept could make—in fact was already making—an important practical contribution.[36] This has led to renewed efforts to find 'a new direction out of the mire in which the debate currently remains trapped'.[37] The most promising of these have relied on a threshold to define the content of human security. For example, Owen has argued that threats should be included in the scope of human security on the basis of their severity, not because they fall into some predetermined category.[38] Similarly, the Commission on Human Security suggested in its report that 'what defines a threat to human security is its depth', regardless of the source or nature of the threat.[39] The concept of human security was deliberately conceived to be holistic and comprehensive so that it can be relevant to people in diverse circumstances.[40] Although some argue that including a range of threats makes it difficult to identify priorities,[41] this could be done on the basis of severity rather than excluding certain types of threats and privileging others on a global basis. MacFarlane and Khong use the analogy of airline luggage tags to illustrate the priority-setting problem that can arise from 'horizontal extension' of the concept: if all luggage has a 'priority' tag, they will arrive in random order at their destination rather than business-class passengers receiving their luggage first.[42] This well illustrates the need to assign priority on some basis, but one might ask: why should the individual threatened by physical violence necessarily be designated a 'business-class passenger' and another, dying of hunger or disease, always travel 'economy class'?

The most expansive definitions of human security are indeed unhelpful to the extent that they equate security with broad notions of well-being or enjoyment of the full range of human rights. It is possible, however, to delineate a more distinctive and precise concept of human security without excluding threats that may be most important to many individuals. Understanding human security as protection from threats of a certain severity is consistent with the meaning of security as being concerned with preservation and survival. Threats to individuals may also be human rights violations or environmental problems, for example, but if they pass the threshold they also become threats to security.[43] This threshold-based

---

[36] D Hubert, 'An Idea that Works in Practice' (2004) 35 *Security Dialogue* 351, at 351.

[37] Roberts, above n 33, at 257.

[38] T Owen, 'Human Security—Conflict, Critique and Consensus: Colloquium Remarks and a Proposal for a Threshold-Based Definition' (2004) 35(3) *Security Dialogue* 373 ['Conflict, Critique and Consensus'], at 382.

[39] CHS, *Human Security Now*, above n 20, at 11.

[40] UNDP, *HDR 1994*, above n 2, at 22.

[41] See, eg, MacFarlane and Khong, above n 28, at 237–40.

[42] *Ibid*, at 240. See also the earlier version of this analogy in YF Khong, 'Human Security: A Shotgun Approach to Alleviating Human Misery?' (2001) 7 *Global Governance* 231, at 233.

[43] Owen, 'Conflict, Critique and Consensus', above n 38, at 384.

approach is by no means new,[44] but has received renewed attention as a way of moving past the definition debate in the literature.[45]

How, then, is the threshold to be defined? A variety of descriptions have been used. Some have specifically referred to risks to life or mortality,[46] or implied this limitation by discussing causes of death as threats to human security.[47] This is consistent with understanding security as ensuring survival, although we might also include threats to individuals' quality of life or life circumstances that severely impair their ability to make meaningful choices or maintain a minimum level of dignity. Along these lines, the Commission on Human Security referred to protection from 'critical (serious)' and 'pervasive (widespread)' threats to the 'vital core' of human lives.[48] This does not necessarily require that threats be immediately life-threatening, although they must be serious and affect vital interests.

Some have further limited the relevant threats to *preventable* sources of harm.[49] This makes sense, since human security is about *protection* from certain threats, and if harms cannot be prevented then protective efforts may be futile. We do need to be careful, however, not to define preventable harms too narrowly here. For example, some have suggested that natural disasters such as the December 2004 tsunami 'are not usefully constructed as a human security problem' because they do not involve deliberate attempts to harm populations.[50] However, while it is true that no one can prevent a tsunami, hurricane, or similar event, the harm that these events cause can quite critically depend on human responses and on differing levels of vulnerability, which may well result from political or economic factors. Both of these were apparent in the aftermath of Hurricane Katrina, which saw greater and probably unnecessary harm resulting from poorly organised relief efforts and a disproportionate impact on lower income and minority groups.[51] We can therefore

---

[44] As Owen argues, it is arguably implicit in the UNDP definition (*ibid*). For a different kind of threshold-based approach, see King and Murray's definition based on 'generalized poverty', meaning falling below a set threshold in any area of human well-being: G King and CJL Murray, 'Rethinking Human Security' (2001–02) 116 *Political Science Quarterly* 585, at 594.

[45] In addition to Owen, 'Conflict, Critique and Consensus', above n 38, see Roberts, above n 33.

[46] See, eg, Roberts, above n 33, at 258; R Thakur, 'A Political Worldview' (2004) 35 *Security Dialogue* 347.

[47] See, eg, UNDP, *HDR 1994*, above n 2.

[48] CHS, *Human Security Now*, above n 20, at 4. Owen's definition is very similar: Owen, 'Conflict, Critique and Consensus', above n 38, at 383.

[49] See, eg, Roberts, above n 33, at 258. Owen does not specifically make preventability part of his definition but does repeatedly refer to preventable threats or harms: Owen, 'Conflict, Critique and Consensus', above n 38, at 379, 382, 385.

[50] MacFarlane and Khong, above n 28, at 245.

[51] See, eg, P Reynolds, 'Multiple Failures Caused Relief Crisis', BBC News 7 September 2005 <http://news.bbc.co.uk/2/hi/americas/4216508.stm> (accessed 27 February 2007); N Scheper-Hughes, 'Katrina: The Disaster and its Doubles' (2005) 21(6) *Anthropology Today* 2;

distinguish between preventable *events* and preventable *harm*, and critical threats to human lives may be properly considered relevant to human security if the harm they cause can be prevented or mitigated by human action. Following Roberts, it is suggested that if we are serious about protecting people's security, we cannot exclude consideration of:

> conscious but unintentional human agency or omission as deeper causes of . . . avoidable mortalities . . . in other words, the acts or omissions of human activity that have an identifiable role in indirectly contributing to far more deaths than are caused by traditional conceptualizations of security.[52]

Even if we limit human security to protection from critical and preventable threats to human lives, it would still give rise to a very broad policy agenda. The human security *agenda* could quite conceivably include elements that are excluded from a limited definition of human security. For example, I would suggest that a definition of human security that includes access to education within its scope is unduly broad.[53] However, education may be critical to reducing people's vulnerability and empowering them to successfully confront threats to their security, so including access to education in a policy agenda directed at human security is quite sensible.[54] This means that even the threshold-limited definition will not satisfy some of the critics of a human security approach, since as we will see in the next section, some of their objections are based on the breadth and ambition of the human security agenda. However, greater clarity can be achieved in the debates about defining human security if we distinguish more carefully between the human security concept or approach itself and the range of policies that might be required to give effect to it.

THE UTILITY OF HUMAN SECURITY

Along with debates about the definition of human security, the literature also contains extensive discussion about its utility. Opinions differ on whether the concept is useful at all, whether it has anything new to offer in terms of analysis or guiding policy, and whether using human security as a framework for issues of concern will ultimately be beneficial. Among those who do accept the utility of human security, there are also different views of what functions it can or should fulfil.

N Human Rights Committee, 'United States of America: Concluding Observations' (27 July 2006) UN Doc CCPR/C/USA/Q/3/CRP.4, at para 26.

[52] Roberts, above n 33, at 258.

[53] See, eg, Kofi Annan defining human security as including 'human rights, good governance, access to education and health care . . . [and] a healthy natural environment' (quoted in CHS, *Human Security Now*, above n 20, at 4).

[54] CHS, *Human Security Now*, above n 20, at ch 7.

Incoherent and Unworkable?

As we have just seen, the more expansive definitions of human security have been criticised as unworkable. Some critics of human security have argued that it is not coherent or useful as currently defined—or worse, that it *cannot* be defined in a way that is coherent or useful. There are, in fact, several related concerns here, from both theoretical and practical perspectives. One concern is that human security is conceptually incoherent, because trying to expand the concept of security beyond the traditional referent (the state) and threats (military force) undermines its analytical precision. Attempting to reconceptualise security in this way is said to 'dilute the established field of security studies' and 'compromise the analytical power of [its] ideas'.[55] Buzan has recognised the appeal of making individuals the referent object of security, but argues that 'the cost to be paid is loss of analytical purchase'.[56] Paris suggests that although human security may be useful as a 'rallying cry', its value for policy or for scholarly research is questionable.[57] While some critics argue that human security could be useful if it were more precisely defined,[58] others seem to suggest that changing the referent object necessarily deprives security of analytical value.

There are several possible responses to this critique. Perhaps the most obvious requires only that we recognise the irony of claims that the concept of human security muddies the previously clear waters of traditional thinking about security. Analysts have been arguing about the meaning of security for decades, even when it was limited to notions of national security from military threats in the realist/neorealist paradigm.[59] Conceptual difficulty and complexity are inherent to thinking about security and as such are unavoidable, perhaps even useful. They are also common to many important concepts, and not usually considered sufficient grounds to reject a concept.[60] Human security may in fact be

---

[55] WT Tow and R Trood, 'Linkages between traditional security and human security' in WT Tow, R Thakur and I Hyun (eds), *Asia's Emerging Regional Order: Reconciling Traditional and Human Security* (Tokyo, United Nations University Press, 2000), at 14 (describing a typical critique from 'traditionalists'). See also Bajpai, above n 23, at 49.

[56] B Buzan, 'A Reductionist, Idealistic Notion that Adds Little Analytical Value' (2004) 35 *Security Dialogue* 369 ['Little Analytical Value'], at 370.

[57] Paris, 'Paradigm Shift', above n 1.

[58] See, eg, MacFarlane and Khong, above n 28, at 236*ff*.

[59] See Bajpai, above n 23, at 50–51, on the complexity and difficulty of the study of security in the realist and neorealist tradition. See also RBJ Walker, 'The Subject of Security' in K Krause and MC Williams (eds), *Critical Security Studies: Concepts and Cases* (Minneapolis, University of Minnesota Press, 1997), at 63. The comments of Wolfers in 'National Security as an Ambiguous Symbol' in A Wolfers, *Discord and Collaboration: Essays on International Politics* (Baltimore, Johns Hopkins Press, 1962), at 147–50 regarding national security are strikingly similar to some contemporary concerns about human security.

[60] See, eg, B McSweeney, *Security, Identity and Interests: A Sociology of International Relations* (Cambridge, Cambridge University Press, 1999), at 200: in discussing whether security is

useful precisely *because* it challenges the previously set boundaries of analysis, and if that is the case then the challenge must be faced: 'it cannot be the case that confronted by a complex and dangerous world that confounds our theoretical and policy "comfort zones", we climb back into those zones'.[61] Whether human security does have distinctive analytical value that merits this effort can only be tested through its application to practical and theoretical problems.

Next, in considering these criticisms it is important to acknowledge, as was done above, that some definitions and uses of human security are indeed so broad and all-encompassing as to compromise their utility as analytical tools. Further, the policy agenda to which human security gives rise, even using a more limited definition, is also broad and ambitious, to the point of being overwhelming. Perhaps the most common criticism of human security is that the concept is too broad and vague to provide useful guidance to policy-makers.[62] Since the concept is holistic in its inclusion of a broad range of threats, the worry is that it does not offer sufficient means for distinguishing or prioritising the various threats.[63] Khong asks: 'Is it not the case that, from the human security perspective, every threat to the well-being of every individual in every state is a security issue? Ironically, in making all individuals a priority, none actually benefits.'[64] On this view, not only do we not know where to begin, but neither do the proponents of a human security approach have the resources or political will to follow through on such an ambitious policy agenda.[65] Even when the commitment is there, the 'human security agenda' seems to demand a capacity for 'social engineering' that we are not likely to possess.[66] As a result, invoking human security may only give 'false hope',[67] while

'essentially contested', he suggests that 'the error lies in the presumption that other social concepts in general—like the state—are any more stable, any less prone to the slippage of meaning which is a condition of the social'.

[61] Bajpai, above n 23, at 51.

[62] See, eg, H Owens and B Arneil, 'Human Security paradigm shift: a new lens on Canadian foreign policy?' (1999) 7(1) *Canadian Foreign Policy* 1, at 2; Paris, 'Paradigm Shift', above n 1, at 88–93; A Hammerstad, 'Whose Security? UNHCR, Refugee Protection and State Security After the Cold War' (2000) 31 *Security Dialogue* 391, at 399; Bajpai, above n 23, at 50; M McDonald, 'Human Security and the Construction of Security' (2002) 16 *Global Society* 277, at 280; E Lammers, *Refugees, Gender and Human Security: A Theoretical Introduction and Annotated Bibliography* (Utrecht, International Books, 1999), at 48.

[63] See, eg, Paris, 'Paradigm Shift', above n 1, at 92; MacFarlane and Khong, above n 28, at 237–40.

[64] Khong, above n 42, at 233. See also MacFarlane and Khong, above n 28, at 240; Paris, 'Paradigm Shift', above n 1, McDonald, above n 63, at 281.

[65] Khong, above n 42, at 233; D Stairs, 'Canada and the Security Problem' (1999) 54 *International Journal* 386, at 399, 401.

[66] Stairs, above n 65, at 400–401.

[67] Khong, above n 42, at 236.

allowing states to pick and choose among agenda items according to their perceived national interests.[68]

It would be futile to deny that the human security agenda is daunting. It requires action across a range of interrelated areas, and to large extent does defy attempts to identify discrete and limited priorities. The scope of this action increases even more if we include not just protection from immediate danger but also efforts to address 'creeping vulnerabilities'[69] and to empower populations.[70] As if this were not enough, in order to be effective, preventive action by its very nature often needs to be taken under conditions of uncertainty, when information about causal relationships and the likely effectiveness of available strategies is limited. The holistic nature of human security, especially on its more expansive definitions, makes understanding causation even more difficult.[71] The task facing policy-makers is challenging, to say the least. Dan Henk has rightly cautioned:

> It is important that participants take a long-term view of future benefits. A human security agenda almost by definition requires consistency and patience. The coherence and comprehensiveness of the effort must be matched by its persistence.[72]

Again, though, this difficulty is hardly unique to human security. Efforts to ensure national security—or any other kind of security—require multiple strategies, difficult judgements, and the taking of calculated risks. Narrowing the scope of security to military threats and military means does limit the field, but the complexity of strategic choices remains significant. An entire academic sub-discipline of strategic studies has been devoted to analysing this complexity. National security policies within the military realm are certainly not immune to difficult predictions or unintended negative consequences;[73] quite to the contrary, these are so common that the term 'blowback' was coined to refer to the unintended negative effects of security strategies, especially covert operations, creating or exacerbating new sources of insecurity.[74] Nor does the breadth

[68] J Jockel and J Sokolsky, 'Lloyd Axworthy's Legacy: Human Security and the Rescue of Canadian Defence Policy' (2000–2001) 56 *International Journal* 1, at 18.

[69] PH Liotta, 'Through the Looking Glass: Creeping Vulnerabilities and the Reordering of Security' (2005) 36 *Security Dialogue* 49.

[70] CHS, *Human Security Now*, above n 20, at 10–12.

[71] MacFarlane and Khong, above n 28, at 240–41.

[72] D Henk, 'Human Security: Relevance and Implications' (2005) 35 *Parameters* 91, at 103.

[73] The past US strategies of supporting the Mujahideen and the Taliban in Afghanistan and providing military assistance to Iraq come to mind as notorious recent examples: see, eg, N Nojumi, *The Rise of the Taliban in Afghanistan: Mass Mobilization, Civil War, and the Future of the Region* (New York, Palgrave, 2002), at 222–3; R Hollis, 'The US Role: Helpful or Harmful?' in LG Potter and GG Sick (eds), *Iran, Iraq, and the Legacies of War* (New York, Palgrave Macmillan, 2004).

[74] See, eg, P Bergen and A Reynolds, 'Blowback Revisited' (2005) 84(6) *Foreign Affairs* 2; C Johnson, *Blowback: The Costs and Consequences of American Empire* (New York, Henry Holt, 2004).

or difficulty of the policy agenda attached to a concept of security necessarily reflect an inherent weakness of that concept. In fact, we might even suggest the opposite: an approach or concept that purported to identify clear and manageable policy prescriptions in response to complex global problems should immediately be suspect.

The kind and degree of clarity that we require from a concept will ultimately depend on how we intend to use it. While breadth in itself may present difficulties for policy-makers, it is problematic for analytical purposes only if it is indicative of conceptual vagueness and indeterminacy. Does the concept of human security have a determinate core of meaning that is sufficient to make it potentially useful in analysing issues—for our purposes, issues of international law? And how precise need this meaning be in order for the concept to serve as a reference point in this analysis? In attempting to answer these questions—final judgement on which must be suspended until the end of this project and even beyond—it is useful to look at some suggestions about the use of human security as a conceptual approach or orientation rather than a policy agenda, the former use being more relevant to the present project. An early Canadian policy paper, for example, suggested that 'human security is perhaps best understood as a shift in perspective or orientation' or as 'an alternative way of seeing the world, taking people as its point of reference'.[75] Human security can be understood—in the opinion of some, *best* understood—as a 'normative' or 'critical' project, and uncertainty about definitions or policy prescriptions need not undermine this function.[76] From this perspective, questions about the scope of relevant threats or definition of policy agendas are secondary to the essential idea of giving priority to the security of individuals, an idea which is neither unusually complex nor particularly vague, no matter how challenging it may be to give effect to it in practice. While this basic idea may be difficult to translate into a foreign policy agenda, it may be sufficient for use as an analytical tool. Some of the various ways in which human security can be used will be explored below, and throughout the subsequent chapters.

Old Wine in New Bottles?

Another common and important critique of human security is that it adds nothing new to our analysis of the issues that fall within its scope. Some argue that the so-called 'new' concept of human security is not new at all,

---

[75] Canada, *Human Security*, above n 12, at 5.

[76] McDonald, above n 63, at 277–8; H Hudson, '"Doing" Security As Though Humans Matter: A Feminist Perspective on Gender and the Politics of Human Security' (2005) 36(2) *Security Dialogue* 155, at 162, 164. See also M Zambelli, 'Putting People at the Centre of the International Agenda: The Human Security Approach' <http://hei.unige.ch/ped/docs/Human-security.doc> (accessed 27 February 2007), at 9.

but redundant and unnecessary.[77] If human security is merely a way of revisiting familiar ideas, we may be better off using the frameworks we already have rather than adding to the 'long line of neologisms' in international affairs.[78] Even if we do accept that human security could contribute something novel, it is important to understand how it relates to existing frameworks.

As explained in chapter one, human security was developed as a complement to human development, and these two concepts can be described as distinct but 'mutually reinforcing' concepts.[79] The *Human Development Report* described human development as 'a process of widening the range of people's choices' and human security as their ability to 'exercise these choices safely and freely . . . [being] relatively confident that the opportunities they have today are not totally lost tomorrow'.[80] Although they are interdependent, each has a different focus: human development focuses on creating and enhancing opportunities and capabilities, and human security is more concerned with protection against risks and reduction of vulnerability.[81] The Commission on Human Security has suggested that human security furthers and broadens human development through its emphasis on 'downside risks'.[82]

Human rights and human security have also been presented as mutually reinforcing, but the relationship between them is more problematic. One of the most obvious questions for lawyers approaching the concept of human security is how it relates to the conceptual and legal framework of human rights. The response of human rights advocates to human security has been mixed, but generally cautious.[83] Some would argue that human security simply represents a 'repackaging' of human rights, rather than a substantively new concept.[84] Refocusing security on the individual produces an agenda that may be little different from that of human rights.[85] If human security 'means no more (nor less) than protecting individual rights and freedoms, [then] the distinction between it and the human rights approach is unclear'.[86] At best, then, human security may be redundant, or perhaps only of marginal value as an

[77] Eg, C Tomuschat, 'Human Rights between Idealism and Realism' (Academy of European Law, 13th Session, Florence, Italy, 18 June 2003).

[78] Paris, 'Paradigm Shift', above n 1, at 87.

[79] Canada, *Freedom from Fear*, above n 13, at 3; Canada, *Human Security*, above n 12, at 7.

[80] UNDP, *HDR 1994*, above n 2, at 23.

[81] Commission on Human Security, 'Report: Second Meeting of the Commission on Human Security' (16–17 December 2001) <http://www.humansecurity-chs.org/activities/meetings/second/report.pdf> (accessed 27 February 2007), at 5.

[82] CHS, *Human Security Now*, above n 20.

[83] K Vignard, 'Editor's Note' (2004) 3 *Disarmament Forum* 1.

[84] D Petrasek, 'Human Rights "Lite"? Thoughts on Human Security' (2004) 3 *Disarmament Forum* 59, at 59.

[85] Buzan, 'Little Analytical Value', above n 57, at 369.

[86] Petrasek, above n 84, at 60.

additional way of arguing for respect for human rights,[87] or allowing human rights issues to be discussed in contexts where the language of human rights faces resistance.[88]

The degree of overlap between a 'human security approach' and a 'human rights approach' will, of course, depend on how each of these is defined. As we saw above, the nature and scope of human security is still much contested; although human rights are better established and more clearly defined in a body of law and scholarship, the limits of human rights and a human rights approach are still open to debate. It does appear that much of the ground central to human security has already been covered from the perspective of human rights. As we saw in chapter one, part of the justification for shifting our focus from state to human security is that states do not always protect the security of their people and in fact may threaten individuals' security. None of this, of course, is news to those with an interest in human rights, and so one can understand their impatience if it is sometimes treated as a new insight by those advocating a human security approach. A central objective of human rights is to protect individuals from abuses by the state; international human rights law also includes principles specifically governing the extent to which individuals' rights may be limited for the sake of national security.[89] The fact remains, however, that many analyses of security have ignored the ambivalent relationship between state and individual security, and therefore part of the value of human security has been to point out this 'blind spot'[90]—in a sense, to make the connection between what has long been obvious in human rights, on one hand, and parallel concerns in security, on the other. This is an important function, albeit a modest one, which would then open up space for consideration of the relevant human rights provisions in discussions of security.

The Commission on Human Security, among others, has suggested that human rights and human security are 'mutually reinforcing'[91] and can 'fruitfully supplement each other'.[92] One way of linking human security and human rights is to see the protection of human rights as a means of ensuring human security, and human security as a goal or objective of

---

[87] Petrasek, above n 84, at 61.

[88] Buzan, 'Little Analytical Value', above n 57, at 369–70.

[89] See, eg, International Covenant on Civil and Political Rights (adopted 16 December 1966, entered into force 23 March 1976) 999 UNTS 171, arts 4, 12(3), 13, 14(1), 19(3)(b), 21, 22(2); UN Sub-Commission on the Prevention of Discrimination and Protection of Minorities, 'Siracusa Principles on the Limitation and Derogation Provisions in the International Covenant on Civil and Political Rights' (28 September 1984) UN Doc E/CN.4/1985/4, Annex.

[90] MacFarlane and Khong, above n 28, at 237.

[91] CHS, *Human Security Now*, above n 20, at 10.

[92] *Ibid*, at 9.

human rights protection.[93] Some see this so-called 'rights-based' approach to human security as just one possible approach, contrasting with others more concerned with safety or development,[94] but many view rights as central to human security. Human rights are often said to constitute part of the normative or conceptual foundation of human security,[95] and the Commission on Human Security report referred to respect for human rights as the 'core' of human security.[96] A link with human rights is also thought to lend greater power to human security, because of the duties that are commonly associated with rights.[97] If the relationship is supposed to be mutual, what can human rights gain from a link with human security? Suggestions include resolving tensions or divisions within human rights,[98] and helping to define the content, importance, and relevance of basic rights.[99] These have been met with some scepticism, however.[100]

Even if there are some potential benefits to adding a new concept of human security and linking it to human rights, there are also problems and risks. Human security may in fact be worse than redundant if it has the effect of undermining commitments to human rights. Could human security be simply 'human rights lite',[101] a watered-down version of human rights made more palatable for regimes that have traditionally

---

[93] See, eg, *ibid*, at 10; BG Ramcharan, *Human Rights and Human Security* (The Hague, Martinus Nijhoff, 2002), especially at 3–4, 9–10; Commission on Human Security, 'Relación entre Derechos Humanos y Seguridad Humana' (Documento de trabajo) (Comisión sobre Seguridad Humana—Universidad para la Paz—Instituto Interamericano de Derechos Humanos, Reunión de Expertos, San José, Costa Rica, 1 December 2001) <http://www. humansecurity-chs.org/activities/outreach/sanjosedoc.pdf> (accessed 27 February 2007); Canada, *Freedom from Fear*, above n 13, at 3–4.

[94] FO Hampson, *Madness in the Multitude: Human Security and World Disorder* (Don Mills, Ontario, Oxford University Press, 2002), at 17*ff*. Hampson calls an approach that emphasises strengthening human rights and legal frameworks and institutions the 'rights-based' or 'human rights/rule-of-law' approach to human security. See also A Acharya and A Acharya, 'Human Security in Asia Pacific: Puzzle, Panacea or Peril?' (2000) 27 *CANCAPS Bulletin/Bulletin du CONCSAP* 1 <http://www.cancaps.ca/cbul27.pdf> (accessed 6 March 2007).

[95] See, eg, Ramcharan, above n 93, at 3, 5, 9; Commission on Human Security, 'Declaration on Human Rights as an Essential Component of Human Security' (Workshop on Relationship Between Human Rights and Human Security, San Jose, Costa Rica, 2 December 2001) <http://www.humansecurity-chs.org/activities/outreach/sanjosedec.pdf> (accessed 27 February 2007), at para 2; Lodgaard, above n 30, at 8.

[96] CHS, *Human Security Now*, above n 20, at 10.

[97] *Ibid*, at 9; E Seidensticker, 'Human Security, Human Rights, and Human Development' (5 February 2002) <http://www.humansecurity-chs.org/activities/outreach/0206harvard. pdf> (accessed 6 March 2007).

[98] Seidensticker, above n 97.

[99] CHS, *Human Security Now*, above n 20, at 9, 10.

[100] See, eg, Petrasek, above n 84, at 61, who is especially critical of the CHS report's contention that human security can contribute to human rights by defining what should receive protection.

[101] Petrasek, *ibid*.

been hostile to rights discourse?[102] Some point to the example of Japan and other Asian countries as evidence that human security may, indeed, be displacing rather than complementing human rights. It has been argued that Japan's advocacy of human security has allowed it to claim support for human rights without offending 'sensitive' neighbours,[103] and even, perhaps, without showing much real commitment to human rights.[104] Some Asian governments have been more receptive to formulations of human security that do not explicitly make the link with human rights protection.[105] The concern is not limited to any particular region, however:

> We need to be watchful lest the focus on human security and the 'Millennium Development Goals' at the UN takes us backward to the 1970s–1980s framework of basic needs as opposed to rights. Rather, we need to ensure that basic needs are seen as human rights and that rights are respected in the pursuit of meeting those needs.[106]

Replacing human rights with a weaker and more limited concept of human security would be a significant step backwards, so the concern is understandable.

One way of minimising this risk may be to articulate and maintain separate roles for human rights and human security, despite their inter-relatedness.[107] The terms 'human rights approach' and 'human security approach' are both sometimes used in a very general way to refer to a human-centred approach to a particular issue, and in this sense they could be very similar, even interchangeable. However, this would not do justice to either approach. At the risk of stating the obvious, human rights are about *rights* and therefore have a particular function. Human rights comprise a body of legal norms, and a human rights approach is concerned with the elaboration, implementation, and enforcement of legal rights and duties. Human security is not unconcerned with rights; indeed they feature prominently in most definitions of the concept. However, human security, rather than being a body of norms, is a concept that is designed to be used in a variety of ways, including in the interpretation and development of legal norms. Human security is also narrower than human rights in that it is most concerned with a limited set of basic or fundamental rights pertaining to 'survival, to livelihood, and to basic dignity' as opposed to the more expansive rights and obligations that

---

[102] Buzan, 'Little Analytical Value', above n 57, at 370.

[103] Edström, above n 26, at 221.

[104] M Fujioka, 'Japan's Human Rights Policy at Domestic and International Levels: Disconnecting Human Rights from Human Security?' (2003) 15 *Japan Forum* 287.

[105] Acharya, above n 24, at 448.

[106] C Bunch, 'A Feminist Human Rights Lens' (2004) 16 *Peace Review* 29, at 31.

[107] See, eg, K Boyle and S Simonsen, 'Human Security, Human Rights and Disarmament' (2004) 3 *Disarmament Forum* 5, at 5, arguing that human security and human rights are conceptually linked, but 'are separate ideas and have separate functions'.

remain even when people are secure.[108] This should not be understood as an attempt to narrow the scope of human rights or deny the importance of rights that fall outside the sphere of human security; it merely reflects a different focus. At the same time, a human security approach in some respects extends beyond human rights, at least as they are currently embodied in international law.[109] One of the goals of subsequent chapters will be to tease out and evaluate the distinct scope and functions of human security as compared to human rights.

The Risks of Human Security Discourse

Part of the rationale for introducing the concept of human security was that it would shift attention and resources away from military concerns toward other areas important to human survival and well-being. To designate something as a security issue lends it a degree of importance and urgency that may be useful from an advocate's perspective. The term 'securitisation' has been coined to refer to this process (or 'speech act').[110] Securitisation presents an issue 'as so important that it should be dealt with decisively by top leaders prior to other issues'[111] and is therefore attractive as a strategy. However, it also has negative connotations and consequences. The effect of securitisation is to justify emergency action or extraordinary measures, beyond the ordinary rules; these have tradi-tionally included such things as secrecy, rights violations, and a lack of democratic accountability.[112] As a result, it is argued that securitisation 'should be seen as negative, as a failure to deal with issues as normal politics'.[113] The 'problematic side effects' of securitising issues must therefore be weighed against its potential advantages.[114] With this caution in mind, it could be that a human security approach simply 'reinforces a

---

[108] S Alkire, 'Conceptual Framework for Human Security (Excerpt: Working Definition and Executive Summary)' (16 February 2002) <http://www.humansecurity-chs.org/activities/outreach/frame.pdf> (accessed 27 February 2007), at 2, 6. Alkire's notion of fundamental rights here bears some resemblance to Shue's definition of basic rights as those rights that 'specify the line below which no one is to be allowed to sink' or that are 'everyone's minimum reasonable demands upon the rest of humanity', the enjoyment of which is 'essential to the enjoyment of all other rights': H Shue, *Basic Rights: Subsistence, Affluence, and U.S. Foreign Policy*, 2nd edn (Princeton, NJ, Princeton University Press, 1996), at 18–19.

[109] R McRae, 'Human Security in a Globalized World' in R McRae and D Hubert (eds), *Human Security and the New Diplomacy: Protecting People, Promoting Peace* (Montreal and Kingston, McGill-Queen's University Press, 2001), at 16; Hampson, above n 94, at 15.

[110] See B Buzan, O Wæver and J de Wilde, *Security: A New Framework for Analysis* (Boulder, Lynne Rienner, 1998); O Wæver, 'Securitization and Desecuritization' in RD Lipschutz, *On Security* (New York, Columbia University Press, 1995).

[111] Buzan, Wæver and de Wilde, above n 110, at 29.

[112] *Ibid*, at 24, 29.

[113] *Ibid*, at 29.

[114] *Ibid*, at 19.

mistaken tendency to idealize security as the desired end goal'.[115] However, others have pointed out that securitisation may not necessarily be as negative as it is made out to be, and that discouraging securitisation of new issues may serve the interests of those who wish to maintain the status quo.[116]

Related concerns are that reframing issues in terms of security could also be harmful because of security's association with militarisation and an 'us and them' mentality. Krause asks: 'does it actually lead us down the wrong path when we treat certain problems—such as migration or HIV/AIDS—as threats to "our own" security, building walls between people where we could be building bridges?'[117] Even though human security was introduced as a way of diverting attention and resources from military responses, the association between securitisation and militarisation may be so strong that it will tend to creep back in. If this happens, then 'the human security approach, by introducing and legitimizing a whole new set of issues (e.g., the environment) that can be securitized, may unwittingly lead to military solutions to political and socioeconomic problems'.[118] Although it should be possible to minimise these risks, we do need to take into consideration the fact that any security concept carries with it some 'baggage' that may lead the discourse in unexpected and problematic directions.

Feminist critiques have also raised several concerns about recent attempts to reframe issues in terms of human security. One is that an emphasis on protection could cast individuals, and especially women, in a passive role as victims, rather than recognising and supporting their agency.[119] The report of the Commission on Human Security has gone some way to addressing this concern by emphasising empowerment along with protection, and this is perhaps one of its most significant contributions.[120] Another concern is that a focus on 'human' security may lose sight of differences and 'conceal the gendered underpinnings of security practices'.[121] However, having voiced this concern, Hudson suggests that, with feminist perspectives acting as a corrective to this tendency, human security could serve important critical functions.[122] Others are profoundly sceptical of claims that human security represents a new approach. Crosby contrasts it to earlier feminist attempts to redefine security and dismisses human security as part of a 'charade' designed to

---

[115] Buzan, 'Little Analytical Value', above n 57, at 369.
[116] G Hoogensen and SV Rottem, 'Gender Identity and the Subject of Security' (2004) 35 *Security Dialogue* 155, at 162.
[117] Krause, above n 31, at 368.
[118] MacFarlane and Khong, above n 28, at 242.
[119] Hudson, above n 76, at 170.
[120] See, eg, CHS, *Human Security Now*, above n 20, at 10–12.
[121] Hudson, above n 76, at 157.
[122] *Ibid*, at 157, 164. See also Bunch, above n 106, at 33.

'give the appearance of security having taken on a human face' while remaining 'the face of power acting in its own interests'.[123] Critiques like this aim not so much at the concept of human security itself, as at the ways in which it can be used (or misused) as part of discourse and practice.[124] Even Crosby acknowledges that although (in her opinion) the Canadian government 'has it all wrong' in its human security approach, 'even having it wrong opens spaces for change'.[125] In later chapters, some examples of the potential for misuse, distortion, or co-option of human security will be critically examined.

Potential Uses of Human Security

Obviously, what constitutes an adequate definition of human security and whether it can make a valuable contribution depends largely on how one expects it to be used. Human security is variously referred to as a concept, an approach, a perspective, or an agenda. While the distinctions between these are not always sharply drawn, they do indicate different potential functions. There are several possible ways of classifying these; some commentators have distinguished 'analytical' and 'policy' or 'political' functions.[126] There seem to be at least three basic functions that human security could usefully serve in relation to international law, which can briefly be described as 'agenda-setting', 'question-framing', and 'critical' functions.[127]

The human security *agenda* can be understood as an agenda for action that is intended to protect human security or elaborated by reference to the concept of human security. Items are included on the agenda and assigned priority because of their importance for human security. A human security agenda has been developed by various governments and organisations, comprised of the areas that need to be addressed in order to increase the level of security enjoyed by individuals worldwide. These could include particular threats to security, vulnerable groups whose security is of special concern, and means or agents with an important role in increasing human security. Notwithstanding the debates about scope and definition described above, there is a high degree of consistency in the items

[123] AD Crosby, 'Myths of Canada's Human Security Pursuits: Tales of Tool Boxes, Toy Chests, and Tickle Trunks' in CT Sjolander, H Smith and D Steinstra (eds), *Feminist Perspectives on Canadian Foreign Policy* (Don Mills, Ontario, Oxford University Press, 2003), at 91.

[124] On the danger of co-option, see also A Burke, 'Caught between National and Human Security: Knowledge and Power in Post-crisis Asia' (2001) 13 *Pacifica Review* 215, at 222.

[125] Crosby, above n 123, at 106.

[126] MacFarlane and Khong, above n 28, at 236–7; Hudson, above n 76, at 155.

[127] B von Tigerstrom, 'International Law and the Concept of Human Security' in T Dolgopol and J Gardam (eds), *The Challenge of Conflict: International Law Responds* (Leiden, Brill, 2006).

proposed for inclusion on the agenda. It brings together an otherwise diverse set of issues, concerns, and initiatives, including: landmines; transnational organised crime; terrorism; small arms; illicit drugs; environmental degradation; infectious diseases (especially HIV/AIDS); poverty; gender-based violence; natural disasters; war-affected children; protection of civilians in armed conflict; internally displaced persons and refugees; peacekeeping and peacebuilding; humanitarian intervention; the International Criminal Court; conflict prevention; corporate social responsibility; and the role of non-state actors.[128] As Lloyd Axworthy, one of the concept's leading proponents, has suggested, when human security is taken as the point of departure, the 'road forward has many paths. What unites them is a very simple aspiration—security for all people, everywhere. It is, in essence, an effort to construct a global society where the safety of the individual is the central priority.'[129] Human security has been described as a 'unifying concept'[130] and can be used to bring diverse issues together in a single agenda. Although this exacerbates the risk of overwhelming breadth and complexity, it also allows policy-makers and analysts to see connections between issues that might not otherwise be recognised. In fact, some commentators have suggested that this ability to link diverse issues and encourage a coordinated approach constitutes the most important contribution of a human security approach.[131]

The agenda-setting function is related to what others have identified as the political or policy function of human security—at its simplest, human security as a 'slogan' or 'rallying cry'.[132] It serves to draw attention to

[128] For some examples of the range of issues considered to be part of the human security agenda, see CHS, *Human Security Now*, above n 20; Canada, *Freedom from Fear*, above n 13; Japan, MOFA, *The Trust Fund for Human Security: For the 'Human-centered' 21st Century* (Tokyo, MOFA, 2006) <http://www.mofa.go.jp/mofaj/press/pr/pub/pamph/pdfs/t_fund21.pdf> (accessed 27 February 2007); Human Security Network, 'A Perspective on Human Security: Chairman's Summary' (Lysøen, Norway, 20 May 1999) <http://www.humansecuritynetwork.org/docs/Chairman_summaryMay99-e.php> (accessed 6 March 2007); Human Security Network, 'Second Ministerial Meeting: Chairman's Summary' (Lucerne, 11–12 May 2000) <http://www.humansecuritynetwork. org/docs/Chairman_summary-e.php> (accessed 25 April 2007); Human Security Network, 'Report on the Status of the Human Security Network's Main Action Areas' (2002) <http://www.humansecurity network.org/docs/santiago_annex2-e.php> (accessed 27 February 2007); and R McRae and D Hubert (eds), *Human Security and the New Diplomacy: Protecting People, Promoting Peace* (Montreal and Kingston, McGill-Queen's University Press, 2001).

[129] L Axworthy, 'Introduction' in R McRae and D Hubert (eds), above n 128, at 12. Similarly, see CHS, *Human Security Now*, above n 20, at 4, 6–7: human security integrates a diverse set of concerns and agendas.

[130] K Annan, 'The Quiet Revolution' (1998) 4 *Global Governance* 123, at 136.

[131] K Graham, '"We Have Come to a Fork in the Road . . . Now We Must Decide": Human Security in Context' (Opening Address at the 17th Annual Meeting of the Academic Council of the United Nations System, 30 June–2 July 2004; UN-CRIS Occasional Paper 0-2004/17) <http://www.cris.unu.edu/admin/documents/OP%20KENNEDY%20GRAHAM%20Geneva%203%20Short.pdf> (accessed 27 February 2007), at 6; Henk, above n 72, at 102.

[132] MacFarlane and Khong, above n 28, at 237; Paris, 'Paradigm Shift', above n 1, at 88–9, 102.

issues and mobilise resources to respond to them. However, it also plays a role in analysis by determining what is considered a relevant issue for study. Reference to the concept of human security can be especially helpful in drawing attention to issues that may have been neglected because they have not seemed significant for national or international security, yet have serious consequences for the security of individuals. Through the agenda-setting function of human security, we may also be better able to identify areas where the protection of a vulnerable group or response to a threat may be inadequate, and where we might attempt to 'fill the gap' with specific initiatives such as the development or adaptation of an institution or set of norms. In a human security approach, attention is focused on identifying and preventing or mitigating, through collective action, sources of threats to individuals' security. This offers a way of identifying and prioritising issues to be addressed. As suggested above, a threshold-based definition of human security would encourage prioritisation on the basis of severity of threats, which may be quite context-specific.

Although identifying issues as part of a human security agenda may be useful in itself, it also entails bringing a particular perspective to bear upon them and approaching them in a particular way. Just getting items on the agenda may not be enough; the risk of negative effects of securitisation is greatest if we do not follow through and also frame the issues using the conceptual and normative framework of human security. Here the roles of human security as a concept and approach come into play in informing analysis. Human security is most often discussed as a *concept*, or occasionally as a conceptual framework. In this sense it encompasses a set of interrelated ideas that can be used as a point of reference, a guide to interpretation, and a way of organising discussion. It could be compared to sustainable development, for example: a concept that integrates several main ideas and that can be used to derive principles or to guide decision making and reform.[133] In legal analysis, the concept of human security can serve to orient analysis and development of the law.

Closely related to this is the notion of human security as an approach or perspective. A human security *approach* is one that takes human security as a reference point or primary objective. A certain methodological

---

[133] See, eg, P Sands, *Principles of International Environmental Law*, Vol 1: Frameworks, Standards and Implementation (Manchester, Manchester University Press, 1995), at 13–14; D Vander Zwaag, 'The Concept and Principles of Sustainable Development: "Rio-Formulating" Common Law Doctrines and Environmental Laws' (1993) 13 *Windsor Yearbook of Access to Justice* 39. Other examples might be the concept of common heritage: see, eg, AE Boyle, 'International Law and the Protection of the Global Atmosphere: Concepts, Categories and Principles' in R Churchill and D Freestone (eds), *International Law and Global Climate Change* (London, Graham and Trotman, 1991), at 9–10 and CC Joyner, 'Legal Implications of the Concept of the Common Heritage of Mankind' (1986) 35 *ICLQ* 190; or 'democratic inclusion': see S Marks, *The Riddle of all Constitutions: International Law, Democracy, and the Critique of Ideology* (Oxford, Oxford University Press, 2000), at 111.

orientation also follows from a concern with people's security and the recognition that it is not automatically enhanced when the state's security is protected. This requires that we devote specific and deliberate attention to the ways in which all people, including those who may be most vulnerable, are affected by laws and policies. That is, we should explicitly consider the impact of measures from the perspectives of those they most affect. According to McRae, the concept of human security 'takes the individual as the nexus of its concern, the life *as lived*, as the true lens through which we should view the political, economic, and social environment'.[134] He further suggests, with respect to the body of international agreements aimed at tackling problems relevant to human security, that:

> By focusing on human security, we focus on the actual impact of these inter-governmental agreements, where the individual is the nexus of competing and sometimes conflicting international and national laws and treaties, or even policies (e.g., the IMF or World Bank strictures). We are just now coming to terms with the unintended effects on people's lives of this plethora of national and international instruments.[135]

Similarly, Burke suggests that 'human security implies a radical shift from the abstract imagery of the nation state, and its interests, to the visceral distress of the human'.[136] In this respect there is an affinity between the human security approach and some kinds of feminist theory which emphasise the importance of attention to individuals' diverse experiences.[137] To look at a particular issue from a human security *perspective*, then, is to approach it from the perspective of affected individuals, focusing specifically on the impact on their security. Some scholarship on human security focuses on the collection of empirical data to aid in such analyses.[138] For the purposes of legal analysis, the most important implication is a need to consider in specific contexts how people's security may actually be affected, rather than relying on unquestioned assumptions.

[134] McRae, above n 109, at 15. See also Owens and Arneil, above n 63, at 2–3; Lammers, above n 63, at 58; Japan, MOFA, 'Statement by HE Mr Shigeo Uetake, Senior Vice Minister for Foreign Affairs of Japan at the International Conference on Financing for Development' (22 March 2002) <http://www.mofa.go.jp/announce/svm/uetake0203.html> (accessed 27 February 2007).

[135] McRae, above n 109, at 19. See also Owens and Arneil, above n 63, at 2.

[136] Burke, above n 124, at 226. See also McSweeney, above n 61, at 85: 'To say that security policy must be formulated with reference to human individuals is . . . to say that some assessment of human needs derived from empirical observation and philosophical analysis must be the reference for security policy; and it is to deny that the collective good can be subsumed under the needs and requirements of the organization of the state.'

[137] See, eg, H Charlesworth and C Chinkin, *The Boundaries of International Law: A Feminist Analysis* (Manchester, Manchester University Press, 2000), at 40, 52, and (applying such an approach to the principle of self-determination and Palestinian women), at 155*ff*.

[138] See, eg, Human Security Centre, *Human Security Report*, above n 17; Bajpai, above n 23; S Lonergan, K Gustavson and B Carter, 'The Index of Human Insecurity' (January 2000) 6 *Aviso* <http://www.gechs.org/aviso/06/index.html> (accessed 9 March 2007).

Consideration of issues from the perspective of those individuals most affected can influence the way issues and questions are framed, which in turn influences potential outcomes. Human security also provides a useful perspective from which to re-examine existing or proposed efforts, to determine whether they may be having unintended negative effects on people's security 'on the ground' in spite of good intentions, or whether they are achieving the goals articulated in terms of benefit to affected populations. In this role human security is better seen as a useful way of asking questions than as an answer to problems, but this question-framing function can be significant. Framing issues in a particular way—especially a way that departs from traditional approaches to familiar problems—can also be a step towards usefully critiquing existing approaches. Like its precursor concept human development, human security is particularly well suited to providing a critical perspective. The underlying rationale of both concepts is that we cannot accept certain assumptions at face value if we are genuinely concerned with human well-being: a country's economic growth will not *automatically* benefit individuals living in that country; the security of a state does not *necessarily* ensure, and its pursuit may even undermine, the security of its inhabitants. By focusing on the actual, 'visceral' state of human beings we are forced to question assumptions and test the reality of 'abstract' theories and concepts.

THE CONCEPTUAL AND NORMATIVE CONTENT OF HUMAN SECURITY

No matter how its scope is defined, in essence a human security approach shifts the primary referent of security to the individual from some higher level, usually the state. In some respects this is a fairly simple idea, but in order to understand how it might relate to international law we need to have a better understanding of what it means in conceptual and normative terms. The first, and most obvious, component is the 'human-centred' approach, which is normally taken to mean privileging the individual as the ultimate value or beneficiary of our efforts and legal framework. The second is less obvious but, it will be argued, equally important: when the focus of security shifts from the state to the individual, human security becomes a matter of common concern such that in some situations the government of one state will legitimately be concerned with and even, to some extent, responsible for the security of individuals in another state, as well as that of its own people.

The 'Human-centred' Approach

Human security was introduced as one element of a 'people-centred' or 'human-centred' world order.[139] As its name suggests, *human* security is distinguished from other security concepts above all by this human-centred approach. What precisely do we mean, though, by 'human-centred'?

Human security was developed in reaction to views of security dominated by realist and neorealist perspectives, which, as we saw in chapter one, focus on states as the primary actors in the international system and define the interests of states in terms of power, especially military power. The underlying rationale is that in an anarchical system composed of self-interested, naturally aggressive actors, states need to ensure their survival as autonomous entities by maximising their power and preparing for war. This 'traditional' conception of national security is not necessarily indifferent to the security of individuals. National security is given priority because if the state does not ensure its own survival, it will be unable to carry out any of its other functions, including the protection of its people. However, the traditional approach has been criticised for its tendency to treat national security as an end in itself rather than merely as an instrument for the protection of individuals, and to assume that individuals' security will automatically be ensured 'by virtue of our membership in a particular political community'.[140] It also either discounted the potential for the pursuit of national security to threaten individuals' security, or accepted it as a necessary evil.[141] This model thus allows the security of individuals to be treated as secondary and to be disregarded for the sake of state security. If protection for individuals is the reason we value the state's survival in the first place, this is somewhat ironic and unsatisfactory. Booth, for example, has argued that:

> It is illogical to place states at the centre of our thinking about security because even those which are producers of security . . . represent the means and not the ends . . . An analogy can be drawn with a house and its inhabitants. A house requires upkeep, but it is illogical to spend excessive amounts of money and effort to protect the house against flood, dry rot and burglars if this is at the cost of the well-being of its inhabitants. There is obviously a relationship between

---

[139] UNDP, *Human Development Report 1993* (Oxford, Oxford University Press, 1993), at 2.

[140] W Bain, 'The Tyranny of Benevolence: National Security, Human Security, and the Practice of Statecraft' (2001) 15 *Global Society* 277, at 277–8.

[141] See, eg, B Buzan, *People, States and Fear: An Agenda for International Security Studies in the Post-Cold War Era*, 2nd edn (New York, Harvester Wheatsheaf, 1991), at 38, 44–7; Walker, above n 60, at 67; M Ayoob, 'Defining Security: A Subaltern Realist Perspective' in K Krause and MC Williams (eds), *Critical Security Studies: Concepts and Cases* (Minneapolis, University of Minnesota Press, 1997), at 132–3.

the well-being of the sheltered and the state of the shelter, but can there be any question as to whose security is primary?[142]

This argument takes for granted that what we really care about is the well-being of the individuals (inhabitants) and not that of the state (house). This is a moral judgement about the relative value of the two possible referents, and thus the argument, as McSweeney suggests, is fundamentally a moral rather than a logical one.[143] It postulates that although states have legal rights in international and domestic law and have *instrumental* value, they do not have *intrinsic* moral value. That position is reserved for human beings, as reflected in the recognition of human rights. The concept of human security is based on the argument that, because of this privileged moral position, individual human beings rather than states should be the primary referent objects of security.

The adoption of human security as a conceptual framework, then, can be explained as the result of a judgement about the relative moral value of states and human beings. From this we can derive the nature of its relationship with state security. It is a truism that the people of an insecure state are unlikely to enjoy much security. The security of the state is *necessary* for human security. Even the strongest advocates of human security acknowledge the importance of state security for this reason.[144] However, part of the function of human security is to draw attention to the fact that ensuring the state's security may not make individuals more secure, and in some cases, it may even have the opposite effect. Thus, the pursuit of state security cannot be *sufficient* for human security. Furthermore, it should be seen as a means to an end, not as an end in itself. State security cannot simply be used as a proxy for individual security, just as economic growth cannot be used as a proxy for human development. This means that both the sufficiency of state security and the methods used to protect it must be measured against the ultimate justification and objective of human security.

It might be asked whether state security does not also protect people, not just as in the traditional understanding of national security, but because the state, after all, is only a human construct and its institutions and power structures are made up of human beings. There is another way of explaining what is meant by the human-centred approach from this perspective. The state as a legal and political institution is meant to represent, and to protect, the security and interests of all of its people (potentially including future as well as current members of its

---

[142] K Booth, 'Security and Emancipation' (1991) 17 *Review of International Studies* 313, at 320.

[143] McSweeney, above n 61, at 87.

[144] Compare FO Hampson and DF Oliver, 'Pulpit Diplomacy: A Critical Assessment of the Axworthy Doctrine' (1998) 53 *International Journal* 383, at 386 (arguing that a preoccupation with human security ignores the role of the state).

population). However, in reality, protection of the institution of the state may sometimes ignore or injure the security and interests of some—even the majority—of the population, while protecting only the security of a small elite. As a result, human security is deliberately (if implicitly) egalitarian and universalist in its human-centred approach. To pursue human security means attempting to ensure the security of *all* people, including 'ordinary' people, not just the security of elites.[145]

A further question is whether the human-centred focus of human security is necessarily individualistic or whether it also refers to the security of communities or groups. The *Human Development Report 1994* included 'community security' as one of the seven areas of human security, noting that '[m]ost people derive security from their membership in a group—a family, a community, an organization, a racial or ethnic group'.[146] The report of the Commission on Human Security mentions both individuals and communities as the concern of human security and the subject of threats.[147] Many discussions of human security refer generally to 'people' without specifying whether this means individuals or groups, although some specifically mention individuals as the referent in human security.[148] To some degree, vagueness on this point may be a deliberate or at least a convenient way to sidestep debates about individualism and communitarianism, and to avoid alienating those who may be suspicious of an individualistic approach. However, it is also somewhat unsatisfactory, given that 'the relationship between individuals and collectivities is central to the discourse of human security'.[149] The reason for a 'people-centred' approach to security is the ambivalent relationship between state security and people's security: a secure state is necessary to protect its people but may still neglect or even threaten their security. The same would seem to be true of any of the groups mentioned by the Human Development Report, from families to ethnic groups. The report does acknowledge that some groups may 'perpetuate oppressive practices',[150] but does not draw any conclusions from this about the place of community security as part of human security. The conclusion that would seem to follow is that the security of communities or groups, like the security of states is important to human security but instrumental to the more fundamental value of individual security. The rationale for displacing the

[145] Commission on Global Governance, *Our Global Neighborhood: The Report of the Commission on Global Governance* (Oxford, Oxford University Press, 1995), at 81; UNDP, *HDR 1994*, above n 2, at 22.

[146] UNDP, *HDR 1994*, above n 2, at 31.

[147] CHS, *Human Security Now*, above n 20, at 4, 11.

[148] See, eg, Canada, *Freedom from Fear*, above n 13, at 1–2; Human Security Centre, *Human Security Report*, above n 17, at vii.

[149] Hudson, above n 76, at 163.

[150] UNDP, *HDR 1994*, above n 2, at 31. This comment is with reference to 'traditional communities', but presumably any community, whether 'traditional' or not, could have the potential to perpetuate oppressive practices.

state as a referent object of security in its own right would apply to other kinds of groups, which can also either contribute to or threaten individuals' security. Human security, on this view, *is* fundamentally individualistic; it is concerned with the security of communities, but as instrumental to the security of individuals.[151]

This points to an affinity between the concept of human security and liberal individualism, and indeed some have made this link, even suggesting that human security is no more than a 'repackaging' of liberalism.[152] Normative individualism, described as 'the premise that the primary normative unit is the individual',[153] is the main common thread between them. Human security also shares with at least some accounts of liberalism a particular concern with the relationship between individuals and states. Whereas realism and neorealism tend to treat states as unitary actors that have the same functions and characteristics regardless of their internal organisation,[154] liberalism is concerned with relations within states and sees these as having important implications for international relations.[155] In part this is because of a belief that liberal states—that is, those with democratic political arrangements, respect for individual freedoms, and free markets—are less inclined to go to war with each other (the so-called 'liberal peace' or 'democratic peace').[156] On some accounts, the nature of a state's domestic regime also determines its legitimacy and the respect to which it is entitled in the international system. A state that does not respect the rights of its people, on this view, ceases to be a legitimate member of the international community of 'just' states and is

---

[151] Compare Acharya, above n 24, at 449, asserting that the security of 'people' in human security includes both individuals and communities, and that this understanding is 'eminently compatible' with communitarian perspectives. While I fully agree that a human security approach can include concern for communities, its underlying rationale suggests that this concern would still treat community security as instrumental to individual security, and that it would not justify treating community security as an objective where that might prejudice the security of individual members of the community.

[152] C Thomas, 'A Bridge Between the Interconnected Challenges Confronting the World' (2004) 35 *Security Dialogue* 353, at 353 (presenting this as the perception of human security from a Marxist point of view). See also Liotta, above n 70, at 58; T Owen, 'Challenges and Opportunities for Defining and Measuring Human Security' (2004) 3 *Disarmament Forum* 15, at 15, citing E Rothschild, 'What is Security?' (1995) 124(43) *Daedalus* 53.

[153] FR Tesón, *A Philosophy of International Law* (London, Westview Press, 1998).

[154] See, eg, S Burchill, 'Realism and Neo-realism' in S Burchill and A Linklater (eds), *Theories of International Relations* (New York, St Martin's Press, 1995), at 87; M Sheehan, *International Security: An Analytical Survey* (Boulder, Colorado, Lynne Rienner, 2005), at 17.

[155] For this reason Burchill describes realism/neorealism and liberalism as 'outside-in' and 'inside-out' views of international relations, respectively: S Burchill, 'Liberal Internationalism' in S Burchill and A Linklater (eds), *Theories of International Relations* (New York, St Martin's Press, 1995) ['Liberal Internationalism'], at 30. See also A-M Slaughter, 'A Liberal Theory of International Law' (2000) 94 *American Society of International Law Proceedings* 240 ['Liberal Theory'], at 241 ('top-down' versus 'bottom-up' views).

[156] See, eg, Burchill, 'Liberal Internationalism', above n 155, at 29*ff*; A-M Slaughter, 'International Law in a World of Liberal States' (1995) 6 *EJIL* 503 ['Liberal States'], at 509.

not entitled to respect for its sovereignty. A state's sovereignty is thus seen as *conditional* upon its compliance with certain requirements of a liberal state.[157]

Other understandings of liberalism in international law or international relations pay less attention to internal state–individual relations, treating states as the equivalent of individuals in the international sphere, with 'sovereign equality as the concomitant of individual autonomy' and little regard for individuals within states.[158] To the extent that liberalism is concerned with international peace and security in the sense of avoiding conflict between states, and with securing liberal democracies from external challenges, the protection of individuals is secondary to the interests of states.[159] For this reason human security could be considered 'a departure from traditional liberal internationalism'.[160] Even those accounts of liberalism that most clearly parallel human security do not exhaust the normative content of human security, and one cannot simply be equated with the other. For instance, liberalism is generally considered to give priority to individual freedom, which may not amount to ensuring individual *security*. In addition, its focus on the legitimacy of states and conditional sovereignty only partially captures the concerns of human security.

Human Security as a Matter of Common Concern

The other key implication of the shift from state to individual security is the idea of human security as a common concern or common responsibility. This is not as obvious as the human-centred approach, although others have made a similar connection.[161] It is apparent in two distinct but complementary tendencies in the current uses of human security in official and academic discourse. The first is the recognition that the security of individuals in different parts of the world is interrelated or mutually dependent, and that collective action will often be essential to ensuring human security because of the transnational nature of many important threats to human security. Human security is thus a common concern in the sense that the security of others, even in a distant part of the world,

---

[157] Tesón, above n 153, at 40, 57–8. See also Slaughter, 'Liberal States', above n 156, at 534*ff*, suggesting that sovereignty be disaggregated and non-intervention be understood as protecting the integrity and capacity of certain institutions to carry out their functions and act as checks and balances to each other.

[158] Slaughter, 'Liberal Theory', above n 155, at 240.

[159] Hampson, above n 94, at 5–6, 47.

[160] *Ibid*, at 5.

[161] See, eg, CHS, *Human Security Now*, above n 20, at 12; Alkire, above n 108, at 5; Hampson, above n 94, at ch 3 (human security as a 'global public good'); JE Fossum, '*Gidsland* and Human Security' (2006) 61 *International Journal* 813.

may affect the security of any of us, and no one's security can adequately be ensured without common effort. In this respect human security is a successor to the earlier idea of common security, which grew out of the recognition that states could only ensure their security cooperatively, since their fates are interdependent. In recognising the need for cooperation in security matters it also has something in common with collective security:

> Although broadening the focus of security policy beyond citizens may at first appear to be a radical shift, it is a logical extension of current approaches to international peace and security. The Charter of the United Nations embodies the view that security cannot be achieved by a single state in isolation . . . A human security perspective builds on this logic by noting that the security of people in one part of the world depends on the security of people elsewhere.[162]

As noted in chapter one, perceptions about globalisation, including the global reach of threats to security and the global effects of insecurity, stimulated interest in the concept of human security. They have also influenced use of the concept in current discourse by emphasising interdependence and the need for cooperation.

The second tendency takes this a step further and implies some form of common responsibility for the security of all people in all parts of the world. In the first instance, each state is responsible for ensuring the security of its own people. The division of responsibility on the basis of territory and nationality reflects an expectation that national governments will 'take care of their own'. However, part of the rationale for the shift to human security is the acknowledgment that states do not always fulfil this responsibility. If we value the security of individuals, and we know that we cannot always rely on people's own governments to keep them safe, it would seem to follow that there must be some international aspect to protection within the framework of human security.[163] Some degree of common responsibility must be accepted if human security is to be adequately protected. To put it another way, the security responsibilities of each state would extend, at least in some instances and to some degree, to individuals over whom it does not have jurisdiction. Although actors other than states obviously have important impacts on human security, the international legal system still treats states as having the primary responsibility for ensuring security for individuals. Whether and how this responsibility should also be shared with other actors is a question that deserves attention, but does not necessarily follow from the shift to human security. This analysis will focus on the implications of this concept for

---

[162] Canada, *Human Security*, above n 12, at 6. See also CHS, *Human Security Now*, above n 20, at 12.

[163] See, eg, McRae, above n 109, at 19–20; CHS, *Human Security Now*, above n 20, at 12; Fossum, above n 161, at 823.

states' obligations, exploring how these are affected by changing the referent object of security.

This 'strong' form of common responsibility for human security can be found in the discourse on human security alongside the 'weak' form of common concern which emphasises interdependence and the need for collective action to address transnational threats. It might be possible to view human security as simply a redefinition of national security to mean the security of individuals within each state. On this view, the government of a state would be exclusively responsible for the security of its population and would be concerned with threats to individuals in another state only to the extent that they might affect its own people. Appeals to 'enlightened self-interest' and insistence on interdependence or 'mutual vulnerability' in the context of human security appear to be directed at expanding the scope of states' policy agendas on this basis. However, these would not always justify concern with human security beyond national boundaries. Although people's security is indeed more inter-dependent than ever in a globalised world, in many cases the potential global impact of threats to human security is speculative, at best.[164] And although vulnerability may be more mutual than ever, it is still by no means equal. Many people are relatively insulated from the effects of insecurity in other countries, while others are extremely vulnerable. The content of even the narrower versions of the human security agenda cannot be derived on the basis of mutual vulnerability alone. If we look at the analyses and policy agendas that have been grounded in the concept of human security, it is clear that concern with human security commonly extends beyond this to threats affecting distant individuals, including in situations where there is no significant impact on security 'at home'. The ways in which human security has been used in contemporary discourse suggest that while the traditional view of 'state security largely concerns territorial units and the persons who dwell in them', human security 'addresses all people'.[165]

Perhaps more importantly, a view of common concern based on interdependence and self-interest alone does not fit as well with the normative foundations of human security. It could be consistent with giving priority to security of human beings over states' security. However, it treats the security of some human beings (those in one's own country or region) as more important than that of others. As we saw above, the human-centred approach inherent in the concept is implicitly egalitarian, in that it gives equal weight to the security of all individuals in a society, not just that of elites or certain groups. At the global level, this egalitarian orientation leads more logically to a sense of common concern based on

---

[164] See, eg, Khong, above n 42, at 234 (questioning, as a 'false causal assumption', the impact of human security on international peace and security).

[165] Alkire, above n 108, at 5.

equal value and concern, rather than self-interest. In this view, all human beings have inherent and equal moral worth, so their security is intrinsically and equally important, and should be ensured, if necessary, through international cooperation.

Some have referred to this as an understanding of human security based on morality or 'common values'.[166] It could be described as a cosmopolitan perspective insofar as it assumes that all individuals form a single moral community for whom each actor bears some responsibility.[167] Just as we saw above regarding liberalism, it is difficult to draw simple parallels between human security and cosmopolitan theories, not least because of the variation among those theories.[168] However, certain basic features shared by cosmopolitan approaches resonate with the idea of common concern and responsibility for human security. Moral cosmopolitanism has been described as having three core elements: individualism, universality or equality, and generality or global scope.[169] The first, individualism, is the idea that human beings are the ultimate units of moral concern.[170] The second feature of equality or universality means that every human being has this special moral status, and the claims of each individual should have equal weight.[171] According to the third feature, this equality of moral worth is to be understood on a global scale. The moral claims that individuals can make on one another, and the equal weight to be given to all claims, are not dependent on relationships of nationality or other group membership.[172] Putting these three components together, the core of moral cosmopolitanism is that 'every human being has a global stature as an ultimate unit of moral concern'.[173] As we

[166] M Glasius and M Kaldor, 'Individuals First: A Human Security Strategy for the European Union' (2005) 1 *Internationale Politik und Gesellschaft* 62, at 68 (the 'moral case' for interest in human security beyond Europe, as opposed to the 'legal case' or 'enlightened self-interest case'); G Oberleitner, 'Human Security: A Challenge to International Law?' (2005) 11 *Global Governance* 185, at 190 (human security based on 'common values' as opposed to national security based on 'national interest').

[167] Others have also noted a connection between this aspect of human security and cosmopolitanism. See, eg, P Hayden, 'Constraining War: Human Security and the Human Right to Peace' (2004) 6(1) *Human Rights Review* 35, at 39–40; Bajpai, above n 23, at 52; Fossum, above n 161; WW Bain, 'Against Crusading: The Ethic of Human Security and Canadian Foreign Policy' (1999) 6(3) *Canadian Foreign Policy* 85, at 88.

[168] See, eg, the typology and discussion of various approaches to cosmopolitanism in C Jones, *Global Justice: Defending Cosmopolitanism* (Oxford, Oxford University Press, 1999), at 14 and chs 2–4.

[169] T Pogge, 'Cosmopolitanism and Sovereignty' (1992) 103 *Ethics* 48, at 48–9. See also P Hayden, *Cosmopolitan Global Politics* (Aldershot, Ashgate, 2005), at 11.

[170] Pogge, *ibid*, at 48; B Barry, 'International Society from a Cosmopolitan Perspective' in DR Mapel and T Nardin (eds), *International Society: Diverse Ethical Perspectives* (Princeton, Princeton University Press, 1998).

[171] Barry, above n 170, at 146; Jones, above n 168, at 15; D Miller, 'The Limits of Cosmopolitan Justice' in DR Mapel and T Nardin (eds), *International Society: Diverse Ethical Perspectives* (Princeton, Princeton University Press, 1998), at 165.

[172] Barry, above n 170, at 145; Jones, above n 168, at 16.

[173] Pogge, above n 169, at 49. See also Hayden, *Cosmopolitan Global Politics*, above n 169, at 34.

saw above, individualism is also a feature of liberal theories, but the insistence on moral equality on a global scale sets cosmopolitanism apart from other theoretical perspectives.[174] It is quite clear that human security treats individuals as the units of ultimate moral value, and arguably it gives equal weight to the moral claims of all individuals. The question remains whether it also implies that rights, responsibilities, and moral claims have global scope. The fact that repeated concerns are expressed about states' failure to protect their own people suggests that it may, although some ambivalence on this point remains. This ambivalence is not surprising, since the idea that there is some collective responsibility for human security throughout the world is arguably 'the most radical or demanding feature' of the human security concept.[175] The way in which we understand human security as a matter of common concern—the version based on interdependence and self-interest, or the cosmopolitan sense—has important implications for the use of the concept, some of which will be discussed in later chapters.

The 'human-centred' and 'common concern' elements of a human security approach clearly raise issues with respect to central concepts in international law, such as state sovereignty, human rights, and the extent of obligations to cooperate with respect to issues of common concern. They may also have significant implications for the understanding and development of areas of international law that are directly relevant to human security threats. Furthermore, the different ways of defining and using human security that were discussed above may affect the roles it might play in relation to international law. The following chapter will begin to explore these links in a broad survey of norms and principles, setting the stage for consideration of specific issues in the remaining chapters.

---

[174] See, eg, Jones, above n 168, at 16; Barry, above n 170, at 145; Miller, above n 171, at 165.
[175] E Regehr, 'Reshaping the Security Envelope' (2005) 60 *International Journal* 1033, at 1039.

3

Human Security and International Law

INTRODUCTION

STATEMENTS ABOUT HUMAN security in official documents and academic literature show a degree of ambivalence about international law and its role. International law is seen as both a useful tool and an impediment to promoting human security. On one hand, the rule of law, enforcement of international law, and legal accountability are valued as essential components of a human security approach.[1] In addition, legal developments and initiatives have addressed most elements of the human security agenda. Thus, international law has an important and positive role as a means of advancing human security. On the other hand, the discussions of human security sometimes reflect a perception that international law acts as a constraint on actions that are necessary to ensure human security. In some respects the law is seen to be a hindrance to the pursuit of human security, rather than a help. While in some respects human security is consistent with developments in international law, at the same time, it is also seen as representing a challenge to international law,[2] requiring a 'paradigm shift' or revolutionary change in current legal structures.[3]

---

[1] See, eg, UN, *'We the Peoples' The Role of the United Nations in the 21st Century: Millennium Report of the Secretary-General of the United Nations* (New York, United Nations, 2000) [*Millennium Report*], at 46; OAS, General Assembly, 'Human Security in the Americas' (Document presented by the Delegation of Canada, 30th Regular Session) (26 April 2000) OEA/SER.P, AG/doc.3851/00, at 3; Canada, DFAIT, *Freedom from Fear: Canada's Foreign Policy for Human Security* (Ottawa, Department of Foreign Affairs and Trade (DFAIT), 2000) <http://www.humansecurity.gc.ca/pdf/freedom_from_fear-en.pdf> (accessed 27 February 2007) [*Freedom from Fear*], at 1; Canada, DFAIT, *Human Security: Safety for People in a Changing World* (Ottawa, DFAIT, 1999) [*Human Security*], at 10.

[2] G Oberleitner, 'Human Security: A Challenge to International Law?' (2005) 11 *Global Governance* 185.

[3] See, eg, UNDP, *Human Development Report 1994* (Oxford, Oxford University Press, 1994) [*HDR 1994*], at 22; H Owens and B Arneil, 'Human Security Paradigm Shift: A New Lens on Canadian Foreign Policy?' (1999) 7(1) *Canadian Foreign Policy* 1, at 1, 11; WT Tow and R Trood, 'Linkages between Traditional Security and Human Security' in WT Tow, R Thakur and I Hyun (eds), *Asia's Emerging Regional Order: Reconciling Traditional and Human Security* (Tokyo, United Nations University Press, 2000), at 13; Canada, *Freedom from Fear*, above n 1,

Before I turn in later chapters to explore particular topics illustrating the role of human security in legal analysis and development, this chapter will seek to better understand this complex relationship in more general terms, by exploring the relationship between the key components of a human security approach and the norms and principles of international law.

INTERNATIONAL LAW AND THE HUMAN SECURITY AGENDA

As we saw in previous chapters, human security has been used to define a foreign policy agenda. One way of approaching the relationship between human security and international law is to examine the use of law as an instrument to further this agenda. Virtually all of the items on the human security agenda have been addressed by legal norms and institutions, and some have been the subject of important recent developments. For example, international agreements on arms, transnational organised crime, illicit drugs, and terrorism have sought to address these threats to human security. A range of binding and non-binding instruments have been developed to respond to important threats beyond physical violence, including infectious diseases, poverty, natural disasters, and environmental degradation. The protection of civilians in armed conflict is a central aim of humanitarian law, and the special vulnerability of children in armed conflict has been the subject of a recent Protocol.[4] The law is increasingly called upon to respond to the particular vulnerabilities to which women are subject, in conflict and other situations, as a result of their gender. Displaced persons are another vulnerable group whose situation is addressed by an evolving legal framework, as will be seen below in chapter five.

The human security agenda also includes means of ensuring human security, such as specific measures to be used and actors whose participation is critical. With regard to the latter, the role of non-state actors is important, given that various actors other than state governments, including corporations and armed groups, have significant impacts on human security. Recent developments in the traditionally state-centred framework of international law include attempts to develop codes and

at 16; R McRae, 'Human Security in a Globalized World' in R McRae and D Hubert (eds), *Human Security and the New Diplomacy: Protecting People, Promoting Peace* (Montreal and Kingston, McGill-Queen's University Press, 2001), at 15; WW Bain, 'Against Crusading: the Ethic of Human Security and Canadian Foreign Policy' (1999) 6(3) *Canadian Foreign Policy* 85 ['Against Crusading'], at 85–6.

[4] Optional Protocol to the Convention on the Rights of the Child on the Involvement of Children in Armed Conflicts (opened for signature 25 May 2000, entered into force 12 February 2002) UNGA Res 54/263 (16 March 2001) UN Doc A/RES/54/263. See also Rome Statute of the International Criminal Court (opened for signature 17 July 1998, entered into force 1 July 2002) 2187 UNTS 3 [Rome Statute], art 8(2)(b)(xxvi).

guidelines for multinational corporations and to expand the interpretation of international criminal law to take greater account of non-state actors.[5] One of the most important examples of the way the law can be used as an instrument for ensuring human security is the establishment of international criminal tribunals and especially the International Criminal Court. The UN Charter provides a legal structure for actions in pursuit of human security, including Security Council-authorised responses to threats to international peace and security, UN peace-keeping missions, and conflict prevention efforts. More contentious is the legal basis for 'humanitarian intervention' as a potential means of ensuring human security, which will be discussed below in chapter four.

These examples illustrate some ways in which international law can be seen to serve as an instrument or framework for ensuring human security. However, much more is needed to determine the extent to which international law effectively contributes to the protection of people's security. Even initiatives that appear to have human security objectives may have unintended negative effects, whether because they are simply ill conceived, or because they trade off one type of security against another. The 'war on terrorism' would seem to be a prime example of both of these: although the prevention of terrorism is a valid objective that would enhance human security, the strategies chosen have significantly increased other forms of insecurity for individuals in many countries, whether directly, by threatening their lives and physical and psychological security through detention or deportation, or indirectly, through the exacerbation of poverty and economic insecurity resulting from the diversion of resources. Although this is perhaps an extreme example, it illustrates the caution with which we should approach efforts to further one part of the human security agenda without a comprehensive and critical analysis of their impact.

In addition to examining specific initiatives to develop the law in relevant areas, we also need to understand something of the broader legal context—the framework of concepts, principles, and norms operating in international law—within which these initiatives and a human security foreign policy agenda would be pursued. Some commentators who have explicitly considered the relationship between human security and international law have found parallels in, for example, the UN Charter and human rights law, but also tensions, especially with the fundamental principle of state sovereignty. The remainder of this chapter will begin to

[5] Regarding the former, see, eg, OECD, 'The OECD Guidelines for Multinational Enterprises: Text, Commentary and Clarifications' (31 October 2001) OECD Doc DAFFE/IME/WPG(2000)15/FINAL; UN Sub-Commission on the Protection and Promotion of Human Rights, 'Norms on the Responsibilities for Transnational Corporations and Other Business Enterprises With Regard to Human Rights' (26 August 2003) UN Doc E/CN.4/Sub.2/2003/12/Rev.2. Regarding the latter, see Rome Statute, above n 4, art 7(2)(a); *Prosecutor v Tadić (Opinion and Judgment)* ICTY-94-1 (7 May 1997), at paras 654–5.

explore some of these complex relationships between human security and the norms and principles of international law. As we shall see, precursors and parallels to the central elements of human security can be identified in existing international law. The survey of relevant norms and principles here is intended to be wide-ranging, but obviously not exhaustive. The examples given do not necessarily relate to specific areas or elements of the human security agenda. The concern is more with identifying general principles and norms of international law that resonate with a human security approach.[6]

THE HUMAN-CENTRED APPROACH IN INTERNATIONAL LAW

Traditionally, international law has been concerned primarily with regulating the relationships between states. At the same time, though, many assume the individual to be 'the ultimate beneficiary of the international legal system'.[7] What would it mean, then, for international law to be or become (more) 'human-centred'? The human-centred focus inherent in the concept of human security demands explicit attention to the needs and interests of individuals, and gives analytical and moral priority to individuals' needs and interests over those of states. We could also understand a 'people-centred world order' as emphasising the role and participation of individuals and (non-state) groups in the inter-national arena.[8] This is relevant to human security, in the sense that participation may allow people to voice their concerns about the threats that most affect them, and to have a role in addressing those threats. However, in this context individual participation has instrumental value for its potential contribution to human security, rather than as an end in itself. The core of the human-centred approach in human security is the normative priority of people's security, especially in relation to states' security. Furthermore, as we saw in the last chapter, it is best understood as giving priority to individuals, although it does not exclude an

---

[6] Note that this is not intended to refer to 'general principles of law' in the strict sense but rather general principles of international law that serve as guides to interpretation, to inspire or coordinate the development of specific norms, or to describe the structure of the international legal framework. See A Cassese, *International Law in a Divided World* (Oxford, Clarendon Press, 1986) [*Divided World*], at 86; FX Perrez, *Cooperative Sovereignty: From Independence to Interdependence in the Structure of International Environmental Law* (The Hague, Kluwer, 2000), at 265.

[7] G Van Bueren, 'Deconstructing the Mythologies of International Human Rights Law' in C Gearty and A Tomkins (eds), *Understanding Human Rights* (London, Pinter, 1996), at 596. Compare R Higgins, *Problems and Process: International Law and How We Use It* (Oxford, Clarendon Press, 1994), at 95.

[8] See, eg, C Grossman and DD Bradlow, 'Are We Being Propelled Towards a People-centered Transnational Legal Order?' (1993) 9 *American University Journal of International Law and Policy* 1.

instrumental concern with communities. We are therefore looking to identify aspects of international law that explicitly consider and give priority to the needs and interests of individual people, particularly valuing these above the needs or interests of states.

As will be seen below, we can find many parallels in international law to this human-centred approach to security. Before examining some of these, though, it is important to explore briefly why it is sometimes seen to be fundamentally in conflict with the existing system of international law. Human security has been described as a challenge to the existing international order and to international law.[9] It has also been invoked as a framework or impetus for rethinking key aspects of the international legal order, especially state sovereignty.[10]

The perceived tension between international law and human security arises from a view of the existing international legal system as according primary legal and moral status to the state, and giving priority to the protection of states' security, while the concept of human security asserts the priority of individuals' security.[11] The constitutive norms of international society are said to protect the security of states, even those that threaten the security of their people.[12] The state-centred system seems to be based on the very assumptions that the concept of human security is meant to question: that the 'state aggregates, protects and promotes the interests of its individual citizens' and therefore states' security can be equated with the security of their inhabitants.[13] The idea that states are morally valued entities worth preserving 'in their own right' is said to be 'deeply entrenched in the constitution and practice of international society'.[14]

---

[9] Oberleitner, above n 2; Bain, 'Against Crusading', above n 3, at 86.

[10] T Owen, 'Human Security—Conflict, Critique and Consensus: Colloquium Remarks and a Proposal for a Threshold-based Definition' (2004) 35(3) *Security Dialogue* 373, at 377; International Commission on Intervention and State Sovereignty, *Responsibility to Protect: Report of the International Commission on Intervention and State Sovereignty* (Ottawa, International Development Research Centre, 2001) <http://www.iciss.ca/pdf/Commission-Report.pdf> (accessed 26 February 2007), at 13.

[11] McRae, above n 3, at 15.

[12] W Bain, 'The Tyranny of Benevolence: National Security, Human Security, and the Practice of Statecraft' (2001) 15 *Global Society* 277 ['Tyranny of Benevolence'], at 279–80. See also Bain, 'Against Crusading', above n 3, at 87–8.

[13] SN MacFarlane and TG Weiss, 'The United Nations, Regional Organisations and Human Security: Building Theory in Central America' (1994) 15 *Third World Quarterly* 277, at 279. See also K Bajpai, 'Human Security: Concept and Measurement' (August 2000) Kroc Institute Occasional Paper 19:OP:1 <http://www.nd.edu/~krocinst/ocpapers/op_19_1.pdf> (accessed 1 March 2007), at 38.

[14] Bain, 'Tyranny of Benevolence', above n 12, at 278. See also Tesón's description of 'statist' international law and its incompatibility with the normative priority of individuals: FR Tesón, *A Philosophy of International Law* (London, Westview Press, 1998), at 1, 39–41; FR Tesón, *Humanitarian Intervention: An Inquiry into Law and Morality*, 2nd edn (Irvington-on-Hudson, NY, Transnational Publishers, 1997), at ch 3.

State sovereignty is one of the 'oldest concepts of modern international law',[15] and the principle of sovereign equality, one of the fundamental principles of the UN Charter,[16] has been described as 'the linchpin of the whole body of international legal standards, the fundamental premise on which all international relations rest'.[17] The legal concept of state sovereignty is closely connected to the traditional conception of security. As we saw in chapter one, national security is traditionally conceived of as being concerned with preserving the survival of the state as an autonomous entity against external threats. The value that the pursuit of national security aims to protect is essentially the sovereignty of the state, including control over its territory and political autonomy.[18] The legal protection of state sovereignty in international law therefore functions to protect the security of the state, and its centrality in the international legal system tends to suggest that state security also has a privileged position. Other fundamental legal principles also protect national security as traditionally understood. For example, the prohibition on the threat or use of force as articulated in article 2(4) of the UN Charter specifically refers to the territorial integrity and political independence of states. The right of self-defence is also said to give 'practical effect to the doctrine of national security'[19] by allowing states to use force in response to an armed attack, even at the expense of individuals' security.[20]

This very brief review illustrates that, in some respects, international law seems designed, as some suggest, to protect the security of states and to reflect the assignment of moral value to states. The fact that the international legal framework provides protection for the security of states does not in itself make international law incompatible with human security. For human security, protecting the security of the state is necessary but not sufficient, ideally complementary but sometimes detrimental. As a result, the degree of incompatibility is determined by the extent to which the law allows state security to be protected at the expense of individuals' security. Much, then, depends on the interpretation of such fundamental principles as sovereignty and the prohibition on the use of

---

[15] B Fassbender and A Bleckmann, 'Article 2(1)' in B Simma (ed), *The Charter of the United Nations: A Commentary*, 2nd edn (Oxford, Oxford University Press, 2002), vol I, at 70.

[16] *Ibid.*

[17] A Cassese, *International Law* (Oxford, Oxford University Press, 2001), at 88. See also Perrez, above n 6, at 13.

[18] S Lodgaard, 'Human Security: Concept and Operationalisation' (Expert Seminar on Human Rights and Peace) (15 November 2000) UN Doc PD/HR/11.1 <http://www.upeace.org/documents/resources/report_lodgaard.doc> (accessed 7 March 2007), at 2, 6; Bajpai, above n 13, at 22–4. See also Canada, *Freedom from Fear*, above n 1, at 1.

[19] Bain, 'Tyranny of Benevolence', above n 12, at 278.

[20] See *ibid*, at 278–9. Bain suggests that the prevailing view of the right of self-defence protects the security of states even at the expense of other important principles, including humanitarian law, when the state's 'supreme interests' are at stake, with particular reference to the *Nuclear Weapons* case: *Legality of the Threat or Use of Nuclear Weapons* [1996] ICJ Rep 226.

force, as will be discussed in subsequent chapters. At the same time, other aspects of international law parallel the human-centred approach.

Human Rights and the Human-centred Approach

A human-centred orientation can be discerned in several areas of international law, most obviously refugee law, humanitarian law, and human rights. Some have attempted to show the consistency of human security with international law by placing human security within an evolving legal tradition that includes these areas of law and is said to reflect a growing 'recognition that people's rights are at least as important as those of states'.[21] It has been suggested that linking human security with this tradition could lend it greater force or legitimacy, as well as providing a legal framework and conceptual point of reference from which it can develop.[22] As will be argued below, the concept of human security cannot simply be equated with any particular area of the law. However, one would expect to find some important parallels between the concept of human security and the legal recognition and protection of human rights in international law.

The regime of human rights norms and institutions that has developed in international law is designed to protect the rights of individual human beings (and, to a lesser extent, groups or communities). It has been described as 'strikingly different' from 'classical' international law, which appears to have had 'relatively little to offer' with respect to addressing the needs of individuals.[23] The norms set out in human rights treaties and other major documents recognise the rights of individuals and impose obligations on states with respect to those rights. In some cases the institutions established by these instruments also grant standing to individuals to submit complaints of alleged violations of their rights.[24]

---

[21] L Axworthy, 'Human Security and Global Governance: Putting People First' (2001) 7 *Global Governance* 19, at 19. See also Canada, *Human Security*, above n 1, at 3; Canada, *Freedom from Fear*, above n 1, at 1; Commission on Human Security, Declaration on Human Rights as an Essential Component of Human Security (Workshop on Relationship Between Human Rights and Human Security, San Jose, Costa Rica, 2 December 2001) <http://www.humansecurity-chs.org/activities/outreach/sanjosedec.pdf> (accessed 1 March 2007) [CHS, Declaration on Human Rights]; Lodgaard, above n 18, at 8.

[22] Lodgaard, above n 18, at 14; Owens and Arneil, above n 3, at 3, 9; CHS, Declaration on Human Rights, above n 21; Commission on Human Security, *Human Security Now: Protecting and Empowering People* (New York, Commission on Human Security, 2003) <http://www.humansecurity-chs.org/finalreport/index.html> (accessed 26 February 2007), at 9.

[23] Higgins, above n 7, at 95.

[24] See, eg, Optional Protocol to the International Covenant on Civil and Political Rights (opened for signature 16 December 1966, entered into force 23 March 1976) 999 UNTS 171; Optional Protocol to the Convention on the Elimination of All Forms of Discrimination against Women (opened for signature 6 October 1999, entered into force 22 December 2000) 2131 UNTS 83; Convention Against Torture and Other Cruel, Inhuman or Degrading

This unprecedented degree of recognition of individuals' status in international law has been said to reflect 'the acknowledgement of the worth of human personality as the ultimate unit of all law' and the need to consider 'the good of the individual human beings who comprise the collectivity' of the state.[25] That a 'human-centred' orientation is the essential foundation of human rights norms is apparent in such documents as the Vienna Declaration, which affirms that 'all human rights derive from the dignity and worth inherent in the human person, and that the human person is the central subject of human rights and fundamental freedoms, and consequently should be [their] principal beneficiary'.[26] Following the adoption of the UN Charter and key international human rights instruments such as the Universal Declaration of Human Rights and the 1966 Covenants (ICESCR and ICCPR), many human rights obligations have become part of customary international law, and a prohibition on at least some serious violations of fundamental human rights has emerged as a general principle of international law.[27] This represents a baseline of protection for individuals among the essential principles of the international legal order.

The effect that the development of human rights law has had on international law more generally is also important here. It has been suggested that:

> The international human rights program is more than a piecemeal addition to the traditional corpus of international law, more than another chapter sandwiched into traditional textbooks of international law. By shifting the fulcrum of the system from the protection of sovereigns to the protection of people, it works qualitative changes in virtually every component.[28]

This effect of human rights on international law has been described as a 'revolution'[29] because of the ways in which it has challenged fundamental

Treatment or Punishment (adopted 10 December 1984, entered into force 26 June 1987) 1465 UNTS 85 [CAT], art 22; European Convention for the Protection of Human Rights and Fundamental Freedoms (4 November 1950) ETS No 5 (as amended) [ECHR], art 34; American Convention on Human Rights (22 November 1969) OASTS No 36 [ACHR], art 44.

[25] H Lauterpacht, *International Law and Human Rights* (London Stevens and Sons, 1950), at 62, 70, excerpted in HJ Steiner and P Alston, *International Human Rights in Context: Law, Politics, Morals*, 2nd edn (Oxford, Oxford University Press, 2000), at 147–8.

[26] UNGA, 'Vienna Declaration and Programme of Action' (12 July 1993) UN Doc A/CONF.157/23, preamble. See also the preambles to the International Covenant on Economic, Social and Cultural Rights (adopted 16 December 1966, entered into force 3 January 1976) 993 UNTS 3 [ICESCR] and the International Covenant on Civil and Political Rights (adopted 16 December 1966, entered into force 23 March 1976) 999 UNTS 171 [ICCPR]: 'these rights derive from the inherent dignity of the human person'.

[27] Cassese, *International Law*, above n 17, at 104; I Brownlie, *Principles of Public International Law*, 6th edn (Oxford, Oxford University Press, 2003), at 537.

[28] WM Reisman, 'Sovereignty and Human Rights in Contemporary International Law' (1990) 84 *AJIL* 866, at 872.

[29] See, eg, D McGoldrick, 'The Principle of Non-Intervention: Human Rights' in V Lowe and C Warbrick (eds), *The United Nations and the Principles of International Law: Essays in*

principles of international law, in particular the related principles of sovereignty and non-intervention, and its effect on the scope of domestic jurisdiction.[30] In simple terms, the development of human rights law 'has made human rights a matter of international law'.[31] To be more precise, intervention is permissible to the extent that it is provided for in human rights treaties to which a state is a party,[32] and consistent patterns of gross human rights violations, at least, are considered to be matters of international concern rather than domestic jurisdiction.[33]

The influence of human rights can also been seen in a variety of areas of international law, including the law of treaties, recognition of states, and humanitarian law.[34] In the context of humanitarian law, the Appeals Chamber of the International Criminal Tribunal for the former Yugoslavia has stated that:

> [T]he impetuous development and propagation in the international community of human rights doctrines, particularly after the adoption of the Universal Declaration of Human Rights in 1948, has brought about significant changes in international law, notably in the approach to problems besetting the world community. A State-sovereignty-oriented approach has been gradually supplanted by a human-being-oriented approach. Gradually the maxim of Roman law *hominum causa omne jus constitutum est* (all law is created for the benefit of human beings) has gained a firm foothold in the international community as well.[35]

Although one might do well to be cautious of overstating the revolutionary impact of human rights, the development of human rights is an

memory of *Michael Akehurst* (London, Routledge, 1994), at 85; LB Sohn, 'The New International Law: Protection of the Rights of Individuals Rather than States' (1982) 32 *American University Law Review* 1, at 1.

[30] Reisman suggests that 'because the human rights norms are constitutive, other norms must be reinterpreted in their light, lest anachronisms be produced' (above n 28, at 873). See, eg, McGoldrick, above n 29, and J Donnelly, 'State Sovereignty and International Intervention: The Case of Human Rights' in GM Lyons and M Mastanduno (eds), *Beyond Westphalia?: State Sovereignty and International Intervention* (Baltimore, Johns Hopkins University Press, 1995) ['State Sovereignty'] for discussions of the relationship between human rights, non-intervention, and domestic jurisdiction.

[31] McGoldrick, above n 29, at 94.

[32] *Ibid*, at 102.

[33] *Ibid*, at 97–8, 103. Donnelly argues that despite increasing international interest and non-coercive interference in human rights, it is only in rare cases that human rights will be accepted as a subject of coercive intervention: 'State Sovereignty', above n 30.

[34] See Cassese, *International Law*, above n 17, at 372, for references to these and other areas. Regarding humanitarian law and impact of human rights, see also *Prosecutor v Tadić (Interlocutory Appeal)* ICTY-94-1 (2 October 1995); T Meron, 'The Humanization of Humanitarian Law' (2000) 94 *AJIL* 239. Regarding human rights and peacekeeping, see J Donnelly, 'The Social Construction of International Human Rights' in T Dunne and NJ Wheeler (eds), *Human Rights in Global Politics* (Cambridge, Cambridge University Press, 1999) ['Social Construction'], at 89–90. Donnelly notes, however, that the integration of human rights norms has not yet occurred in some important areas (*ibid*, at 91).

[35] *Prosecutor v Tadić (Interlocutory Appeal)*, above n 34, at para 97. See Cassese, *International Law*, above n 17, at 330, 372.

important example of a human-centred approach and has clearly had a significant effect on the body of international law.

Humanitarian Principles

International law also includes a cluster of norms and principles that can be described as humanitarian, based on concern and compassion for humanity. This is the basis of humanitarian law, generally,[36] and of norms in areas such as arms control, protection of civilians in armed conflict, and protection of sick, wounded, or captured members of armed forces. These norms establish important, albeit limited, protections for individuals' security as a matter of priority where states or sub-state groups attempt to protect their own security by engaging in military activities. Apart from the specific rules of the law of armed conflict and humanitarian law that are set out in the relevant Conventions, basic humanitarian principles apply in any conflict regardless of whether those involved are parties to the Conventions. Common article 3 to the Geneva Conventions establishes minimum humanitarian standards applicable in non-international conflicts.[37] Furthermore, the rules set out in the Conventions are not exhaustive and, according to the 'Martens clause',[38] principles of international law derived from custom and the laws or principles of humanity continue to protect affected persons.[39] As well as preserving customary

[36] R Provost, *International Human Rights and Humanitarian Law* (Cambridge, Cambridge University Press, 2002), at 5; H McCoubrey, *International Humanitarian Law* (Aldershot, Dartmouth, 1998), at 1; LC Green, *The Contemporary Law of Armed Conflict*, 2nd edn (Manchester, Manchester University Press, 2000), at 348.

[37] Geneva Convention for the Amelioration of the Condition of the Wounded and Sick in Armed Forces in the Field (signed 12 August 1949, entered into force 21 October 1950) 75 UNTS 31 [First Geneva Convention]; Geneva Convention for the Amelioration of the Condition of Wounded, Sick and Shipwrecked Members of Armed Forces at Sea (signed 12 August 1949, entered into force 21 October 1950) 75 UNTS 85 [Second Geneva Convention]; Geneva Convention Relative to the Treatment of Prisoners of War (signed 12 August 1949, entered into force 21 October 1950) 75 UNTS 135 [Third Geneva Convention]; Geneva Convention Relative to the Protection of Civilian Persons in Time of War (signed 12 August 1949, entered into force 21 October 1950) 75 UNTS 287 [Fourth Geneva Convention].

[38] The clause is restated in, among other instruments, the Geneva Conventions, above n 37, and its Additional Protocols: Protocol Additional to the Geneva Conventions of August 12, 1949, and relating to the Protection of Victims of International Armed Conflicts (adopted 8 June 1977, entered into force 7 December 1978) 1125 UNTS 3 [Protocol I]; Protocol Additional to the Geneva Conventions of August 12, 1949, and relating to the Protection of Victims of Non-International Armed Conflicts (adopted 8 June 1977, entered into force 7 December 1978) 1125 UNTS 609 [Protocol II]. See T Meron, 'The Martens Clause, Principles of Humanity, and Dictates of Public Conscience' (2000) 94 *AJIL* 78 ['Martens Clause'], at 78.

[39] See Green, above n 36, at 17, 349. See also the International Court of Justice in *Military and Paramilitary Activities in and against Nicaragua (Nicaragua v United States of America), Merits* [1986] ICJ Rep 14 [*Nicaragua*], at para 218: 'the Geneva Conventions are in some respects a development, and in other respects no more than the expression' of 'fundamental general principles of humanitarian law'.

norms that have not been codified, the clause supports interpretations of humanitarian law consistent with the principles of humanity and what has been called a 'homocentric focus'.[40] The principle of humanity is a fundamental principle of the International Committee of the Red Cross (ICRC) and the Red Cross and Red Crescent Movement, and under this principle their purpose is to 'prevent and alleviate human suffering . . . to protect life and health and to ensure respect for the human being'.[41] The ICRC's right of humanitarian initiative, allowing it to offer humanitarian services to parties to a conflict, is recognised in its constitutive documents and the Geneva Conventions.[42] The 'principles of humanity' are also applicable to humanitarian assistance in the event of natural disasters and other emergencies.[43]

Humanitarian principles have also been referred to as 'considerations of humanity'.[44] The International Court of Justice (ICJ) in the *South West Africa* case accepted that considerations of humanity may be the 'inspirational basis for rules of law', although they do not themselves 'generate legal rights and obligations'.[45] The Court had earlier referred to 'elementary considerations of humanity' as among the 'general and well-recognized principles' that obliged Albania to warn of the presence of mines in the *Corfu Channel* case.[46] The more recent advisory opinion of the Court on the legality of nuclear weapons made reference to 'the overriding consideration of humanity' and 'the cardinal principles' of humanitarian law.[47] Considerations of humanity are not limited to the context of armed

[40] Meron, 'Martens Clause', above n 38, at 87–8.

[41] Statutes of the International Committee of the Red Cross, (8 May 2003) <http://www.icrc.org/Web/Eng/siteeng0.nsf/html/icrc-statutes-080503> (29 March 2007), art 4(1)(a); Statutes of the International Red Cross and Red Crescent Movement, (1986, as amended 1995) <http://www.icrc.org/Web/eng/siteeng0.nsf/htmlall/statutes-movement-220506/$File/Mvt-Statutes-ENGLISH.pdf> (29 March 2007), preamble. See JW Samuels, 'Organized Responses to Natural Disasters' in R St John Macdonald, DM Johnston and GL Morris (eds), *The International Law and Policy of Human Welfare* (Alphen aan den Rijn, Netherlands, Sijthoff and Noordhoff, 1978), at 678; R Coupland, 'Humanity: What is It and How Does It Influence International Law' (2001) 83 *IRRC* 969, at 972–3. See Coupland, *ibid*, for discussion of the origins and interpretation of this principle.

[42] Statutes of the International Committee of the Red Cross, above n 41, art 4(2); Statutes of the International Red Cross and Red Crescent Movement above n 41, art 5(3); common art 3 of the four Geneva Conventions and art 9 of the First, Second and Third Geneva Conventions, above n 37.

[43] UNGA Res 43/131 (8 December 1988) UN Doc A/RES/43/131, preamble; UNGA Res 45/100 (14 December 1990) UN Doc A/RES/45/100, preamble; UNGA, 'Guiding Principles on Humanitarian Assistance', UNGA Res 46/182 (19 December 1991), Annex, at para 2.

[44] Meron, 'Martens Clause', above n 38, at 82. It has been suggested that 'considerations of humanity' are a 'minor' source of law: see H Thirlway, 'The Law and Procedure of the International Court of Justice 1960–1989: Part Two' (1990) 61 *BYBIL* 3, at 6, citing G Fitzmaurice (at fn 8). See also Brownlie, above n 27, at 26–7.

[45] *South West Africa, Second Phase* [1966] ICJ Rep 6, at 34.

[46] *Corfu Channel, Merits* [1949] ICJ Rep 4, at 22.

[47] *Nuclear Weapons*, above n 20, at paras 95, 78. The cardinal principles or fundamental rules of humanitarian law are said to be 'intransgressible principles of international customary law': *ibid*, at para 79.

conflict and are 'even more exacting in peace than in war'.[48] Thus, the use of weapons against civilian aircraft was condemned as being 'incompatible with elementary considerations of humanity' by a Resolution of the Security Council.[49] According to most interpretations, the principles or considerations of humanity referred to in the Martens clause and the decisions of the ICJ do not themselves establish rules of international law. They can play a role, though, as principles of interpretation supporting a more human-centred approach.

International Peace and Security

A more recent development that could be said to show a shift in concern from the state to individuals is the evolving interpretation of threats to international peace and security within the meaning of the UN Charter. This development is important given that the Security Council is responsible for maintaining international peace and security, and the existence of a 'threat to the peace' provides a legal basis for measures taken by the Security Council under chapter VII of the Charter.[50] The definition of threats to international peace and security has become progressively wider, potentially including non-military threats;[51] situations of internal armed conflict, disruption of democracy, and humanitarian crisis; and gross violations of human rights.[52] Of particular interest here is the tendency for the Security Council to consider gross human rights violations or a humanitarian crisis as constituting threats to international peace and security. An oft-cited example regarding human rights violations is the series of resolutions on South Africa's policies of apartheid, in which the Security Council referred to the situation as 'endanger[ing]' or 'seriously disturbing international peace and security'.[53] Humanitarian

---

[48] *Corfu Channel*, above n 46, at 22.

[49] UNSC Res 1067 (26 July 1996) UN Doc S/RES/1067. See Meron, 'Martens Clause', above n 43, at 83, and at 82–3 on other uses of elementary considerations of humanity.

[50] Article 39 provides: 'The Security Council shall determine the existence of any threat to the peace, breach of the peace, or act of aggression and shall make recommendations, or decide what measures shall be taken in accordance with Articles 41 [non-military measures] and 42 [military measures], to maintain or restore international peace and security.' Chapter VI, regarding pacific settlement of disputes, also deals with situations that 'endanger the maintenance of international peace and security' (art 33) and provide for certain actions to be taken by states and the Security Council in such situations (arts 34–8).

[51] UNSC, 'Note by the President of the Security Council' (31 January 1992) UN Doc S/23500. Compare J Frowein and N Krisch, 'Article 39' in B Simma (ed), *The Charter of the United Nations: A Commentary*, 2nd edn (Oxford, Oxford University Press, 2002), vol I, at 720.

[52] See, eg, Frowein and Krisch, above n 51, at 723–5; S Chesterman, *Just War or Just Peace? International Law and Humanitarian Intervention* (Oxford, Oxford University Press, 2001), at 128ff.

[53] UNSC Res 134 (1 April 1960) UN Doc S/4300; UNSC Res 181 (7 August 1963) UN Doc S/5386; UNSC Res 182 (4 December 1963) UN Doc S/5471. On the distinction and

crises have been cited in chapter VII resolutions on numerous occasions in the last few decades, including with regard to Iraq,[54] Somalia,[55] Zaire and later the Democratic Republic of the Congo,[56] Haiti,[57] and the Sudan.[58] The Security Council has stated that systematic, flagrant, and widespread violations of international humanitarian law and human rights in situations of armed conflict and the deliberate targeting of civilians may constitute a threat to international peace and security, and expressed its willingness to take appropriate measures in such situations.[59]

It is a matter of debate to what extent these resolutions really demonstrate a new interpretation of threats to international peace and security. Most of the resolutions that find a threat to international peace and security in relation to a humanitarian crisis also note potential impacts on peace and stability in the region. There are often grounds for concern that the transboundary effects of such situations, for example the impact of refugee flows or tensions with neighbouring states, could threaten peace and security in the traditional sense, that is, it could lead to armed conflict between states.[60] It will be difficult to separate these concerns and establish that the Security Council's exclusive concern is with the internal humanitarian situation. However, the descriptions of situations constituting a threat to international peace and security as well as the actions authorised in response suggest that concern for the impact on individuals in these crisis situations is a significant and genuine, if not exclusive, motivation for the determination. This can be seen as evidence of an evolving understanding of threats to peace and security that includes threats to people within states as well as conflicts between states. This, in turn, could be described as a movement toward a human-centred interpretation of the Charter's provisions.[61]

---

relationship between a 'danger' to the peace and a 'threat' to the peace, see Frowein and Krisch, above n 51, at 723.

[54] UNSC Res 688 (5 April 1991) UN Doc S/RES/688. For discussion see, eg, Higgins, above n 7, at 255–6.

[55] UNSC Res 794 (3 December 1992) UN Doc S/RES/794.

[56] UNSC Res 1078 (9 November 1996) UN Doc S/RES/1078; UNSC Res 1080 (15 November 1996) UN Doc S/RES/1080; UNSC Res 1484 (19 May 2003) UN Doc S/RES/1484.

[57] UNSC Res 1542 (30 April 2004) UN Doc S/RES/1542.

[58] UNSC Res 1556 (30 June 2004) UN Doc S/RES/1556; UNSC Res 1564 (18 September 2004) UN Doc S/RES/1564; UNSC Res 1593 (31 March 2005) UN Doc S/RES/1593; UNSC Res 1679 (16 May 2006) UN Doc S/RES/1679.

[59] UNSC Res 1296 (19 April 2000) UN Doc S/RES/1296; UN SC Res 1314 (11 August 2000) UN Doc S/RES/1314.

[60] Compare Higgins, above n 7, at 255, describing these resolutions as resting on a 'legal fiction' that humanitarian crises or human rights violations cause threats to peace and security.

[61] See, eg, Frowein and Krisch, above n 51, at 725; C Greenwood, 'International Law and the NATO Intervention in Kosovo' (2000) 49 *ICLQ* 926, at 930.

COMMON CONCERN AND RESPONSIBILITY
IN INTERNATIONAL LAW

The previous chapter suggested that in addition to a human-centred approach, the concept of human security as currently used in international discourse entails the idea that the security of the world's people is a matter of common concern and, perhaps, common responsibility. Since people's own governments cannot always be relied on to protect them and many threats transcend national boundaries, states and other actors must act collectively in pursuit of human security if it is to be effectively ensured. States may act primarily out of self-interest or concern for their own people, in which case they will be motivated to take action where their own population seems likely to be vulnerable to the effects of human security threats outside their borders. In this situation a threat to human security anywhere in the world may be a matter of common concern to all states attempting to protect their own population. It was argued in chapter two that a more ambitious understanding of common concern, which includes a degree of common *responsibility* for the security of individuals anywhere in the world, is more consistent with the normative and conceptual basis of human security which respects the inherent and equal value of each individual. Although this cosmopolitan understanding of common concern for human security is more radical, both dimensions challenge accepted principles of international law to some extent.

As was noted above, state sovereignty is one of the central principles of the international legal order. The external aspect of state sovereignty protects the state's independence and shields it from interference in its domestic affairs or within its territory.[62] The human security agenda includes many matters which have traditionally been 'thought of as within the realm of domestic and not international responsibility'.[63] The idea of common concern and responsibility for human security suggests the possibility that outside intervention with respect to these matters may sometimes be called for. When people's security is threatened within a

---

[62] See, eg, UNGA, 'Declaration on Principles of International Law Concerning Friendly Relations and Co-operation Among States in Accordance with the Charter of the United Nations', UNGA Res 2625 (XXV) (24 October 1970) UN Doc A/8028 [Declaration on Friendly Relations] (subpara (d) of the 'principle of sovereign equality of states'); Fassbender and Bleckmann, above n 19, at 70–73; Cassese, *International Law*, above n 17, at 89; Perrez, above n 6, at 14*ff*.

[63] G MacLean, 'The Changing Perception of Human Security: Coordinating National and Multilateral Responses' (1998) <http://www.unac.org/en/link_learn/canada/security/perception.asp> (accessed 7 March 2007), at 3. See also OAS, 'Human Security in the Americas', above n 1, at 1; L Axworthy, 'Towards a New Multilateralism' in MA Cameron, RJ Lawson and BW Tomlin (eds), *To Walk Without Fear: The Global Movement to Ban Landmines* (Toronto, Oxford University Press, 1998), at 451; G MacLean, 'Instituting and Projecting Human Security: A Canadian Perspective' (2000) 54 *Australian Journal of International Affairs* 269, at 271.

particular state, other states and international actors may feel compelled to act, whether out of sole concern for those people or because they fear the potential transboundary impact of security threats (or both). However, the 'shield' of sovereignty stands as a barrier to such action.[64]

The idea of common concern for human security thus seems to bring the human security approach into conflict with state sovereignty and the related principle of non-intervention. The principle of non-intervention involves 'the right of every sovereign State to conduct its affairs without outside interference'[65] and has been described as an affirmation of a state-centred legal order.[66] It is recognised as a principle of customary international law,[67] reflected in the principles of the UN Charter and reiterated in the 1970 Declaration on Friendly Relations, which prohibits states from intervening in each others' affairs 'for any reason whatever'.[68] Presented in these stark terms, the principle of non-intervention would indeed appear to be a constraint on efforts to promote human security and to conflict with the idea of human security as a common concern. As with sovereignty and the human-centred approach, though, the degree of conflict depends on several factors. The first is the scope and effect of the principles; it is well accepted that neither sovereignty nor the principle of non-intervention is absolute, and their limits are defined and redefined as international law evolves. The scope of domestic jurisdiction, that is, what is considered to be solely a matter of domestic law and therefore protected from interference, depends on the development of international law.[69] The second factor is the degree to which collective action for human security really does entail the need for intervention by states (or international organisations acting at their behest) in the territory and affairs of others. This question will be explored in later chapters.

---

[64] S Ogata, 'International Security and Refugee Problems after the Cold War, Assuring the Security of People: the Humanitarian Challenge of the 21st Century' (Olof Palme Memorial Lecture, Stockholm, 14 June 1995) <http://www2.sipri.se/sipri/Lectures/Ogata.html> (accessed 7 March 2007); UN, *Millennium Report*, above n 1, at 48; Canada, DFAIT, 'Notes for an Address by the Honourable Lloyd Axworthy, Minister of Foreign Affairs, to the G-8 Foreign Ministers' Meeting' Statement 99/40 (9 June 1999) <http://w01.international.gc.ca/minpub> (accessed 26 February 2007); Canada, DFAIT, 'Notes for an Address by the Honourable Lloyd Axworthy, Minister of Foreign Affairs, to the 55th UN General Assembly' Statement 2000/31 (14 September 2000) <http://w01.international.gc.ca/minpub> (accessed 26 February 2007).

[65] *Nicaragua*, above n 39, at paras 202, 207.

[66] McGoldrick, above n 29, at 85, 88.

[67] *Nicaragua*, above n 39, at para 202.

[68] UNGA, Declaration on Friendly Relations, above n 62; UN Charter, art 2(7). Although this article refers to the competence of the UN it is usually seen as reflecting the general principle of non-intervention: see McGoldrick, above n 29, at 88. The principle is also found in the Charter of the Organization of American States, (signed 30 April 1948, entered into force 13 December 1951) OASTS No 1-C, 61; 119 UNTS 48 (as amended), arts 3(e), 19.

[69] See Brownlie, above n 27, at 291, and McGoldrick, above n 29, at 86, citing *Nationality Decrees in Tunis and Morocco* (1923) PCIJ Ser B, No 4. See also the decision of the ICJ in the *Nicaragua* case, above n 39, at para 205.

The idea of common responsibility for human security suggests that states may bear some responsibility for the security of individuals regardless of whether those individuals are within their jurisdiction. This also runs up against two central features of international law. First, international law has traditionally consisted of reciprocal obligations between states, rather than to or among individuals. Although this is increasingly challenged by human rights, or international criminal law, in particular, most international law still consists of obligations owed by states to other states, even if individuals may be the ultimate beneficiaries. Second, where a state does owe duties to individuals, generally speaking those duties are only owed to individuals within its territory or tied to it by nationality, as a corollary of a state's sovereign authority over its territory and population. As we will see below, human rights obligations have typically been conceived of as pertaining to the relationship between a state and the people within its territory and subject to its jurisdiction. Absent these territorial or jurisdictional links, a state has few legal obligations towards individuals, even if those individuals are affected by its actions. Other areas of law such as humanitarian law and refugee law do offer some broader protections, but these are limited in their content and scope of application.

Notwithstanding the tensions between the international legal framework and the ideas of common concern and responsibility for human security, parallels to these ideas can be identified in international law. This section will trace some of these parallels, first in general principles and obligations and then in relation to specific areas of law. International environmental law offers some cognate concepts, since the law in this area has long sought to address transnational threats requiring collective action. The scope of common responsibility for the protection of individuals in human rights, humanitarian, and refugee law will also be considered.

General Principles of Cooperation and Common Concern or Responsibility

States have always cooperated on a variety of matters in their common interest, but a general duty of cooperation is thought to have emerged only since the adoption of the UN Charter.[70] Article 1(3) establishes as one of the purposes of the United Nations '[t]o achieve international cooperation in solving international problems of an economic, social, cultural, or humanitarian character, and in promoting and encouraging respect for human rights and for fundamental freedoms for all without

---

[70] Cassese, *Divided World*, above n 6, at 150.

distinction as to race, sex, language, or religion'. In article 56, members of the UN 'pledge themselves to take joint and separate action in co-operation with the Organization for the achievement of the purposes set forth in article 55'.[71]

The general duty or principle of cooperation was restated in the 1970 Declaration on Friendly Relations in the following terms:

> States have the duty to co-operate with one another, irrespective of the differences in their political, economic and social systems, in the various spheres of international relations, in order to maintain international peace and security and to promote international economic stability and progress, the general welfare of nations and international co-operation free from discrimination based on such differences.[72]

The Declaration also imposes specific obligations to cooperate in maintaining international peace and security and in the promotion of human rights, and, for members of the United Nations, to 'take joint and separate action in co-operation with the United Nations in accordance with the relevant provisions of the Charter'. Apart from the last of these (addressed only to UN members), the obligations are framed as those of all states, thereby extending the principle of cooperation 'to the whole international community'.[73]

Questions remain about the content and scope of the principle of co-operation, however. It does not prescribe any particular measures or actions on the part of states,[74] but requires states 'to take into consideration the legitimate interests of others and to contribute generally to the solution of common problems'.[75] An obligation to cooperate per se may have quite minimal content, for example, not to obstruct the efforts of others and perhaps to share such information as is necessary to allow for cooperative action. Although article 56 has been treated as imposing some

---

[71] The purposes in art 55 include promoting, '[w]ith a view to the creation of conditions of stability and well-being':

(a) higher standards of living, full employment, and conditions of economic and social progress and development;
(b) solutions of international economic, social, health, and related problems; and international cultural and educational co-operation; and
(c) universal respect for, and observance of, human rights and fundamental freedoms for all without distinction as to race, sex, language, or religion.

[72] Above n 62.

[73] Cassese, *Divided World*, above n 6, at 151. See also B Babovič, 'The Duty of States to Cooperate with One Another in Accordance with the Charter' in M Šahovič (ed), *Principles of International Law Concerning Friendly Relations and Cooperation* (Dobbs Ferry, NY, Oceana Publications, 1972), at 290*ff*; Perrez, above n 6, at 258. Cassese notes, however, that the principle is 'still in a rudimentary form' (*Divided World*, above n 6, at 152). For a discussion of differing views of states on the status of the duty, see Babovič, above, at 280*ff*.

[74] See, eg, Cassese, *Divided World*, above n 6, at 151; Perrez, above n 6, at 261, 264, 271.

[75] Perrez, above n 6, at 264.

binding obligations, its function and content are therefore limited.[76] An obligation to cooperate *for a specific purpose*, though, arguably entails some obligation to take positive action towards the fulfilment of that purpose.[77] Still, the obligation is a very general one, making it difficult to use as the basis for more specific duties.[78] Acknowledging the existence of a principle or duty of cooperation, therefore, would still leave unanswered crucial questions about what type and extent of action is required in various situations.

The idea that some matters are of universal concern and interest is most notably apparent in the concept of obligations *erga omnes* or obligations owed 'to the international community as a whole'. These apply to a limited range of cases in which, '[i]n view of the importance of the rights involved, all States can be held to have a legal interest in their protection'.[79] Examples include prohibitions on aggression and genocide, 'basic rights of the human person' such as protection from slavery and racial discrimination,[80] the right to self-determination,[81] and at least some of the rules of humanitarian law.[82] The concept of obligations *erga omnes* specifically recognises that all states may have an interest in the enforcement of certain forms of protection, entitling them to invoke the responsibility of the offending state, despite not being able to demonstrate that they have been injured by the breach.[83]

That all states have certain *obligations* in some cases is less well established, but receives support from the International Law Commission's Draft Articles on State Responsibility. Here the category of cases is defined by reference to the related but distinct concept of

---

[76] R Wolfrum, 'Article 56' in B Simma (ed), *The Charter of the United Nations: A Commentary*, 2nd edn (Oxford, Oxford University Press, 2002), vol II, at 942–3.

[77] For example, art 55(c) of the UN Charter, as well as setting an agenda for UN activity, also 'legally obligates not only the world Organization but also the member States to respect and protect human rights': E Riedel, 'Article 55(c)' in B Simma (ed), *The Charter of the United Nations: A Commentary*, 2nd edn (Oxford, Oxford University Press, 2002), vol II, at 920.

[78] R Wolfrum, 'Article 1' in B Simma (ed), *The Charter of the United Nations: A Commentary*, 2nd edn (Oxford, Oxford University Press, 2002), vol I, at 45: the question has arisen whether 'Art 1(3) contained sufficiently precise standards to be invoked as a basis for specific recommendations' (footnotes omitted).

[79] *Barcelona Traction, Light and Power Company, Limited, Second Phase* [1970] ICJ Rep 3, at para 33.

[80] *Ibid*, at para 34.

[81] *Ibid*, at para 34; *East Timor (Portugal v Australia)* [1995] ICJ Rep 90, at para 29; *Legal Consequences of the Construction of a Wall in the Occupied Palestinian Territory (Advisory Opinion)*, Advisory Opinion of 9 July 2004 [*Legal Consequences*], at paras 88, 156.

[82] *Legal Consequences*, above n 81, at para 157.

[83] See, eg, International Law Commission, 'Draft Articles on State Responsibility', UNGA Res 56/83 (28 January 2002) UN Doc A/RES/56/83, Annex ['State Responsibility'], art 48 (on 'Invocation of responsibility by a State other than an injured State'), in particular para (1)(b); and the discussion at 38–41 and 278 in J Crawford, *The International Law Commission's Articles on State Responsibility: Introduction, Text and Commentaries* (Cambridge, Cambridge University Press, 2002).

peremptory norms.[84] In the event of a serious breach of an obligation arising under a peremptory norm,[85] other states are obliged to 'cooperate to bring [the breach] to an end through lawful means', as well as to refrain from recognising or helping to maintain a situation created by such a breach.[86] The commentary to this article suggests that it 'may reflect the progressive development of international law', since it is not certain that an obligation to cooperate to bring the breach to an end in such circumstances presently exists in general international law, but notes that 'such cooperation . . . is carried out already in response to the gravest breaches of international law and it is often the only way of providing an effective remedy'.[87] More recently, in the advisory opinion of the ICJ regarding *Legal Consequences of the Construction of a Wall in the Occupied Palestinian Territory*, 13 of the 15 judges determined that:

> Given the character and the importance of the rights and obligations involved, the Court is of the view that all States are under an obligation not to recognize the illegal situation resulting from the construction of the wall in the Occupied Palestinian Territory, including in and around East Jerusalem. They are also under an obligation not to render aid or assistance in maintaining the situation created by such construction. It is also for all States, while respecting the United Nations Charter and international law, to see to it that any impediment, resulting from the construction of the wall, to the exercise by the Palestinian people of its right to self-determination is brought to an end.[88]

The majority opinion did not elaborate on the source of these obligations or their specific implications.

Common Interests and Responsibilities in International Environmental Law

International environmental law contains norms, concepts, and principles relating to cooperation and common responsibility which are designed to address the reality that the need for environmental protection transcends state boundaries. A duty to cooperate is 'affirmed in virtually all environmental agreements of bilateral and regional application, and global instruments'.[89] The Stockholm Declaration emphasises the importance of

[84] The precise nature of the relationship between obligations *erga omnes* and peremptory norms of international law is an open question which need not be settled here. The categories of cases defined by reference to each of them are similar, however.

[85] International Law Commission, 'State Responsibility', above n 83, art 40. According to para 2 of this article, a breach is serious 'if it involves a gross or systematic failure by the responsible State to fulfil the obligation'.

[86] *Ibid*, art 41(1), (2).

[87] Crawford, above n 83, at 249.

[88] *Legal Consequences*, above n 81, at para 159.

[89] P Sands, *Principles of International Environmental Law*, vol 1: Frameworks, Standards and Implementation (Manchester, Manchester University Press, 1995), at 197 (footnotes omitted).

cooperation in environmental matters,[90] and the obligation to cooperate is mentioned several times in the Rio Declaration, including in principle 7 which requires states to 'cooperate in a spirit of global partnership to conserve, protect and restore the health and integrity of the Earth's ecosystem'.[91] States also commit to cooperating with respect to transboundary environmental risks and shared resources.[92] This includes specific commitments regarding notification, information sharing, consultation, and negotiation.[93]

The principle of prevention (also referred to as the protective or preventive principle, or principle of preventive action) requires states to prevent harm to the environment beyond their borders. It is expressed in principle 21 of the 1972 Stockholm Declaration as follows:

> States have, in accordance with the Charter of the United Nations and the principles of international law, . . . the responsibility to ensure that activities within their jurisdiction or control do not cause damage to the environment of other States or of areas beyond the limits of national jurisdiction.

This principle has since been reiterated in numerous international legal instruments, including the Rio Declaration,[94] the UN Framework Convention on Climate Change,[95] the Convention for the Protection of the Ozone Layer ('the Vienna Convention'),[96] and the Convention on

---

[90] Declaration of the United Nations Conference on the Human Environment, Report of the United Nations Conference on the Human Environment, Stockholm, 5–16 June 1972 (UN publication, Sales No E.73.II.A.14 and corrigendum), ch I [Stockholm Declaration], principle 24.

[91] Rio Declaration on Environment and Development, Report of the United Nations Conference on Environment and Development, Rio de Janeiro, 3–14 June 1992, vol I, Resolutions Adopted by the Conference (UN publication, Sales No E.93.I.8 and corrigendum), Resolution 1, Annex I [Rio Declaration]. See also principle 27 ('States and people shall cooperate in good faith and in a spirit of partnership in the fulfilment of the principles embodied in this Declaration and in the further development of international law in the field of sustainable development') and obligations to cooperate for specific purposes in principles 5, 9, 13, and 14.

[92] See, eg, AE Boyle, 'The Principle of Co-operation: The Environment' in V Lowe and C Warbrick (eds), *The United Nations and the Principles of International Law: Essays in memory of Michael Akehurst* (London, Routledge, 1994). See also International Law Commission, 'Draft Articles on Prevention of Transboundary Harm from Hazardous Activities', UNGA, Report of the International Law Commission, Fifty-third session (2001) GAOR 56th Session Supp 10, 370 [ILC, 'Transboundary Harm'], art 4.

[93] See, eg, *Lac Lanoux Arbitration (Spain v France)* (1957) 12 RIAA 281; Sands, above n 89, at 198; Boyle, above n 92, at 122*ff*; P Birnie and A Boyle, *International Law and the Environment*, 2nd edn (Oxford, Oxford University Press, 2002), at 126*ff*. Obligations of notification and consultation in case of possible transboundary effects are codified in the Rio Declaration, above n 91, principles 18 and 19. See also ILC, 'Transboundary Harm', above n 92, arts 7, 8, 9, 12 and 17.

[94] Rio Declaration, above n 91, principle 2.

[95] UN Framework Convention on Climate Change (adopted 9 May 1992, entered into force 21 March 1994) 1771 UNTS 107 [Climate Change Convention], preamble.

[96] Vienna Convention for the Protection of the Ozone Layer (adopted 22 March 1985, entered into force 22 September 1988) 1513 UNTS 293 [Vienna Convention], preamble.

Biological Diversity.[97] The principle of prevention is widely accepted as a principle of customary law, based on state practice and international instruments both pre-dating and subsequent to the Stockholm Declaration.[98] In 1996 the ICJ affirmed that the 'existence of the general obligation of States to ensure that activities within their jurisdiction and control respect the environment of other States or of areas beyond national control is now part of the corpus of international law relating to the environment'.[99]

Given that the emphasis is on transboundary harm, the origins of the principle are closely related to a more general principle of 'good neighbourliness', which enjoins states from using their territory in such a way as to harm other states,[100] and respect for the sovereignty and territorial integrity of other states.[101] The scope of the principle also extends beyond harm to another state, since it includes harm to common areas and also, according to some, harm within a state's own jurisdiction.[102] There are some grounds for saying, then, that the principle, if originally rooted in sovereignty concerns, has moved beyond those roots to focus on harm to the environment *per se,* and global rather than merely bilateral relationships.[103] Furthermore, it emphasises proactive prevention rather than reacting to harm after the fact.[104] It is supported by other principles of international environmental law, including the requirement of environmental impact assessment, the obligation of immediate notification of emergencies, and obligations of prior consultation and information sharing.[105]

Other principles directly address the question of common responsibility. Principle 7 of the Rio Declaration, just mentioned, also refers to

[97] Convention on Biological Diversity (adopted 5 June 1992, entered into force 29 December 1993) 1760 UNTS 79, art 3.

[98] J Vessey, 'The Principle of Prevention in International Law' (1998) 3 *Austrian Review of International and European Law* 181, at 189; Sands, above n 89, at 194; Birnie and Boyle, above n 93, at 109–10. See also ILC, 'Transboundary Harm', above n 92, especially art 3; ILC, 'Commentaries to the Draft Articles on Prevention of Transboundary Harm from Hazardous Activities', UNGA, Report of the International Law Commission, Fifty-third session (2001) GAOR 56th Session Supp 10, 377, at 378*ff*.

[99] *Nuclear Weapons,* above n 20, at para 29. This passage was subsequently cited by the Court in *Gabcíkovo-Nagymaros Project (Hungary /Slovakia)* [1997] ICJ Rep 7, at para 53.

[100] See the *Trail Smelter Case (United States v Canada)* (1941) 3 RIAA 1905 regarding the obligation in the environmental context, and the *Corfu Channel* case, above n 51, at 22 regarding this obligation generally.

[101] Vessey, above n 98, at 185.

[102] Sands, above n 89, at 195.

[103] See, eg, Vessey, above n 98, at 185; Birnie and Boyle, above n 93, at 111; Sands, above n 89, at 194–5. Sands in fact distinguishes between principle 21, which is concerned with transboundary harm only, and the preventive principle, which is distinguishable in that it 'seeks to minimise environmental damage as an objective itself' and therefore may oblige a state 'to prevent damage to the environment *within its own jurisdiction'*: *ibid,* at 195 (emphasis in original).

[104] Vessey, above n 98, at 181–2.

[105] Rio Declaration, above n 91, principles 17, 18, and 19. See Vessey, above n 98, at 194.

'common but differentiated responsibilities' of states.[106] The principle of common but differentiated responsibility has two key elements:

> The first concerns the common responsibility of states for the protection of the environment, or parts of it, at the national, regional, and global levels. The second concerns the need to take account of differing circumstances, particularly in relation to each state's *contribution* to the creation of a particular environmental problem and its *ability* to prevent, reduce and control the threat. In practical terms [its application] has at least two consequences. First, it entitles, or may require, all concerned states to participate in international response measures aimed at addressing environmental problems. Second, it leads to environmental standards which impose differing obligations on states.[107]

The first element, global common responsibility, is said to be nearly universally accepted, while states' responses to the differentiation of responsibilities have been more cautious,[108] although the differentiated approach 'is reflected in many treaties'.[109] The differentiation of responsibilities is the result of the application of other principles, most notably equity and solidarity, to the principle of common responsibility.[110]

The idea of common responsibility has a long history and has been invoked in relation to fish and other marine resources, waterfowl, wildlife, outer space, the moon, and more recently climate change and biological diversity.[111] Common responsibility can be considered a generic term which refers to 'the shared obligations of two or more states towards the protection of a particular environmental resource'.[112] Within this, there is a cluster of related concepts, principles, and special legal regimes that have been developed to deal with areas beyond the territorial jurisdiction of any state, common or globally significant resources, and matters of

---

[106] See also Climate Change Convention, above n 95, preamble and art 3(1). The principle is also reflected in the Vienna Convention, above n 96, and the Convention on Biological Diversity, above n 97.

[107] Sands, above n 89, at 217 (emphasis in original). See also Perrez, above n 6, at 295.

[108] Birnie and Boyle, above n 93, at 100 and 102–3, respectively.

[109] Sands, above n 89, at 219.

[110] See, eg, *ibid*, at 217; Birnie and Boyle, above n 93, at 102; Perrez, above n 6, at 295. Solidarity is sometimes discussed as a separate principle, although it is closely related to the principle of cooperation, and its status as a legal principle is unclear: see Perrez, *ibid*, at 52, 295 (text and fn 344). Solidarity is sometimes also invoked in the context of refugee law (see below n 191 and accompanying text) and human rights (see below n 186 and accompanying text). See EMG Denters, 'IMF Conditionality: Economic, Social and Cultural Rights, and the Evolving Principle of Solidarity' in PJIM de Waart, P Peters and E Denters (eds), *International Law and Development* (Dordrecht, Martinus Nijhoff, 1988), at 242, for a brief discussion of the principle's potential implications in the area of balance of payment adjustment. Note that solidarity is sometimes also used in reference to a right of all parties to a treaty to take action against a state that breaches an obligation under a treaty: see DN Hutchinson, 'Solidarity and Breaches of Multilateral Treaties' (1988) 59 *BYBIL* 151.

[111] Sands, above n 89, at 218; Perrez, above n 6, at 292–3; Birnie and Boyle, above n 93, at 97.

[112] Sands, above n 89, at 218.

universal concern. Designations include 'common concern' (of human-kind), 'common heritage' (of mankind or humankind), 'international resource', 'province of all mankind', or 'for the good of mankind'.[113] These various 'attributions of commonality' have some of the same consequences, such as a legal responsibility to prevent damage to the resource at issue.[114] At least some of them, in particular common heritage and common concern, may ground obligations *erga omnes*.[115] There are also significant differences, however: for example, the concept of common heritage as applied to the moon[116] and the deep sea bed[117] has a specific meaning which entails equitable sharing of the benefits of resource exploitation, shared management, and prohibition of military uses.[118]

Of particular relevance to human security is the idea of 'common concern' as it has been articulated in the context of climate change and biological diversity.[119] Birnie and Boyle describe common concern as a concept used 'to designate those issues which involve global responsibilities' because of 'their universal character and the need for common action by all states if measures of protection are to work'.[120] The designation of matters as being of common concern has two important effects. First, it 'declares them to be a legitimate object of international regulation and supervision', removing them from the reserved domain of domestic jurisdiction or the sphere of 'exclusive territorial sovereignty of individual

---

[113] See *ibid*; Perrez, above n 6, at 293, and the sources cited therein.

[114] Sands, above n 89, at 218.

[115] Birnie and Boyle, above n 93, at 99; FL Kirgis, Jr, 'Standing to Challenge Human Endeavours that Could Change the Climate' (1990) 84 *AJIL* 525, at 527. The concept of common concern has the same effect regarding standing as common heritage, according to Kirgis (*ibid*, at 529). For a discussion of obligations *erga omnes* in international environmental law, see M Ragazzi, *The Concept of International Obligations Erga Omnes* (Oxford, Clarendon Press, 1997), at 154–62.

[116] Agreement Governing the Activities of States on the Moon and Other Celestial Bodies (adopted 5 December 1979, entered into force 11 July 1984) 1363 UNTS 3, arts 3, 4, 11.

[117] UN Convention on the Law of the Sea (opened for signature 10 December 1982, entered into force 16 November 1994) 1833 UNTS 3, arts 136–42.

[118] See CC Joyner, 'Legal Implications of the Concept of the Common Heritage of Mankind' (1986) 35 *ICLQ* 190, at 191–2. The other key elements are the prohibition on national or private appropriation and free sharing of scientific research (*ibid*). See Birnie and Boyle, above n 93, at 141, 143 on the distinction between common heritage and common property (eg the high seas) which can be used reasonably by any state without provision for international administration or sharing of benefits. Note, however, that the term 'common heritage' is not always used in this precise sense, which tends to blur the distinctions: see Perrez, above n 6, at 292, who discusses common heritage and common concern together without explicitly distinguishing between them, and Birnie and Boyle, above n 93, at 143, commenting on the tendency to use the term 'common heritage' loosely.

[119] Climate Change Convention, above n 95, preamble; Convention on Biological Diversity, above n 97, preamble; UNGA, 'Declaration on Protection of the Global Climate for Present and Future Generations of Mankind', UNGA Res 43/53 (6 December 1988) UN Doc A/RES/43/53. The original proposal for this Declaration used the terminology of 'common heritage of mankind': see Kirgis, above n 115, at 525.

[120] Birnie and Boyle, above n 93, at 97.

states'.[121] It establishes the legitimate *interest* of states in matters of global significance.[122] Second, it imposes common *responsibility* for assistance and protection.[123] These closely parallel the two dimensions of common concern for human security that were outlined earlier. The concept of common concern has also been suggested as a way of reconciling respect for state sovereignty and the legitimate interests of other states in matters within one state's jurisdiction.[124]

Common Responsibility for the Protection of Individuals

As we have just seen, the concept of common concern in international environmental law, which parallels the idea of common concern for human security, entails two main consequences: legitimate interest (the interest of one state in what would otherwise be the domestic affairs of another state) and common responsibility (obligations of assistance and protection). Both of these aspects are also present in the context of human rights, but the first seems rather better developed than the second. That is, the focus to date has been largely on establishing that states have the *right* to interfere in others' domestic affairs where human rights are concerned, and much less on determining what *responsibility* they have to do anything to help prevent or respond to violations. It is now well established that the protection of human rights is a matter of legitimate concern for the whole international community, including states having no direct connection (for example of nationality) to the victims of violations. As we saw above, violations of human rights, at least serious and large-scale violations, are matters of international concern.[125] In addition, the category of obligations owed to the international community (obligations *erga omnes*) contains at least some fundamental human rights.

States' duties with respect to human rights generally apply to individuals within their territory or subject to their jurisdiction.[126] Their responsibilities toward individuals in and of other states have been described as 'vague and weak';[127] indeed, some deny that they exist at

---

[121] Birnie and Boyle, above n 93, at 100.

[122] *Ibid*, at 99.

[123] *Ibid*, at 99.

[124] J Brunnee and SJ Toope, 'Environmental Security and Freshwater Resources: Ecosystem Regime Building' (1997) 91 *AJIL* 26, at 41. See also I Mgbeoji, 'Beyond Rhetoric: State Sovereignty, Common Concern, and the Inapplicability of the Common Heritage Concept to Plant Genetic Resources' (2003) 16 *Leiden Journal of International Law* 821, at 837.

[125] See above n 33 and accompanying text.

[126] See, eg, ICCPR, above n 26, art 2(1) ('all individuals within its territory and subject to its jurisdiction'); ECHR, above n 24, art 1 ('everyone within their jurisdiction'); ACHR, above n 24, art 1(1) ('all persons subject to their jurisdiction').

[127] M Gibney, K Tomašcevski and J Vedsted-Hansen, 'Transnational State Responsibility for Violations of Human Rights' (1999) 12 *Harvard Human Rights Journal* 267, at 267.

all.[128] A few authors have explored the idea of 'transnational' human rights obligations, by which is meant 'the possibility that states may have obligations relating to the human rights effects of their external activities, such as trade, development cooperation, participation in international organizations, and security activities'.[129] However, these seem generally to be considered as matters of foreign policy or morality rather than legal obligation. Human rights 'in the classical sense' are understood to involve 'an obligation running between a person, or persons, and the state which has jurisdiction over them'.[130] This classical understanding of human rights as a matter of 'state–citizen relations' can be traced back to the liberal social contract theory which heavily influenced modern conceptions of human rights.[131] Some have criticised the fact that human rights obligations are limited by territoriality and citizenship, suggesting that it is a paradox that inhibits the 'universal enforcement of nominally universal human rights'.[132]

Jurisprudence interpreting the ICCPR and regional human rights agreements has extended their application beyond a state's territory and nationals in some situations, but so far these remain quite limited. Duties may be owed even to non-nationals outside the state's territory if the state exercises effective control over the area in which the alleged violation occurs, for example due to military occupation.[133] It has been accepted that ICCPR obligations apply where a state exercises jurisdiction outside its territory,[134] as do those under the ECHR.[135] However, attempts to extend this to states' actions outside their territory which do not amount to the exercise of jurisdiction or effective control have generally been unsuccessful.[136] In the case of *Banković et al v Belgium et al*, the claimants

---

[128] See, eg, Donnelly, 'Social Construction', above n 34, at 85: 'Foreign states simply have no internationally recognised human rights obligation to protect foreign nationals abroad from, for example, torture.'

[129] SI Skogly and M Gibney, 'Transnational Human Rights Obligations' (2002) 24 *Human Rights Quarterly* 781, at 781. See also Gibney, Tomaševski and Vedsted-Hansen, above n 127.

[130] Higgins, above n 7, at 104.

[131] Donnelly, 'Social Construction', above n 34, at 86.

[132] Gibney, Tomaševski and Vedsted-Hansen, above n 127, at 267–8.

[133] *Loizidou v Turkey (Preliminary Objections)*, Series A No 310 (1995).

[134] *Legal Consequences*, above n 81, paras 108–11. See also *Lopez Burgos v Uruguay* (29 July 1981) UN Doc CCPR/C/13/D/52/1979; UN Human Rights Committee, 'General Comment No 31: The Nature of the General Legal Obligation Imposed on States Parties' (26 May 2004) UN Doc CCPR/C/21/Rev.1/Add.13, at para 10: 'a State party must respect and ensure the rights laid down in the Covenant to anyone within the power or effective control of that State Party, even if not situated within the territory of the State Party . . . This principle also applies to those within the power or effective control of the forces of a State Party acting outside its territory, regardless of the circumstances in which such power or effective control was obtained.'

[135] ECHR, above n 24. See, eg, *Öcalan v Turkey*, Judgment, 12 May 2005 (Application No 46221/99), at para 91.

[136] *Banković et al v Belgium et al*, Admissibility Decision, 12 December 2001 (Application No 52207/99). However, compare *Alejandre v Cuba*, American Commission on Human Rights

argued that NATO countries involved in the bombing of Kosovo could owe obligations to the injured individuals under the ECHR, appropriate to the degree of control they exercised in carrying out the bombings, even though this did not amount to effective control. The ECHR rejected this position, stating that this amounted to arguing that:

> anyone adversely affected by an act imputable to a Contracting State, wherever in the world that act may have been committed or its consequences felt, is thereby brought within the jurisdiction of that State for the purpose of Article 1 of the Convention.[137]

This, in the opinion of the Court, would unduly distort the ordinary and intended meaning of the Convention.

There are other indications of states' responsibilities for human rights protection on a global scale. We have already seen that the general duty of cooperation in the UN Charter includes an obligation to cooperate for purposes including the 'universal respect for, and observance of, human rights and fundamental freedoms for all'.[138] Provisions in some human rights instruments impose a duty to act cooperatively for the realisation of human rights.[139] The International Covenant on Economic, Social and Cultural Rights (ICESCR) and the Convention on the Rights of the Child (CRC) have been held to apply where a state exercises jurisdiction, even if it does not have sovereignty over those areas.[140] In addition, article 4 of the CRC requires states parties to undertake measures for the implementation of economic, social, and cultural rights recognised in the Convention 'within the framework of international cooperation'. Other provisions require states parties to promote and encourage international cooperation in respect of particular rights, taking account of the needs of developing countries.[141] Under the ICESCR, states parties undertake 'to take steps, individually and *through international assistance and cooperation*, especially economic and technical . . . with a view to achieving progressively the full

Report No 86/99, OEA/Ser.L/V/II.106 Doc 3 (1999) (holding that shooting down an aeroplane can constitute placing the victims under the attacking state's authority so that its human rights obligations apply; decided under the American Declaration of the Rights and Duties of Man, OAS Res XXX adopted by the Ninth International Conference of American States (1948) reprinted in Basic Documents Pertaining to Human Rights in the Inter-American System OEA/Ser L V/II.82 Doc 6 Rev 1 at 17 (1992).

[137] *Banković et al v Belgium et al*, above n 136, at 356.

[138] Art 55(c).

[139] Convention on the Rights of the Child, (adopted 20 November 1989, entered into force 2 September 1990), 1577 UNTS 3 [CRC]. See also art 22 of the Universal Declaration of Human Rights (adopted 10 December 1948) UN GA Res 217A (III), UN Doc A/810, which states: 'Everyone, as a member of society, has the right to social security and is entitled to realization, through national effort and international cooperation and in accordance with the organization and resources of each State, of the economic, social and cultural rights indispensable for his dignity and the free development of his personality.'

[140] *Legal Consequences*, above n 81, at paras 112–13.

[141] CRC, above n 139, arts 23 (disabled children), 24 (health), and 28 (education).

realization of the rights recognized in the present Covenant'.[142] They also recognise 'the essential importance of international cooperation based on free consent' in taking 'appropriate steps to ensure the realization' of the right to an adequate standard of living.[143] The Committee on Economic, Social and Cultural Rights, in commenting on these provisions, has emphasised that 'international cooperation for development and thus for the realization of economic, social and cultural rights is an obligation of all States'.[144] More recently, it has considered the effect of economic sanctions and concluded that 'the party or parties responsible for the imposition, maintenance or implementation of the sanctions' have certain obligations under the Covenant, which require them to take account of economic, social, and cultural rights when designing sanctions regimes, to monitor the effects of sanctions on these rights, and to respond to 'disproportionate suffering experienced by vulnerable groups within the targeted country'.[145]

The principle of non-refoulement, which prohibits states from returning an individual to a state where he or she is likely to suffer certain serious human rights violations,[146] also has a transnational element. States' obligations under this principle imply some recognition that a state has a responsibility to ensure that human rights violations do not occur outside its territory (notwithstanding the fact that there is also a clear link with the state's jurisdiction in the sense that the individual is presently located within its territory).[147] Finally, the right of self-determination and the so-called 'third generation' rights to peace, development, and a healthy environment would seem to imply some degree of transnational responsibility for their

[142] ICESCR, above n 26, art 2(1) (emphasis added).

[143] *Ibid*, art 11(1).

[144] UN Committee on Economic, Social and Cultural Rights, 'General Comment 3: The Nature of States Parties Obligations' (14 December 1990) UN Doc E/1991/23, at para 14. See also 'Limburg Principles on the Implementation of the International Covenant on Economic, Social and Cultural Rights', reprinted in (1987) 9 *Human Rights Quarterly* 122, at paras 29–34; UN Committee on Economic, Social and Cultural Rights, 'General Comment 14: The Right to the Highest Attainable Standard of Health' (11 August 2000) UN Doc E/C.12/2000/4, at para 45; UN Committee on Economic, Social and Cultural Rights, 'Poverty and the International Covenant on Economic, Social and Cultural Rights, Statement of the Committee on Economic, Social and Cultural Rights to the Third United Nations Conference on the Least Developed Countries' (4 May 2001) UN Doc E/C.12/2001/17, Annex VII, at paras 15–18.

[145] UN Committee on Economic, Social and Cultural Rights, 'General Comment 8: The Relationship Between Economic Sanctions and Respect for Economic, Social and Cultural Rights' (12 December 1997) UN Doc E/CN.12/1997/8, at paras 11–14.

[146] For example torture, in the CAT, above n 24, art 3, and also held to be implied in art 3 of the ECHR, above n 24; threat to life or freedom based on one's race, religion, nationality, membership of a particular social group, or political opinion, in the Convention Relating to the Status of Refugees (adopted 28 July 1951, entered into force 22 April 1954) 189 UNTS 150 [Refugee Convention], art 33(1).

[147] Gibney, Tomaševski and Vedsted-Hansen, above n 127, at 271: 'The clearest transnational duty that X possesses [in a hypothetical situation where human rights abuses are carried out by state Y] is the prohibition against returning a person to a country if there is likelihood that this person would face persecution there.'

fulfilment. Higgins has suggested that the right to development, for example, goes beyond the 'classical' pattern of human rights obligations, as 'a purported right of one state to receive benefits from others—and indeed, from international institutions—for the good of its citizens',[148] or phrased in terms of obligations, the responsibility of one state to contribute to benefits for the good of another state's citizens. These 'third generation' rights have been referred to as solidarity rights, in part because they are collective as well as individual rights, but also because their fulfilment seems to require the imposition of joint responsibility on all states and even other actors in the international community.[149] However, the status of these as legal rights has always been controversial.

In the field of humanitarian law, there is an element of common responsibility in the obligation of parties to the Geneva Conventions to 'ensure respect for the Convention[s]', which has been said to include a duty to take some measures to ensure that parties to a conflict respect humanitarian law.[150] This provision 'provides the nucleus for a system of collective responsibility' and 'has come to be seen by many as implying a universal obligation for States and international organizations (be they regional or universal) to ensure that this body of law is implemented wherever a humanitarian problem arises'.[151] The ICJ has emphasised the obligation to ensure respect for humanitarian law in several recent decisions, and in the *Wall* case, found it to be the basis of an obligation on the part of all states parties to the Fourth Geneva Convention 'to ensure compliance by Israel with international humanitarian law as embodied in that Convention'.[152] Although the ICJ here limited the obligation to states parties to the Convention, some have suggested that it is also a matter of customary international law.[153] Although the precise extent of the obligation is not clear, it can be carried out by means of, for example, resolutions by international bodies, prosecutions in ad hoc criminal

---

[148] Higgins, above n 7, at 104.

[149] See discussion in C Wellman, 'Solidarity, the Individual and Human Rights' (2000) 22 *Human Rights Quarterly* 639.

[150] Art 1 of the four Geneva Conventions, above n 37, and art 1(1) of Protocol I, above n 38: 'The High Contracting Parties undertake to respect and ensure respect for [the present Convention/this Protocol] in all circumstances.' Although the provision does not appear in Protocol II, above n 38, Boisson de Chazournes and Condorelli suggest that the same obligation is indirectly incorporated in that Protocol: L Boisson de Chazournes and L Condorelli, 'Common Article 1 of the Geneva Conventions Revisited: Protecting Collective Interests' (2000) 837 *IRRC* 67, at 69. For further discussion of the scope of the obligation, see *ibid*; F Azzam, 'The Duty of Third States to Implement and Enforce International Humanitarian Law' (1997) *Nordic Journal of International Law* 55; U Palwankar, 'Measures Available to States for Fulfilling Their Obligation to Ensure Respect for International Humanitarian Law' (1994) 298 *IRRC* 9.

[151] Boisson de Chazournes and Condorelli, above n 150, at 68, 70.

[152] *Legal Consequences*, above n 81, at para 159. *Armed Activities on the Territory of the Congo (Democratic Republic of the Congo v Uganda)*, Judgment of 19 December 2005, at para 211.

[153] J-M Henckaerts and L Doswald-Beck, *Customary International Humanitarian Law* (Cambridge, Cambridge University Press, 2005), vol 1, at 511–12.

tribunals or the ICJ, sanctions, peace-keeping forces, and the establishment and exercise of universal jurisdiction over grave breaches of
humanitarian law.[154]

The Genocide Convention also contains obligations on states parties to
protect individuals, although the punishment of genocide has historically
been emphasised more than its prevention.[155] Under article 1, the parties
undertake to 'prevent and punish' the crime of genocide, and article 8
allows parties to call upon UN organs to take action for the prevention and
suppression of genocide.[156] The ICJ recently confirmed that the undertaking in article 1 of the Convention does give rise to a distinct obligation
to prevent genocide.[157] This obligation requires a state that is able to
influence the conduct of relevant actors to 'take all measures to prevent
genocide which [are] within its power, and which might [contribute] to
preventing the genocide'.[158] While geographical distance may be relevant
to a state's ability to effectively influence the persons committing or likely
to commit genocide,[159] the obligation to prevent genocide is not otherwise
limited to the state's territorial jurisdiction: the state's obligations under
article 1 'apply to a State wherever it may be acting or may be able to act
in ways appropriate to meeting the obligations in question'.[160]

Finally, the principle of 'burden sharing' in refugee law 'requires states
to cooperate in dealing with the global refugee problem'.[161] The need for
international cooperation 'to share the burdens and responsibilities of
hosting refugees and to find solutions to refugee problems' is said to be
'essential to achieving effective protection under the Convention'.[162]
Burden sharing is also expressed as a matter of international solidarity.[163]

---

[154] *Ibid*, at 512.

[155] WA Schabas, *Genocide in International Law: The Crime of Crimes* (Cambridge, Cambridge
University Press, 2000), at 447.

[156] Convention on the Prevention and Punishment of Genocide (opened for signature 9
December 1948, entered into force 12 January 1951) 78 UNTS 277.

[157] *Application of the Convention on the Prevention and Punishment of the Crime of Genocide
(Bosnia and Herzegovina v Serbia and Montenegro)*, Judgment of 26 February 2007, at para 427.

[158] *Ibid*, at para 430.

[159] *Ibid*, at para 430.

[160] *Ibid*, at para 183. But see the Separate Opinion of Judge Tomka in that case, stating that
the obligation to prevent genocide outside a state's own territory is limited to situations in
which the state exercises jurisdiction or control outside its territory: *ibid*, at paras 66–7.

[161] BS Chimni, 'The Principle of Burden-sharing' in BS Chimni (ed), *International Refugee
Law: A Reader* (London, Sage Publications, 1999), at 146.

[162] UNHCR, 'Note on International Protection' (13 September 2001) UN Doc
A/AC.96/951 ['International Protection'], at para 6. See also the preamble to the 1951
Refugee Convention, above n 146, which states that 'the grant of asylum may place unduly
heavy burdens on certain countries' and 'a satisfactory solution of a problem of which the
United Nations has recognised the international scope and nature cannot therefore be
achieved without international cooperation'.

[163] UNHCR, 'International Protection', *ibid*, at para 6; UNHCR, 'International Solidarity
and Burden-sharing in All Its Aspects: National, Regional and International Responsibilities
for Refugees' (7 September 1998) UN Doc A/AC.96/904. See also Chimni, above n 161, at 148.
See above n 110 regarding the principle of solidarity.

It has been used as a basis for discussion of collective responses to situations of mass influx which may place heavy burdens on certain states, for example.[164] The concept of burden sharing in the context of refugees and internally displaced persons will be discussed further in chapter five.

CONCLUSION

We saw at the beginning of this chapter that specific initiatives and developments in international law have addressed a broad range of issues and concerns forming part of the human security agenda. At the level of general principles, though, the literature reveals divergent perceptions of the degree of consistency between the human security concept and international law. Concerns have been expressed that certain fundamental principles, most notably state sovereignty and non-intervention, give primacy to state security and impede efforts to protect the security of individuals. At the same time, however, a particular legal tradition which includes human rights, humanitarian law, and refugee law is thought to be evolving in a direction that is consistent with the underlying rationale of a human security approach. In subsequent sections, we saw that even if some tension exists between human security and aspects of international law, there are also parallels between elements of the concept and certain international legal norms and principles.

It might seem, then, that elements of international law can be identified in fairly broad terms which either conflict with or support the pursuit of human security, and that international law is evolving in a direction that would make it more consistent with a human security approach. On one view, the traditional state-centred model of international law is being challenged and giving way to a new human-centred legal regime. In relation to the human-centred approach, one could cite the historical development of norms of humanitarian, refugee, and human rights law over the last century, the evolution of international and regional human rights regimes and their impact on the scope of domestic jurisdiction, and the movement towards a more inclusive interpretation of threats to international peace and security. At the same time, international law has been described as evolving within the last century from a law of co-existence[165] to a law of cooperation, and even beyond, as the law responds

---

[164] See UNHCR, 'Mechanisms of International Cooperation to Share Responsibilities and Burdens in Mass Influx Situations' (19 February 2001) UN Doc EC/GC/01/7.

[165] The law of 'coexistence' has been described as 'a limited set of neighborly rules designed to regulate the peaceful coexistence of the independent and equal nation states' and 'characterized by its individualistic focus': Perrez, above n 6, at 255. See also Fassbender and Bleckmann, above n 15, at 72–3.

to an ever greater degree of global integration.[166] The UN Charter can be seen in some respects as a watershed in this development.

However, a closer look confirms that this view is altogether too simplistic. Although we can identify some broad tendencies in the development of international law, it is clear that so-called 'old' and 'new' elements coexist, rather than forming stages in a linear evolution.[167] It is also evident that a strict dichotomy between opposing elements oversimplifies complex phenomena and thus can be misleading. This is especially apparent in relation to human-centred as opposed to state-centred elements in international law. For example, the rationale of the 1951 Refugee Convention has been referred to as 'fundamentally humanitarian, human rights and people-oriented',[168] but this view is not uncontested. Some argue that, in fact, the regime of refugee law is profoundly state-centred, and is designed to protect the right of states to control entry to their territory more than the rights or needs of displaced individuals.[169] It must also be acknowledged that, although humanitarian principles are intended to prevent harm to individuals by regulating the conduct of armed conflict, not everyone agrees that the effect on individuals is actually beneficial; for example, some argue that international humanitarian law may actually increase human suffering by legitimating violence in some circumstances.[170] Even the human rights regime, arguably the central pillar of human-centred international law, has been described as reinforcing the strength and central position of the state,[171] and has been criticised for the way in which it leaves unchallenged many factors which profoundly affect human well-being and for its undue emphasis on formalisation of norms and institutional mechanisms at the expense of attention to outcomes.[172] Such critiques highlight the need for scrutiny of the impact of legal norms and principles, even those which seem, on their face, to operate for the benefit of individuals.

---

[166] See, eg, Fassbender and Bleckmann, above n 165, at 72–3, 89 (citing W Friedmann and C Tomuschat).

[167] Cf Cassese, *International Law*, above n 17, at 18.

[168] UNHCR, 'International Protection', above n 162, at para 4.

[169] See JC Hathaway, 'Reconsideration of the Underlying Premise of Refugee Law' (1990) 31 *Harvard International Law Journal* 129. Hathaway argues that 'neither a humanitarian nor a human rights vision can account for refugee law as codified in [the Refugee Convention and Protocol]' (*ibid*, at 130). See also TA Aleinikoff, 'State-centred Refugee Law: From Resettlement to Containment' (1992) 14 *Michigan Journal of International Law* 120; JC Hathaway, 'Reconceiving Refugee Law as Human Rights Protection' (1991) 4 *Journal of Refugee Studies* 113, at 114. Further discussion in the context of preventive action and internally displaced persons will be found in ch 5. See also the critique of refugee law in D Kennedy, 'The International Human Rights Movement: Part of the Problem?' [2001] *European Human Rights Law Review* 245, at 256.

[170] See, eg, McCoubrey, above n 36, at 2–5 for a discussion of some arguments. See also Kennedy, above n 169, at 261.

[171] Kennedy, above n 169, at 255–6.

[172] *Ibid*, at 252–3, 255–6. See also P Allott, *Eunomia: New Order for a New World* (Oxford, Oxford University Press, 1990), at paras 15.66–15.67, 16.97–16.98.

The search for norms and principles relating to common concern for human security also painted a mixed picture, and here the parallels to this aspect of human security appear to be weaker. For the most part, the scope of obligations under human rights law remains limited to individuals under a state's jurisdiction, despite the fact that others may be vulnerable in important ways to the state's actions, and in contrast to the idea that states could bear some responsibility for the security even of those outside their jurisdiction. There are some obligations which might have wider application, in human rights law as well as humanitarian and refugee law, but their implications remain unclear and contested. General duties of cooperation are likewise unclear, and all of these run up against the basic structure of international law that continues to tie responsibility to sovereign jurisdiction in a state-based system.

The point here is that it is not adequate simply to rely on human rights, humanitarian law, and refugee law to give effect to a human security approach and to challenge countervailing tendencies in international law. These areas of law do reflect the normative foundations and approach of the concept to a certain degree and are significant in that respect. However, there are limits and ambiguities apparent in each of them, and one cannot assume that they will always operate in ways that are beneficial from a human security perspective. This also means that it cannot be assumed that human security is merely redundant or has nothing to add to existing frameworks. Furthermore, the survey in this chapter has shown that norms and principles which resonate with aspects of the concept in important ways can also be found outside these specific fields, for example in international environmental law and at the level of general principles of international law.

The concept of human security, although new, is not entirely alien to international law, but rather can be found reflected in diverse elements of the law. At the same time, the concept can also be used critically to scrutinise developments in the law that appear to be designed to give priority to the protection of individuals. Whether and to what extent the law actually advances human security through these and other developments are empirical questions which, if they can be answered at all, would require a different sort of investigation from the present study. However, some of the apparent problems and weaknesses of legal responses will be examined with respect to particular issues in later chapters.

4

Human Security and 'Humanitarian Intervention'

INTRODUCTION

HUMANITARIAN INTERVENTION has long been, and continues to be, the subject of vigorous debate. Is there a right or duty to intervene to stop serious and widespread violations of human rights? If so, when, how, and by whom should such action be undertaken, and who decides? These questions have exercised the minds of philosophers, political scientists, and international lawyers, and have yet to be answered with any significant degree of consensus. Government positions on this issue are also divided. The ongoing controversy can be explained by the fact that humanitarian intervention touches on critical issues involving the use of force, ethical obligations in foreign policy, and North–South relations. Debates about the legality of intervention engage fundamental questions about the nature and limits of sovereignty, the status and interpretation of the UN Charter, and the relationship between morality, legitimacy, and legality.

Humanitarian intervention is a proposed response where individuals' security is threatened, and involves intervening on the territory of a sovereign state. As a result, there is an obvious connection between this debate and human security. It is less clear, however, just how the connection should be made and what its implications are. Is humanitarian intervention, as some have suggested, an example of human security 'in action'? What would be the implications of viewing the humanitarian intervention debate through a human security 'lens'? This chapter will discuss a few aspects of the debate which are of particular relevance to human security, and will explore some ways in which the concept might contribute to their analysis.

THE LEGAL DEBATE

The term 'humanitarian intervention', in itself controversial,[1] is generally understood to refer to the use of force in a state (the target state), without its consent, by one or more other states (the intervening state or states) for humanitarian purposes, that is, to prevent or stop gross human rights violations, especially threats to life and physical security. The term is usually, though not consistently, used to refer to such interventions taken in the absence of Security Council authorisation, which has crucial legal significance.[2] The legality of humanitarian intervention has been the subject of lengthy and heated debate among international lawyers.[3] Intervention of any kind, whether forcible or not, runs up against the principle of non-intervention, a corollary of the principle of sovereign equality of states which prohibits one state from intervening in another's affairs.[4] The prohibition on intervention is not absolute, since it applies only, as the International Court of Justice (ICJ) put it in the *Nicaragua* case, to 'matters on which each state is permitted, by the principles of state sovereignty, to decide freely'.[5] The significant developments in international law relating to human rights, particularly in and since the UN Charter, have 'made human rights a matter of international law'.[6] It has been argued that, as a result, 'humanitarian intervention cannot be unlawful *intervention* at all, because human rights do not fall within any state's domestic jurisdiction'.[7]

[1] See, eg, International Commission on Intervention and State Sovereignty, *Responsibility to Protect: Report of the International Commission on Intervention and State Sovereignty* (Ottawa, International Development Research Centre, 2001) [ICISS, *Responsibility to Protect*], at 9. This chapter uses the term despite acknowledging that it is problematic, since it is the commonly accepted shorthand term.

[2] The extent to which humanitarian crisis within a state can legitimately ground Security Council action under chapter VII is a related but distinct issue, which was briefly discussed in chapter three. This chapter focuses on the much more contentious question of whether military intervention can be legally justified on some basis other than Security Council authorisation.

[3] For a useful recent overview of positions, see A Rogers, 'Humanitarian Intervention and International Law' (2004) 27 *Harvard Journal of Law and Public Policy* 725.

[4] See ch 3, nn 65–9 and accompanying text for a brief discussion of this principle.

[5] *Military and Paramilitary Activities in and against Nicaragua (Nicaragua v United States of America)*, Merits [1986] ICJ Rep 14 [*Nicaragua*], at para 205.

[6] D McGoldrick, 'The Principle of Non-Intervention: Human Rights' in V Lowe and C Warbrick (eds), *The United Nations and the Principles of International Law: Essays in memory of Michael Akehurst* (London, Routledge, 1994), at 94. See also, eg, R Higgins, 'Intervention and International Law' in H Bull (ed), *Intervention in World Politics* (Oxford, Clarendon Press, 1984) ['Intervention'], at 35.

[7] FR Tesón, *Humanitarian Intervention: An Inquiry into Law and Morality*, 2nd edn (Irvington-on-Hudson, NY, Transnational Publishers, 1997) [*Humanitarian Intervention*], at 304. A more nuanced version of this argument, based on an analysis of UN and state practice, is that the concept of exclusive domestic jurisdiction cannot be invoked, at least in the case of gross or systematic human rights abuses: see McGoldrick, above n 6, at 98 and at 103–4, citing B Ramcharan.

The legality of intervention, though, depends not only on the nature of the affairs being interfered with but also on the means used to intervene. Here, because the focus of the discussion is *forcible* intervention, the prohibition on the threat or use of force is central to the debate.[8] This prohibition is enshrined in article 2(4) of Charter, which states: 'All Members shall refrain in their international relations from the threat or use of force against the territorial integrity or political independence of any state, or in any other manner inconsistent with the Purposes of the United Nations.' The principle of non-use of force is now recognised as a general rule of customary international law and as part of *jus cogens*.[9] The only explicit exceptions in the Charter are article 51, which preserves the right of individual or collective self-defence in the event of an armed attack on a member state and pending Security Council measures, and chapter VII (in particular, article 42), providing for military (or other) measures authorised by the Security Council to maintain or restore international peace and security.[10]

The question which is then raised is whether a military intervention for humanitarian purposes can be legal if it does not fall within one of these exceptions. One position is that no threat or use of force can be lawful unless it is covered by an explicit exception; the prohibition was meant to be otherwise comprehensive and absolute.[11] This position may be bolstered by cautions that any exceptions permitted would be liable to abuse.[12] Recent attempts to interpret the right of self-defence expansively

[8] On the relationship between intervention and use of force, see *Nicaragua*, above n 5, at paras 205, 227–8.

[9] See, eg, A Randelzhofer, 'Article 2(4)' in B Simma (ed), *The Charter of the United Nations: A Commentary*, 2nd edn (Oxford, Oxford University Press, 2002), vol I ['Article 2(4)'], at 133–5; A Randelzhofer, 'General Introduction to Article 2' in B Simma (ed), *The Charter of the United Nations: A Commentary*, 2nd edn (Oxford, Oxford University Press, 2002), vol I, at 66; A Cassese, *International Law* (Oxford, Oxford University Press, 2001), at 101; I Brownlie, *International Law and the Use of Force by States* (Oxford, Clarendon Press, 1963), at 120–1; B Simma, 'NATO, the UN and the Use of Force: Legal Aspects' (1999) 10 *EJIL* 1, at 3; C Gray, *International Law and the Use of Force* (Oxford, Oxford University Press, 2000), at 24 (and sources cited therein at fn 1).

[10] In addition, art 53 allows enforcement actions to be taken by regional agencies with the authorisation of the Security Council.

[11] See, eg, M Akehurst, 'Humanitarian Intervention' in H Bull (ed), *Intervention in World Politics* (Oxford, Clarendon Press, 1984), at 106; Simma, above n 9, at 2; I Brownlie and CJ Apperley, 'Kosovo Crisis Inquiry: Memorandum on the International Law Aspects' (2000) 49 *ICLQ* 878 ['Memorandum'], at 885–6. This position is said to be supported by reference to the *travaux préparatoires*: see, eg, Akehurst, above; Cassese, *International Law*, above n 9, at 101; JI Charney, 'Anticipatory Humanitarian Intervention in Kosovo' (1999) 93 *AJIL* 834, at 835; Brownlie and Apperley, 'Memorandum', above, at 884–5 (although for a contrary interpretation of the *travaux*, see Tesón, *Humanitarian Intervention*, above n 7, at 154–5).

[12] On the danger of abuse, see, eg, TM Franck and NS Rodley, 'After Bangladesh: The Law of Humanitarian Intervention by Military Force' (1973) 67 *AJIL* 275, at 284, 290; L Henkin, 'Kosovo and the Law of "Humanitarian Intervention"' (1999) 93 *AJIL* 824, at 825; Charney, above n 11, at 837–9; M Ayoob, 'Humanitarian Intervention and State Sovereignty' (2002) 6 *International Journal of Human Rights* 81, at 92; R Higgins, *Problems and Process: International Law and How We Use it* (Oxford, Clarendon Press, 1994) [*Problems and Process*], at 247 (rebutting this argument).

as including broader pre-emptive use of force, and to claim a humanitarian justification for the invasion of Iraq, have only heightened critics' concerns about abuse.[13] An opposing view holds that there can be some situations in which a threat or use of force which falls outside chapter VII and article 51 may be lawful. One argument is that there is a right of humanitarian intervention in customary international law, and that this right continues to exist notwithstanding the Charter.[14] Not everyone agrees that such a right did or does exist,[15] however, or that it could continue to exist despite article 2(4).[16] Then, there are arguments that the prohibition on the use of force should be narrowly construed so as not to include humanitarian intervention. For example, it could be said that humanitarian intervention (at least in some cases) is not really a use of force 'against the territorial integrity or political independence of any state'[17] or that, given its humanitarian objective, it is not a use of force 'inconsistent with the Purposes of the United Nations'.[18] The persuasiveness of such arguments, even if accepted in principle,[19] undoubtedly

---

[13] See, eg, R Thakur, 'Developing Countries and the Intervention–Sovereignty Debate' in RM Price and MW Zacher (eds), *The United Nations and Global Security* (New York, Palgrave MacMillan, 2004), at 200; AJ Bellamy, 'Responsibility to Protect or Trojan Horse? The Crisis in Darfur and Humanitarian Intervention after Iraq' (2005) 19 *Ethics and International Affairs* 31, at 37*ff*, 48, 51–2; TG Weiss, 'The Sunset of Humanitarian Intervention? The Responsibility to Protect in a Unipolar Era' (2004) 35 *Security Dialogue* 135, at 143.

[14] C Greenwood, 'International Law and the NATO Intervention in Kosovo' (2000) 49 *ICLQ* 926, at 930, 931; WM Reisman, 'Humanitarian Intervention to Protect the Ibos' in R Lillich (ed), *Humanitarian Intervention and the United Nations* (Charlottesville, University of Virginia Press, 1973) ['Protect the Ibos'], at 171; Tesón, *Humanitarian Intervention*, above n 7, at 157, 175 (see also his assessment of state practice at 175*ff*).

[15] See, eg, Randelzhofer, 'Article 2(4)', above n 9, at 130–31 (text and n 155); Brownlie, above n 9, at 339–40; Franck and Rodley, above n 12, at 299; Cassese, *International Law*, above n 9, at 321; Brownlie and Apperley, 'Memorandum', above n 11, at 894; I Brownlie and CJ Apperley, 'Kosovo Crisis Inquiry: Further Memorandum on the International Law Aspects' (2000) 49 *ICLQ* 905 ['Further Memorandum'], at 908–9. The disagreement on this point turns mainly on differing interpretations of state practice. See, for example, the contrasting accounts by Akehurst, above n 11, at 95–104, and Franck and Rodley, above n 12, on one hand, and Tesón, *Humanitarian Intervention*, above n 7, at 175*ff*, on the other.

[16] See, eg, Randelzhofer, 'Article 2(4)', above n 9, at 130–31; Brownlie, above n 9, at 342.

[17] See, eg, Tesón, *Humanitarian Intervention*, above n 7, at 150–51; Higgins, *Problems and Process*, above n 12, at 245; Higgins, 'Intervention', above n 6, at 39; Reisman, 'Protect the Ibos', above n 14, at 177; A D'Amato, 'The Invasion of Panama was a Lawful Response to Tyranny' (1990) 84 *AJIL* 516, at 520. This was the position taken by Belgium before the ICJ in *Legality of the Use of Force (Yugoslavia v Belgium)*, Request for the Indication of Provisional Measures, Verbatim Record, CR 99/15, 10 May 1999.

[18] See, eg, Tesón, *Humanitarian Intervention*, above n 7, at 151; Higgins, *Problems and Process*, above n 12, at 246 (regarding a military action to end a hijacking, since it is 'directed towards the preservation of human life'); Reisman, 'Protect the Ibos', above n 14, at 177.

[19] For contrary views, see, eg, Randelzhofer, 'Article 2(4)', above n 9, at 123–4, 130; Akehurst, above n 11, at 105–6; Cassese, *International Law*, above n 9, at 321; Charney, above n 11, at 835. The United Kingdom unsuccessfully argued for a narrow interpretation of art 2(4) in *Corfu Channel, Merits* [1949] ICJ Rep 4, although as Chinkin notes, the argument 'is stronger in the context of human rights': C Chinkin, 'The Legality of NATO's Action in the Former Republic of Yugoslavia (FRY) under International Law' (2000) 49 *ICLQ* 910 ['Legality'], at 917. The ICJ stated in the *Nicaragua* case that 'the use of force could not be the

depends in each case on the exact nature and circumstances of the military action. Alternatively, it has been argued that humanitarian intervention should be recognised as an implicit exception to the prohibition on the use of force,[20] or that the application of article 2(4) depends on the effective functioning of the chapter VII provisions.[21] Finally, some argue that while humanitarian intervention has traditionally been prohibited, a breach of the prohibition may sometimes be 'justified' or 'legitimate' according to morality or an 'emerging' customary rule.[22] These arguments maintain that although the principle regarding the use of force may appear to be comprehensive, humanitarian intervention is a special case because of its purpose.

A right of humanitarian intervention, if it exists, would apply only to certain circumstances, and not everyone agrees how those should be defined. The threshold for intervention can be defined according to the severity of the threat (including both its scope and the type of threat) and its immediacy. Most seem to agree that in order to justify intervention, there must be widespread or systematic violations that are serious and irreparable.[23] This is typically taken to refer to 'large scale threatened or actual loss of life' or severe threats to physical integrity.[24] However, a few commentators have argued that intervention could also be justified in a

appropriate method to monitor or ensure [respect for human rights]' (above n 5, at para 268), although it has been noted that, given the context, this statement 'can be seen as either a complete rejection of any right to use force to protect human rights or as merely a finding that the particular US action did not further any humanitarian objective': Gray, above n 9, at 28.

[20] The legal basis for this suggested exception is not always clear. One example is WM Reisman, 'Kosovo's Antinomies' (1999) 93 *AJIL* 860, in which he argues that in the absence of Security Council authorisation, the use of force to protect human rights is not only permitted but a 'legal requirement' (at 862). The basis for this argument is apparently that the development of human rights law makes protection of human rights an 'imperative objective' (at 862) and has affected the scope of both art 2(7) and art 2(4) (at 861).

[21] See Gray, above n 9, at 24–5 and the sources cited therein at fn 3; Randelzhofer, 'Article 2(4)', above n 9, at 130 (text and fns 149, 150), 136.

[22] See, eg, A Cassese, '*Ex iniuiria ius oritur*: Are we Moving towards International Legitimation of Forcible Humanitarian Countermeasures in the World Community?' (1999) 10 *EJIL* 23 ['*Ex iniuiria*']; A Cassese, 'A Follow-up: Forcible Humanitarian Countermeasures and *Opinio Necessitatis*' (1999) 10 *EJIL* 791 ['Follow-up']; R Wedgwood, 'NATO's Campaign in Yugoslavia' (1999) 93 *AJIL* 828, at 828; Chinkin, 'Legality', above n 19, at 918, 920; V Lowe, 'International Legal Issues Arising in the Kosovo Crisis' (2000) 49 *ICLQ* 934, at 941; United Kingdom, Foreign and Commonwealth Office, quoted in Gray, above n 9, at 29. See also the discussion of NATO countries' positions in the case brought against them by Yugoslavia in the ICJ, in Gray, *ibid*, at 39; Brownlie and Apperley, 'Memorandum', above n 11, at 881–2.

[23] See, eg, Tesón, *Humanitarian Intervention*, above n 7, at 123; Independent International Commission on Kosovo, *The Kosovo Report: Conflict, International Response, Lessons Learned* (Oxford, Oxford University Press, 2000), at 193; ICISS, *Responsibility to Protect*, above n 1, at 32–3; SD Murphy, *Humanitarian Intervention: The United Nations in an Evolving World Order* (Philadelphia, University of Pennsylvania Press, 1996), at 16; United Kingdom, Foreign and Commonwealth Office, 'Guiding Humanitarian Intervention' (Speech by the Foreign Secretary, Robin Cook, American Bar Association Lunch, QEII Conference Centre, London, 19 July 2000) <http://www.fco.gov.uk> (accessed 9 March 2007).

[24] ICISS, *Responsibility to Protect*, above n 1, at 33; some examples of situations that would qualify are also listed by the Commission (*ibid*).

broader class of cases, for example, for the protection or restoration of democracy.[25] The criterion of immediacy requires that the violations be occurring or imminent.[26] It is related to the idea that humanitarian intervention should be a last resort, attempted only when no other option is available. The condition that intervention should be a last resort is one on which virtually all commentators agree, although its interpretation and application can be problematic. Although it could be taken literally to mean that all other possible options have actually been tried, this may be unrealistic or counterproductive in a situation of urgency. Instead, it requires that potential interveners must have explored all non-forcible alternatives that seem likely to be effective.[27] The significance of the principle that forcible intervention should be a last resort will be discussed further below.

THE DEBATE THROUGH THE LENS OF HUMAN SECURITY

Some scholars and government representatives have pointed to humanitarian intervention as an example of 'human security in action', where concern for the protection of individuals 'trumps' state sovereignty. Canadian government representatives, in particular, pointed to the NATO military intervention in Kosovo as an action motivated by human security and 'an important step in the ascendance of human security as a norm for global action'.[28] This view has been supported by some commentators.[29] It is debatable whether the Kosovo intervention is a good example of an

[25] See, eg, D'Amato, above n 17; WM Reisman, 'Coercion and Self-Determination: Construing Charter Article 2(4)' (1984) 78 *AJIL* 642. Tesón argues that the use of force will sometimes, but not always, be justified to overthrow an undemocratic government, depending on the proportionality between the use of force and the violations committed by the target regime: *Humanitarian Intervention*, above n 7, at 305ff.

[26] See, eg, ICISS, *Responsibility to Protect*, above n 1, at 32; United Kingdom, 'Guiding Humanitarian Intervention', above n 23.

[27] See, eg, ICISS, *Responsibility to Protect*, above n 1, at 36; NJ Wheeler, *Saving Strangers: Humanitarian Intervention in International Society* (Oxford, Oxford University Press, 2000), at 35; RA Falk, 'Kosovo, World Order, and the Future of International Law' (1999) 93 *AJIL* 847, at 856; Tesón, *Humanitarian Intervention*, above n 7, at 122; Chinkin, 'Legality', above n 19, at 921; United Kingdom, 'Guiding Humanitarian Intervention', above n 23.

[28] Canada, DFAIT, 'Notes for an Address by the Honourable Lloyd Axworthy Minister of Foreign Affairs to the Empire Club', Statement 99/43 (28 June 1999) <http://w01. international.gc.ca/minpub> (accessed 26 February 2007). See also Canada, DFAIT, 'Notes for an Address by the Honourable Lloyd Axworthy, Minister of Foreign Affairs, to the G-8 Foreign Ministers' Meeting', Statement 99/40 (9 June 1999) <http://w01.international.gc.ca/minpub> (accessed 26 February 2007); P Heinbecker and R McRae, 'Case Study: The Kosovo Air Campaign' in R McRae and D Hubert (eds), *Human Security and the New Diplomacy: Protecting People, Promoting Peace* (Montreal, McGill-Queen's University Press, 2001), at 125.

[29] E Mendes, 'Human Security, International Organizations and International Law: The Kosovo Crisis Exposes the "Tragic Flaw" in the UN Charter' (1999) 38 *Human Rights Research and Education Centre Bulletin* <http://www.cdp-hrc.uottawa.ca/publicat/bull38.html> (accessed 9 March 2007).

'instrument of human security'[30] or even of humanitarian intervention.[31] The larger question, though, is whether a human security approach logically or necessarily favours humanitarian intervention and would support arguments for its legal or moral justification. It has been suggested that human security is 'interventionist by nature' because it 'extends the security obligations of states beyond their borders' and justifies the use of force for 'cosmopolitan' goals.[32] The International Commission on Intervention and State Sovereignty (ICISS) invoked human security as part of the foundation of the 'responsibility to protect', proposed in its report as the new framework for debates on humanitarian intervention.[33] This shifted the emphasis from the right of intervention to a shared responsibility for the protection of individuals, but still with a view to justifying intervention including, where necessary, military intervention.

Others, however, have debated whether the use of force is 'consistent with the ethos and agenda of human security'[34] and question the invocation of human security to justify intervention.[35] Even those who are generally sympathetic to the concept have expressed reservations about the interventionist tendencies of some human security advocates.[36] The fear that human security will be used to justify intervention has been one of the barriers to its widespread acceptance, especially among non-Western governments who suspect that it may represent a form of neocolonialism.[37] The relationship of the concept to humanitarian

[30] Heinbecker and McRae, above n 28, at 125. For a critique, see W Nelles, 'Canada's Human Security Agenda in Kosovo and Beyond' (2002) 57 *International Journal* 459.

[31] The Kosovo intervention is commonly discussed in recent literature as a test case regarding humanitarian intervention, although some have pointed out that this case does not fit the 'standard schema' of humanitarian intervention and would be better described as 'reprisals, or countermeasures, intended to induce the FRY to comply with its obligations': Simma, above n 9, at 13. See also Cassese, *Ex iniuria*, above n 22; Cassese, 'Follow-up', above n 22. It also raised a number of issues specific to that case which will not be dealt with here.

[32] G Oberleitner, 'Human Security: A Challenge to International Law?' 11 *Global Governance* 185, at 194.

[33] ICISS, *Responsibility to Protect*, above n 1, at 12, 15.

[34] H Owens and B Arneil, 'Human Security Paradigm Shift: A New Lens on Canadian Foreign Policy?' (1999) 7(1) *Canadian Foreign Policy* 1, at 6.

[35] See, eg, SL Woodward, 'Should We Think Before We Leap?: A Rejoinder' (1999) 30 *Security Dialogue* 277; Nelles, above n 30.

[36] See, eg, Japan, MOFA, 'Toward Effective Cross-Sectorial Partnership to Ensure Human Security in a Globalized World' (Statement by Mr Yukio Takasu, Director-General of Multilateral Cooperation Department, at the Third Intellectual Dialogue on Building Asia's Tomorrow, Bangkok, 19 June 2000) <http://www.mofa.go.jp/policy/human_secu/speech0006.html> (accessed 9 March 2007); Commission on Human Security, 'Report: Meeting of the Commission on Human Security' (8–10 June 2001) <http://www.humansecurity-chs.org/activities/meetings/first/report.pdf> (accessed 9 March 2007), at 4; Regional Human Security Centre, 'Pan-Arab Brainstorming Session, August 31, 2000: Narrative Report' (2000) <http://www.id.gov.jo/human/activities2000/report6.html> (accessed 9 March 2007).

[37] See, eg, P Upadhyaya, 'Human Security, Humanitarian Intervention, and Third World Concerns' (2004) 33 *Denver Journal of International Law and Policy* 71.

intervention thus merits closer examination, both to assess these divergent perspectives and to determine whether a human security perspective can usefully contribute to the long-standing debate on this subject.

Human Rights versus Sovereignty?

As the previous section showed, there are a number of specific legal arguments regarding the use of force that have been used to justify military intervention on humanitarian grounds. However, many of those who argue for a right of humanitarian intervention also pose the question in more general terms, as one of the relative weight of state sovereignty and human rights. In this view, sovereignty should not be used as a 'shield' to prevent concerned members of the international community from intervening to protect human rights.[38]

The proposed primacy of human rights over sovereignty, even if not relied on without more to justify humanitarian intervention, underlies many of the arguments surveyed above. For example, Tesón presents a sustained defence of the legality of humanitarian intervention, including an interpretation of the UN Charter and an assessment of state practice, all of which is premised on a normative framework that privileges the rights of individuals over those of states.[39] The position that humanitarian intervention is not a use of force 'inconsistent with the Purposes of the United Nations' depends in part on the increased importance of human rights among these purposes.[40] In addition, the centrality of human rights might generally lend support to the argument that humanitarian intervention should be considered an unwritten exception to the prohibition in article 2(4), since the rationale for treating humanitarian intervention differently from other uses of force rests on the nature and importance of its purpose of protecting human rights. Conversely, opponents of humanitarian intervention are assumed to rely 'on the supposed moral significance of state sovereignty and national borders'.[41]

---

[38] See, eg, UN Secretary-General, 'Statement of the United Nations Secretary-General to the General Assembly on Presenting his Millennium Report' (3 April 2000) <http://www.un.org/millennium/sg/report/state.htm> (accessed 12 March 2007).

[39] Tesón, *Humanitarian Intervention*, above n 7 (for discussion of the normative basis of his argument, see pt 1; regarding the role of the normative framework in analysing the Charter and state practice, see chs 7 and 8, respectively, particularly at 149, 173–4, and 222). See also FR Tesón, *A Philosophy of International Law* (London, Westview Press, 1998), especially ch 2.

[40] Compare, eg, the statement by Cassese, in *International Law*, above n 9, at 321, that although human rights is one of the purposes of the UN, the maintenance of international peace and security is paramount and so the use of force to protect human rights cannot be justified within the Charter framework.

[41] FR Tesón, 'The Liberal Case for Humanitarian Intervention' in JL Holzgrefe and RO Keohane, *Humanitarian Intervention: Ethical, Legal, and Political Dilemmas* (Cambridge, Cambridge University Press, 2003) ['Liberal Case'], at 97.

Viewed in this light, an emerging norm favouring a right of humanitarian intervention could be situated as part of a progressive development recognising the primary importance of human rights. It also seems to mirror the normative basis of the concept of human security, to the extent that human security privileges the rights and needs of individuals over those of states. As we saw in chapter three, the human-centred and common concern aspects of human security bring it into potential conflict with legal norms of sovereignty and non-intervention, while aligning it with developments in international law like human rights obligations, broad interpretations of the Security Council's chapter VII mandate, and shared responsibilities for protecting individuals. It is perhaps not surprising, then, that humanitarian intervention has been advocated by some as a means of protecting human security, and that the concept of human security should be invoked to justify humanitarian intervention. If the conflict is one between human rights and sovereignty, human security would seem clearly to weigh in on the side of human rights. In this view, human security requires that we do something to protect people from violations of their rights and threats to their security, even at the expense of infringing state sovereignty—and that 'something' is, or at least may include, military intervention. Hence the view of the Kosovo intervention as a case of human security winning out over sovereignty and traditional security.[42]

Using the concept of human security in this way is problematic, however, because the underlying framework on which the argument is based is both insufficient and misleading. It is well established, as we saw earlier, that the recognition of human rights in international law does affect the scope of domestic jurisdiction, and thus the scope of permissible intervention or interference with states' sovereignty. This does not fully answer the question of what kind of intervention is permissible, however. In particular, as we also saw, military intervention involves a threat or use of force which is subject to a distinct set of rules. Privileging human rights over sovereignty does not necessarily affect these rules.[43] As Gray explains, in order to establish a right of humanitarian intervention,

> it would be necessary to show not only that human rights are accepted and recognized by the international community of states as a whole as a norm from which no derogation is permitted, *but also that states have accepted the right to use force to protect them.*[44]

---

[42] L Axworthy, 'Human Security: An Opening for UN Reform' in RM Price and MW Zacher, *The United Nations and Global Security* (New York, Palgrave MacMillan, 2004), at 255.

[43] Reisman claims that 'Article 2(4) was changed by the contraction of Article 2(7)' as a result of the development of human rights law ('Kosovo's Antinomies', above n 20, at 861), but the reasoning in support of this claim is not clear.

[44] Gray, above n 9, at 39 (emphasis added).

If the issue is presented as one of sovereignty and intervention, this crucial further step, the acceptance of the use of force, seems to be assumed without argument. At most, then, this approach only addresses half of the legal question.

This view sets up state sovereignty in simple opposition to human rights, although the relationship between them is much more complex and it is a mistake to assume that violating sovereignty will always serve to protect human rights.[45] Chinkin rightly points out that '[t]he doctrine of humanitarian intervention is predicated upon a presumed choice between state sovereignty and the protection of human rights. In reality, both are compromised.'[46] The idea that a right of intervention arises when a state abuses, or fails to protect, its people echoes some liberal views of international relations in which states lose their entitlement to respect for their sovereignty if they do not respect the rights of their people.[47] The problem, however, is that while focusing on what protection states 'deserve', this proposition neglects the question of whether intervention will help to protect people.[48]

The 'human rights versus sovereignty' framework is inadequate to address human security concerns because it sidesteps the issue of the inevitable human costs of a military intervention. The 'down side' of humanitarian intervention is presumed to be an injury to state sovereignty, rather than a threat to the security of individuals who will be harmed as a result of military action. Instead of moving the debate away from a preoccupation with states and their rights, invoking human security within this framework unwittingly reinforces an approach that considers injuries to states but disregards some serious threats to individuals. Focusing on human security could, instead help to displace the debate from the unhelpful human rights/sovereignty dichotomy which assumes that the most significant harm from the intervention is to the state. At the heart of the concept is the shift in referent object from state to human security. In keeping with this, a human security approach should make the risk of harm to individuals the central consideration in this debate.

What would be the consequences of this shift in focus? To begin with, it suggests that the concept of human security may have a useful role to play in encouraging us to critically examine claims to a right to use force on humanitarian grounds. It would especially call into question those claims

---

[45] See K Bennoune, '"Sovereignty vs. Suffering"? Re-examining Sovereignty and Human Rights through the Lens of Iraq' (2002) 13 *EJIL* 243; J Conlon, 'Sovereignty vs. Human Rights or Sovereignty and Human Rights?' (2004) 46 *Race and Class* 75.

[46] CM Chinkin, 'Kosovo: A "Good" or "Bad" War?' (1999) 93 *AJIL* 841 ['Kosovo'], at 845. See also Bennoune, above n 45.

[47] See ch 2, n 157 and accompanying text. See also Tesón, 'Liberal Case', above n 41, at 93.

[48] To be fair, Tesón, one of the leading proponents of this position, has recently begun to address this question more seriously (*ibid*).

that are framed as a right to override state sovereignty for the sake of human rights, given that this structure of argument tends to obscure rather than address threats to human security and human rights. That is, it would remind us that although arguments to intervene for the protection of human rights at the expense of sovereignty may be superficially appealing, they do not take account of the threat to human security that is involved in military action, even if it is undertaken with the best of intentions. While this critical role for human security would not undermine the imperative to protect individuals at risk, it would make us question, rather than take for granted, the value of military force as an option. It follows that only an analysis that gives full weight to the threats to human beings that may *result from* intervention, as well as those *prompting the calls for* intervention, can be consistent with a human security approach.[49] Questions about when and how one can justify using force and harming innocent people for the sake of a saving others have been debated for centuries and will not be resolved by invoking the concept of human security. What the concept can do, though, is to encourage us to frame legal debates in a way that struggles with these questions rather than bypassing them.

Certain other aspects of the legal debate on humanitarian intervention are also affected by adopting this perspective. First there is the issue of abuse of a right of humanitarian intervention. It was noted earlier that fears of abuse by states are sometimes invoked to argue against recognition of a legal right of humanitarian intervention, and these fears have been exacerbated by attempts to justify the invasion of Iraq on humanitarian grounds. In this context, abuse is commonly understood to mean that an intervening state will use humanitarianism as a cover for other motives, and thus intervene to advance its own national interests (however defined), rather than to protect individuals in the target state. The potential for this type of abuse would be of concern from the point of view of human security, since it would expose individuals to a significant risk of harm without justification.

In addition, though, an intervening state may undertake an intervention for which there is a valid humanitarian justification, but conduct it in a manner that causes serious—perhaps unnecessarily serious—harm to the population of the target state.[50] International law does set limits on the

---

[49] See Falk, above n 27, at 848, 853*ff*, for an analysis which is useful, in some respects, from this point of view.

[50] The NATO intervention in Kosovo, for example, was widely criticised for using military tactics that increased the risk of civilian casualties. In particular, the use of high altitude bombing and weapons such as cluster bombs has been criticised for inflicting heavy damage on civilian infrastructure and causing civilian casualties and displacement. See, eg, Independent International Commission on Kosovo, above n 23, at 177*ff*; Falk, above n 27, at 851–2; Human Rights Watch, 'Civilian Deaths in the NATO Air Campaign' (February 2000), Volume 12, Number 1(D) <http://www.hrw.org/reports/2000/nato> (accessed 9 March

conduct of military operations, by imposing general requirements of necessity and proportionality, as well as specific rules about the methods and means of warfare, selection of targets and weapons, and other matters. There is a broad consensus that any humanitarian intervention must adhere to these laws and perhaps even should be held to a higher standard.[51] This body of law speaks to concerns about harm to individuals, although its impact is limited, for example, by the latitude afforded to states in interpreting principles such as proportionality, the possible non-applicability of norms in some circumstances, and of course the potential for non-compliance. More fundamentally, it is one thing to say that an intervention, once undertaken, must comply with these legal norms and principles. To say that the possibility of non-compliance and resulting harm to individuals should figure in the decision to allow military intervention in the first place takes the argument a step further. The fear that a right of humanitarian intervention will be abused is often invoked to caution against recognising such a right. From a human security perspective, the potential for intervening states to abuse the right by causing excessive harm to individuals should also be taken into consideration in the same way. It would therefore influence the decision whether intervention should be allowed at all, rather than being merely a secondary consideration about how the right is exercised.[52]

A second aspect is related to the way in which discussions about humanitarian intervention would deal with cases of so-called 'failed states'. If humanitarian intervention is thought of as an injury to state sovereignty, the injury is obviously less serious (or absent altogether) where the state in question has ceased to function or even to exist, in legal terms.[53] Ayoob, for example, argues that '[h]umanitarian emergencies accompanying state failure are unlikely to pose the normative constraints on international intervention that [human rights violations by functioning states] would pose'.[54] Furthermore, in the context of failed states there might also be a stronger argument that a use of force would not contravene article 2(4), since one could more easily argue that it was not 'against the territorial integrity or political independence of a state'. It might then be possible to take the position that the use of force would be

---

2007); M Foster, 'Kosovo and the 1997 Landmines Treaty' (September 1999) *Ploughshares Monitor* <http://www.ploughshares.ca/libraries/monitor/mons99c.html> (accessed 29 March 2007); Chinkin, 'Kosovo', above n 46, at 844–5.

[51] See, eg, Independent International Commission on Kosovo, above n 23, at 195; ICISS, *Responsibility to Protect*, above n 1, at xiii, 67; Chinkin, 'Kosovo', above n 46, at 844.

[52] Craven makes a similar point about the limited way in which humanitarian arguments have been used in the debates about sanctions, potentially affecting the ways in which sanctions are designed and implemented but not generally questioning whether they should be imposed at all: M Craven, 'Humanitarianism and the Quest for Smarter Sanctions' (2002) 13 *EJIL* 43.

[53] Ayoob, above n 12, at 96–7.

[54] *Ibid*, at 97.

consistent with the purposes of the United Nations, given its purpose of protecting human rights. In this context, traditional arguments against intervention lose much of their potency. However, these arguments can be critically examined by taking into account a concern for the security of affected individuals. Focusing on the security of the individuals at risk rather than that of the state would suggest that the state's status and sovereignty do not lead to any necessary conclusions regarding the use of force. A normative framework that permits intervention whenever there is no sovereign power to be interfered with focuses on the wrong question and does not take sufficient account of the threat to human security that results whenever military force is used.

Further, the prohibition on the use of force protects states from forcible intervention and helps to maintain international peace and security, thereby indirectly protecting individuals from the consequences of war. In the case of a failed state, the prohibition on the use of force seems to have a lesser role to play in these respects, since there is no state authority to protect, and retaliation and an ensuing international conflict may be less likely. We could, however, assume an independent role for the prohibition in *directly* protecting individuals from the harm that results from any use of force. If the prohibition, when it protects states from the use of force, has a primarily instrumental value in protecting individuals, then it could retain this function even when there is no state to protect. We could understand the basis of the principle of non-use of force as human-centred rather than state-centred. In that case, humanitarian intervention is not a question of pitting the protection of human security against state security. Instead, one form of protection for human security has to be balanced against another. This point comes into focus if we examine the possibility of intervention in a failed state from a human security perspective. However, its significance is broader than this, because it could fundament-ally change the way we interpret and apply this central principle of international law.

In summary, increasing acceptance of a right of unilateral humanitarian intervention is characterised by some as a progressive and positive development, consistent with, and indeed reflective of, a human security approach to international affairs. Awareness of the importance of human rights and the need to respond to violations, generally speaking, certainly could be characterised in this way. However, the view that international law is more consistent with human security to the extent that it allows humanitarian intervention has to be approached with some scepticism. The dichotomy between human rights and state sovereignty is not a helpful way of framing the debate or of using the concept of human security. When the use of force is at issue, human security can more productively be used to critically assess proposals for intervention and refocus the analysis on injuries to individuals rather than states. Trying to use human security as an 'answer' to the question of whether to intervene—human security trumps state security, hence intervention is justified—only leads to a false resolution that could actually undermine individuals' security. Instead, the concept has most value as a way of reorienting the questions that we should ask.

Right and Responsibility

As we saw above, the debate regarding humanitarian intervention has largely focused on the question of whether such intervention (absent authorisation by the Security Council) is legally permitted under the UN Charter and/or customary international law. The preoccupation with debating the existence of a right of humanitarian intervention seems to assume that states will intervene if they are not hampered by legal concerns. One author explains the need to establish the legality of humanitarian intervention in these terms:

> No-one, no State, should be driven by the abstract and artificial concepts of State sovereignty to watch innocent people being massacred, refraining from intervention because they believe themselves to have no legal right to intervene.[55]

Yet past experience gives us little reason to believe that states will always intervene provided they are (or believe themselves to be) legally justified in doing so.[56] Surveys of state practice reveal the selectivity of states' responses and the many cases where intervention might have seemed justified but did not occur.[57] If Kosovo is often taken as the paradigm case of unilateral military intervention, Rwanda stands as a reminder of the possibility and consequences of inaction. In view of the slow and inadequate response to the humanitarian crisis in the Sudan, promises that the international community would 'never again' stand aside when populations were threatened with genocide have seemed hollow. Other recent instances have shown that states are often slow to respond even when the state concerned has consented to outside assistance, which suggests that concerns about sovereignty and non-intervention are not the main barrier to action.[58] It therefore seems unlikely that legal recognition of the right to

---

[55] Lowe, above n 22, at 941. See also Canada, DFAIT, 'Canada and Human Security', Statement No 2000/8 (17 February 2000) <http://w01.international.gc.ca/minpub> (26 March 2007); UN Secretary-General, above n 38.

[56] See, eg, TM Franck, 'Lessons of Kosovo' (1999) 93 *AJIL* 857, at 859; D Archibugi, 'Cosmopolitan Guidelines for Humanitarian Intervention' (2004) 29 *Alternatives* 1, at 5.

[57] See, eg, Franck and Rodley, above n 12, at 290*ff*. In this analysis, the authors conclude that 'the balance of practice is clearly on the side of abstention. This abstention is particularly notable in situations where the genuine humanitarian needs seem greatest' (*ibid*, at 302). For more recent examples, see Chinkin, 'Kosovo', above n 46, at 847.

[58] TS Hataley and KR Nossal, 'The Limits of the Human Security Agenda: The Case of Canada's Response to the Timor Crisis' (2004) 16 *Global Change, Peace & Security* 5, at 7.

intervene will necessarily encourage recourse to it. As Wheeler notes, '[c]hanging norms provide actors with new public legitimating reasons to justify actions, but they do not determine that an action will take place'.[59]

The inconsistency of states' responses is troubling, given that, in principle, all human lives are equally worthy of protection.[60] Would it be better, then, to focus on whether states have a duty to intervene? Generally speaking, the literature on humanitarian intervention (particularly the Anglo-American literature) has, at least until recently, paid more attention to debating the existence of a right of intervention than to the question of whether there might be a legal obligation to intervene.[61] The idea that there is a moral or ethical duty to help threatened individuals has been in the background as the justification for a legal right of intervention: surely states should not be legally prohibited from doing that which they are morally obliged to do when faced with a humanitarian crisis? It is the sense that states are somehow obliged to undertake humanitarian intervention in some circumstances—the 'moral position that, in the face of atrocity, one cannot simply do nothing'[62]—that makes an uncertain or negative answer to the question of legality seem so problematic. Yet the troubling cases of inaction might suggest that we should focus directly on an obligation to intervene.

There are some legal obligations to which we could point in support of an argument that states, either individually or collectively through the United Nations, have an obligation to intervene in a case of massive human rights violations. As we saw in the previous chapter, there has been more emphasis on the right of states to intervene in others' affairs for the protection of human rights than on their responsibility to do so—a pattern we see replicated here with respect to humanitarian intervention.

---

[59] Wheeler, above n 27, at 9–10.

[60] D Hubert and M Bonser, 'Humanitarian Military Intervention' in R McRae and D Hubert (eds), *Human Security and the New Diplomacy: Protecting People, Promoting Peace* (Montreal and Kingston, McGill-Queen's University Press, 2001), at 117. The failure to intervene in Rwanda (among others) was seen by some as evidence that all lives are not, in fact, considered to be equally worthy: see, eg, ICISS, *Responsibility to Protect*, above n 1, at 1; Chinkin, 'Kosovo', above n 46, at 847.

[61] There are some notable exceptions: see, eg, WA Schabas, *Genocide in International Law: The Crime of Crimes* (Cambridge, Cambridge University Press, 2000), at 491*ff*; Murphy, above n 23, at 294-97. The possibility of legal duty is raised and dismissed by Gray, above n 9, at 40, fn 47. The question has received more attention in Continental, especially French, literature, in discussion of the 'droit et devoir d'ingérence'. However, even here, the 'devoir d'ingérence' is not necessarily considered to be a *legal* duty, as opposed to an ethical one, and its applicability to states (as distinct from non-governmental organisations) is uncertain: see, eg, Y Sandoz, '"Droit" or "devoir d'ingérence" and the right to assistance: the issues involved' (1992) 228 *IRRC* 215, at 215–16; B Bowring, 'The "droit et devoir d'ingérence": A Timely New Remedy for Africa?' (1995) 7 *Revue africaine de droit international et comparé* 493, at 493, 502–3; M Bettati, 'Un droit d'ingérence?' (1991) 3 *Revue générale de droit international public* 639, at 643.

[62] S Chesterman, *Just War or Just Peace? International Law and Humanitarian Intervention* (Oxford, Oxford University Press, 2001), at 236.

However, it has been suggested that 'a more general obligation to ensure human rights within other territories' can be derived from states' obligations under human rights instruments and the obligation to cooperate for the protection of human rights in the UN Charter.[63] We also saw that, according to article 41(1) of the International Law Commission's Articles on State Responsibility, states have an obligation to 'cooperate to bring to an end through lawful means any serious breach' of a peremptory norm.[64] In addition, it has been suggested that humanitarian law imposes obligations on states to protect individuals, even in other states.[65] Perhaps the strongest argument can be made in the case of genocide, since the Genocide Convention includes an undertaking to prevent the crime of genocide.[66]

All of these obligations, however, are general in nature. It is not clear what they entail, and specifically, whether they ground a right or duty of intervention.[67] In short, the law arguably requires states to 'do something' to prevent genocide or serious violations of human rights or humanitarian law, but does not specify whether this 'something' must—or even may— be military intervention. Would using existing obligations to argue for a duty to intervene be an appropriate way of promoting human security? The report of the ICISS encouraged a shift in focus from the right of intervention to a 'responsibility to protect'.[68] As already mentioned, it

[63] Chinkin, 'Legality', above n 19, at 918. See also ICISS, *Responsibility to Protect*, above n 1, at 16.

[64] International Law Commission, 'Draft Articles on State Responsibility', UNGA Res 56/83 (28 January 2002) UN Doc A/RES/56/83, Annex. A serious breach of a peremptory norm is defined for these purposes in art 40. See the discussion in ch 3, nn 85–6 and accompanying text.

[65] ICISS, *Responsibility to Protect*, above n 1, at xi, 16. Although it is not explicitly stated in this report, the most likely basis for this argument is common art 1 of the Geneva Conventions, which imposes an obligation to 'ensure respect for' the Conventions. See the discussion and sources cited in ch 3, nn 150–53 and accompanying text.

[66] Convention on the Prevention and Punishment of Genocide (opened for signature 9 December 1948, entered into force 12 January 1951) 78 UNTS 277, art 1. See *Application of the Convention on the Prevention and Punishment of the Crime of Genocide (Bosnia and Herzegovina v Serbia and Montenegro)*, Judgment of 26 February 2007 [*Genocide Convention*], at para 427ff. See also the discussion in ch 3, nn 157–60 and accompanying text; Schabas, above n 61, at 491ff; Simma, above n 9, at 2; Hubert and Bonser, above n 60, at 114; SJ Toope, 'Does International Law Impose a Duty Upon the United Nations to Prevent Genocide?' (2000) 46 *McGill Law Journal* 187.

[67] Regarding genocide, see the ICJ's statement that in fulfilling their obligation to prevent genocide, states 'may only act within the limits permitted by international law': *Genocide Convention*, above n 66, at para 430; See also Schabas, above n 61, at 447, 491ff. Regarding humanitarian law, see Sandoz, above n 61, at 219 (text and fn 11); F Azzam, 'The Duty of Third States to Implement and Enforce International Humanitarian Law' (1997) *Nordic Journal of International Law* 55, at 55–6; L Boisson de Chazournes and L Condorelli, 'Common Article 1 of the Geneva Conventions Revisited: Protecting Collective Interests' (2000) 837 *IRRC* 67, at 76ff. Regarding art 41(1) of the ILC Draft Articles on State Responsibility, see J Crawford, *The International Law Commission's Articles on State Responsibility: Introduction, Text and Commentaries* (Cambridge, Cambridge University Press, 2002), at 249.

[68] ICISS, *Responsibility to Protect*, above n 1, at 11–12.

cited human security as part of the basis for this shift. This is consistent with the common concern element of human security that was outlined in chapter two. A key aspect of the concept is the idea that states share responsibility for the security of people, regardless of where they are. This should prompt us to move the question of obligations from the margins to the centre of the debate on humanitarian intervention. The ICISS also urged that humanitarian crises be viewed from the perspective of those affected, rather than that of potential interveners, which also echoes a human security approach.[69]

The ICISS report appears to have had some success in its aim of shifting the terms of both academic and political discourse towards the responsibility to protect, and this is widely recognised as its most important contribution. Yet some worry that the change in focus will make little difference in practice,[70] and in fact may simply provide new ways of articulating spurious humanitarian justifications[71] or resisting proposals for action. In recent debates about the Sudan, for example, arguments both for and *against* intervention were framed in terms of the responsibility to protect, with opponents arguing that the primary responsibility lay with the Sudanese government and denying that it had failed in that responsibility.[72] Despite these concerns, the focus on responsibilities is a positive development. Reframing the debate in terms of a responsibility to protect will not guarantee that states will agree on whether intervention is appropriate. The framework contemplates other states stepping in only when the threatened people's state is unable or unwilling to fulfil its responsibility, and whether this is the case or not is essentially a factual question on which there may be disagreement. Like human security, the responsibility to protect cannot be used to answer the question of whether intervention is necessary or desirable; instead, it provides a better way of asking the question.

Focusing on the responsibility to protect in the context of humanitarian intervention still does not fully address human security concerns, however. We need to consider not only what obligations states might have to protect the security of individuals in other states, but also how we should best understand the implications of those obligations. As we saw above, the option of military intervention carries serious risks for human security, so invoking states' obligations to protect individuals as support for the right to use force is profoundly problematic from this point of view. The idea of an obligation to intervene may seem to be more compelling

---

[69] *Ibid*, at 11, 15.

[70] See, eg, SN MacFarlane, CJ Thielking and TG Weiss, '*The Responsibility to Protect*: Is Anyone Interested in Humanitarian Intervention?' (2004) 25 *Third World Quarterly* 977, at 980.

[71] See Weiss, above n 13, at 143, discussing attempts to use the responsibility to protect to justify pre-emptive use of force along the lines advocated by the Bush administration.

[72] See Bellamy, above n 13, for a detailed and useful account of the debates.

because it is directly concerned with states' obligations to respond when human security is threatened. However, it is equally problematic as long as it is understood to mean a duty to undertake military intervention. Looking at the issue with reference to the concept of human security therefore suggests that we need to question the connection made between obligations to protect human rights or prevent genocide, on one hand, and the right or duty of humanitarian intervention, on the other, rather than taking this connection for granted. Instead of engaging in the humanitarian intervention debate, we should use it merely as a point of departure and move beyond it. If we are serious about protecting human security, the aim of devoting greater attention to obligations should not be to argue for a right or duty to forcibly intervene, but to open up a broader discussion about responsibilities and their possible implications.

Prevention of Harm and the Use of Force as a Last Resort

The fundamental principle that the use of force should be a last resort speaks to the concerns about military intervention that have been discussed in the last two sections. The point of that discussion is not to deny that it can *ever* be necessary or right to use force, but rather to draw attention to the risks entailed by any use of force, thereby emphasising that it should be contemplated only when there truly is no alternative. Although its application in practice may be difficult, as a matter of principle, the rule that force should be used only as a last resort is uncontroversial.[73] It is a fundamental precept of 'Just War theory',[74] which has influenced discussions of humanitarian intervention, and is one of the few points in these discussions on which commentators seem to be virtually unanimous.

The effective operation of this rule is essential if human security concerns about harm resulting from the use of force are to be addressed, but this effectiveness depends on the structure of the debate about humanitarian intervention. There is, for example, a danger that emphasis on establishing a right of humanitarian intervention may tend to undermine the last resort rule by concentrating attention on the military option to the exclusion of other possibilities. That is, although the use of force is said to be a last resort, the impulse to 'do something' in response to a humanitarian emergency tends to become equated too easily with military action because this has been the primary focus of debate. The ICISS report noted that one of the reasons that the traditional terms of debate on humanitarian intervention are inadequate is that they do not

---

[73] See the discussion above, nn 26–7 and accompanying text.
[74] See, eg, RL Holmes, 'Can War Be Morally Justified? The Just War Theory' in JB Elshtain (ed), *Just War Theory* (Oxford, Blackwell, 1992), at 213, 222.

'adequately take into account the need for either prior preventive effort or subsequent follow-up assistance'.[75] The last resort rule may also be undermined by lack of consideration of other obligations that states may have to prevent harm to individuals. Military intervention may seem to be a last resort only when measured against options actually attempted or evaluated, while a broader discussion might reveal many other possibilities that were not considered. There will always be a significant degree of uncertainty in assessing whether all other preventive measures that might be effective have been attempted. However, the last resort rule will be best able to operate where there is the fullest possible consideration of other alternatives, causal factors, and relevant obligations.

A concern with preventing harm, and specifically with giving effect to the last resort rule, therefore reinforces the approach suggested in the last section, that is, the need to consider obligations to protect, but not as directed toward justifying or encouraging military intervention. The focus should not be on finding support for military intervention but on avoiding the need for it. Human security is clearly better protected if a crisis can be dealt with by non-military means or, better still, if a crisis never arises. Taking a human security approach seriously, as a shared responsibility for protecting individuals from threats to their security, suggests that the most important element of the debates regarding humanitarian intervention, from a human security perspective, may be discussion of states' responsibilities to prevent harm by measures other than, and prior to, military intervention. The ICISS report endorsed calls for a 'renewed focus on cooperation for prevention' and urged the international community to do 'more to close the gap between rhetorical support for prevention and tangible commitment'. This would require increased efforts on early warning, an understanding of the range of preventive policy options, and the political will to apply available measures.[76]

Furthermore, if one is concerned with preventing harm to individuals, consideration should not be limited to other types of formal intervention. Some analyses have tried to draw attention to the ways in which states are already effectively intervening in each other's affairs and to the impact their actions may have, apart from any deliberate attempt to intervene for individuals' protection. For example, Orford has explored the role of 'monetary interventions' (the impact of international financial institutions and international trade law) in contributing to the humanitarian crisis in the former Yugoslavia.[77] Others have examined the impact of foreign

---

[75] ICISS, *Responsibility to Protect*, above n 1, at 16.

[76] *Ibid*, at 20*ff*. See also UN, *A More Secure World: Our Shared Responsibility*, Report of the Secretary-General's High-Level Panel on Threats, Challenges and Change (New York, UN Department of Public Information, 2004), at 35*ff*.

[77] A Orford, 'Locating the International: Military and Monetary Interventions after the Cold War' (1997) 38 *Harvard International Law Journal* 443.

governments' actions and policies on the domestic situation in Rwanda leading up to the 1994 genocide. Although Rwanda is commonly portrayed as a paradigm case of non-intervention, the full picture shows not just a failure to intervene to stop the genocide, but foreign financial assistance and arms supplies that helped to make it possible.[78] From this perspective, the choice between humanitarian intervention ('doing something') and inaction ('doing nothing') is revealed as a false one which does not take into account the 'ways in which international institutions and actors contribute to the conditions leading to the outbreak of violence'.[79] Discussion of states' obligations to prevent harm to individuals in other states must therefore consider these broader impacts and the ongoing effects of states' actions and policies, rather than just direct responses to actual or impending crises.[80] This view of prevention would try to give effect to the idea that 'any intervention, by definition, is an admission of failure of prevention'.[81] Although this idea is often expressed, effectively protecting human security would require further serious and sustained attention to explore its implications and translate it into practice.

Furthermore, the analysis here challenges another view that is sometimes expressed about the relationship between prevention and the rule that forcible intervention should be a last resort. It has been suggested that a preventive approach and the last resort rule tend to work at cross purposes, because prevention favours early intervention, while the last resort rule requires that we refrain from intervening until other options have been exhausted.[82] If we wait for evidence to be collected and other options to be attempted or assessed, the window of opportunity for early intervention will have passed and irreparable harm may already have been done.[83] Should a desire to prevent harm not therefore encourage intervention to be taken as soon as practicable, and even in anticipation of possible threats to human security?[84] The considerations that have been explored above suggest that this solution is based on too narrow a view of prevention, equating it with military intervention and discounting the

---

[78] LM Melvern, *A People Betrayed: The Role of the West in Rwanda's Genocide* (London, Zed Books, 2000); SD Goose and F Smyth, 'Arming Genocide in Rwanda' (1994) 73(5) *Foreign Affairs* 86; Small Arms Survey, *Small Arms Survey 2001: Profiling the Problem* (Oxford, Oxford University Press, 2001), at 206–7.

[79] Orford, above n 77, at 444.

[80] This is reinforced by awareness of the fact that attempts to intervene may backfire (see, eg, Wheeler, above n 28, at 214, regarding Rwanda and the Arusha peace process); if (even non-forcible) intervention risks doing more harm than good, that is all the more reason to focus more attention on what states are already doing and the effects of their actions.

[81] United Kingdom, 'Guiding Humanitarian Intervention', above n 23. See also discussion of this speech in Gray, above n 9, at 41.

[82] Wheeler, above n 27, at 35.

[83] Chinkin, 'Legality', above n 19, at 921; Lowe, above n 22, at 940.

[84] Chinkin, 'Legality', above n 19, at 921. For an opposing view, see Charney, above n 11, at 841 (arguing against 'anticipatory humanitarian intervention' as a 'particularly dangerous permutation of an already problematic concept').

need to prevent the harm that would ensue from an intervention. According to the account given here, the last resort rule supports a preventive approach to protecting human security by attempting to minimise the likelihood of military intervention. In addition, a broad approach to prevention that addresses the conditions contributing to humanitarian crises would extend the idea of forcible intervention as a last resort from the context of crisis intervention to crisis avoidance. In this view, prevention and the last resort rule are complementary rather than conflicting.

The essence of the above discussion is that whereas the legal debates have emphasised the right of humanitarian intervention, a human security approach would place more emphasis on exploring responsibilities, as well as requiring careful attention to the nature and scope of those responsibilities. As we saw above, the harms to be prevented must include those caused by military intervention itself. Rather than using states' obligations to support calls for military intervention, then, we should instead engage in discussion about those obligations and their implications. This discussion should take a comprehensive view of how states' actions and inactions contribute to the safety of people in other states. It should not be seen as 'taking sides' in the humanitarian intervention debate, in support of intervention. Instead, it should reframe this debate through an awareness that these obligations could help to avoid the need for intervention. This would give the fullest possible effect to the principle that the use of force should be a last resort.

CONCLUSION

The aim of this chapter has been to re-examine aspects of the legal debates on the subject of humanitarian intervention in the light of human security and some of the ways in which human security has been invoked in these debates. It has been suggested by some that humanitarian intervention is an important means of protecting human security and that recognising a right of humanitarian intervention would align the law more closely with human security. It might also appear that a duty to intervene would further recognise the notion of human security as a matter of common concern and responsibility. These arguments have a certain appeal, since the concept of human security privileges the security of human beings over that of states and implies a degree of shared responsibility for the security of people everywhere. A closer look reveals, however, that such arguments are in fact problematic because they do not take sufficient account of the threat to human security that is involved in military intervention, even when it is undertaken with the best of intentions.

The concept of human security can be used instead to critically examine arguments in the humanitarian intervention debate. Arguing that humanitarian intervention should be allowed because the protection of human rights should take precedence over sovereignty appears mistakenly to assume that the injury caused by humanitarian intervention is primarily to the state rather than to human beings who may be harmed. This has implications for the way we conceptualise intervention in the case of failed states and concerns about abuse of a purported right of humanitarian intervention. It was suggested that a human security approach might prompt us to reconsider the purpose of the prohibition on the use of force, shifting it from an instrumental concern for state security to the direct protection of individuals.

Next, we saw that focusing on the concept of human security would encourage explicit attention to the question of states' obligations in the event of a humanitarian crisis, but that using these obligations as a foundation for arguments in favour of a right or even a duty to undertake military intervention also raised the problem of threats to people's security from the use of military force. From the point of view of human security, it would be more useful to frame the discussion of these obligations more broadly. The fullest possible consideration of states' obligations, encompassing non-forcible means of intervention but also attention to the ongoing impact of their actions, is important in preventing harm to individuals and ensuring that the use of force really is a last resort.

Taking the security of individuals as the primary concern certainly does not resolve all of the difficult questions about humanitarian intervention. In fact, this chapter has suggested that trying to use human security to *answer* these questions is unhelpful and perhaps even misguided. Privileging human security does not necessarily lead to any particular conclusion about whether and when it is appropriate to intervene, and where it appears to do so, this is usually at the expense of a full consideration of threats to individuals' security. The real value of human security here is to provide or encourage an alternative way of framing and prioritising the questions to be asked.

5

Human Security and Forced Displacement

INTRODUCTION

PEOPLE WHO HAVE been forcibly displaced from their homes are a vulnerable group whose security has been the subject of special attention in the human security agenda.[1] Displacement is an important indicator of human insecurity, being both a cause and a consequence of insecurity.[2] It is also related to other parts of the human security agenda, including the protection of civilians in armed conflict, war-affected children, the impact of anti-personnel mines and small arms, and the observance of human rights and humanitarian law. An international regime concerned with displaced persons has been developing over the last half-century, with the Refugee Convention and Protocol,[3] and some protections in international humanitarian law. More recently, the legal framework specifically relating to internally displaced persons has been discussed and developed. Internally displaced persons (IDPs) have been described as 'the largest "at-risk" population in the world'[4]: according to some estimates, there are more than twice as many IDPs as refugees.[5]

[1] See, eg, Commission on Human Security, *Human Security Now: Protecting and Empowering People* (New York, Commission on Human Security, 2003) <http://www.human security-chs.org/finalreport/index.html> (accessed 26 February 2007), at ch 3; Canada, DFAIT, *Freedom from Fear: Canada's Foreign Policy for Human Security* (Ottawa, DFAIT, 2000) <http://www.humansecurity.gc.ca/pdf/freedom_from_fear-en.pdf> (accessed 27 February 2007), at 4; SN MacFarlane and YF Khong, *Human Security and the UN: A Critical History* (Bloomington, Indiana University Press, 2006), at 219–23.

[2] UNHCR, 'Human Security: A Refugee Perspective' (Keynote Speech by Mrs Sadako Ogata, United Nations High Commissioner for Refugees, at the Ministerial Meeting on Human Security Issues of the 'Lysoen Process' Group of Governments, Bergen, Norway, 19 May 1999) <http://www.unhcr.org/admin/ADMIN/3ae68fc00.html> (accessed 25 April 2007).

[3] Convention Relating to the Status of Refugees (adopted 28 July 1951, entered into force 22 April 1954) 189 UNTS 150 [Refugee Convention]; Protocol Relating to the Status of Refugees (adopted 31 January 1967, entered into force 4 October 1967) 606 UNTS 267 [Refugee Protocol].

[4] R Cohen and FM Deng, *Masses in Flight: The Global Crisis of Internal Displacement* (Washington, DC, Brookings Institution, 1998), at 15.

[5] UNHCR, *The State of the World's Refugees: A Humanitarian Agenda* (Oxford, Oxford University Press, 1997), at 153. Estimates vary, due to not only operational difficulties of obtaining accurate numbers but also the lack of any consistent or universal definition of IDPs.

These people have been forced to leave their homes, but remain within the borders of their countries of origin, and thus are not eligible to be considered 'refugees'. Awareness of the plight of IDPs has increased in recent years, due in part to the widespread concern that violent conflict within states and its impact on civilians have increased.

Although all aspects of forced displacement are important to human security, recent discussions about international protection for IDPs have special relevance because they intersect with the two key dimensions of the shift to human security: the human-centred approach, giving priority to the security of individuals over states; and common concern for human security, suggesting the need for international protection efforts. Since IDPs by definition are located in their home country, to propose that external actors such as international organisations or other states should have a role in their protection immediately raises issues of sovereignty and intervention. It also requires consideration of what kinds of obligations those external actors might have and what the source of those obligations might be. This topic therefore provides an opportunity to explore further some of the themes discussed in the previous chapter, as well as the areas of tension and complementarity between human security and international law that we saw in chapter three.

This area is also one in which the use of the human security concept has provoked some controversy. Apart from familiar concerns about the interventionist tendencies of powerful Western states, some have been critical of the use of human security discourse, in particular by the UN High Commissioner for Refugees (UNHCR), as a way of framing and reconciling security concerns relating to displacement.[6] It is therefore important to scrutinise the roles that human security has played and could play in this context.

INTERNALLY DISPLACED PERSONS AND INTERNATIONAL LAW

There is no universally accepted definition of IDPs. The Guiding Principles on Internal Displacement (discussed below) describe IDPs as

> persons or groups of persons who have been forced or obliged to flee or to leave their homes or places of habitual residence, in particular as a result of or in order to avoid the effects of armed conflict, situations of generalized violence,

---

[6] See, eg, A Hammerstad, 'Whose Security? UNHCR, Refugee Protection and State Security After the Cold War' (2000) 31 *Security Dialogue* 391; A Suhrke, 'Human Security and the Protection of Refugees' in E Newman and J van Selm, *Refugees and Forced Displacement: International Security, Human Vulnerability, and the State* (Tokyo, United Nations University Press, 2003), at 93.

violations of human rights or natural or human-made disasters, and who have not crossed an internationally recognized State border.[7]

Although internal displacement is by no means a new phenomenon, explicit attention to IDPs as a distinct group within the sphere of international law is a relatively recent development. In the late 1980s and through the 1990s, people became more aware of the problem of internal displacement and some began to question why refugees and IDPs were treated so differently by the law. The definitions of a refugee in the 1951 Convention and related Protocol and in relevant regional instruments include only persons who have crossed an international border and who meet certain other criteria.[8] In legal terms, if not always in common usage, the term 'refugee' therefore refers only to these persons, and the refugee regime is designed to address their specific needs. Amidst widespread, more general questions about the restrictive definition of refugees, the validity of excluding IDPs was raised as an issue.[9] Why, it was asked, if IDPs are displaced by the same causes as refugees, and equally vulnerable, are they not equally protected?[10] Surely it would be inhumane, and in some cases impractical or impossible, to single out refugees for international assistance and protection, leaving IDPs unprotected.[11]

These criticisms have sparked discussion about the extent to which the existing institutional and normative framework already does address the

[7] UNCHR, 'Guiding Principles on Internal Displacement, Report of the Representative of the Secretary-General, Mr Francis Deng, submitted pursuant to Commission resolution 1997/39: Addendum' (11 February 1998) UN Doc E/CN.4/1998/53/Add.2, Annex ['Guiding Principles'], at para 2. For a discussion of some of the difficulties and controversies in defining IDPs, see M Vincent, 'IDPs: Rights and Status' (2000) 8 *Forced Migration Review* 29 ['Rights and Status']; N Geissler, 'The International Protection of Internally Displaced Persons' (1999) 11 *International Journal of Refugee Law* 451, at 455–6.

[8] Refugee Convention, above n 3, art 1(A)(2); Refugee Protocol above n 3, art 1(2); Convention Governing the Specific Aspects of Refugee Problems in Africa (adopted 10 September 1969, entered into force 20 June 1974) 1001 UNTS 45, art 1; Cartagena Declaration on Refugees (22 November 1984) Annual Report of the Inter-American Commission on Human Rights, OAS Doc OEA/Ser.L/V/II.66/doc.10, Rev 1 at 190, at para 3.

[9] The exclusion of many other people who are *externally* displaced but do not meet the other criteria for refugee status is, of course, the other main issue. Some of the concerns raised with respect to IDPs might also apply to this group of externally displaced persons. However, there are also some distinct legal issues relating to IDPs, which are the primary focus of this chapter. For the sake of clarity, the text here will therefore refer to 'IDPs' and 'refugees' (the latter meaning refugees as defined in the relevant legal instruments).

[10] See, eg, UNHCR, 'Internally Displaced Persons: The Role of the United Nations High Commissioner for Refugees' (20 June 2000) UN Doc EC/50/SC/INF.2 ['Internally Displaced Persons'], at 1, 3–4; UNGA Res 49/169 (24 February 1995) UN Doc A/RES/49/169, preamble; United States, Mission to the United Nations, 'Statement by Ambassador Richard C Holbrooke, United States Permanent Representative to the United Nations' USUN Press Release #44(00) (28 March 2000) <http://www.un.int/usa/00_044.htm> (accessed 10 March 2007); LT Lee, 'Internally Displaced Persons and Refugees: Toward a Legal Synthesis?' (1996) 9 *Journal of Refugee Studies* 27, at 29–30.

[11] See, eg, UNHCR, 'Internally Displaced Persons', above n 10, at 4, 9; UNGA Res 49/169, above n 10, preamble; Lee, above n 10, at 33–4, 38.

situation of IDPs. With respect to institutions, greater attention has been focused on the ways in which the UNHCR is already involved in working with and on behalf of IDPs. The UNHCR's competence as set out in its Statute is limited to refugees as defined by the Refugee Convention and Protocol.[12] However, the Statute also sets out the activities of the UNHCR, including reducing the number of refugees requiring protection and assisting with voluntary repatriation,[13] as well as 'such additional activities . . . as the General Assembly may determine, within the limits of the resources placed at [the High Commissioner's] disposal'.[14] In practice, the UNHCR has frequently provided protection and assistance to other 'persons of concern', including IDPs, within this framework, either in response to a specific request,[15] or as part of its activities relating to refugees. The UNHCR's work tends to involve IDPs especially in the context of voluntary repatriation and prevention of refugee flows, and in situations where it is impractical or unreasonable to distinguish between IDPs and refugees.[16] Assistance and protection for IDPs in such situations follow from the UNHCR's humanitarian mandate.[17] Its activities in relation to IDPs are, however, limited by the terms set by the General Assembly and by the UNHCR's own policy.[18] Critics and even the agency itself have been divided on the question of whether UNHCR's mandate should be extended to give it primary responsibility for IDPs.[19] As will

---

[12] Statute of the Office of the United Nations High Commissioner for Refugees, UNGA Res 428(V) (14 December 1950), Annex, art 6.

[13] *Ibid*, art 8.

[14] *Ibid*, art 9. In UNGA Res 2956(XXVII) (12 December 1972), the General Assembly requested the High Commissioner to participate in UN activities for which UNHCR has particular experience and expertise, at the request of the Secretary-General.

[15] General Assembly resolutions have supported the UNHCR's actions, at the request of the Secretary-General or other competent principal organ of the United Nations, on behalf of IDPs: eg, UNGA Res 47/105 (26 April 1993) UN Doc A/RES/47/105, at para 14; UNGA Res 48/116 (24 March 1994) UN Doc A/RES/48/116, at para 12; UNGA Res 49/169, above n 10, at para 10.

[16] See, eg, UNHCR, 'UNHCR's Role with Internally Displaced Persons' (23 April 1993) UN Doc IOM-FOM/33/93 ['UNHCR's Role'], at para 8; UNHCR, 'Protection Aspects of UNHCR Activities on Behalf of Internally Displaced Persons' (17 August1994) UN Doc EC/SCP/87 ['Protection Aspects'], at paras 1–3; UNHCR, 'UNHCR's Operational Experience with Internally Displaced Persons' (1 September 1994) <http://www.unhcr.org/publ/PUBL/3d4f95964.pdf> (accessed 25 April 2007) ['Operational Experience'], at paras 6, 228–9, and the case studies summarised therein; UNHCR, 'Internally Displaced Persons', above n 10, at 4.

[17] UNHCR, 'Internally Displaced Persons', above n 10, at 1.

[18] UNHCR, 'UNHCR's Role', above n 16, at para 7; UNHCR, 'Internally Displaced Persons', above n 10, at 3; UNGA Res 47/105, above n 15, at para 14; UNGA Res 48/116, above n 15, at para 12. These limits include the need for authorisation by a competent UN organ; the availability of adequate resources, expertise, and experience within the UNHCR; and the consent of the state concerned and any other relevant entities.

[19] See, eg, UNHCR, *The State of the World's Refugees 2006: Human Displacement in the New Millennium* (Oxford, Oxford University Press, 2006) [*Refugees 2006*], at 166–7; C Phuong, *International Protection of Internally Displaced Persons* (Cambridge, Cambridge University Press, 2004), at 84–90.

seen below, some of the controversy surrounding this question is tied to concerns that more formalised protection for IDPs could undermine the UNHCR's refugee protection mandate if it is used by potential destination states as an excuse to deny entry to refugees.[20]

In addition to the UNHCR, numerous organisations and UN agencies are involved in protecting and assisting IDPs as part of their responses to armed conflict, natural disasters, or other humanitarian crises. Recent institutional developments within the UN have attempted to respond to the need for greater coordination between these bodies and for explicit attention to IDP issues. The UN Emergency Relief Coordinator has overall responsibility for coordinating activities of UN agencies.[21] An IDP Unit and subsequently the Inter-Agency Internal Displacement Division have been established within the UN Office for the Coordination of Humanitarian Affairs (OCHA), in order to assist and support the Emergency Relief Coordinator, Inter-Agency Standing Committee (IASC), and other bodies in effectively responding to the needs of IDPs.[22] The IASC has also published guidelines for implementing a collaborative approach to internal displacement.[23] These developments reflect a perception that what is needed is not a new organisation dedicated to IDPs, but rather increased attention and improved coordination on the part of those already involved with IDPs in various ways. This approach is appealing, given the controversy about extending the UNHCR's mandate and the recognition that multiple agencies will usually be involved in relevant crisis situations. However, 'nearly every UN and independent evaluation that has examined the collaborative approach has found that it works poorly' and, according to one expert, 'the steps needed to strengthen it for the most part have not been taken'.[24]

The focal point for discussion about the norms applicable to IDPs has been the work of the Representative of the Secretary-General on internally displaced persons [the UN Representative],[25] in particular the

---

[20] See Phuong, above n 19, at 88–9; R Cohen, 'Developing a System for Internally Displaced Persons' (2006) 7 *International Studies Perspectives* 87 ['Developing a System'], at 95. Cohen notes that there is also an element of 'turf protection' in some objections to an expanded UNHCR mandate.

[21] Cohen, 'Developing a System', above n 20, at 96; MR Islam, 'The Sudanese Darfur Crisis and Internally Displaced Persons in International Law: The Least Protection for the Most Vulnerable' (2006) 18 *International Journal of Refugee Law* 354, at 359.

[22] UN OCHA, 'Terms of Reference for an IDP Unit within OCHA' (2002) <http://www.reliefweb.int/IDP/docs/references/IDPUnitTORFinal.pdf> (accessed 10 March 2007); UN OCHA, 'Inter-Agency Internal Displacement Division' <http://www.reliefweb.int/idp/> (accessed 10 March 2007).

[23] UN IASC, *Implementing the Collaborative Response to Situations of Internal Displacement: Guidance for United Nations Humanitarian and/or Resident Coordinators and Country Teams* (Geneva, United Nations, 2005).

[24] Cohen, 'Developing a System', above n 20, at 96. See also Islam, above n 21, at 375.

[25] The first UN Representative, Mr Francis Deng, was appointed in 1992 at the request of the UN Commission on Human Rights, and his mandate was extended a number of times; he was succeeded in 2004 by Walter Kälin.

Compilation and Analysis of Legal Norms[26] and the drafting of Guiding Principles on Internal Displacement [the Guiding Principles].[27] The Compilation and Analysis of Legal Norms surveyed human rights, humanitarian, and refugee law relevant to displaced persons and applicable in a variety of contexts.[28] The study found that existing norms cover many aspects of importance to IDPs, including non-discrimination; protection of life, physical security, and liberty; subsistence; movement; personal identification, documentation, and registration; protection of property; protection of family and community; and self-reliance.[29] It also found, however, that there are some gaps in protection or 'grey areas', since certain norms are not applicable in all situations, others are of a general nature and have not been interpreted to apply specifically to IDPs, and in some situations relevant norms can only be deduced by developing, extending, or applying by analogy other existing norms.[30]

In order to address these perceived deficiencies in the law and to make the existing provisions more effective for IDPs by setting out the relevant norms in a single document,[31] the UN Representative subsequently drafted the Guiding Principles. These set out principles to be applied by all relevant actors in the areas of protection from displacement, protection during displacement, humanitarian assistance, and return, resettlement, and integration. They are intended to reflect existing law, or where gaps were found, to follow 'what could be said was implicit in the law'.[32] Although some states have expressed reservations about the Guiding Principles and have sought to emphasise their non-binding status, they

[26] UNCHR, 'Compilation and Analysis of Legal Norms, Report of the Representative of the Secretary-General' (5 December 1995) UN Doc E/CN.4/1996/52/Add.2 ['Compilation and Analysis']; UNCHR, 'Compilation and Analysis of Legal Norms, Part II: Legal Aspects Relating to Protection from Arbitrary Displacement, Report of the Representative of the Secretary-General' (11 February 1998) UN Doc E/CN.4/1998/53/Add.1 ['Compilation and Analysis II'].

[27] UNCHR, Guiding Principles, above n 7. For a useful review of the development of the Guiding Principles, see R Cohen, 'The Guiding Principles on Internal Displacement: An Innovation in International Standard Setting' (2004) 10 *Global Governance* 459 ['Guiding Principles']. Another effort to compile the relevant rights and obligations is the International Law Association's 'London Declaration of International Law Principles on Internally Displaced Persons' (July 2000), reprinted in (2001) 12 *International Journal of Refugee Law* 672.

[28] UNCHR, 'Compilation and Analysis', above n 26, at para 27*ff*. See also Cohen and Deng, above n 4, at 77–85.

[29] UNCHR, 'Compilation and Analysis', above n 26, at para 47*ff*. See also Cohen and Deng, above n 4, at 85–113.

[30] UNCHR, 'Compilation and Analysis', above n 26, at para 411*ff*. See also W Kälin, 'The *Guiding Principles* on Internal Displacement—An Introduction' (1998) 10 *International Journal of Refugee Law* 557, at 560–61; Cohen and Deng, above n 4, at 74–5, 122–4.

[31] UNCHR, Guiding Principles, above n 7, 'Introductory note to the Guiding Principles', at para 7.

[32] Cohen, 'Guiding Principles', above n 27, at 467–8. It has been suggested, however, that the Guiding Principles did create new law in some respects: Phuong, above n 19, at 60–61.

have been widely used and referred to by states, international agencies, and non-governmental organisations (NGOs).[33]

There are various opinions about the role and usefulness of the Guiding Principles. According to one view, the Guiding Principles simply restate existing law; while they may be a useful tool for advocacy and operational application, they are unnecessary and redundant from a legal perspective.[34] Others understand the Guiding Principles to be a more significant development in the articulation and application of norms.[35] Underlying this difference of opinion is a more fundamental one about the validity of defining IDPs as a separate category. Some argue that there is no need to give IDPs special status,[36] and question whether it is appropriate to distinguish between IDPs and other civilians who should also be protected by humanitarian law in the event of armed conflict.[37] Defining IDPs as a separate category is said to 'entail the risk of diminishing the scope of the protection to which the civilian population is entitled'.[38] There are also fears that action on behalf of IDPs, particularly by the UNHCR, may undermine its central goal of protecting refugees.[39] Others acknowledge these fears but argue that undermining asylum or protection of other civilians need not necessarily follow from recognising and addressing the specific situation of IDPs.[40] Even if there is no need for

[33] Cohen, 'Guiding Principles', above n 27, at 467–75; Cohen, 'Developing a System', above n 20, at 93–4.

[34] M Barutciski, 'Tensions Between the Refugee Concept and the IDP Debate' (1998) 3 *Forced Migration Review* 11, at 13; EE Ruddick, 'The Continuing Constraint of Sovereignty: International Law, International Protection, and the Internally Displaced' (1997) 77 *Boston University Law Review* 429, at 439; International Committee of the Red Cross (ICRC), 'Internally Displaced Persons: The Mandate and Role of the International Committee of the Red Cross' (2000) 82 *IRRC* 491, at 492. The ICRC insists that international humanitarian law 'remains fully adequate to address most problems of internal displacement' associated with situations of armed conflict, 'in spite of the fact that the term 'internally displaced persons' does not appear anywhere in that law': *ibid*, at 494.

[35] See, eg, M Kingsley-Nyinah, 'What May Be Borrowed; What Is New?' (1999) 4 *Forced Migration Review* 32, at 33.

[36] See, eg, Geissler, above n 7, at 457.

[37] J-P Lavoyer, 'Guiding Principles on Internal Displacement' (1998) 324 *IRRC* 463, at 471–2; Barutciski, above n 34, at 13. See also ICRC, above n 34, at 492: '[the ICRC] seeks to give priority to those in most urgent need, in accordance with the principle of impartiality. In this respect, the ICRC considers an internally displaced person to be first and foremost a civilian, who as such is protected by international humanitarian law.'

[38] Lavoyer, *ibid*, at 474.

[39] See, eg, Barutciski, above n 34, at 14; UNHCR, *The State of the World's Refugees 2000: Fifty Years of Humanitarian Action* (Oxford, Oxford University Press, 2000) [*Refugees 2000*], at 282.

[40] See, eg, B Rutinwa, 'How tense is the tension between the refugee concept and the IDP debate?' (1999) 4 *Forced Migration Review* 29, at 31; Kingsley-Nyinah, above n 35, at 33; R Plender, 'The Legal Basis of International Jurisdiction to Act with Regard to the Internally Displaced' (1994) 6 *International Journal of Refugee Law* 345, at 360. The Guiding Principles themselves state that they 'shall not be interpreted as restricting, modifying or impairing the provisions of any international human rights or international humanitarian law instrument' and, in particular, 'are without prejudice to the right to seek and enjoy asylum in other countries': UNCHR, Guiding Principles, above n 7, principle 2(1).

special legal status, they argue, the needs of IDPs must be taken into account.[41]

HUMAN SECURITY AND FORCED DISPLACEMENT

People who have been forcibly displaced from their homes, whether by human rights violations, armed conflict, or environmental catastrophes, experience a high degree of insecurity as both a cause and a consequence of their displacement. Those who remain within the borders of their home state (the state of their nationality and/or habitual residence) should be able to rely on the protection of their government. However, they may not enjoy that protection, either because the government lacks the capacity to provide it or because that same government is responsible for creating or exacerbating their insecurity. As we have seen earlier, the realisation that we cannot always rely on governments to protect their people and that effective protection will require some kind of shared responsibility underlies the idea of human security as a common concern. It is this same insight that led to calls for international protection for IDPs.

The prospect of international involvement in IDP protection raises issues of sovereignty and non-intervention. Once again the problem could be characterised as a conflict between state security, protected by the legal principles of sovereignty and non-intervention, and human security. Military intervention, with or even without Security Council authorisation, is not ruled out as an option, and to the extent that the use of force is contemplated, the analysis of humanitarian intervention in chapter four would apply. In that chapter, it was argued that framing the question of humanitarian intervention as a conflict between human rights or human security and state sovereignty missed the point because what was at stake was not just sovereignty but the prohibition on the use of force and potential threats to human security from military action. There remains a question as to whether other types of non-forcible intervention to protect human security can legitimately override state sovereignty. This question has been central to discussions of international protection for IDPs. It was in this context that the concept of 'sovereignty as responsibility' originated as a way of legitimising external intervention where a state fails to protect people at risk.[42] This view of sovereignty mirrors the human security approach in that it treats the protection of states as instrumental to protection for individuals. It also posits a protection role for external actors similar to the idea of common concern for human security, although, as will be seen below, the prevailing understanding of sover-

[41] See, eg, Cohen and Deng, above n 4, at 27.

[42] FM Deng et al, *Sovereignty as Responsibility: Conflict Management in Africa* (Washington, DC, Brookings Institution, 1996). See the discussion below at nn 67ff and accompanying text.

eignty as responsibility may unduly limit the scope of shared responsibilities.

The increased attention to providing security for IDPs has come at a
time when security has also been invoked in other ways in relation to
displaced persons. Many have noted that in the post-Cold War era refugee
flows have been characterised as a threat to the security of destination
states.[43] This is especially true where mass influxes threaten to overwhelm
neighbouring states, which may lack capacity to deal with them and may
themselves be vulnerable to some of the same problems as the source state.
Since the advent of the 'war on terror', refugees have faced additional
barriers to entry on security grounds.[44] States' efforts to protect their
security may conflict with efforts to ensure the security of displaced
individuals, for example when people are encouraged or forced to remain
within their home state in unsafe conditions to avoid refugee flows.
Concerns about this 'containment' approach have made critics suspicious
of efforts at 'prevention'. Although prevention of displacement could
obviously contribute to human security if it addresses the causes of
displacement, as an end in itself, directed at containing refugee flows, it
could seriously undermine human security. As we will see below, these
tensions have raised doubts about efforts by the UNHCR to devote more
attention to preventive strategies and IDPs. It has also complicated the use
of human security discourse in the displacement context.

Sovereignty and International Protection

The sustained attention that the problem of internal displacement has
received in recent years has been motivated in part by a concern that IDPs
suffer from many of the same kinds of insecurity as refugees but lacked an
equivalent legal regime for their protection. This concern with people's
lived experiences could be described as part of a human-centred approach
to displacement, even if the label 'human security' was not attached to it
originally. It uses people's actual experiences of insecurity to identify
apparent gaps in legal protection. Although extremely important, it needs
to be followed by analysis of the nature of the gap and the implications of
particular attempts to fill it. It does not get us very far to say that from the
individual's perspective there is 'no real difference' between being
internally displaced and being a refugee, and that the distinction between
them is merely 'bureaucratic'.[45] Putting in question the legal distinction

---

[43] See generally G Loescher, 'Refugee Protection and State Security: Towards a Greater
Convergence' in RM Price and MW Zacher (eds), *The United Nations and Global Security* (New
York, Palgrave MacMillan, 2004).

[44] See, eg, R Freitas, 'Human Security and Refugee Protection after September 11: A
Reassessment' (2002) 20(4) *Refuge* 34.

[45] United States, Mission to the United Nations, above n 10.

between IDPs and refugees is only a first step, which raises a series of related and difficult questions about the extension of international protection to IDPs.[46]

As a starting point, then, we need to look more closely at what it means to question this legal distinction. It cannot mean that IDPs and refugees should be treated just the same by international law, or that IDPs should be assimilated into the refugee regime, since that regime is designed specifically to address the situation of being outside one's country of origin.[47] To understand the implications of international protection for IDPs, we need to acknowledge both what they share with refugees and what makes them different. What refugees and IDPs have in common is the failure of their own state to adequately protect their rights and their personal security. This failure is the reason that refugees have fled their home state and cannot return; it is the reason that IDPs may need assistance or protection from outsiders even though they remain in their home country. If we are concerned about human security, it is not enough to say that IDPs may be *entitled* to the protection of their own government, when we know that this will not provide *effective* protection.[48] Of course, this will not necessarily be true of everyone who is internally displaced, since some may, in fact, be sufficiently provided for by their home government.[49] When we speak of international protection for IDPs, then, we are concerned with those who require some outside assistance for adequate protection of their security.

[46] Although 'protection' is sometimes used to mean specifically protection from violence and human rights violations affecting physical security and liberty, as distinct from 'assistance' which is understood to refer to provision of food, shelter, medical care, etc., the term 'protection' will be used in this chapter in a general sense which could include both aspects, since they are in many respects inseparable: see Ruddick, above n 34, at 456, n 137; Geissler, above n 7, at 469–70; Cohen and Deng, above n 4, at 255–6.

[47] See, eg, Vincent, 'Rights and Status', above n 7, at 30; M Vincent, 'Protection and Assistance to IDPs' (1999) 4 *Forced Migration Review* 34, at 34; Rutinwa, above n 40, at 30; J Bennett, 'Rights and Borders' (1999) 4 *Forced Migration Review* 33, at 33; Kingsley-Nyinah, above n 35, at 32. At most, some argue that certain aspects of refugee law should be applicable by analogy; for example, the essence of the principle of non-refoulement, protection from return to situations where one's life or safety is threatened, is also relevant to IDPs: Kingsley-Nyiah, *ibid*. Even Lee, who proposes a 'legal synthesis' of refugees and IDPs, essentially argues that refugees and IDPs should be *equally* protected, not necessarily that they should be protected in the same way: Lee, above n 10.

[48] The position of the ICRC, for example, is that refugees and IDPs are different because '[w]hile refugees are victims of persecution and as such are in need of a specific legal regime, the internally displaced are in their own country and accordingly remain fully entitled to the full range of protection provided by international human rights law, humanitarian law and domestic law': ICRC, above n 34, at 494. This, however, misses the point that *entitlement* to protection does not necessarily mean *effective* protection.

[49] This will be unlikely where their forced displacement is a result of human rights violations, but may be the case where it results from a natural disaster or perhaps in some conflict situations. By the same token, the category of IDPs is under-inclusive as a delineation of those in need of international protection, since those who have remained in their homes may be equally, or in some cases even more, at risk. Some have objected to the focus on IDPs on this basis: see, eg, Lavoyer, above n 37, at 471–2; ICRC, above n 34, at 493.

At the same time, we cannot ignore the fact that there are other people who may be equally vulnerable, without being displaced.[50] The experience of being displaced will usually bring with it a degree of vulnerability, associated with lack of housing, health care, and other basic needs, and the disruption of livelihoods and support systems.[51] It is not out of the question, though, that those who are unable to move at all may be at equal or even greater risk. If the key criterion is insufficient local protection giving rise to international concern, the category of IDPs is both over- and under-inclusive. It remains the case that displacement is a useful indicator of insecurity, if not a perfect one, so it may still be useful and legitimate as a focus for international protection efforts.[52] However, we also need to be aware that the discussion of international protection for IDPs will have broader implications. As one authority has suggested:

> If we are serious that we are now in a position to enter behind the wall of sovereignty, we ought not to privilege those who are displaced, effectively doing a disservice to those who are trapped in their own homes, and we ought simply to get about the business of enforcing international human rights law internally if we honestly believe that is a possibility.[53]

The logic that requires the extension of international protection to IDPs also may demand the same for other individuals in need of protection.

If we accept that refugees and IDPs (at least) share a need for international protection, it still cannot be denied that '[i]n an international system still organized around sovereign states, there is a world of difference between being within the jurisdiction of the state where persecution takes place and being outside it'.[54] This means that international protection of IDPs will have to mean something different from protection for refugees. In the case of refugees, the legal framework is precisely designed to provide an alternative form of protection for individuals when their rights are not respected and they cannot rely on their own government to protect them.[55] The protection of other countries

---

[50] Lavoyer, above n 37, at 471–2; ICRC, above n 34, at 493. In addition, as mentioned above in n 9, there are also persons who are *externally* displaced but who fall outside the refugee regime because their circumstances do not fit the legal definitions; these persons may also be extremely vulnerable.

[51] See, eg, UNCHR, Report of the Representative (1995), above n 65, at para 14 for an overview of some of the risks to which IDPs tend to be more vulnerable. The report cites studies indicating that the death rates for displaced persons are much higher (as much as 60 times) than for non-displaced persons in the same country: *ibid*.

[52] Vincent, for example, usefully draws a distinction between legally significant *definitions* of categories (such as refugees) and *descriptions* (such as IDPs), where the latter is used not to assign legal status but merely to recognise vulnerability and the potential need for protection: Vincent, 'Rights and Status', above n 7, at 29–30.

[53] J Hathaway, quoted in Phuong, above n 19, at 27.

[54] UNHCR, *Refugees 2000*, above n 39, at 282. See also Barutciski, above n 34, at 12.

[55] See, eg, JC Hathaway, 'Reconceiving Refugee Law as Human Rights Protection' (1991) 4 *Journal of Refugee Studies* 113, at 120–21 (describing the 'palliative' function of refugee law) and 123–24.

is a surrogate for the protection lacking in their home country. The internally displaced may be in the same position of not being able to reasonably expect protection from their state, but there is no equivalent regime providing for surrogate protection. Since IDPs have not entered other states' territory or jurisdiction, the obligations central to refugee law are inapplicable, and it is not necessarily obvious what international protection should involve.[56] Means of protection that have been suggested include humanitarian assistance, human rights monitoring and other volunteer presence, the establishment of safe areas, and measures to protect individuals upon return and reintegration, such as security assessments and monitoring.[57]

Many of these forms of international protection assume that states will intervene in some way in another state's territory, since that is where the internally displaced are, by definition, located. There is thus an 'inherent tension' between international protection and internal displacement.[58] The sovereignty of the IDPs' state is widely perceived to be a significant barrier to providing protection.[59] A central question is whether respect for sovereignty can or should block access to a displaced population that is not being adequately provided for internally. There have been numerous examples of states invoking their sovereignty to bar external access to threatened populations.[60] In these situations the question arises whether the state's consent is required for others to step in to assist, and whether the state can validly refuse to give this consent. The UNHCR will act with respect to IDPs only with the consent of their state,[61] and humanitarian assistance by UN agencies has generally been understood to require state consent, although the positions of states and organisations on this point have sometimes been conflicting or ambivalent.[62] The International

---

[56] UNHCR, 'Operational Experience', above n 16, at para 239; Cohen and Deng, above n 4, at 255.

[57] Phuong, above n 19, at 125–42.

[58] *Ibid*, at 208.

[59] See, eg, Ruddick, above n 34; J Fitzpatrick, 'The Human Rights of Refugees, Asylum-Seekers, and Internally Displaced Persons: A Basic Introduction' in J Fitzpatrick (ed), *Human Rights Protection for Refugees, Asylum seekers, and Internally Displaced Persons: A Guide to International Mechanisms and Procedures* (Ardsley, NY , Transnational Publishers, 2002), at 5; UNHCR, *Refugees 2000*, above n 39, at 215; Lee, above n 10, at 37, 39; UNCHR, 'Internally Displaced Persons: Report of the Representative of the Secretary-General' (2 February 1995) UN Doc E/CN.4/1995/50 ['Report 1995'], at para 14; Islam, above n 21, at 367*ff*.

[60] See, eg, Cohen, 'Developing a System', above n 20, at 91; UNHCR, *Refugees 2006*, above n 19, at 160.

[61] See above n 18.

[62] See UNGA, 'Guiding Principles on Humanitarian Assistance', UNGA Res 46/182 (19 December 1991) UN Doc A/RES/46/182, Annex, at para 3; UNGA Res 43/131 (8 December 1988) UN Doc A/RES/43/131; UNGA Res 45/100 (14 December 1990) UN Doc A/RES/45/100; Z Coursen-Neff, 'Preventive Measures Pertaining to Unconventional Threats to the Peace such as Natural and Humanitarian Disasters' (1998) *New York University Journal of International Law and Politics* 645, at 675; JW Samuels, 'Organized Responses to Natural Disasters' in R St John Macdonald, DM Johnston and GL Morris (eds), *The*

Committee of the Red Cross (ICRC) and other non-governmental and international organisations have a 'right of initiative' which allows them to offer assistance, but the provision of relief remains subject to the consent of the state or of parties to a conflict.[63] Some have suggested, however, that states may have an obligation to accept offers of international assistance, unless they are able and willing to take adequate measures on their own.[64] It is argued that states' obligations under human rights and humanitarian law may ground an obligation to seek and accept assistance if it is required for adequate protection of the population, or at least an obligation not to deny offers of assistance without a valid reason.[65] The Guiding Principles on Internal Displacement state that offers of assistance are not to be regarded as unfriendly acts or interference in a state's domestic affairs, and consent 'shall not be arbitrarily withheld, particularly when authorities concerned are unable or unwilling to provide the required humanitarian assistance'.[66]

The former UN Representative Francis Deng has championed the concept of 'sovereignty as responsibility' as a way of understanding and supporting these obligations.[67] This concept views sovereignty as 'an instrument for ensuring the protection and welfare of all those under a state's jurisdiction', and entails accountability to the state's own population and to other states for the protection of human rights and respect for international law.[68] In this account, a state bears the primary responsibility for protecting its population, including, if necessary, by requesting or accepting assistance from others.[69] State sovereignty cannot be invoked to

International Law and Policy of Human Welfare (Alphen aan den Rijn, Netherlands, Sijthoff and Noordhoff, 1978), at 675; Plender, above n 40, at 354; Ruddick, above n 34, at 456–61 (noting some ambivalence on this point but a general acceptance of the need for consent or at least acquiescence).

[63] UNCHR, 'Compilation and Analysis', above n 26, at para 367*ff*; Geissler, above n 7, at 470–71. See also ch 3, n 42 and the sources cited therein.

[64] See, eg, UNCHR, 'Compilation and Analysis', above n 26, at para 365 (but noting, at para 366, that the international community has been reluctant to recognise a duty to accept offers of humanitarian assistance); UNCHR, 'Internally displaced persons: Report of the Representative of the Secretary-General' (22 February 1996) UN Doc E/CN.4/1996/52 ['Report 1996'], at para 34; Geissler, above n 7, at 474–5; Plender, above n 40, at 356; Ruddick, above n 34, at 462*ff* (surveying various arguments); Coursen-Neff, above n 62, at 693*ff*; Samuels, above n 62, at 686–7 (suggesting that such a principle may be emerging).

[65] See, eg, K Luoparjärvi, 'Is there an Obligation on States to Accept International Humanitarian Assistance to Internally Displaced Persons under International Law' (2003) 15 *International Journal of Refugee Law* 678; UNCHR, 'Compilation and Analysis', above n 26, at para 361*ff*; Coursen-Neff, above n 62, at 699–702; Geissler, above n 7, at 474–5.

[66] UNCHR, Guiding Principles, above n 7, principle 25(2).

[67] See, eg, Deng *et al*, above n 42, at ch 1 for a discussion of the origins and development of this concept.

[68] Cohen and Deng, above n 4, at 275–6.

[69] UNCHR, 'Internally displaced persons: Report of the Representative of the Secretary-General' (25 January 1994) UN Doc E/CN.4/1994/44, at paras 41–2; UNCHR, 'Report 1995', above n 59, at para 38; UNCHR, 'Report 1996', above n 64, at para 34.

obstruct the provision of humanitarian assistance.[70] If a state fails in its responsibility, other states are entitled and indeed obliged to provide protection, even against the state's will. Respect for a state's sovereignty depends on its fulfilment of essential responsibilities.[71] Redefining sovereignty as responsibility rather than as exclusive control makes the possibility of intervention by other states a corollary of sovereignty rather than its negation. This concept of 'conditional' sovereignty is said to be the 'philosophical foundation' of the Guiding Principles on Internal Displacement,[72] and has been central to discussions of international protection for IDPs. It echoes some liberal views of sovereignty and human rights which, as we have seen, hold that states are only entitled to respect for their sovereignty if they respect the fundamental rights of their inhabitants.[73] Despite the influence that the development of human rights law has had on the principle of state sovereignty, this remains a 'bold proposal'.[74] It does appear to be gaining some ground: sovereignty as responsibility is an important component of the 'responsibility to protect' as articulated by the International Commission on Intervention and State Sovereignty (ICISS),[75] and some recent UN documents have endorsed the concept.[76] However, many states are predictably resistant to the idea, so it has not yet achieved widespread acceptance.[77]

According to the ICISS, human security and human rights are the impetus for reconceiving sovereignty as responsibility, which in turn is the foundation for the responsibility to protect.[78] Its report suggested that the 'case for thinking of sovereignty in these terms is strengthened by . . . the increasing impact in international discourse of the concept of human

---

[70] Deng *et al*, above n 42, at 28.

[71] Cohen and Deng, above n 4, at 276–7; UNCHR, 'Report 1995', above n 59, at para 38; UNCHR, 'Report 1996', above n 64, at para 34.

[72] Cohen, 'Developing a System', above n 20, at 93.

[73] See the discussion in ch 2, n 157 and accompanying text, and ch 4, n 47 and accompanying text.

[74] Phuong, above n 19, at 218.

[75] International Commission on Intervention and State Sovereignty, *Responsibility to Protect: Report of the International Commission on Intervention and State Sovereignty* (Ottawa, International Development Research Centre, 2001) [ICISS, *Responsibility to Protect*], at 13.

[76] UN, *A More Secure World: Our Shared Responsibility* (Report of the Secretary-General's High-Level Panel on Threats, Challenges and Change) (New York, UN Department of Public Information, 2004), at 65–6; UNGA, 'In Larger Freedom: Toward Development, Security and Human Rights for All, Report of the Secretary-General' (21 March 2005) UN Doc A/59/2005 ['In Larger Freedom'], at para 135.

[77] For example, the Secretary-General proposed (UNGA, 'In Larger Freedom', above n 76, Annex, para 7(b)) that the responsibility to protect be endorsed by the 2005 World Summit, but the Summit document committed only 'to continue consideration of the responsibility to protect populations' and to help, 'as necessary and appropriate', states to build their capacity to protect their populations: UNGA, 'World Summit Outcome' (12 September 2005) UN Doc A/RES/60/1, at para 139.

[78] ICISS, *Responsibility to Protect*, above n 75, at 13.

security'.[79] There is indeed a significant degree of similarity between the two frameworks. As is frequently acknowledged, the security of states has value for human security because it is expected that a secure state is normally the best provider of security for its people. At the same time, though, a human security approach entails the recognition that states do not always ensure the security of their people and may even be the greatest threat to human security. Under these circumstances human security is a matter of shared interest and responsibility, and concern for the security of people, not of states, must take precedence.

In the last chapter we saw that privileging human rights over sovereignty—a more simplistic version of this framework—was deeply problematic where it was used to justify the use of force, since it obscured the fact that the intervention thus justified could itself be a serious threat to human security. To the extent that non-forcible measures are contemplated in the context of IDPs, this concern is minimised, although one still cannot assume that even a non-forcible intervention will necessarily be beneficial to human security in all respects, and its effects must therefore be subject to scrutiny. The sovereignty as responsibility approach is more useful than a simple dichotomy between human rights and sovereignty, because it understands sovereignty in a more nuanced way. That is, it recognises that state sovereignty is not necessarily antithetical to human rights and it integrates both the positive and negative potential of state action for human security: governments can be both protectors of and threats to human security. It also considers the implications of this for other states, and therefore incorporates an element of common responsibility for human security. It remains to be seen, however, whether the distribution of responsibilities in the sovereignty as responsibility framework is adequate as an expression of shared responsibility for human security.

Common Responsibility and Displacement

The concept of sovereignty as responsibility acknowledges that the primary or 'default' responsibility for a population's security rests with that population's own government, which is normally in the best position to provide it. It also implies, however, a 'residual' responsibility on the part of other actors to step in when the primary mechanism for ensuring

[79] *Ibid*, at 13. See also the statement made by Deng at the 2000 meeting of the Human Security Network: 'Human Security provides an umbrella for both the normative meaning of sovereignty as responsibility and the basis for holding Governments accountable and providing people with the international protection and assistance': Human Security Network, 'Second Ministerial Meeting: Chairman's Summary' (Lucerne, 11–12 May 2000) <http://www.humansecuritynetwork.org/docs/Chairman_summary-e.php> (accessed 25 April 2007).

security has failed, which is what the ICISS report refers to as the international community's responsibility to protect. This arguably extends the concept beyond the liberal notion of conditional sovereignty and parallels the cosmopolitan dimension of human security as a common concern, which makes ensuring individuals' security a matter of common responsibility.[80] How should we conceptualise states' obligations with respect to the protection of IDPs? What would be the implications of shared responsibility for their protection?

As we saw in chapter three, a general duty or principle of cooperation in international law, based especially on the UN Charter, requires states to work together towards the solution of common problems, including in the areas of peace and security and the protection of human rights. This duty is of a very general nature, though, and does not prescribe the measures to be taken by states in response to particular problems. Therefore, it is necessary to further explore states' obligations within a specific context. Refugee law is one area where the duties of states as part of a collective response to the refugee problem have been extensively discussed, and the concept of burden sharing in refugee law was briefly introduced in chapter three as an example of common responsibility for the protection of individuals in the international legal regime. Burden sharing (or responsibility sharing, as it is sometimes called) refers to the distribution of responsibilities among states in response to refugee flows. Underlying the concept are the notions that cooperation is required to address refugee problems effectively and that the burdens of providing protection for refugees should be equitably shared by states. The narrow meaning of burden sharing refers to arrangements regarding the distribution of refugees, especially in resettlement. Prominent examples include the resettlement of refugees after the Second World War[81] and of Vietnamese refugees in the late 1970s and the 1980s,[82] as well as, more recently, a scheme to transfer Kosovan refugees from Macedonia to third countries.[83] The UNHCR's scheme to resettle 'quota refugees', whereby relatively small numbers of especially vulnerable refugees are resettled in third countries each year, is another example.[84]

Although the term 'burden sharing' is often used narrowly to refer to these resettlement schemes, the concept also has broader dimensions. An

---

[80] See ch 2, nn 163–75 and accompanying text.

[81] See, eg, A Hans and A Suhrke, 'Responsibility Sharing' in JC Hathaway (ed), *Reconceiving International Refugee Law* (The Hague, Martinus Nijhoff, 1997), at 86–7; A Suhrke, 'Burden-sharing During Refugee Emergencies: The Logic of Collective Versus National Action' (1998) 11 *Journal of Refugee Studies* 396 ['Burden-sharing'], at 403–5.

[82] See, eg, Hans and Suhrke, above n 81, at 99–102; Suhrke, 'Burden-sharing', above n 81, at 405–6.

[83] See M Barutciski and A Suhrke, 'Lessons from the Kosovo Refugee Crisis: Innovations in Protection and Burden-sharing' (2001) 14 *Journal of Refugee Studies* 95.

[84] Suhrke, 'Burden-sharing', above n 81, at 397.

important UNHCR document suggests that measures to more effectively share responsibilities with respect to refugee protection could include, in addition to resettlement: arrangements to share the burden of first asylum countries (including financial assistance); cooperation to strengthen the protection capacity of refugee-receiving countries (including financial and technical assistance); partnerships with civil society; empowering refugee communities; and addressing refugee issues in development (allocation of development funds, including refugees in development plans).[85] States share the responsibility for refugee protection to some degree by contributing financially to multilateral institutions such as the UNHCR[86] or through the redistribution of resources globally from North to South.[87] The disproportionate burden borne by countries of first asylum is of particular concern, since developing countries host by far the largest numbers of refugees, while at the same time having the least resources to cope with the costs involved.[88] African states have proposed (without much success) that their burden should be shared by wealthier states. Not only are wealthier states better able to bear part of the cost but, at the same time, they also benefit from the relatively generous asylum policies within the African region that prevent large influxes of refugees into Western countries.[89]

Burden sharing in this broader sense is arguably just as relevant in the case of internal displacement. Measures such as financial assistance to the host state and contributions to multilateral institutions and organisations are equally applicable in the case of IDPs. In certain circumstances, granting first asylum and providing resettlement opportunities may help to alleviate the burden on the home state just as resettlement alleviates the burden on states of first asylum, so even this form of burden sharing is potentially applicable by analogy. Extending burden sharing to IDP protection would be ambitious, given that even in the refugee context, states do not appear to accept that they owe shared responsibilities. States' responses to burden-sharing initiatives for refugees have been inconsistent, and they have not recognised legal obligations to contribute to the costs of refugee protection, as evidenced by the chronic under-funding of UNHCR and its reliance on

---

[85] UNHCR, 'Agenda for Protection' (26 June 2002) UN Doc AC/AC.96/965/Add.1, at 13–16.

[86] A Acharya and DB Dewitt, 'Fiscal Burden Sharing' in JC Hathaway (ed), *Reconceiving International Refugee Law* (The Hague, Martinus Nijhoff, 1997), at 125–6.

[87] *Ibid*, at 128–30.

[88] UNHCR, *Statistical Yearbook 2001* (UNHCR, Geneva, 2002), at 12–13, 65. See also Acharya and Dewitt, above n 86, at 116; G Martin, 'International Solidarity and Co-operation in Assistance to African Refugees: Burden-Sharing or Burden-Shifting?' (1995, Special Issue) *International Journal of Refugee Law* 250, at 250, 257.

[89] Acharya and Dewitt, above n 86, at 129; Hans and Suhrke, above n 81, at 91. See also Martin, above n 88, at 254.

voluntary contributions.[90] Furthermore, unlike in the case of refugees, where at least one other state is automatically involved as soon as refugees even attempt to cross the border, international response to internal displacement is not inevitable, and the effects of internal displacement are indirect and likely to be less intense. However, both the residual international responsibilities inherent in the sovereignty as responsibility framework and common responsibility for human security would require the recognition of some form of burden sharing in this context.

In order to understand what shared responsibility for IDPs might mean, we also need to take a closer look at the manner in which the sovereignty as responsibility framework and discussions of international protection have framed the respective obligations of the home state and of other actors. The state whose population is at risk has the primary responsibility to ensure that population's security, sometimes referred to as a 'default' responsibility,[91] reflecting the assumption that in the usual course of events, it will be able, willing, and best placed to provide security for its people. This is reiterated in the Guiding Principles, which state that the 'primary duty and responsibility for providing humanitarian assistance to internally displaced persons lies with national authorities'.[92] The responsibility to protect that is shared by other states is said to be a 'residual' or 'fallback'[93] responsibility, which comes into play only if and when this normal condition is disrupted. Similarly, burden sharing in the refugee regime concerns the distribution of responsibility among states in their role as surrogate protectors.

As we saw in the last chapter, though, some commentators have usefully drawn attention to the ways in which states' actions (on their own or through international organisations) can be implicated in causing insecurity for others' populations.[94] Consideration of shared responsibility for human security is arguably incomplete if it does not take account of this dimension. In the context of displacement this is equally apparent. In addition to contributing to the causes or severity of armed conflicts or other forms of violence, the actions and policies of other states and of international organisations may play a particularly important role in 'development-induced' displacement, whereby millions of people are involuntarily displaced by development projects, often with inadequate provision for resettlement or 'rehabilitation'.[95] It is also widely recognised

---

[90] The UNHCR is financed almost entirely by voluntary contributions from governments, NGOs, and individuals. See Hathaway, above n 55, at 126–7 (arguing for a legally binding system of resource sharing to replace the current system of voluntary funding).

[91] ICISS, *Responsibility to Protect*, above n 75, at 17.

[92] UNCHR, Guiding Principles, above n 7, principle 25(1).

[93] See also ICISS, *Responsibility to Protect*, above n 71, at 17.

[94] See ch 4, nn 77–80 and accompanying text.

[95] See, eg, B Pettersson, 'Development-induced displacement: internal affair or international human rights issue?' (2002) 12 *Forced Migration Review* 16; TE Downing,

that the 'natural' disasters that displace further millions often have a human element which contributes to their occurrence or exacerbates their effects. This human element may include foreign states' policies with respect to areas such as trade, finance, and especially the environment, in addition to negligent or deliberate actions by the population's own government.[96] Foreign states are therefore often implicated in the causes of displacement and threats to security experienced by the displaced. Furthermore, the UN Representative has suggested that states are to some degree responsible for the magnitude of the crisis of internal displacement because the 'growing reluctance on the part of States in the post-Cold War era to admit large numbers of refugees or to finance their stay in third countries is forcing greater numbers of persons to remain displaced within their own countries and in need of international assistance and protection'.[97]

If we take into account the full range of actions which have a significant impact on human security, this seems to suggest that sharing responsibility should mean something more than merely 'residual' responsibilities. It is unrealistic to assume that all actions by other states will be beneficial to people's security, or that they will only have an impact when they are deliberately intervening in the case of a failure by the people's own government. Shared responsibility can mean helping to protect the displaced and providing humanitarian assistance, but it could also include a broader view of how foreign states' actions affect the security of people by contributing to the causes of their displacement or affecting the conditions they experience once displaced. The primary responsibility of the home state and these responsibilities of other states are not mutually exclusive. The possibility that other states might have obligations, both to

'Creating Poverty: The Flawed Economic Logic of the World Bank's Revised Involuntary Resettlement Policy' (2002) 12 *Forced Migration Review* 13; UNCHR, 'Compilation and Analysis II', above n 26, at para E.1*ff*. The number of people displaced as a result of the construction of large hydroelectric dams alone has been estimated at 40–60 million: Pettersson, above, at 16. These numbers are not normally included in the estimates of numbers of IDPs, although these displaced persons could be considered as falling within the UN Representative's definition of IDPs as 'persons . . . who have been forced or obliged to flee or to leave their homes or places of habitual residence, . . . as a result of . . . violations of human rights or natural or human-made disasters' (UNCHR, Guiding Principles, above n 7).

[96] For example, trade policies may encourage certain forms of agricultural or industrial production that may increase vulnerability to disasters or their effects; policies of international financial institutions may have the unintended effect of reducing governments' abilities to undertake preventive or mitigating measures; policies contributing to or failing to prevent environmental harms may have global effects, as, for example, in the case of climate change. Coursen-Neff points out that international organisations may also be involved in the latter (negligent or deliberate actions by the population's own government); for example, in the Ethiopian famine in 1972–73, 'every major international relief agency and donor organization, including the U.N. agencies, went along with the Ethiopian government's cover-up', apparently due to 'a diplomatic practice that valued working relationships with the government above humanitarian concerns': Coursen-Neff, above n 62, at 677–8.

[97] UNCHR, 'Report 1995', above n 59, at para 13.

assist in the case of a crisis and to ensure that their own actions and policies do not contribute to displacement or security threats for the displaced, need not undermine the assumption that the state whose people are affected has the primary responsibility for protecting them and will normally be in the best position to do so. Insistence on the home state's primary responsibility should therefore not be used as a way of closing off a broader discussion about other obligations. The notion of common responsibility for human security merely addresses those cases where protection by one state is inadequate, and recognises that sole responsibility does not reflect the reality of an interdependent world.

This approach would also, more realistically, recognise that whether the home state's protection is adequate is not a simple all-or-nothing matter. It could help to avoid the kind of debate that seems to have been problematic in the case of Sudan, where some states (including, of course, Sudan itself) insisted that the threshold of failed responsibility had not been met.[98] If we see all states' obligations as always subsisting, with the *content* and *implications* of those obligations varying according to circumstances, the question is not whether the home state has failed to meet some threshold which is bound to be contentious, but rather whether there are specific areas or forms of protection that are lacking and could be provided by external actors. Finally, as we saw in the previous chapter, preventive measures are crucial to protecting human security. In order to be effective, such measures need to be implemented as early as possible and on an ongoing basis, rather than waiting for a failure of domestic protection. Consequently, there is a tension between limiting the responsibility to protect to a fallback role for the international community, on one hand, and expanding the responsibility to protect to include a greater focus on prevention, on the other, which does not seem to have been fully recognised.[99] It may be appropriate to consider that an individual's own state has the primary responsibility for their protection, but it does not necessarily follow that other states' responsibilities only come into play when the primary responsibility fails.

To summarise, the extension of international protection to IDPs would be a way of giving effect to common responsibility for human security. If we explore the meaning of international protection further from the perspective of human security, though, it becomes apparent that the narrower view—that states should intervene to provide protection in the case of a failure of protection by the home state—only partially captures what is required to ensure effective protection. The dichotomy between default and residual responsibilities is inadequate to describe the varied nature of states' responsibilities, which will depend on their roles and relationships to the displaced population.

[98] See ch 4, n 72 and accompanying text.
[99] See ICISS, *Responsibility to Protect*, above n 75, at 17.

Prevention and Security

Discussions of international protection for IDPs are part of a wider phenomenon of increased interest in a broad preventive approach which includes preventing displacement altogether and addressing the root causes of refugee flows.[100] The UNHCR has taken a more proactive approach to refugee issues, with a greater focus on protection within the country of origin.[101] The root causes of refugee flows are often the same as those of internal displacement, so efforts to address these causes will affect both refugees and IDPs. Providing effective protection for IDPs could be one way of preventing refugee flows. Such an approach could help to ensure human security by aiming to prevent harm before it occurs, preferably by tackling root and precipitating causes and, failing this, by providing effective protection at the earliest possible stage. Nevertheless, it has been viewed with scepticism, and even alarm, by advocates and scholars who fear that, far from contributing to individuals' security, this approach might protect only states' security at their expense. It is widely acknowledged that the willingness of states (particularly developed states) to host refugees has declined in recent years, for a variety of reasons, and that refugees are often perceived as threats to the security of host countries.[102] The conjunction between these states' desire to reduce the number of refugees and the new enthusiasm for a preventive approach has raised suspicions that the real aim of prevention is containment of potential refugees and asylum-seekers.[103]

The UNHCR and the UN Representative have attempted to allay these fears by insisting that protection of IDPs must not be understood to

---

[100] See, eg, P Kourula, *Broadening the Edges: Refugee Definition and International Protection Revisited* (The Hague, Martinus Nijhoff, 1997), at 1–3; TA Aleinikoff, 'State-Centred Refugee Law: From Resettlement to Containment' (1992) 14 *Michigan Journal of International Law* 120, at 128–9.

[101] See, eg, ED Mooney, 'In-country Protection: Out of Bounds for UNHCR?' in F Nicholson and P Twomey (eds), *Refugee Rights and Realities: Evolving International Concepts and Regimes* (Cambridge, Cambridge University Press, 1999).

[102] See, eg, Loescher, above n 43; Freitas, above n 44; GS Goodwin-Gill, 'After the Cold War: Asylum and the Refugee Concept Move On' (2001) 10 *Forced Migration Review* 14, at 14–15; GS Goodwin-Gill, 'Refugees and Security' (1999) 11 *International Journal of Refugee Law* 1, at 3–4; J Crisp, 'Refugees and International Security: An Introduction to Some Key Issues and Policy Challenges' (Geneva, 4th International Security Forum, 15–17 November 2000) <http://www.isn.ethz.ch/4isf/4/Papers/ISF_WS_II-4_Crisp.pdf> (accessed 10 March 2007). On the more general tendency to frame refugee issues in terms of security, see Hammerstad, above n 6, at 392.

[103] See Mooney, above n 101, at 206–7 (discussing and to some extent rebutting such concerns with respect to the work of the UNHCR) and at 213–26. See also Barutciski, above n 34, at 14, expressing the fear that extending protection to IDPs will be used as a justification for further restricting asylum, by allowing states to claim that this protection makes asylum unnecessary.

undermine or reduce the need for asylum.[104] Despite these efforts, serious concerns persist, and cast a shadow over not only the preventive approach but also any optimistic assessment of the developments discussed in the last two sections. Humanitarian access and intervention to protect IDPs are argued to be justifiable limitations on state sovereignty for humanitarian purposes, but could also be seen as attempts by powerful states to protect their own sovereignty—specifically their right to exclude aliens from their territory—at the expense of the sovereignty of less powerful states.[105] Assistance to developing states hosting large numbers of displaced persons could be seen as a less burdensome alternative to accepting asylum or resettlement, rather than the recognition of shared responsibility.[106] Long-term preventive solutions may be 'less threatening' to states because the obligations they entail seem less immediate and concrete.[107] In sum, states' efforts to protect IDPs might be motivated primarily by concerns for their own national security, not the security of vulnerable displaced persons. The developments with respect to protection of IDPs could be part of a 'troubling use of a humanitarian discourse to mask a reaffirmation of state-centeredness'.[108]

The use of human security discourse in the context of forced displacement has been caught up in these concerns. The plight of displaced persons has been discussed as a human security issue, given the insecurity that usually attaches to displacement, and the close relationship between displacement and other parts of the human security agenda. As we have seen throughout this chapter, there are numerous parallels between a human security approach and recent discussions of international protection for IDPs. However, reference to human security in this context is part of a more general tendency to frame displacement issues in security terms.[109] This includes the security of displaced persons but also that of UNHCR personnel and affected states; not only human security but also

[104] The UNHCR has stated that one of its basic principles of operation is that its involvement with IDPs should not limit or detract from the availability of asylum: UNHCR, 'UNHCR's Role', above n 16, at para 10; UNHCR, 'Protection Aspects', above n 16, at para 14. See also UNHCR, 'Internally Displaced Persons', above n 10, at 7–8, suggesting that UNHCR's involvement should include upholding the right to seek asylum, but also that states may actually be '*more* inclined to maintain their asylum policies if something is done to alleviate the suffering of the internally displaced, reduce their compulsion to seek asylum and create conditions conducive to return' (emphasis added); UNCHR, Guiding Principles, above n 7, principle 2(2).

[105] Aleinikoff, above n 100, makes a similar argument at 130–31.

[106] Similarly, see the discussion of burden-sharing and developing countries of first asylum in Acharya and Dewitt, above n 86, at 128–30.

[107] Hathaway, above n 55, at 117.

[108] Aleinikoff, above n 100, at 134. See also Hathaway, above n 107, at 114: 'Its rhetoric of humanitarianism aside, refugee law as it exists today is fundamentally concerned with the protection of powerful states.'

[109] See, eg, Hammerstad, above n 6; H Adelman, 'From Refugees to Forced Migration: The UNHCR and Human Security' (2001) 35(1) *The International Migration Review* 7; Loescher, above n 43.

national and international security.[110] It has been argued that the way in which the UNHCR conceptualises security is affected by conflicting influences:

[T]he discourse [of security] must be seen in the context of the agency's perpetual quest for the right balance between serving donor states, on which the agency depends for its existence, and protecting and assisting refugees, the task for which the agency exists.[111]

As a result, this discourse is said to legitimise the new paradigm of prevention and containment by showing that refugee flows threaten the security of host states and regions as well as refugees themselves.[112] Within this framework, it is argued, the UNHCR 'has employed the concept of "human security" as a means by which to establish harmony between the security concerns of states and the protection needs of refugees'.[113] Some commentators have also argued that state and human security can be complementary and that preventive strategies can play a dual role in protecting both.[114]

While it is easy to understand the pragmatic motivations underlying this view, the attempt to merge state and individual security is problematic because it obscures the potential contradictions between them.[115] The use of human security in this context has therefore been criticised as supporting a containment approach to displacement. This is a serious concern, since it would mean that human security discourse has been coopted to encourage strategies which are likely to be *harmful* to people's security. If the concept of human security has been used within the UNHCR to elide human security with state security, this would run contrary to common understandings about the concept and the relationship between the security of people and the security of states. We can, however, identify this as a distortion of what is normally meant by a human security approach, and we could guard against such negative effects by being vigilant about how the concept is used and pointing out contradictions when they appear.

Perhaps more problematic is the possibility that states might use human security in this context to mean that they are protecting the security of their own people, when this amounts to imposing increased insecurity on

---

[110] Loescher, above n 43, at 163*ff*. Adelman suggests that this does not represent a radical change in the UNHCR's approach, but in fact is consistent with the organisation's history and development: Adelman, above n 109.

[111] Hammerstad, above n 6, at 395.

[112] *Ibid*, at 396.

[113] *Ibid*, at 398. See also Loescher, above n 43, at 171.

[114] See, eg, S Schmeidl, 'The Early Warning of Forced Migration: State or Human Security?' in E Newman and J van Selm, *Refugees and Forced Displacement: International Security, Human Vulnerability, and the State* (Tokyo, United Nations University Press, 2003), at 149–50; Loescher, above n 43, at 173–4.

[115] Hammerstad, above n 6, at 399.

others. For example, although the perception of refugees as a threat to security is not new, since the attacks of September 11, 2001, exclusionary policies on security grounds have become more widespread.[116] Such policies are said to protect internal security (or 'homeland security' in the US discourse), and are based on 'the opposition between refugees and citizens as referent object of security'.[117] Proponents of such policies could claim that they are protecting human security, meaning the security of individuals in their own state. Freitas argues that since 'the concept of human security is at this stage so loose and all-encompassing', it can be used to justify these restrictions. This seems plausible, given that this position does focus on the security of individuals, which is at least part of the concept of human security. The crucial point, however, is that it clearly privileges the security of some individuals (nationals or inhabitants of the state using restrictive policies) over that of others (potential refugee claimants from other states). Therefore, whether the concept of human security can be used to support restrictive policies depends on whether it is understood to entail the 'cosmopolitan' view of common concern for human security—that is, that everyone's security is of equal value. Although there is support for this understanding of human security, some ambiguity remains, and this ambiguity could allow the concept to be used to support policies which are detrimental to individuals' security.

If we accept the view of human security that entails both a shift to the individual as referent object and the 'strong' or cosmopolitan version of common responsibility for human security, the concept could usefully function as a critique of a containment approach, rather than as a justification for it. Prevention of displacement, in itself, is neither good nor bad; it must be assessed according to its value in protecting human security. Therefore, using human security as a reference point prompts us to consider what it is that we are trying to prevent. The objective is always protection of people's security, rather than prevention of displacement as an end in itself. The concept could thus be used to evaluate preventive measures, seeking to ensure that they primarily enhance human security. Certain means of preventing displacement, such as closing borders in a situation of mass displacement, are almost certain to threaten people's security. However, many strategies, from early warning to humanitarian assistance to the establishment of safe areas, can serve dual purposes of containment and effective protection, depending on the factual context and how they are implemented.[118] They should be designed and evaluated with reference to protection of human security as the primary goal.

---

[116] Freitas, above n 44.

[117] *Ibid*, at 41.

[118] Schmeidl, above n 14; Islam, above n 21, at 381–3. See also Phuong, above n 19, at 124: 'There is always a fine line between prevention of refugee flows and containment.'

This will not necessarily provide easy answers, especially where, for example, there is a genuine and plausible concern that an influx of refugees into a neighbouring country will contribute to insecurity for its inhabitants. Echoing more general critiques of the concept, some have suggested that human security is not helpful in dealing with displacement issues because it provides insufficient policy guidance to UNHCR and other actors.[119] As was noted in the last chapter, however, the role that human security can play as a way of framing questions may be just as important, and more productive, than looking to it for answers to complex policy dilemmas.

CONCLUSION

International protection for IDPs has been the subject of ongoing discussion. As we have seen in this chapter, the concept of human security can be used to contribute to this discussion in a number of ways. Consideration of individuals' experiences of insecurity serves as a starting point for exploring the questions that have been raised about the legal framework relating to refugees and IDPs. These questions are related to broader concerns about the implications of states' inability or unwillingness to provide security, and how we can reconcile international protection with the dominant principle of state sovereignty. The interpretation of sovereignty as responsibility has been proposed as a way of understanding and resolving this dilemma: sovereignty entails the responsibility to protect one's population, and if this responsibility is neglected, the international community will have a right and a responsibility to intervene. The concept of human security would support this approach, with the proviso that the intervention itself must also be scrutinised to ensure that it is in fact beneficial to individuals' security.

A concern with preventing threats to people's security also suggests, however, that a discussion of states' obligations must go beyond the model of sovereignty as responsibility, at least in its dominant formulation. This model has characterised the responsibilities of people's home state and other states as default and residual responsibilities, respectively. Effective protection of human security must instead take full account of the ways in which states affect the security of each other's populations, including by contributing to causes of displacement, and consider what duties would be required to give effect to their common responsibility for human security. These responsibilities would coexist with the primary responsibility of the home state and not be dependent on a failure of that state to fulfil its own responsibilities.

[119] Suhrke, 'Burden-sharing', above n 81; Hammerstad, above n 6; Loescher, above n 43.

Focusing on human security therefore provides a way of approaching the discussion of obligations and revealing some of the limits of the current approach. In the last section, it was seen that concerns raised about the UNHCR's use of human security, and more recently reference to human security in the context of security-based restrictions on refugees, highlight the need for cautious examination of the precise way in which the concept is invoked and for attention to the discursive and political context surrounding its use. However, the concept as commonly under-stood can be used to assess and critique preventive approaches to displacement, helping to ensure that they are focused on the protection of individuals' security. While this will not necessarily provide clear guides to policy in difficult cases, it would ensure that the relevant questions are framed in a way that gives appropriate weight to the security of vulnerable individuals.

6

Human Security and the 'Small Arms Pandemic'

INTRODUCTION

THE PROLIFERATION AND misuse of small arms and light weapons (SALW) present a grave threat to human security. It has been estimated that as many as 500,000 people are killed by SALW annually (up to 300,000 in armed conflict and at least 200,000 in homicides and suicides),[1] and further millions permanently disabled,[2] prompting references to a small arms 'pandemic'.[3] SALW have been the primary instruments of violence in recent conflicts.[4] They are sometimes referred to as the 'real weapons of mass destruction' because of the harm they cause.[5] Widespread availability of small arms is believed to facilitate violations of humanitarian law, increase risks for civilians,[6] and make

---

[1] Small Arms Survey, *Small Arms Survey 2001: Profiling the Problem* (Oxford, Oxford University Press, 2001) [*SAS 2001*], at 1, 197. Later reports have confirmed this as a conservative estimate of non-conflict deaths, but reduced the estimated number of direct conflict deaths from SALW: Small Arms Survey, *Small Arms Survey 2004: Rights at Risk* (Oxford, Oxford University Press, 2004) [*SAS 2004*]; Small Arms Survey, *Small Arms Survey 2005: Weapons at War* (Oxford, Oxford University Press, 2005) [*SAS 2005*].

[2] WHO, 'Small Arms and Global Health: WHO Contribution to the UN Conference on Illicit Trade in Small Arms and Light Weapons, July 9–20, 2001' (August 2001) UN Doc WHO/NMH/VIP/01.1 ['Small Arms and Global Health'].

[3] See, eg, N Arya, 'Confronting the Small Arms Pandemic' (2002) 324 *British Medical Journal* 990.

[4] Small Arms Survey, *SAS 2005*, above n 1; A Latham, 'Taking the Lead? Light Weapons and International Security' (1997) 52 *International Journal* 316, at 316.

[5] K Krause, 'Facing the Challenge of Small Arms: The UN and Global Security Governance' in RM Price and MW Zacher (eds), *The United Nations and Global Security* (New York, Palgrave MacMillan, 2004) ['Facing the Challenge'], at 23 (citing several annual reports by the Small Arms Survey).

[6] International Committee of the Red Cross (ICRC), *Arms Availability and the Situation of Civilians in Armed Conflict* (Geneva, ICRC, 1999) <http://www.icrc.org> (accessed 13 March 2007) [*Arms Availability*], at pt 5.F. See also P Herby, 'Arms Transfers, Humanitarian Assistance and International Humanitarian Law' (1998) 325 *IRRC* 685, at 685–7; C Wyatt, 'The Forgotten Victims of Small Arms' (2002) 22 *SAIS Review* 223, at 224; UN, 'Programme of Action to Prevent, Combat and Eradicate the Illicit Trade in Small Arms and Light Weapons in All Its Aspects', Report of the Conference on the Illicit Trade in Small Arms and Light Weapons in All Its Aspects (2001) UN Doc A/CONF.192/15, 7 ['Programme of Action'], at para I.5.

armed conflicts more likely, lethal, and prolonged.[7] In addition to their direct impact in causing human death and disability, the proliferation of these weapons has serious indirect effects, including economic costs, displacement, disruption of communities and political processes, and impeding development.[8] The proliferation of SALW is also of great concern to humanitarian organisations because the risks it creates for field staff make their activities in some areas difficult or impossible.[9] Even if 'humanitarian access' to threatened populations such as IDPs is permitted, as discussed in chapter five, it will be of little practical use if conditions on the ground are too dangerous to provide assistance.

Traditionally, disarmament and arms control efforts focused on major weapons systems and weapons of mass destruction, largely ignoring SALW because they were not perceived to be a significant risk to international peace and security.[10] In the last decade, however, increasing attention has been paid to SALW. The campaign against one particular category of SALW, anti-personnel mines, was an early cornerstone of the human security agenda, and the conclusion of the Ottawa Convention banning anti-personnel mines has been widely viewed as a victory for human security over national security. Many hoped that an effective campaign targeting the broader category of SALW would be able to build on the momentum of the mines ban movement.[11] However, this has proved to be challenging and contentious. This chapter will discuss some of the recent international developments with respect to SALW, and the role that a human security perspective has played and could play in the analysis of these developments.

---

[7] ICRC, 'UN Conference on Illicit Trade in Small Arms: ICRC Statement' (New York, 12 July 2001) <http://www.icrc.org> (accessed 13 March 2007) [Conference Statement]; A Latham, 'Light Weapons and Human Security—A Conceptual Overview' in J Dhanapala *et al* (eds), *Small Arms Control: Old Weapons, New Issues* (Aldershot, Ashgate, 1999) ['Conceptual Overview'], at 16; WHO, 'Small Arms and Global Health', above n 2, at 13; UN, 'Programme of Action', above n 6, at para I.5.

[8] WHO, 'Small Arms and Global Health', above n 2, at 10, 14–15; Arya, above n 3, at 990; Small Arms Survey, *SAS 2001*, above n 1, at 214–17, 229–34; Small Arms Survey, *Small Arms Survey 2003: Development Denied* (Oxford, Oxford University Press, 2003) [*SAS 2003*], at ch 4; Latham, 'Conceptual Overview', above n 7, at 13–15.

[9] ICRC, Conference Statement, above n 7; Herby, above n 6, at 686; Small Arms Survey, *SAS 2001*, above n 1, at 226–9; UN, 'Programme of Action', above n 6, at para I.5.

[10] See, eg, M Klare, 'An Overview of the Global Trade in Small Arms and Light Weapons' in J Dhanapala *et al* (eds), *Small Arms Control: Old Weapons, New Issues* (Aldershot, Ashgate, 1999), at 3; UN Secretary-General, 'Supplement to an Agenda for Peace: Position Paper of the Secretary-General on the Occasion of the Fiftieth Anniversary of the United Nations' (25 January 1995) UN Doc S/1995/1 ['Supplement'], at para 65; Herby, above n 6, at 689.

[11] See, eg, FO Hampson, *Madness in the Multitude: Human Security and World Disorder* (Don Mills, Ontario, Oxford University Press, 2002), at 98.

THE EVOLVING LEGAL FRAMEWORK

Generally the term 'small arms' refers to weapons that can be carried and used by one person, and 'light weapons' by several persons. The former include revolvers, pistols, rifles, submachine guns, assault rifles and light machine guns; the latter, heavy machine guns, hand-held grenade launchers, portable anti-aircraft guns and portable missile launchers.[12] The associated ammunition and explosives are usually (though not always) included in this category, as are anti-personnel and anti-tank mines. The impact of SALW is attributed to their particular characteristics: they are relatively inexpensive, portable, durable, easy to operate and to conceal, and lethal.[13] These characteristics make SALW amenable to illicit trafficking, illegal and covert use, and acquisition and use by non-state actors.[14] These weapons account for a relatively small proportion of the global arms trade,[15] and for many years were not considered a serious security concern. However, in the last decade there has been growing awareness that they have a significant impact which demands specific attention.[16] The legal framework has been evolving in response to these concerns.

Many arms control agreements focus on specific types of weapons, the most prominent example being nuclear weapons.[17] Since the late 1800s,

[12] UN, 'Report of the Panel of Governmental Experts on Small Arms' (27 August 1997) UN Doc A/52/298, Annex [Panel Report], at paras 25–6. Note that use of these terms is not consistent; for example, some authors use either 'light weapons' or 'small arms' as a general term which includes both categories.

[13] *Ibid*, at para 27; UN, 'Report of the Group of Governmental Experts on Small Arms' (19 August 1999) UN Doc A/54/258 [Group Report], at para 13; Klare, above n 10, at 4–5; O Greene, 'Examining International Responses to Illicit Arms Trafficking' (2000) 33 *Crime, Law and Social Change* 151, at 154; E Regehr, 'Small Arms and Light Weapons: A Global Humanitarian Challenge' (Working Paper No 01-4, June 2001) <http://www.ploughshares.ca/libraries/WorkingPapers/wp014.html> (accessed 29 March 2007); ICRC, *Arms Availability*, above n 6, at pt 2.E.

[14] UN, Panel Report, *ibid*, at para 27; Greene, above n 13, at 154; Regehr, above n 13, Latham, 'Conceptual Overview', above n 7, at 12; Klare, above n 10, at 5.

[15] One estimate is that small arms purchases account for $10 billion (US) of a total arms spending of $850 billion annually: Arya, above n 3, at 990, although the UN Secretary-General suggests that SALW account for almost one third of the total arms trade: UN Secretary-General, 'Supplement', above n 10, at para 61. Data on the arms trade, including trade in SALW, are notoriously difficult to collect, so substantial variation in estimates is not surprising.

[16] In 1995 the Secretary-General's Supplement to An Agenda for Peace was released, its discussion of 'micro-disarmament' and light weapons (above n 10, at paras 60–65) signalling a higher profile for the issue. African initiatives and research on small arms also gained momentum around this time: Krause, 'Facing the Challenge', above n 5, at 23.

[17] Nuclear weapons have been the subject of a number of conventions to limit testing, emplacement, and proliferation. For a list of these and other arms control and disarmament agreements compiled by the UN Department of Disarmament Affairs (DDA), see UN DDA, Multilateral Arms Regulation and Disarmament Agreements (no date) <http://disarmament.un.org/TreatyStatus.nsf> (accessed 13 March 2007).

attempts have been made to elaborate and implement legal restrictions on certain types of weapons based on humanitarian principles, in particular the principle of discrimination between combatants and non-combatants or civilians, and the prohibition on the infliction of unnecessary suffering.[18] Examples include prohibitions or restrictions on expanding bullets, incendiary weapons, blinding laser weapons, and chemical and biological weapons.[19] Even in the absence of a specific norm prohibiting a certain class of weapon, international humanitarian law remains applicable, and restricts the use of means and methods of warfare which are indiscriminate or cause unnecessary suffering.[20] Some prohibited weapons fall within the category of SALW, including certain types of bullets or ammunition and, most notably, anti-personnel mines. Although they are a subcategory of SALW, anti-personnel mines are often given separate consideration, being of special concern because of their lack of discrimination and resulting impact on civilians. Their use was restricted in Protocol II to the Convention on Certain Conventional Weapons, and later banned in the Ottawa Convention, which will be discussed below.[21]

Legal measures specifically directed at SALW have been developing since the mid-1990s. Many meetings, conferences, and workshops have been devoted to the topic, and a vast array of non-binding declarations, action plans, resolutions, and other documents have been produced at the sub-regional, regional, and global levels, as well as a few binding instruments. These efforts have been described as a 'patchwork . . . involving a multitude of state actors and organizations with varying interests and objectives'.[22] The majority of measures have been directed at curbing illicit transfers, although, as we will see below, the predominant focus on illicit trade and even the meaning of 'illicit' in this context have been contentious.

Measures to address illicit transfers have been a priority for the Organization of American States, in part because of the link between arms

---

[18] See, eg, RJ Mathews and TLH McCormack, 'The Influence of Humanitarian Principles in the Negotiation of Arms Control Treaties' (1999) 834 *IRRC* 331; H McCoubrey and ND White, *International Law and Armed Conflict* (Aldershot, Dartmouth, 1992), at ch 15.

[19] Mathews and McCormack, above n 18; McCoubrey and White, above n 18, at ch 15.

[20] *Legality of the Threat or Use of Nuclear Weapons* [1996] ICJ Rep 226, at paras 85–7, 95; Mathews and McCormack, above n 18, at 349.

[21] Protocol on Prohibitions or Restrictions on the Use of Mines, Booby-Traps and Other Devices (adopted 10 October 1980, amended 3 May 1996, entered into force 3 December 1998) UN Doc CCW-CONF.I-16 (Part I), Annex B (1996); Convention on Prohibitions or Restrictions on the Use of Certain Conventional Weapons Which May Be Deemed to Be Excessively Injurious or to Have Indiscriminate Effects (adopted 10 October 1980, entered into force 2 December 1983) 1342 UNTS 137; Convention on the Prohibition of the Use, Stockpiling, Production and Transfer of Anti-personnel Mines and on Their Destruction (opened for signature 18 September 1997, entered into force 1 March 1999) 2056 UNTS 211 [Ottawa Convention].

[22] Hampson, above n 11, at 99; see also *ibid*, at 118.

trafficking, organised crime, and illicit drugs.[23] The Inter-American Convention Against the Illicit Manufacturing of and Trafficking in Firearms, Ammunition, Explosives, and Other Related Materials was adopted in 1997 and came into force the following year.[24] It sets out measures regarding marking of firearms; export, import, and transit licences; export controls; security measures; establishment of criminal offences for illicit manufacturing and trafficking; and information exchange and cooperation in relevant areas. The Inter-American Convention was the model for the 2001 Protocol against the Illicit Manufacturing of and Trafficking in Firearms, Their Parts and Components and Ammunition.[25] Adopted as a Protocol under the UN Convention on Transnational Organized Crime,[26] again reflecting the link with organised crime and a 'law enforcement approach' to the problem,[27] it contains provisions similar to those of the Inter-American Convention.

The central initiative in the UN system regarding illicit transfers of SALW is the Programme of Action of the 2001 UN Conference on the Illicit Trade in Small Arms and Light Weapons in All Its Aspects.[28] The non-binding Programme of Action provides for national, regional, and global measures on matters including: the establishment and prosecution of relevant criminal offences; marking of weapons; record-keeping and tracing; effective regulation of export, transit, and brokering; security of authorised stockpiles; destruction of confiscated, seized, collected, or surplus weapons; post-conflict disarmament, demobilisation, and reintegration programmes; and inter-state cooperation and coordination. In the period following the 2001 Conference, a UN working group also produced a non-binding instrument on marking and tracing, which was adopted by the UN General Assembly in December 2005.[29] The 5-year Review Conference in 2006 took stock of the implementation of the Programme of Action, but failed to reach consensus on key issues or produce an outcome document. As we will see below, states remain divided about the scope of the agenda, with the most contentious issue being whether to include measures to restrict civilian possession and the 'legal' trade in SALW as well as illicit

---

[23] Greene, above n 13, at 175–6; Small Arms Survey, *SAS 2001*, above n 1, at 252.

[24] Inter-American Convention Against the Illicit Manufacturing of and Trafficking in Firearms, Ammunition, Explosives, and Other Related Materials (adopted 14 November 1997, entered into force 1 July 1998) OAS 24th Special Sess, AG/doc.7 (XXIV-E/97), rev 1.

[25] Small Arms Survey, *SAS 2001*, above n 1, at 278. Protocol against the Illicit Manufacturing of and Trafficking in Firearms, Their Parts and Components and Ammunition, supplementing the United Nations Convention against Transnational Organized Crime (adopted 31 May 2001, entered into force 3 July 2005) UN Doc A/55/383/Add.2.

[26] UN Convention against Transnational Organized Crime (adopted 15 November 2000, entered into force 29 September 2003) UN Doc A/55/25.

[27] Small Arms Survey, *SAS 2001*, above n 1, at 278.

[28] UN, 'Programme of Action', above n 6.

[29] International Instrument to Enable States to Identify and Trace, in a Timely and Reliable Manner, Illicit Small Arms and Light Weapons, UNGA Res 60/81 (8 December 2005) UN Doc A/RES/60/81.

trade. Member states did agree to pursue efforts to control illicit arms brokering, and this issue is to be studied by an intergovernmental expert group.[30] Other regional and international initiatives outside the UN have also begun to address SALW brokering.[31]

A few initiatives have tackled the more contentious issues beyond illicit transfers, including restrictions on state transfers and criteria for export controls. The Organization for Security and Co-operation in Europe (OSCE) Document on Small Arms and Light Weapons, as well as containing measures on illicit transfers similar to the Programme of Action, also contains fuller treatment of related matters such as early warning, conflict prevention, and post-conflict 'rehabilitation'. The OSCE Document and the European Union (EU) Code of Conduct on Arms Exports set out criteria for the approval of arms export licences.[32] A Code of Conduct recently adopted in Central America restricts transfers of arms including SALW based on their likely impact or misuse.[33] Finally, Africa has been the site of significant regional and sub-regional measures with respect to SALW that also extend beyond combating illicit trade.[34] In 1998, the Economic Community of West African States (ECOWAS) declared a Moratorium on the Importation, Exportation and Manufacture of Light Weapons, which was renewed and then recently converted into a binding Convention, adopted in June 2006.[35] The Nairobi Protocol[36] and the

[30] UN Secretary-General, 'Secretary-General Disappointed Small Arms Conference Ended Without Agreement, but Says Global Community Committed to Action Plan to Curb Illicit Trade', Press Release SG/SM/10558 (10 July 2006).

[31] OSCE, 'OSCE Principles on the Control of Brokering in Small Arms and Light Weapons' (24 November 2004) Decision No 8/04, FSC.DEC/8/04; Wassenaar Arrangement, 'Statement of Understanding on Arms Brokerage' (11–12 December 2002) <http://www.wassenaar. org/publicdocuments/2002_statementofunderstanding.html> (accessed 25 April 2007); Wassenaar Arrangement, 'Elements for Effective Legislation on Arms Brokering' (12 December 2003) <http://www.wassenaar.org/publicdocuments/2003_effectivelegislation. html> (accessed 25 April 2007).

[32] OSCE, 'OSCE Document on Small Arms and Light Weapons' (24 November 2000) FSC.DOC/1/00 ['OSCE Document']; EU, EU Code of Conduct on Arms Exports (8 June 1998) Council Doc 8675/2/98, Rev 2, 8.6.1998. See below nn 111–17 and accompanying text.

[33] Code of Conduct of Central American States on the Transfer of Arms, Ammunition, Explosives and Other Related Materiel (adopted and in force 2 December 2005), 'Working Paper Submitted by Nicaragua' (30 June 2006) UN Doc A/CONF.192/2006/RC/WP.6.

[34] See, eg, A Vines, 'Combating Light Weapons Proliferation in West Africa' (2005) 81 *International Affairs* 341; Small Arms Survey, *SAS 2003*, above n 8, at 237–46; E Kytömäki, 'Regional Approaches to Small Arms Control: Vital to Implementing the UN Programme of Action' (2005–06) 2005(4)/2006(1) *Disarmament Forum* 55, 58–60.

[35] ECOWAS, Declaration of a Moratorium on Importation, Exportation and Manufacture of Light Weapons in West Africa (31 October 1998) <http://www.iss.co.za/AF/ RegOrg/unity_to_union/pdfs/ecowas/1ECOWASFirearms.pdf> (accessed 25 April 2007); ECOWAS Convention on Small Arms and Light Weapons, Their Ammunition and Other Related Materials (adopted 14 June 2006) <http://www.iansa.org/regions/wafrica/ documents/CONVENTION-CEDEAO-ENGLISH.PDF> (accessed 25 April 2007).

[36] Nairobi Protocol for the Prevention, Control and Reduction of Small Arms and Light Weapons in the Great Lakes Region and the Horn of Africa (adopted 21 April 2004) <http://www.recsasec.org/pdf/Nairobi%20Protocol.pdf> (accessed 25 April 2007).

Southern African Development Community (SADC) Protocol[37] include provisions on civilian possession as well as illicit trafficking, marking and tracing, transfers, brokering, and the control and disposal of stockpiles.

Although progress has been made on the implementation of the UN Programme of Action and regional instruments, their practical impact in terms of reducing human deaths and injuries remains difficult to assess, and appears to be limited.[38] In addition, both states and civil society continue to be deeply divided on crucial parts of the SALW agenda.

SALW AND HUMAN SECURITY

The acquisition and use of military weapons are traditionally considered to be 'at the heart of state sovereignty'.[39] However, they have also been central to concerns about the impact of states' pursuit of security on the security of individuals. Much of the dissatisfaction with traditional notions of military and national security originated from concerns about arms control and disarmament, the potential for divergence between national and human security being particularly apparent in the context of the nuclear arms race.[40] Given the profound and widespread impact of SALW on the security of individuals, curbing the flow of small arms has been described as 'perhaps one of the clearest and most pressing human security concerns facing the international community today'.[41] Not only do SALW cause harm to many individuals, but the most vulnerable people tend to be disproportionately affected.[42] It is therefore not surprising that SALW have a prominent place on the human security agenda.[43] Furthermore, this is a

[37] Protocol on the Control of Firearms, Ammunition and Other Related Materials (adopted 2001, entered into force 2004) <http://www.sadc.int/english/documents/legal/protocols/firearms.php> (accessed 25 April 2007).
[38] See, eg, P McCarthy, 'Scratching the Surface of a Global Scourge: The First Five Years of the UN Programme of Action on Small Arms' (2005–06) 2005(4)/2006(1) *Disarmament Forum* 5, at 11–12; Kytömäki, above n 34, at 61; Vines, above n 34, at 344–6 (noting poor compliance with the ECOWAS Moratorium).
[39] S Brem and K Rutherford, 'Walking Together or Divided Agenda? Comparing Landmines and Small-Arms Campaigns' (2001) 32 *Security Dialogue* 169, at 171.
[40] See ch 1, n 13 and accompanying text.
[41] Hampson, above n 11, at 98.
[42] Poorer people are more likely to be killed or injured, and have worse outcomes when injured (WHO, 'Small Arms and Global Health', above n 2, at 5); the costs associated with small arms are particularly high among vulnerable populations in both industrialised and developing countries: W Cukier, A Chapdelaine and C Collins, 'Globalization and Small Firearms: A Public Health Perspective' (1999) 42(4) *Development* 40, at 40.
[43] See, eg, Human Security Network, 'Statement of the Human Security Network to the United Nations Conference on the Illicit Trade in Small Arms and Light Weapons in All its Aspects' (2001) <http://www.humansecuritynetwork.org/docs/SALW_Statement-e.php> (accessed 25 April 2007); Canada, DFAIT, *Freedom from Fear: Canada's Foreign Policy for Human Security* (Ottawa: DFAIT, 2000) <http://www.humansecurity.gc.ca/pdf/freedom_from_fear-en.pdf> (accessed 27 February 2007), at 9; Hampson, above n 11, at ch 6; Commission on

problem that fits within both 'broad' and 'narrow' versions of the human security concept or agenda, since it is directly relevant to violence and armed conflict, but also has a serious impact on people's livelihoods and their health.

One way in which the concept of human security has been invoked is simply to raise the profile of the problem and motivate efforts to address it. At the 2001 UN Conference, the impact of SALW on individuals' security was the concern most frequently cited by states (albeit closely followed by concerns about threats to stability and crime).[44] This in itself is significant, but it would be possible, having raised the issue of SALW, to deal with it in ways that would ignore or even undermine a human security approach.[45] Attempts to address the problem of SALW have been characterised by a diversity of approaches and, in some cases, bitter controversies. The 'SALW problem' actually encompasses several problems, including the global or regional accumulation of stockpiles and surplus weapons, proliferation and diffusion of weapons (that is, the spread of weapons among and within countries), and the misuse of SALW to commit criminal acts and violations of human rights and humanitarian law. Proposed solutions are therefore likely to be complex, and it can even be difficult to reach agreement about how best to define 'the problem' and the policy agenda. Because of this complexity, it has been suggested that: 'More so than any issue in disarmament before, small arms compel those who would control their destructiveness to answer fundamental questions about what exactly they hope to achieve.'[46] In this context, human security has been used, along with complementary approaches such as human rights and public health, to define the agenda and critique the evolving legal response.

Small Arms, Anti-personnel Mines, and Human Security

In order to better understand the debates on SALW and the role of human security in those debates, it is important to recall briefly the campaign leading up to the Ottawa Convention on anti-personnel mines.[47] As noted earlier, although they are a subcategory of SALW, mines have been the

Human Security, *Human Security Now: Protecting and Empowering People* (New York, Commission on Human Security, 2003) [CHS, *Human Security Now*].

[44] Small Arms Survey, *SAS 2003*, above n 8, at 228–9.

[45] For example, Krause notes that little of a draft Human Security Network document on the subject 'actually deals with *human security* issues': K Krause, 'Lucerne Presentation, Lysoen Network' (11 May 2000, Lucerne, Lysoen Network Second Ministerial Meeting) <http://humansecuritynetwork.org/docs/report_may2000_1-e.php> (accessed 13 March 2007) [Lucerne Presentation].

[46] A Karp, 'Negotiating Small Arms Restraint: The Boldest Frontier for Disarmament?' (2000) 2000(2) *Disarmament Forum* 5, at 5.

[47] Ottawa Convention, above n 21.

subject of special concern for many years. The effort to address the problem of SALW is commonly viewed as a successor to the mines campaign, and comparisons between the two are both inevitable and revealing.

The Ottawa Convention bans the use, stockpiling, production, and transfer of anti-personnel mines, and commits states to destroying mines in stockpiles or mined areas within their jurisdiction or control and to providing assistance for mine victims. The Convention was an early centrepiece of the human security agenda, particularly for the Canadian government.[48] Among the distinctive features of the 'Ottawa process' leading up to the Convention,[49] a human security approach was evident in a number of ways. First, the problem was defined by reference to the human impact of anti-personnel mines, in terms of civilian deaths and injuries and the effect on communities' livelihoods and prospects for development. The Ottawa process

> differed at a fundamental conceptual level from other international efforts to limit or ban landmines because it looked at the issue from a human security viewpoint rather than a disarmament viewpoint. It took as its starting point the effect of anti-personnel mines on the ground—a massive humanitarian crisis—rather than the disarmament aspects of the problem.[50]

The campaign's objectives followed from this definition of the problem: first, only a complete ban was viewed as an acceptable outcome,[51] and second, measures to prevent and mitigate the human impact of mines were required, including demining, mine awareness programmes, and obligations regarding the care, rehabilitation, and reintegration of mine victims.

The campaign to ban anti-personnel mines and the resulting Convention were seen by many as a concrete example of 'human security in practice', an example of humanitarian concerns prevailing over military and national security interests.[52] Some optimistically suggested that the

[48] CJ Ungerer, 'Approaching Human Security as "Middle Powers": Australian and Canadian Disarmament Diplomacy after the Cold War' in WT Tow, R Thakur and I Hyun (eds), *Asia's Emerging Regional Order: Reconciling Traditional and Human Security* (Tokyo, United Nations University Press, 2000), at 79, 89–90.

[49] The most important of these are the integral role played by NGOs and the decision to develop the Ottawa Convention outside the UN and traditional consensus-based multilateral negotiations.

[50] L Axworthy, 'Towards a New Multilateralism' in MA Cameron, RJ Lawson and BW Tomlin (eds), *To Walk Without Fear: The Global Movement to Ban Landmines* (Toronto, Oxford University Press, 1998), at 451. See also M Gwozdecky and J Sinclair, 'Case Study: Landmines and Human Security' in R McRae and D Hubert (eds), *Human Security and the New Diplomacy: Protecting People, Promoting Peace* (Montreal and Kingston, McGill-Queen's University Press, 2001), at 28; L Axworthy and S Taylor, 'A Ban for All Seasons: The Landmines Convention and Its Implications for Canadian Diplomacy' (1998) 53 *International Journal* 189, at 191.

[51] Axworthy, above n 50, at 451; Mathews and McCormack, above n 18, at 351.

[52] JM Beier and AD Crosby, 'Harnessing Change for Continuity: The Play of Political and Economic Forces Behind the Ottawa Process' in MA Cameron, RJ Lawson and BW Tomlin

successful completion of the Convention might provide a precedent and signal 'the emergence of a new approach within international law'.[53] In particular, it was hoped that 'similar tools' could be applied next to the broader problem of SALW.[54] During the 1997 signing conference for the Ottawa Convention, the first attempts were made to coordinate action by non-governmental organisations (NGOs) on small arms.[55]

Efforts to deal with SALW do follow on from the Ottawa process in some respects. As in the case of mines, the human security approach here emphasises the importance of the human impact of weapons and its role in defining the problem. Human security is also used to measure the value of proposed or attempted measures: the ultimate end is ensuring the safety of people.[56] A human security approach is said to be distinguished from an arms control approach by its focus on the extent to which measures directly contribute to people's safety.[57] It emphasises the need to pay particular attention to the ways in which people are affected by SALW and by measures to control them.[58] These are some ways in which the human security concept has been used in relation to SALW, and they have much in common with the human security approach to mines as developed during the Ottawa process. The greater complexity of the SALW issue is, however, revealed in the definition of objectives.

In the case of anti-personnel mines, it was argued that any utility of such weapons from the point of view of state security was outweighed by the threat they posed to human security, and so the appropriate objective was a complete ban. There is virtually universal agreement that this objective is unsuitable for the larger category of SALW. The important differences between the two issues have been well summarised by Egeland:

> We are not talking [in the case of SALW] about arms which are prohibited, but about ordinary weapons which everyone agrees are needed by the public

---

(eds), *To Walk Without Fear: The Global Movement to Ban Landmines* (Toronto, Oxford University Press, 1998), at 272, 276. See also Axworthy, above n 50, at 448; CHS, *Human Security Now*, above n 43, at 30; Mathews and McCormack, above n 18, at 346–7; Karp, above n 46, at 9; Gwozdecky and Sinclair, above n 50 at 30, 34–5, 39.

[53] Axworthy and Taylor, above n 55, at 200.

[54] *Ibid*, at 201. See also Hampson, above n 11, at 98.

[55] Brem and Rutherford, above n 39, at 177.

[56] Centre for Humanitarian Dialogue, *Putting People First: Human Security Perspectives on Small Arms Availability and Misuse* (Geneva, Centre for Humanitarian Dialogue, 2003) <http://www.hdcentre.org/datastore/PPFeng.pdf> (29 March 2007), at 3, 45; D Hubert, 'Small Arms Demand Reduction and Human Security: Towards a People-Centred Approach to Small Arms' (Ploughshares Briefing 01/5, 2001) <http://www.ploughshares.ca/libraries/Briefings/brf015.html> (accessed 13 March 2007) ['Demand Reduction']; Krause, Lucerne Presentation, above n 45.

[57] See, eg, Krause, Lucerne Presentation, above n 45.

[58] J Loten, 'Case Study: The Challenge of Microdisarmament' in R McRae and D Hubert (eds), *Human Security and the New Diplomacy: Protecting People, Promoting Peace* (McGill-Queen's University Press, Montreal and Kingston, 2001); Hubert, 'Demand Reduction', above n 56.

authorities to defend themselves and maintain order. It is thus not a question of mobilizing against an indiscriminate, particularly cruel weapon of limited military value, as was the case with anti-personnel landmines. We are getting into a much more sensitive area when it comes to the issue of small arms because of the way it relates to State security and national sovereignty. Nor are the economic stakes inconsiderable.[59]

The mines campaign had been able to focus on the nature of the weapon involved, which was already considered to be illegal under international humanitarian law and had been the subject of a restrictive protocol, and characterise it as a threat rather than a legitimate tool for security. In effect, this allowed the campaigners to portray the weapons themselves as the problem and avoid larger questions about states' responsibilities and their pursuit of security.[60] To the extent that this is true, it could lead us to question whether the Ottawa Convention really represents a substantial shift in international law or in understandings of security.[61] Furthermore, even agreeing to give priority to human security has not resolved contro- versies about the Convention, because some critics have argued that the campaign diverted energy and resources away from ongoing demining work that provides more immediate benefits to individuals at risk.[62] The practical impact of the Convention is also difficult to predict, given that some key states withdrew from the process and are unlikely to become parties.

All of these points suggest that we should be cautious about the value of the Ottawa Convention as a precedent for the campaign against SALW, which is even more complex and challenging. In this context, it is much more difficult to avoid engaging broader and more contentious questions about states' practices and responsibilities. The weapons themselves—a larger and more diverse category than anti-personnel mines—cannot be dismissed as illegitimate, so we are required to ask what actions in relation to the weapons are illegitimate. To put this into human security terms, in the case of mines it was essentially argued that the use of these weapons, regardless of any advantage it might provide from the point of view of

[59] J Egeland, 'Arms Availability and Violations of International Humanitarian Law' (1999) 81 *IRRC* 673, at 677. Regarding the economic stakes, it has been remarked that the absence of any significant resistance to the anti-personnel mines ban on the part of the defence production industry can likely be attributed to the fact that it did not 'seriously compromise their economic interests'; in fact, the industry stands to profit more from demining than it did from production of mines (Beier and Crosby, above n 52, at 280–81).

[60] See, eg, Beier and Crosby, above n 52, at 276–7. Regarding the recharacterisation of mines during the campaign, see M de Larrinaga and C Turenne Sjolander, '(Re)presenting Landmines from Protector to Enemy: The Discursive Framing of a New Multilateralism' in MA Cameron, RJ Lawson and BW Tomlin (eds), *To Walk Without Fear: The Global Movement to Ban Landmines* (Toronto, Oxford University Press, 1998).

[61] Beier and Crosby, above n 52, at 269, 285.

[62] See, eg, MJ Flynn, 'Political Minefield' in RA Matthew, B McDonald and KR Rutherford (eds), *Landmines and Human Security: International Politics and War's Hidden Legacy* (Albany, State University of New York Press, 2004).

national security, is never justified because of the threat it poses to human security. In the case of SALW, however, the use and proliferation of the weapons often threatens human security, but these same weapons can also be used in ways that do not threaten human security and can even help the state to fulfil its role as protector of its people's security. Exploring the limits of legitimate acquisition and use is therefore unavoidable in this context. Furthermore, SALW are integral to states' military and police powers and economic interests to a much greater degree than anti-personnel mines. As a result, we can expect greater resistance to scrutiny of state security practices and to the argument that human security should prevail over competing interests. Because the problem is multi-faceted, even adopting a human security approach will leave open many difficult questions about priorities and strategies. In addition, as we will see in the next section, analysing the issues in terms of the tensions between national security and human security is also more complex.

Defining the Small Arms Agenda: Human Security or National Security?

Multilateral efforts to address the SALW problem have focused on illicit transfers of weapons. From the outset, views on the proper scope of the UN Conference on small arms were mixed.[63] Agreement was reached at an early stage on a limited range of measures strictly related to illicit trade.[64] Resistance from certain states kept the agenda narrow and precluded consensus on several key issues, notably controls over civilian possession, transfers to non-state groups and limits on state-to-state or 'legal' transfers.[65] The resulting Programme of Action therefore does not directly address these issues. At the 2006 Review Conference, similar differences prevented states from even agreeing on an outcome document to guide future implementation and review of the Programme of Action.

There is widespread consensus that illicit trade in SALW is a serious problem which requires attention. In the face of the complex issues

---

[63] UNGA, 'Convening of an International Conference on the Illicit Arms Trade in All Its Aspects: Report of the Secretary General' (20 August 1999) UN Doc A/54/260. Compare UN, Panel Report, above n 12, at para 80(k) (recommending that the UN convene a conference focusing on illicit trade); UN, Group Report, above n 13, at para 126 (recommending a broad agenda).

[64] Small Arms Survey, *Small Arms Survey 2002: Counting the Human Cost* (Oxford, Oxford University Press, 2002) [*SAS 2002*], at 207.

[65] UN, 'Report of the Conference on the Illicit Trade in Small Arms and Light Weapons in All Its Aspects' (2001) UN Doc A/CONF.192/15, Annex; Small Arms Survey, *SAS 2002*, above n 64, at 203, 219–20, 220*ff*; SD Murphy (ed), 'Contemporary Practice of the United States Relating to International Law' (2001) 95 *AJIL* 873, at 901–3; K Krause, 'Multilateral Diplomacy, Norm Building, and UN Conferences: The Case of Small Arms and Light Weapons' (2002) 8 *Global Governance* 247.

relating to SALW, the need to curtail illicit trade is one question on which interested parties (including a broad range of both states and NGOs) can agree.[66] It is believed that illicit arms may be disproportionately implicated in armed conflict and crime,[67] so addressing illicit transfers is an important part of reducing the human cost of SALW. Curbing illicit trade would also protect states' monopoly on military power, helping to keep SALW out of the hands of illegitimate users who might threaten national security, like armed insurgents or terrorists.

However, the fact that illicit trade has dominated the international agenda has provoked considerable controversy. It seems likely that efforts within the UN have focused on illicit trade not entirely because of its relative importance but because this issue is perceived as least challenging to states' interests and therefore most likely to elicit some agreement.[68] Even by generous estimates, illicit transfers account for only about half of global trade in SALW,[69] and it is widely recognised that legal transfers 'can contribute to destabilizing small arms accumulations, as well as feeding into illegal markets'.[70] Furthermore, it is clear that legally acquired arms may be used to abuse human rights or otherwise threaten human security.[71] Consequently, while virtually everyone agrees that addressing illicit trade is a valid goal, a decision to focus on illicit transfers while marginalising other issues is an ongoing point of contention. Some observers criticised the UN Conference and Programme of Action on the basis that the debate was framed in 'traditional security and disarmament terms', while failing to address the humanitarian dimension that some saw as 'the core of the problem'.[72] Whereas the Ottawa process largely succeeded in reframing anti-personnel mines as an issue of human rather than state or military security, the UN Conference saw an issue that had gained attention because of its human impact being channelled back into a traditional security and arms control effort. Although the Programme of Action recognised the humanitarian impact of the illicit trade in SALW,[73]

[66] Karp, above n 46, at 7–8, 11; Greene, above n 13, at 151.

[67] L Lumpe, S Meek and RT Naylor, 'Introduction to Gun-Running' in L Lumpe (ed.), *Running Guns: The Global Black Market in Small Arms* (London, Zed Books, 2000), at 2. The same authors acknowledge that due to the level of secrecy regarding both licit and illicit arms transfers, it is impossible to determine what percentage of transfers are licit or illicit and which contribute most to conflict and repression (*ibid*).

[68] See, eg, Karp, above n 46, at 8.

[69] UN DDA, 'Disarmament Issues' (no date) <http://disarmament.un.org/issue.htm> (13 March 2007) (estimating 40%–60%). Other estimates are much lower: see Small Arms Survey, *SAS 2001*, above n 1, at 141, 145 (estimating 10%–20%).

[70] Small Arms Survey, *SAS 2001*, above n 1, at 141.

[71] See, eg, Amnesty International and Human Rights Watch, 'Address to the United Nations Conference on the Illicit Trade in Small Arms and Light Weapons in All Its Aspects' (New York, 16 July 2001) <http://disarmament.un.org/cab/smallarms/statements/Ngo/aisl.html> (accessed 13 March 2007).

[72] Wyatt, above n 6, at 223.

[73] UN, Programme of Action, above n 6, at paras I.2, I.4, I.5.

the Conference was described as essentially 'an arms control and disarm-ament undertaking'.[74] According to some critics, the Conference showed that 'most States are not prepared to put human security before national security'.[75]

A more comprehensive agenda aiming to effectively combat illicit trade and directly address its human impact would include: more stringent and systematic efforts on issues associated with illicit trade, like marking and tracing or regulation of arms brokering; limits on transfers of SALW, especially taking into account human rights concerns; regulation of civilian possession of SALW; integration of SALW measures into development cooperation; support for survivors of SALW violence; and demand reduction.[76] Most of these matters are at least mentioned in the Programme of Action, but advocates have been pushing for better imple-mentation and elaboration of commitments in these areas. Besides being non-binding, the Programme of Action contains very general provisions that leave much room for differences in interpretation. Attempts to flesh these out were, however, met with resistance at the Review Conference. Several states referred to the Programme of Action as a 'delicate balance' between state security concerns and humanitarian concerns, and argued that this balance should not be disturbed by further elaboration of its provisions or extension of the agenda.[77] To some degree, the differing

[74] UN DDA, 'About the Conference' (2001) <http://disarmament.un.org/cab/smallarms/about.htm> (accessed 13 March 2007).

[75] UN Sub-Commission on the Promotion and Protection of Human Rights, 'The Question of the Trade, Carrying and Use of Small Arms and Light Weapons in the Context of Human Rights and Humanitarian Norms' (30 May 2002) UN Doc E/CN.4/Sub.2/2002/39, at para 25, quoting Human Rights Watch. See also V Yankey-Wayne, 'The Human Dimension of the United Nations Programme of Action on Small Arms: The Key Role of Africa' (2005–06) 2005(4)/2006(1) *Disarmament Forum* 83, at 83 (critics of the Programme of Action concluded that it did not address human security concerns).

[76] See, eg, Permanent Mission of Canada to the United Nations, 'Statement by Ambassador Gilbert Laurin, Deputy Permanent Representative of Canada to the United Nations, to the Opening of the UN Conference to Review Progress Made in the Implementation of the Programme of Action to Prevent, Combat and Eradicate the Illicit Trade in Small Arms and Light Weapons in all its Aspects' (26 June 2006) <http://www.un.org/events/smallarms2006/pdf/arms060626can-eng.pdf> (13 March 2007); R Peters, 'RevCon IANSA presentations: Vision for 2012' (30 June 2006) <http://www.un.org/events/smallarms2006/pdf/arms060630iansa-rebecca.pdf> (accessed 13 March 2007).

[77] See, eg, Pakistan, Permanent Mission to the United Nations, 'Statement by Brigadier Javed Iqbal Cheema, Director General, Ministry of the Interior at the UN Conference to Review Progress Made in the Implementation of the Programme of Action to Prevent, Combat and Eradicate the Illicit Trade in Small Arms and Light Weapons in all its Aspects' (28 June 2006) <http://www.un.org/events/smallarms2006/pdf/arms060628pakist-eng.pdf> (accessed 25 April 2007), at 4; Permanent Mission of India to the United Nations, 'Statement by Mr. Hamid Ali Rao, Joint Secretary (Disarmament and International Security Affairs) Ministry of External Affairs at the United Nations Conference to Review Progress Made in the Implementation of the Programme of Action to Prevent, Combat and Eradicate the Illicit Trade in Small Arms and Light Weapons in all its Aspects' (26 June 2006) <http://www.un.org/events/smallarms2006/pdf/arms060627Ind-eng.pdf> (accessed 13 March 2007), at para 16.

positions reflect human security concerns opposed to traditional national security perspectives. However, the full picture is somewhat more complex, if we examine the reasons for opposition to specific proposals and try to analyse them in terms of competing conceptions of security.

Some initiatives could be seen as contributing to both national and human security. Elaboration and implementation of more detailed measures on stockpile security, brokering, or 'technical' matters like marking and tracing can make an important, albeit indirect, contribution to addressing the human impact as well as states' security concerns.[78] If states are concerned with controlling the illicit trade and keeping weapons out of the hands of those who might threaten their security, one would expect this to translate into support for a range of comprehensive and effective measures. Progress is being made on these issues but it has been more difficult than expected to reach agreement; for example, negotiations on marking and tracing proved to be quite contentious and in the end produced only a non-binding instrument.[79] The reasons for resistance to more detailed measures are not always easy to discern, but there appear to be at least two broad motivations. In one view, even if these measures might be needed to effectively address directly and indirectly illicit trade, some states are not prepared to invest the effort and resources required because they do not see SALW as a major security priority. At the Review Conference comments were made to the effect that other types of weapons are of greater concern because they are a greater threat to security.[80] This appears to be a hangover from earlier conceptions of national and international security that kept SALW off the disarmament agenda altogether. It would seem, then, that attempts to shift the agenda to give priority to human security concerns have been only partly successful.

Some resistance can also be attributed to the fact that most of the proposed measures would encompass in their scope some impact on 'licit' SALW. From a practical point of view, it is widely accepted that curbing illicit trade will be impossible without a range of measures directed at weapons that are (at least initially) legally produced, owned, and transferred, given the linkages between licit and illicit trade.[81] The

---

[78] On the relevance of 'technical' provisions to the 'human dimension', see Yankey-Wayne, above n 75, at 87.

[79] See above n 29. On the negotiations, see P Batchelor and G McDonald, 'Too Close for Comfort: An Analysis of the UN Tracing Negotiations' (2005–06) 2005(4)/2006(1) *Disarmament Forum* 39.

[80] Islamic Republic of Iran, Permanent Mission to the United Nations, 'Statement by H.E. Mr. Manouchehr Mottaki, Foreign Minister of the Islamic Republic of Iran, Before the UN Conference to Review Progress made in the Implementation of the Programme of Action to Prevent, Combat and Eradicate the Illicit Trade in Small Arms and Light Weapons' (28 June 2006) <http://www.un.org/events/smallarms2006/pdf/arms060628iraneng.pdf> (accessed 3 August 2006).

[81] See, eg, Greene, above n 13, at 152; W Cukier and S Shropshire, 'Domestic Gun Markets: The Licit–Illicit Links' in L Lumpe (ed), *Running Guns: The Global Black Market in Small Arms*

distinction between licit and illicit trade is to a large extent impractical and even artificial, since weapons—SALW in particular, given that they are inexpensive, portable, and easy to conceal—often move from legal to illicit possession. However, controls on legal trade in SALW have been controversial in several respects.

The most contentious points have been regulating civilian possession and transfers to non-state actors, and restrictions on transfers that are 'legal' in the sense that they have official authorisation but that are likely to be used in ways that violate people's rights and security. The need to impose some controls on the acquisition of arms by civilian individuals and non-state groups is widely accepted as part of efforts to address the misuse of SALW. The annual death toll from civilian firearms is thought to equal or exceed the number of conflict deaths from small arms.[82] Although many of the firearms held by civilians are used legally and responsibly, others are implicated in murders, drug trafficking, terrorist acts, and even genocide. Measures to deal with this problem range from prohibiting civilian possession of certain types of weapons to licensing and registration schemes aimed at preventing possession of arms by individuals who are likely to misuse them, such as those with a history of violent crime.[83] Increased concern about terrorist attacks has led to growing support for restrictions on the acquisition of weapons by non-state actors. These include restrictions on transfers of certain types of light weapons.[84] Even some states that otherwise resisted expansion of the Programme of Action agenda at the Review Conference supported the development of these types of restrictions, especially those directed at keeping light weapons out of the hands of terrorist groups.[85]

Given that concerns about terrorist attacks figure prominently in arguments for these restrictions, one might expect them to be supported by the United States. In fact, the United States has strongly and consistently opposed restrictions on civilian and non-state possession of SALW, as well as measures that might indirectly interfere with these. This apparently contradictory position reflects the influence of a strong 'pro-gun' lobby in the United States. The official US position has opposed 'any

---

(London, Zed Books, 2000); V Gamba, 'Problems and Linkages in Controlling the Proliferation of Light Weapons' in J Dhanapala *et al* (eds), *Small Arms Control: Old Weapons, New Issues* (Aldershot, Ashgate, 1999).

[82] Centre for Humanitarian Dialogue, above n 56, at 22; Small Arms Survey, *SAS 2004*, above n 1, at 174–5.

[83] See, eg, Centre for Humanitarian Dialogue, above n 56, at 23–4.

[84] See, eg, Small Arms Survey, *SAS 2005*, above n 1, at 127-29.

[85] See, eg, Israel, 'Statement by Ambassador Miriam Ziv, Deputy Director General for Strategic Affairs, Ministry of Foreign Affairs, Jerusalem, UN Conference to Review Progress made in the Implementation of the Programme of Action to Prevent, Combat and Eradicate the Illicit Trade in Small Arms and Light Weapons' (27 June 2006) <http://www.un.org/events/smallarms2006/pdf/arms060627israel-eng.pdf> (accessed 25 April 2007); Permanent Mission of India to the United Nations, above n 77.

provisions restricting civilian possession, use or legal trade of firearms inconsistent with [American] laws and practices',[86] including a constitutionally protected right to keep and bear arms. The US position was therefore framed as a matter of defending the rights and national institutions of the country and its citizens.[87] The United States also opposed a ban on transfers of SALW to non-state actors, on the basis that it could interfere with 'the rights of the oppressed to defend themselves against tyrannical and genocidal regimes'.[88] The US statement qualifies its position by saying that it will 'of course continue to oppose the acquisition of arms by terrorist groups', without acknowledging the tension between these aims. The US position is open to criticism on a number of grounds, but it is difficult to make sense of this in terms of an opposition between national and human security approaches. Rather, what seems to be at issue is the promotion of a particular ideological position, and a competing vision in which the protection of national institutions (such as the US Constitution) is the overriding duty of the government[89]—even, apparently, at the expense of security.

The other dimension of limits on legal trade in SALW involves restricting SALW transfers on the basis of their potential misuse. Such restrictions are opposed by a larger group of states, and it is here that we see perhaps the most direct conflict between national security and human security or human rights approaches. Traditional realist conceptualisations of security emphasise the protection of the state from external attack and assume that the state, if its integrity is assured, will protect its inhabitants. The UN Programme of Action largely casts states in this protective role, with the majority of its measures designed to ensure states' control over the SALW trade. From this point of view, the state's primary interest is to maximise its own military power while limiting others' access to weapons. Any restrictions on a state's own ability to acquire weapons are therefore considered to threaten the state's capacity to defend itself as well as its autonomy. These concerns are reflected in official positions on SALW that emphasise the right to self-defence and the principles of sovereignty and non-intervention.[90] States may also seek to protect their

---

[86] United States, 'Statement by Robert G. Joseph, Undersecretary of State for Arms Control and International Security, at the United Nations Conference to Review Progress made in the Implementation of the Programme of Action to Prevent, Combat and Eradicate the Illicit Trade in Small Arms and Light Weapons in All Its Aspects' USUN Press Release #137(06) (27 June 2006) <http://www.un.org/events/smallarms2006/pdf/arms060627usa-eng.pdf> (accessed 25 April 2007).

[87] *Ibid*, at 2.

[88] *Ibid*, at 2.

[89] *Ibid*, at 1.

[90] See, eg, Permanent Mission of the Republic of Cuba to the United Nations, 'Statement by the Head of the Delegation of Cuba, H.E. Manuel Aguilera de la Paz, Deputy Minister of Foreign Affairs' (3 July 2006) <http://www.un.org/events/smallarms2006/pdf/arms060703cuba-eng.pdf> (accessed 13 March 2007); Small Arms Survey, *SAS 2002*, above n 64, at 221–5.

ability to transfer weapons without restriction to their allies for strategic reasons. For states that are significant producers of SALW, the fact that the industry increasingly relies on exports for its viability provides another motivation,[91] since military industries have both economic and strategic value.

Maintaining free access to arms carries the risk that potential enemies of the state can acquire them more easily as well, so a state's position ultimately depends on how it weighs the risks and benefits for its security. The unrestricted possession and transfer of SALW cannot be assumed to be unproblematic from the point of view of either state security or human security. The crucial difference between these approaches, though, is that human security also draws attention to the possibility of abuse or lack of protection on the part of the state, something that traditional conceptual-isations of state security would not address. Therefore, the discussion must be broadened to deal with this possibility if our ultimate concern is with the security of individuals. Human rights approaches to SALW have pointed in a similar direction by emphasising the potential for SALW to be used in violation of people's rights and urging that transfers be restricted where this risk is known to exist.[92] From this perspective, it is profoundly problematic to focus only on controlling illicit trade while assuming that states are legitimate users of SALW whose acquisition and transfer of these weapons are always benign.

Restricting SALW transfers on the basis of potential misuse by their recipients is doubly challenging to traditional approaches to security, because it implies that exporting and transit states should invest energy and resources into preventing harm to individuals in foreign countries. It therefore brings into play the dimension of common responsibility for human security. The next section will examine this dimension in the context of recently proposed common principles to govern SALW transfers.

Common Responsibility and Small Arms Transfers

The idea of human security as a matter of common concern encourages states to take responsibility for the effects of their actions on the security of individuals in other states as well as their own. The role of small arms supplies in facilitating humanitarian catastrophes like the Rwandan genocide was noted earlier as a tragic example of such effects.[93] The report

---

[91] Small Arms Survey, *SAS 2004*, above n 1, at 118–25.

[92] See, eg, Amnesty International and Human Rights Watch, above n 71; Wyatt, above n 6; L Eskeland and P Herby, 'United Nations Conference on the Illicit Trade in Small Arms and Light Weapons in All Its Aspects' (2001) 843 *IRRC* 864, at 865.

[93] See ch 4, n 78 and accompanying text.

of the International Commission on Intervention and State Sovereignty suggested that developed countries are 'deeply implicated' in civil conflicts occurring in distant regions, because of their role in supplying the arms that fuel these conflicts.[94] In earlier chapters, it was argued that effectively ensuring human security would require a broad understanding of shared responsibilities, beyond humanitarian intervention or assistance in times of crisis. An important dimension of these responsibilities involves exercising control over arms transfers that are likely to threaten human security. The area of SALW is one in which obligations to avert harm in other jurisdictions have figured prominently in legal debates.[95]

This issue is connected with debates over the scope of the SALW agenda, because the validity of focusing on illicit transfers depends partly on how this category is defined.[96] Some objections to the narrow scope of the UN Conference and Programme of Action argued that it marginalised consideration of states' responsibilities to prevent abuse of SALW, even where these reflect existing obligations under international law.[97] When these obligations are ignored, some transfers are commonly assumed to be legal, and therefore outside the scope of efforts to control illicit transfers, when they may in fact breach states' international legal obligations. In particular, some observers and commentators have sought to raise awareness of obligations under international human rights and humanitarian law that are relevant to transfers of SALW.[98] The UN Programme of Action urges states to apply regulations for export authorisations that 'are consistent with the existing responsibilities of States under relevant international law'.[99] However, discussion within the UN process has

[94] International Commission on Intervention and State Sovereignty, *Responsibility to Protect: Report of the International Commission on Intervention and State Sovereignty* (Ottawa, International Development Research Centre, 2001) <http://www.dfait-maeci.gc.ca/iciss-ciise/pdf/Commission-Report.pdf> (accessed 13 March 2007), at 5.

[95] See, eg, ICRC, 'Arms Transfers, Humanitarian Assistance and International Humanitarian Law' (19 February 1998) <http://www.icrc.org> (accessed 13 March 2007) ['Arms Transfers']; Gamba, above n 81, at 41; Wyatt, above n 6; Human Rights Watch, 'Press Statement: UN Conference on Small Arms Trafficking' (9 July 2001) <http://www.hrw.org/campaigns/mines/2001/arms-press-0710.htm> (accessed 25 April 2007). This discussion will focus on arms supplies by states; the issue of the responsibility of non-state actors such as manufacturers or brokers raises distinct legal questions which will not be dealt with here.

[96] Cf Karp, above n 46, at 7.

[97] See, eg, Human Rights Watch, above n 95; Wyatt, above n 6, at 223; Amnesty International and Human Rights Watch, above n 71.

[98] See, eg, Amnesty International and Human Rights Watch, above n 71; Herby, above n 6; E Gillard, 'What's Legal? What's Illegal?' in L Lumpe (ed), *Running Guns: The Global Black Market in Small Arms* (Zed Books, London, 2000) ['What's Legal']; Wyatt, above n 6; UN Sub-Commission on the Promotion and Protection of Human Rights, above n 95; ICRC, *Arms Availability*, above n 6; ICRC, Conference Statement, above n 7; ICRC, 'Arms Transfers', above n 95.

[99] UN, Programme of Action, above n 6, at para II.11. Export regulations are also to take into account 'in particular the risk of diversion of these weapons into the illegal trade' (*ibid*). International law obligations are also at issue in para II.15, which concerns taking measures against activity violating a Security Council arms embargo.

largely tended to sidestep the question of what transfers are or should be illegal under international law. Attempts to focus attention on this issue were resisted at both the 2001 Conference and the 2006 Review Conference.[100] For states that rely on imports of arms, the prospect of limiting supplies is perceived as a threat to their national security, as we saw above. For suppliers, limits on transfers could undermine their economic and strategic interests. It would also represent an expansion of their security responsibilities, requiring them to invest in efforts to prevent threats to individuals beyond their borders.

It is generally accepted that states have the right to acquire and transfer arms as required for self-defence and security, which is derived from the right of individual and collective self-defence as recognised in article 51 of the UN Charter, and from the principles of sovereign equality and non-intervention.[101] However, this right is not absolute or unlimited. Transfers of any weapons, including SALW, are prohibited where a relevant UN or regional embargo is in place.[102] In some circumstances, a state providing arms to a non-state group in another state without the latter state's consent will violate the customary international law principle of non-intervention in another's domestic affairs.[103] Other restrictions are based on the use to which SALW are put by their recipients, and it is here that we must directly confront questions about the scope of responsibility that supplier states might bear for the effects that the weapons may have on human security in another jurisdiction.

Specific treaty provisions may impose direct obligations on one state to prevent the unlawful infliction of harm on individuals in another state. The obligation to prevent genocide under article 1 of the Genocide Convention, at least in some circumstances, could imply a duty to refrain from or prevent the provision of arms to individuals or groups engaging

---

[100] For example, at the 2001 Conference China opposed even the mention of human rights violations anywhere in the Programme of Action (Small Arms Survey, *SAS 2002*, above n 64, at 221). Regarding the Review Conference, see, eg, Permanent Mission of India to the United Nations, above n 77, paras 10, 16; Permanent Mission of the Russian Federation to the United Nations, 'Statement by Mr Petr G Litavrin, Deputy Head of the Delegation of the Russian Federation at the Conference to Review Progress Made in the Implementation of the Programme of Action to Prevent, Combat and Eradicate the Illicit Trade in Small Arms and Light Weapons (SALW) in All its Aspects' (27 June 2006) <http://www.un.org/events/smallarms2006/pdf/arms060627rus-eng.pdf> (accessed 13 March 2007), at 3–4.

[101] See, eg, EU, above n 32, preamble; UN, Programme of Action, above n 6, at paras I.9–I.10; UNSC, 'Statement by the President of the Security Council' (4 September 2001) UN Doc S/PRST/2001/21.

[102] See, eg, UN, Programme of Action, above n 6, at para II.15. When an embargo is in place, states are required to refrain from transferring arms to the relevant state and to take measures to ensure that private actors within their jurisdiction do likewise.

[103] *Military and Paramilitary Activities in and against Nicaragua (Nicaragua v United States of America), Merits* [1986] ICJ Rep 14, at paras 241–2, 292(3). See also UNGA, 'Declaration on Principles of International Law Concerning Friendly Relations and Co-operation Among States in Accordance with the Charter of the United Nations', UNGA Res 2625 (XXV) (24 October 1970) UN Doc A/8028.

in, or likely to engage in, genocide.[104] It is also possible that the provision of arms could amount to complicity in genocide, although only where the arms supplier had the requisite intent.[105] Similar duties in respect of terrorist acts have been set out more explicitly, for example in the 2001 Security Council resolution on international cooperation against terrorism, which requires states to: 'Refrain from providing any form of support, active or passive, to entities or persons involved in terrorist acts, including by . . . eliminating the supply of weapons to terrorists.'[106] It is argued by the International Committee of the Red Cross (ICRC) and others that the undertaking to ensure respect for humanitarian law in common article 1 of the Geneva Conventions would preclude 'the knowing provision of arms into situations where serious violations of international humanitarian law occur or are likely to occur'.[107]

As we saw in chapter three, the existing human rights obligations of states are generally limited in the sense that they are owed only to individuals within their jurisdiction, which is usually interpreted to include their nationals, individuals within their territory, and those outside their territory who are subject to their jurisdiction or effective control. This means that a supplier state would not be *directly* responsible for violations of, for example, the right to life, which occur outside its jurisdiction using weapons that it was involved in supplying. However, the supplier may still bear some *derivative* responsibility. Where SALW are used in violations of human rights, humanitarian law, or other international norms, the individuals or states committing these violations bear the primary

---

[104] Convention on the Prevention and Punishment of Genocide (opened for signature 9 December 1948, entered into force 12 January 1951) 78 UNTS 277. See *Application of the Convention on the Prevention and Punishment of the Crime of Genocide (Bosnia and Herzegovina v Serbia and Montenegro)*, Judgment of 26 February 2007 [*Genocide Convention*], at paras 430–32, and the discussion in ch 3, nn 157–60 and accompanying text, and ch 4, nn 66–7 and accompanying text. In that case, the ICJ noted the financial and military links between the Federal Republic of Yugoslavia (FRY) and the Bosnian Serbs responsible for the genocidal acts at Srebrenica as establishing a degree of influence on the part of the FRY that required it to use its best efforts to prevent the genocide (at paras 434, 438).

[105] Convention on the Prevention and Punishment of Genocide, above n 104, art 4. See E Gillard, 'What is Legal? What is Illegal? Limitations on Transfers of Small Arms under International Law' <http://www.armstradetreaty.com/att/what.is.legal.what.is.illegal.pdf> (accessed 29 March 2007) ['Limitations on Transfers'], at para 37. Note, however, that the recent decision of the ICJ on this point suggests that it would be sufficient for the accomplice to 'have given support in perpetrating the genocide with full knowledge of the facts': *Genocide Convention*, above n 104, at para 432.

[106] UNSC Res 1373 (28 September 2001) UN Doc S/RES/1373, at para 2(a).

[107] ICRC, *Arms Availability*, above n 6, at pt 5.A. See also ICRC, 'Arms Transfers', above n 95; ICRC, Conference Statement, above n 7; Gillard, 'Limitations on Transfers', above n 105, at para 32; Wyatt, above n 6, at 225. The ICJ in the *Nicaragua* case, above n 103, at paras 220, 292(9), found that the United States had breached its obligation to ensure respect for the principles of humanitarian law by providing the Contras with a manual on psychological operations which encouraged acts contrary to humanitarian principles. The same reasoning could apply in some cases to the provision of weapons. For discussion of the scope of obligations under art 1, see the sources cited in ch 3, n 150.

responsibility for the breach, but another state may be held responsible for aiding or assisting in the commission of this internationally wrongful act.[108] This derivative or secondary responsibility could ground a duty not to transfer SALW where the supplier is aware that they are likely to be used in violation of international law.[109] In addition, the International Law Commission's Draft Articles on State Responsibility suggest that states may have broader responsibilities in the case of a serious breach of a peremptory norm, including the duty to cooperate to bring the breach to an end as well as not to 'render aid or assistance in maintaining [a] situation' created by such a breach, which in some cases could include not providing arms.[110]

Existing and proposed guidelines have sought to translate some of the legal obligations reviewed here into criteria for approving exports. These include the EU Code of Conduct,[111] the OSCE Document on Small Arms and Light Weapons,[112] and more recently, the Code of Conduct adopted by Central American countries, which applies to SALW as well as other arms, ammunition, and explosives.[113] A set of common guidelines for national transfers of SALW produced by a group of states and civil society organisations was presented to the UN Review Conference,[114] and will provide the basis for further discussions.[115] Work has also been progressing on a broader arms trade treaty which would include SALW

[108] This principle is codified in International Law Commission, 'Draft Articles on State Responsibility', UNGA Res 56/83 (28 January 2002) UN Doc A/RES/56/83, Annex, art 16. Issues of individual criminal responsibility may also arise in this context. See, eg, Rome Statute of the International Criminal Court (opened for signature 17 July 1998, entered into force 1 July 2002) 2187 UNTS 3, art 25(3): 'a person shall be criminally responsible and liable for punishment for a crime within the jurisdiction of the Court if that person: . . . (c) For the purpose of facilitating the commission of such a crime, aids, abets or otherwise assists in its commission or its attempted commission, *including providing the means for its commission'* (emphasis added). A full discussion of individual responsibility, as well as of corporate liability, is beyond the scope of this chapter.

[109] See, eg, Gillard, 'What's Legal?', above n 98; Small Arms Survey, *SAS 2003*, above n 8, at 224.

[110] International Law Commission, above n 108, art 41(1), (2). A serious breach of a peremptory norm is defined in art 40. See J Crawford, *The International Law Commission's Articles on State Responsibility: Introduction, Text and Commentaries* (Cambridge, Cambridge University Press, 2002), at 249ff. This article is to be read in conjunction with art 16, and it is presumed that the state would have knowledge of a serious breach of a peremptory norm (*ibid*, at 252).

[111] EU, above n 32.

[112] OSCE, 'OSCE Document', above n 32.

[113] Code of Conduct of Central American States on the Transfer of Arms, Ammunition, Explosives and Other Related Materiel, above n 33.

[114] UN, 'Suggested Common Guidelines for National Controls Governing Transfers of Small Arms and Light Weapons, Working Paper Submitted by Kenya' (22 June 2006) UN Doc A/CONF.192/2006/RC/WP.2.

[115] Canada, DFAIT, 'Informal, Intersessional Programme of Work: Announcement by Canada' (7 July 2006) <http://www.fac-aec.gc.ca/department/can_announcement-en.asp> (accessed 13 March 2007).

transfers.[116] Although there is some variation among these initiatives, a set of common principles which codify and extend existing obligations is emerging. These require, at a minimum, that states refrain from transferring or prevent transfers of SALW where the transfer would breach an international agreement or other binding obligation, or where there is a significant risk or likelihood that the arms will be used to commit serious violations of human rights or humanitarian law, genocide, or crimes against humanity. Other risks would not automatically preclude a transfer but should be taken into account in determining whether the transfer should be authorised, such as ongoing armed conflict in the region, the likelihood of diversion and subsequent use in contravention of international law, adverse effects on development, risk of use in connection with terrorist acts or organised crime, a history of human rights abuses by the proposed recipient, corruption, or lack of transparency.[117]

These existing and emerging principles establish an obligation to consider the human security impact of arms transfers, and are an important manifestation of shared responsibility for human security. The existing direct and secondary obligations in international law, reflected in mandatory criteria for transfers in these principles, address the potential use of SALW in violations of human rights or humanitarian law. However, it is important that the principles also extend responsibility to situations in which we cannot identify a clear violation of international law, but the transfer of arms would contribute to human insecurity through exacerbating risks from armed conflict, crime, or other threats. These broader obligations are not framed as automatic exclusions, but require risks to be taken into account. While this is a weaker obligation than one that would make transfers illegal under these circumstances, the requirement to consider whether they would increase risks to human security is significant. A human security approach will not necessarily provide easy answers where an exporting state is required to assess whether a transfer should be permitted, since it will need to assess evidence of risks and make difficult predictions about likely outcomes. However, human security can be used as the framework of analysis within which to evaluate the various criteria and, where necessary, to weigh them against each other. If the evolving principles are interpreted and applied using a human-centred approach and giving equal weight to the security of affected individuals, even where they might conflict with the economic

---

[116] See, eg, UNGA Res 61/89 (18 December 2006) UN Doc A/RES/61/89; 'Draft Framework Convention on International Arms Transfers' (Working Draft of 24 May 2004) <http://www.iansa.org/documents/2004/att_0504.pdf> (accessed 13 March 2007).

[117] Some of the documents mentioned also include one or more of these as mandatory criteria that require states to prevent a transfer. In particular, the obligation not to transfer arms where they are likely to be used in terrorist acts is legally binding on UN member states according to UNSC Res 1373, above n 106, and should therefore be a mandatory prohibition.

or strategic interests of exporting states, they could be an important expression of common responsibility for human security.

CONCLUSION

In this chapter, we have seen that the role played by the concept of human security in the Ottawa process has been replicated to some extent in relation to SALW, helping to shape the way issues and problems are identified, and setting standards against which the outcomes of proposed or attempted measures should be assessed. However, it is also apparent that the greater complexity of the issues surrounding SALW and the existence of stronger resistance on the part of states has made the task more difficult. Arguably, though, the human security concept could have an even more important function in this context, where the levels of complexity and resistance are greater and where it is essential to carefully identify objectives and to scrutinise and challenge the positions of key actors. In this area it is particularly apparent that the concept has a multi-faceted role to play. Calling attention to the importance of the issue based on its human impact is valuable, but once the profile of an issue has been raised in this way, it can still be addressed in terms of state security or other frameworks, resulting in measures that do not fully address the concerns that arise from a human security perspective. As a result, the role of the concept in framing issues and critiquing arguments or proposals could be even more important. However, the issues surrounding SALW are sufficiently complex that adopting a human security approach would still leave open many questions about the strategies and priorities that are required.

Furthermore, disagreements about the proper scope of the SALW agenda can only partially be understood in terms of an opposition between national and human security. Some states have resisted measures to control SALW that would be likely to advance state security as well as human security, due to entrenched ideological positions or different views about which strategies will best protect their security. One crucial difference between a national security approach to SALW and a human security or human rights approach, however, is that the latter would require the legal framework to acknowledge and respond to the possibility that legal acquisition of small arms by states may result in threats to individuals' security or rights. Because the state has an ambivalent role as protector or threat, closer scrutiny of state acquisition and use is required.

In the last section we saw that the area of SALW is one in which a significant amount of attention has been devoted to exploring the responsibilities that states may have with respect to the effects of their actions on individuals in other states. There are in fact a range of legal obligations that would impose some limits on states' freedom to transfer SALW according to their strategic or economic interests. There are ongoing efforts to codify these into a set of binding principles. In order to give full effect to the idea of common responsibility for human security, it will be important to develop suggestions that states should also be required more generally to take into account whether arms transfers will increase risks to human security (for example by exacerbating conflict). The obligation to consider certain factors is weaker than a prohibition, but if human security is used as the point of reference for decision making in these situations, this could represent a significant development.

7

Health and Human Security

INTRODUCTION

IN THE LAST decade, it has become increasingly common for health issues, especially infectious diseases, to be discussed as matters of security. The devastating impact of HIV/AIDS, the 2003 Severe Acute Respiratory Syndrome (SARS) outbreak, and fears of a coming influenza pandemic have all contributed to a higher profile for public health issues, and in particular, a tendency to discuss health threats among issues of 'high' politics or security rather than solely as public health or development concerns. As recently noted,

> '[h]ealth challenges now feature in national security strategies, appear regularly on the agenda of meetings of leading economic powers, affect the bilateral and regional political relationships between developed and developing countries, and influence strategies for United Nations reform. Although health has long been a foreign policy concern, such prominence is historically unprecedented.[1]

During the same period, the international legal framework governing health has undergone significant changes. These legal developments have both contributed to and been affected by the wide-ranging implications of globalisation for health,[2] and the emergence of 'global health' and 'global health governance'.[3]

A growing number of commentators and policy documents have also made a link between health and human security, using human security as

---

[1] DP Fidler and N Drager, 'Health and Foreign Policy' (2006) 84 *Bulletin of the World Health Organization* 687, at 687. See also C McInnes and K Lee, 'Health, Security and Foreign Policy' (2006) 32 *Review of International Studies* 5, at 6–9.

[2] See, eg, D Yach and D Bettcher, 'The Globalization of Public Health, I: Threats and Opportunities' (1998) 88 *American Journal of Public Health* 735; D Yach and D Bettcher, 'The Globalization of Public Health II: The Convergence of Self-Interest and Altruism' (1998) 88 *American Journal of Public Health* 738 ['Convergence']; D Woodward *et al*, 'Globalization and Health: A Framework for Analysis and Action' (2001) 79 *Bulletin of the World Health Organization* 875; K Lee and R Dodgson, 'Globalization and Cholera: Implications for Global Governance' in K Lee (ed), *Health Impacts of Globalization: Towards Global Governance* (Houndmills, Palgrave Macmillan, 2003).

[3] See, eg, K Lee, S Fustukian and K Buse, 'An Introduction to Global Health Policy' in K Lee, K Buse and S Fustukian (eds), *Health Policy in a Globalising World* (Cambridge, Cambridge University Press, 2002).

an alternative way of analysing threats to health and exploring parallels between human security and public health.[4] Opinions are divided, however, as to whether it is appropriate or useful to link health with either national security or human security. We do not yet have a full understanding of what it means in practical terms to treat health as a security issue or how this would fit with other approaches. This chapter aims to explore some of these questions and, in particular, to determine what implications the link between health and national or human security, respectively, might have for the developing body of international law relating to health.

DEVELOPMENTS IN INTERNATIONAL LAW AND HEALTH

The lead institution for health in the international legal system is the World Health Organization (WHO), established in 1948. The WHO's objective is the 'attainment by all peoples of the highest possible level of health',[5] and it has a wide range of functions, including technical assistance, promoting cooperation, standard-setting, and provision of information on health issues.[6] In recent years there have been several significant legal developments within the scope of the WHO's mandate. For the first time, the World Health Assembly, the highest decision-making body of the WHO, exercised its authority under article 19 of the WHO Constitution to adopt an international Convention, the 2003 Framework Convention on Tobacco Control.[7] This Convention commits states parties to a comprehensive range of tobacco control measures, including education, protection from exposure to tobacco smoke in public places, controls on advertising and labelling, and restricting access by young persons.

The World Health Assembly also has the authority to adopt regulations on matters including 'sanitary and quarantine requirements and other procedures designed to prevent the international spread of disease'.[8] The existing International Health Regulations (IHR) were adopted as the International Sanitary Regulations in 1951 and revised as the IHR in

---

[4] See, eg, Commission on Human Security, *Human Security Now: Protecting and Empowering People* (New York, Commission on Human Security, 2003) <http://www.human security-chs.org/finalreport/index.html> (accessed 26 February 2007) [CHS, *Human Security Now*], at ch 8; L Chen, J Leaning and V Narasimhan (eds), *Global Health Challenges for Human Security* (Cambridge, MA, Harvard University Press, 2003).

[5] Constitution of the World Health Organization (adopted 22 July 1946, entered into force 7 April 1948) 14 UNTS 185, art 1.

[6] *Ibid*, art 2.

[7] WHO Framework Convention on Tobacco Control (adopted 21 May 2003, entered into force 27 February 2005) 2302 UNTS 166.

[8] Constitution of the World Health Organization, above n 5, art 21.

1969.[9] Their objective is 'to ensure the maximum security against the international spread of diseases with a minimum interference with world traffic'.[10] Like the earlier Conventions upon which they were based, the IHR (1969) deal only with a limited set of specific diseases: plague, cholera, and yellow fever.[11] In respect of those diseases, they require states to notify the WHO of any case of the disease within their territory and of measures taken with respect to arrivals from infected areas and vaccination requirements. This information is then to be shared by the WHO with the health administrations of all other member states. The Regulations set out measures to be taken by states to prevent the spread of each of the three diseases. Part III prescribes minimum standards for sanitation and public health facilities at air and sea ports, as well as some land crossings. Other provisions prescribe mandatory and permitted health measures, and article 23 provides that the permitted measures are the maximum measures to be applied.

Concerns about limited effectiveness of the IHR led to a decision to reform the Regulations in 1995.[12] The experience of the SARS epidemic in 2003 and growing fears of the next influenza pandemic provided the catalyst for renewed efforts, and the revised IHR (2005) were adopted in May 2005.[13] The IHR (2005) came into force in June 2007, and according to article 22 of the WHO Constitution, are binding on WHO member states unless they advise the Director-General of their rejection or reservation.[14] A resolution of the World Health Assembly in May 2006 called on member states to 'comply immediately, on a voluntary basis, with provisions of the [IHR (2005)] considered relevant to the risk posed by avian influenza and pandemic influenza' and requested the WHO Director-General to carry out certain responsibilities under the Regulations pending their entry into force.[15]

---

[9] *International Health Regulations (1969)*, 3rd edn (Geneva, WHO, 1983) [IHR (1969)]. The International Sanitary Regulations themselves were a consolidation of a series of International Sanitary Conventions adopted in the second half of the nineteenth century. WHO, 'Global Crises—Global Solutions: Managing Public Health Emergencies of International Concern through the Revised International Health Regulations' (2002) <http://www.who.int/csr/resources/publications/ihr/en/whocdsgar20024.pdf> (accessed 25 April 2007); LO Gostin, 'International Infectious Disease Law: Revision of the World Health Organization's International Health Regulations' (2004) 291 *Journal of the American Medical Association* 2623 ['International Infectious Disease Law'].

[10] IHR (1969), above n 9, foreword.

[11] *Ibid*, art 1. The Regulations originally covered six diseases: the current three as well as smallpox, relapsing fever, and typhus.

[12] WHO, 'Revision and Updating of the International Health Regulations' (12 May 1995) WHA Res 48.7.

[13] WHO, 'Revision of the International Health Regulations' (23 May 2005) WHA Res 58.3 [IHR (2005)].

[14] Constitution of the World Health Organization, above n 7. See also IHR (2005), above n 13, arts 61 and 62 on rejection and reservation, respectively.

[15] WHO, 'Application of the International Health Regulations (2005)' (26 May 2006) WHA Res 59.2.

The IHR (2005) are substantially different from the 1969 version in several respects.[16] First, the scope of the Regulations has been expanded dramatically, and is no longer based on a fixed list of diseases but rather on the concept of a 'public health emergency of international concern', which acts as a trigger for national notification obligations and WHO responsibilities. Two important changes have also been made to the notification and surveillance provisions. First, notification to the WHO can be confidential in the first instance, in order to encourage states to comply with their notification obligations.[17] Second, the Regulations give explicit authorisation to WHO to consider and act on information from unofficial sources, that is, information other than official government notification.[18] A variety of unofficial sources of information has become available with developments in information and communications technology, and is of growing importance in global surveillance, but the WHO's authority to use this information had previously been uncertain.[19] Finally, as will be discussed below, the IHR (2005) contain much more extensive provisions with respect to the minimum capacities for disease surveillance and response that are required of member states.[20]

The HIV/AIDS pandemic has received specific attention due to its overwhelming impact and particular issues associated with it, such as discrimination against HIV-positive individuals. The Joint United Nations Programme on HIV/AIDS (UNAIDS) was established in 1994 to provide global leadership in responding to HIV/AIDS and to coordinate and strengthen relevant activity in the UN system.[21] The UN General Assembly convened a Special Session on HIV/AIDS in 2001 that resulted in the adoption of a Declaration of Commitment on HIV/AIDS;[22] a follow-up Political Declaration on HIV/AIDS was adopted in 2006.[23] As

---

[16] For an overview of the revision process and the new Regulations, see, eg, DP Fidler, *SARS, Governance and the Globalization of Disease* (Houndmills, Palgrave Macmillan, 2004) [*SARS*], at 60–67; Gostin, 'International Infectious Disease Law', above n 9; J Giesecke, 'International Health Regulations and Epidemic Control' in RD Smith *et al*, *Global Public Goods for Health: Health Economic and Public Health Perspectives* (Oxford, Oxford University Press, 2003); DP Fidler and LO Gostin, 'The New International Health Regulations: An Historic Development for International Law and Public Health' (2006) 34 *Journal of Law Medicine and Ethics* 85.

[17] IHR (2005), above n 13, art 11(2). Information will not be made generally available until the WHO Director-General has determined that a public health emergency of international concern exists, international spread of the disease has been confirmed, control measures are unlikely to succeed or cannot be carried out, or immediate international control measures are required.

[18] *Ibid*, art 9.

[19] See Fidler, *SARS*, above n 16, at 64–5.

[20] IHR (2005), above n 13, art 13 and annex 1.

[21] UN ECOSOC Res 1994/24 (26 July 1994) UN Doc E/1994/L.18/Rev.1.

[22] UNGA, 'Declaration of Commitment on HIV/AIDS', UNGA Res S-26/2 (20 August 2001) UN Doc A/RES/S-26/2.

[23] UNGA, 'Political Declaration on HIV/AIDS', UNGA Res 60/262 (15 June 2006) UN Doc A/RES/60/262.

discussed below, the Security Council has considered and adopted resolutions with respect to the impact of HIV/AIDS on international peace and security. The global response to the HIV/AIDS pandemic was also highlighted in the UN's Millennium Declaration, and the follow-up report and outcome document.[24] As part of this process, HIV/AIDS, along with malaria and 'other major diseases', has been targeted in the UN's Millennium Development Goals.[25] The issue of access to medicines, in particular for HIV/AIDS, has been a major point of contention in international law and public health, focusing on the impact of intellectual property and trade agreements on the cost of medicines in developing countries.[26] Although these issues have yet to be fully resolved, the relevant legal documents are significant to the extent that they recognise the importance of public health as an objective of national and international law and policy.[27]

Finally, during this same period increasing attention has been paid to human rights aspects of health, both the right to health in international human rights law and the relevance of human rights to public health law and practice. With respect to the former, the UN Committee on Economic, Social and Cultural Rights adopted a General Comment on the right to health in 2000,[28] and a Special Rapporteur on the right to health was appointed by the Commission on Human Rights in 2002.[29] The development of a 'health and human rights' approach to public health responded to an increasing appreciation of the linkages between health and the protection of human rights, including, for example, non-discrimination and gender equality in the context of HIV/AIDS, and the 'human rights impact' of public health policies.[30] The influence of this approach has been felt in recent initiatives such as the revision of the IHR, as will be seen below.

---

[24] UNGA, 'United Nations Millennium Declaration', UNGA Res 55/2 (18 September 2000) UN Doc A/RES/55/2; UNGA, 'In Larger Freedom: Toward Development, Security and Human Rights for All, Report of the Secretary-General' (21 March 2005) UN Doc A/59/2005 ['In Larger Freedom']; UNGA, 'World Summit Outcome', UNGA Res 60/1 (12 September 2005) UN Doc A/RES/60/1.

[25] See UNGA, 'In Larger Freedom', above n 24, at 9.

[26] See, in particular, World Trade Organization (WTO), 'Declaration on the TRIPS Agreement and Public Health' (20 November 2001) WTO Doc WT/MIN(01)/DEC/2; WTO, 'Amendment of the TRIPS Agreement: Decision of 6 December 2005' (8 December 2005) WTO Doc WT/L/641.

[27] On public health protection in the WTO generally, see, eg, MG Bloche, 'WTO Deference To National Health Policy: Toward an Interpretive Principle' (2002) 5 *Journal of International Economic Law* 825; C Button, *The Power to Protect: Trade, Health and Uncertainty in the WTO* (Oxford, Hart, 2004).

[28] UN Committee on Economic, Social and Cultural Rights, 'General Comment 14: The Right to the Highest Attainable Standard of Health' (11 August 2000) UN Doc E/C.12/2000/4.

[29] UNCHR Res 2002/31 (22 April 2002) UN Doc E/CN.4/2002/200.

[30] See generally, eg, S Gruskin, J Mann and MA Grodin (eds), *Health and Human Rights: A Reader* (New York, Routledge, 1999).

HEALTH, SECURITY, AND INTERNATIONAL LAW

This short review shows that the last decade has been a period of growth and development in international law relating to health; in fact it would hardly be an exaggeration to say that 'international health law' has begun to emerge as a distinct area of international law for the first time. While this is no doubt due to a convergence of factors, it may well be linked to the increasing prominence of health concerns in foreign policy, which in turn is related to the growing tendency to consider threats to health as matters of security. At the same time, as has just been noted, attention to the human rights dimensions of health has also intensified. Given all of this, there seems to be an important opportunity to examine the process of securitisation and the impact it has on the development of international law, as well the difference it might make, in this context, to invoke different concepts of security.

The remainder of this chapter will thus analyse in more detail the links that have been drawn between health and security. Unlike the topics discussed in other chapters, health is not one that has an obvious and long-standing connection with security, so the first part of this section will explore the ways in which health has been treated as a security issue, and the following section will examine some of the questions that have been raised about the 'securitisation' of health. It will also consider some of the implications for international law, and the ways in which a human security approach might relate to critiques of securitisation. Finally, the last section will examine these questions in the specific context of the recent revision of the International Health Regulations.

Health as a Security Issue

The link between health and security is not new, as the impact of disease on military and economic security has been recognised for centuries.[31] However, increasing concern about the threat posed by emerging infectious diseases and by the possibility of biological terrorist attacks has recently renewed interest in the health-security nexus, within the traditional framework of national security.[32]

Disease and ill health may have direct links with military security because of their potential to limit the effectiveness of national armed

---

[31] NB King, 'Security, Disease, Commerce: Ideologies of Postcolonial Global Health' (2002) 32 *Social Studies of Science* 763, at 764–6; GH Bruntland, 'Global Health and International Security' (2003) 9 *Global Governance* 417, at 417.

[32] See, eg, National Intelligence Council, *The Global Infectious Disease Threat and Its Implications for the United States* (National Intelligence Estimate NIE 99-17D, January 2000); L Garrett, 'The Return of Infectious Disease' (1996) 75 *Foreign Affairs* 66.

forces. The high incidence of disease in some populations may contribute to a shortage of new recruits for the armed forces. For example, as levels of HIV infection rise, it is increasingly difficult for some states to find sufficient numbers of healthy young adults for military service.[33] Similarly, the prevalence of disease within armed forces may undermine their effectiveness. Disease has always been a leading cause of disability and death among military personnel, with hospitalisations and deaths from disease outnumbering those from combat by a significant margin.[34] Rates of HIV infection are typically higher in the military than among the general population, and in some national militaries exceed 50 per cent.[35] AIDS is now the leading cause of death in the armed forces of some countries.[36] High rates of HIV infection among soldiers is a particular concern in the context of peace-keeping missions, since in addition to limiting the availability of peace-keeping forces, they raise concerns about infection spreading between soldiers and resident populations.[37] These links between disease and military capacity allow some aspects of health to be considered as part of a traditional approach to national security. Bioterrorism and biological warfare have also received increased attention as threats to national security.[38] In this context disease is considered as one specific type of military or terrorist threat; this threat, like the impact of emerging infectious diseases, is not new but perceived to be increasingly serious.[39]

More controversial have been attempts to analyse disease as a threat to national security in light of its contribution to instability in affected states or regions, or the direct impact of disease outbreaks on domestic populations. Although HIV/AIDS has been the main focus of discussion, other infectious diseases have also been suggested to have significant social, political, and economic effects potentially affecting national and international security.[40] A growing body of literature has attempted to

[33] H Feldbaum, K Lee and P Patel, 'The National Security Implications of HIV/AIDS' (2006) 3 *PLoS Medicine* e171, at 0775. Although this concern is most often cited with respect to HIV/AIDS and to some extent other infectious diseases, chronic conditions and diseases may contribute to shortages in some countries: see R Norton-Taylor, 'Two-thirds of Teenagers Too Fat to Be Soldiers' *The Guardian* (3 November 2006) <http://www.guardian. co.uk/frontpage/story/0,,1938441,00.html> (accessed 29 March 2007).

[34] National Intelligence Council, above n 32, at 58–9.

[35] *Ibid*, at 53; RL Ostergard, 'Politics in the Hot Zone: AIDS and National Security in Africa' (2002) 23 *Third World Quarterly* 333, at 343–4; International Crisis Group, 'HIV/AIDS As a Security Issue' (ICG Report June 2001) <http://www.crisisgroup.org/home/index.cfm? action=login&ref_id=1831> (accessed 25 April 2007), at 19–20.

[36] Feldbaum, Lee and Patel, above n 33, at 0775.

[37] *Ibid*, at 0775; Ostergard, above n 35, at 342.

[38] See, eg, National Intelligence Council, above n 32, at 59–60; DP Fidler, 'Bioterrorism, Public Health and International Law' (2002) 3 *Chicago Journal of International Law* 7.

[39] National Intelligence Council, above n 32, at 59.

[40] See, eg, the extensive study by AT Price-Smith, *The Health of Nations: Infectious Disease, Environmental Change, and Their Effects on National Security and Development* (Cambridge, MA, MIT Press, 2002); ME Wilson, 'Health and Security: Globalization of Infectious Diseases' in

assess the impact of infectious disease, in particular HIV/AIDS, on the capacity and stability of states with high rates of infection. In countries worst affected by the HIV/AIDS pandemic, high rates of AIDS-related morbidity and mortality, especially among young adults, deprive countries of a large proportion of their productive workforce and providers of essential services like education, health care, policing, and government.[41] Many are also concerned about the social and political impact of demographic changes, in particular the increasing proportion of children and older adults in national populations, and growing numbers of orphans.[42] Finally, the health care costs associated with HIV/AIDS place a large and increasing burden on developing countries' economies, which is exacerbated by lost productivity.[43] Various studies have estimated significant decreases in national GDP for countries seriously affected by HIV/AIDS and other diseases.[44] Moreover, economic impacts are not equally distributed, but are likely to increase inequality within national populations,[45] another possible contributor to instability.

Influenced by these analyses, it has become commonplace for official documents and academic commentaries alike to refer to the HIV/AIDS pandemic as a threat to security. A crucial moment in the securitisation of HIV/AIDS was the January 2000 meeting of the UN Security Council focusing on the impact of HIV/AIDS on peace and security in Africa.[46] Statements at this historic meeting suggested that by discussing HIV/AIDS as a security threat, the Security Council was 'exploring a brand-new definition of world security' and establishing 'a precedent for Security Council concern and action on a broader security agenda'.[47] The links drawn between HIV/AIDS and security in these statements have since become familiar: the sheer numbers of human lives threatened by the disease; the potential impact of AIDS on economic, social, and political stability in Africa; and the fear of a vicious cycle between conflict and infection.[48] As one speaker urged: 'AIDS is not just a health issue. AIDS is

L Chen, J Leaning and V Narasimhan (eds), *Global Health Challenges for Human Security* (Cambridge, MA, Harvard University Press, 2003).

[41] UNGA, 'Special Session of the General Assembly on HIV/AIDS: Report of the Secretary-General' (16 February 2001) UN Doc A/55/779 [Special Session Report], at paras 26–38; International Crisis Group, above n 35, at 14–16.

[42] See, eg, UNGA, Special Session Report, above n 41, at para 31; Ostergard, above n 35, at 339.

[43] See, eg, UNGA, Special Session Report, above n 41, at para 30.

[44] A de Waal, 'HIV/AIDS: The Security Issue of a Lifetime' in L Chen, J Leaning and V Narasimhan (eds), *Global Health Challenges for Human Security* (Cambridge, MA, Harvard University Press, 2003), at 130; International Crisis Group, above n 35, at 9.

[45] de Waal, above n 44, at 131; C McInnes, 'HIV/AIDS and Security' (2006) 82 *International Affairs* 315, at 316.

[46] UNSC, 'The Impact of AIDS on Peace and Security in Africa' (10 January 2000) UN Doc S/PV.4087.

[47] *Ibid*, at 2.

[48] *Ibid*, at 2–5.

not just a development issue. It is also an issue that affects the peace and security of people in the continent of Africa and throughout the world.'[49] This was a classic example of securitisation, 'constructing the disease as something extraordinary which demanded international attention and action'.[50] It has been seen as opening the door to a new security agenda and 'for health in general to be looked at through a new lens', as essential to security.[51]

The action by the Security Council that followed the January 2000 meeting in fact reveals a relatively modest approach, addressing the relevance of HIV/AIDS for peacekeeping operations. Security Council Resolution 1308, adopted in July 2000, reiterates that 'the HIV/AIDS pandemic, if unchecked, may pose a risk to stability and security', but its operative paragraphs focus on the 'potential damaging impact of HIV/AIDS on the health of international peacekeeping personnel, including support personnel'.[52] This resolution responded to concerns about links between peacekeeping operations and HIV infection: the possibility of peace-keeping troops deployed to regions with high HIV prevalence becoming infected through contact with the local population, but also the reverse risk of HIV spreading from foreign peacekeeping troops to the conflict region.[53] It urges member states, the Secretary-General, and UNAIDS to develop strategies for HIV prevention and to cooperate in their implementation. Subsequent Security Council resolutions have repeatedly affirmed the importance of integrating HIV/AIDS prevention into peace-keeping preparations.[54] UNAIDS, in cooperation with the UN Department of Peacekeeping Operations, has been engaged in coordinating and supporting HIV/AIDS prevention initiatives since the adoption of Resolution 1308, and has promoted the 'mainstreaming' of these initiatives into UN peace-keeping missions.[55]

---

[49] *Ibid*, at 8.

[50] McInnes, above n 45, at 315. See also D Altman, 'Understanding HIV/AIDS as a Global Security Issue' in K Lee (ed), *Health Impacts of Globalization: Towards Global Governance* (Houndmills, Palgrave Macmillan, 2003), at 40–41.

[51] WHO, 'World Health Day 2007: International Health Security: Invest in Health, Build a Safer Future' (Issues Paper, 2007) <http://www.who.int/world-health-day/2007/en/index.html> (accessed 8 April 2007) ['World Health Day 2007'], at 14.

[52] UNSC Res 1308 (17 July 2000) UN Doc S/RES/1308.

[53] While conclusive evidence is difficult to find, there appear to have been some examples of HIV infection spreading in the context of peacekeeping operations: see McInnes, above n 45, at 322–3; D Bratt, 'Blue Condoms: The Use of International Peacekeepers in the Fight Against AIDS' (2002) 9(3) *International Peacekeeping* 67, at 73–5; UNAIDS, *On the Front Line: A Review of Policies and Programmes to Address AIDS Among Peacekeepers and Uniformed Services* (New York, UNAIDS, 2005) [*Front Line*], at 13.

[54] See, eg, UNSC Res 1318 (7 September 2000) UN Doc S/RES/1318; UNSC Res 1357 (21 June 2001) UN Doc S/RES/1357; UNSC Res 1460 (30 January 2003) UN Doc S/RES/1460; UNSC Res 1528 (27 February 2004) UN Doc S/RES/1528; UNSC Res 1539 (22 April 2004) UN Doc S/RES/1539.

[55] See, eg, UNAIDS, *Front Line*, above n 53.

More recently, the UN Secretary-General's High-Level Panel on Threats, Challenges, and Change discussed infectious disease among the 'economic and social' threats to its comprehensive understanding of international security, which includes both state and human security.[56] In addition to urging the commitment of increased resources for HIV/AIDS and other diseases, rebuilding public health systems in developing countries, and strengthening the WHO's Global Outbreak Alert and Response Network,[57] the Panel called for the Security Council (in cooperation with UNAIDS) to host another session focusing on HIV/AIDS as a threat to international peace and security.[58] The report also proposed a new role for the Security Council, cooperating with the WHO to implement control measures in 'extreme cases of threat posed by a new emerging infectious disease or intentional release of an infectious agent'.[59] It suggested that either an intentional release of an infectious agent or an 'overwhelming natural outbreak' could be a threat to international security. As a result, the Security Council should be prepared to use its powers to ensure states' compliance with WHO investigations and response coordination, and, '[i]n the event that a State is unable to adequately quarantine large numbers of potential carriers, the Security Council should be prepared to support international action to assist in cordon operations'.[60] Subsequently, the Secretary-General stated that he would, in consultation with the Director-General of the WHO, use his powers under article 99 of the UN Charter to bring to the attention of the Security Council 'any overwhelming outbreak of infectious disease that threatens international peace and security'.[61]

Critiques of Securitisation and Implications for International Law

The securitisation of health threats has not been uncontroversial. Some still resist the expansion of security to encompass non-military threats. To the extent that health is a security concern only if it affects defence and stability, this impact is difficult to demonstrate with any certainty, and has been doubted by recent critiques. Barnett and Prins, having traced the source of common claims about HIV/AIDS and security, found that the primary evidence base for many of these claims is narrow and

---

[56] UN, *A More Secure World: Our Shared Responsibility* (Report of the Secretary-General's High-Level Panel on Threats, Challenges and Change) (New York, UN Department of Public Information, 2004), at 23*ff*.

[57] *Ibid*, at 28–30. See also *ibid*, at 46–7 on the need to build public health capacity as a defence against biological weapons attacks.

[58] *Ibid*, at 29.

[59] *Ibid*, at 30.

[60] *Ibid*, at 47.

[61] UNGA, 'In Larger Freedom', above n 24, at 29.

weak.[62] Another analysis found that to date there seems to be no correlation (much less causal relationship) between HIV infection rates and conflict.[63] At the very least, it seems that the relationship between HIV/AIDS prevalence and the risk of conflict or 'failed states' is more complex than early analyses seemed to suggest.[64] The uncertainty about these relationships undermines the case for treating health as a security issue in the traditional sense.

Other critics do not question that health threats could be properly be considered as threats to security, but worry that this may not be beneficial, and in fact may be harmful, to efforts to protect health. The process of labelling an issue as a matter of security has several effects: it raises the profile of the issue, thus attracting attention as well as human and financial resources; but it also implies certain means of dealing with the issue, justifying extraordinary measures outside the usual protections of democratic accountability and human rights protection.[65] Some of these means may not be appropriate or effective in the public health context. For example, to the extent that security carries its traditional associations with strategies of military action and defence of national territory, these may well do more harm than good for public health. Even when health threats are closely linked with traditional security threats, as in the case of potential biological attacks, traditional military security strategies must be adapted. Deterrence and non-proliferation are less likely to be effective, multiple and extremely complex preventive efforts are required, and appropriate defensive measures consist primarily of strengthening public health measures that can also respond to naturally occurring infectious diseases.[66] Treating health threats as requiring exceptional measures might actually be counterproductive if the best way of mitigating them is through more comprehensive efforts to increase overall public health capacity.

Public health has certainly received increased attention, and some additional resources, as a result of the recent focus on infectious disease as a security threat:

> Within a year, the repercussions of the anthrax incident have led to an unprece-
> dented appreciation of problems that have long hindered efforts to improve the

---

[62] T Barnett and G Prins, 'HIV/AIDS and Security: Fact, Fiction and Evidence—A Report to UNAIDS' (2006) 82 *International Affairs* 359. They argue (at 360) that the discourse on this topic is 'plagued with "factoids"—viruses of opinion that have hardened through repetition into assumed fact'. See also McInnes, above n 45.

[63] Human Security Centre, *Human Security Report 2005: War and Peace in the 21st Century* (New York, Oxford University Press, 2005), at 139. See also McInnes, above n 45, at 317.

[64] See, eg, Human Security Centre, above n 63, at 140; McInnes, above n 45, at 318, 326.

[65] See ch 2, nn 111–13 and accompanying text.

[66] See eg CF Chyba, 'Biological Security' (Paper commissioned by the United Nations and Global Security initiative of the United Nations Foundation) <http://www.un-global security.org/pdf/chyba.pdf> (28 January 2007), at 3–4.

detection and containment of naturally occurring outbreaks. Although public health has struggled—with little success—for decades to have these problems acknowledged, it can take some satisfaction from the fact that its experience and advice are now guiding the way forward in a joint public health and security policy endeavor ... Equally important is the understanding that strong national and international public health must be considered as elements of national security, and that increased funding for strengthening national and international public health must come from government sectors that go beyond health to include national security, defense, and international development aid.[67]

Optimistic views of the impact of securitisation on public health have emphasised the fact that the public health capacities required to effectively respond to a bioterrorist attack are much the same as those used to contain naturally occurring threats, so although the attention and funds devoted to bioterrorism as a security threat are likely to be disproportionate to the actual risk, the whole public health surveillance and response system should benefit.[68]

However, there are concerns that focusing on those aspects of health that can be connected with security will divert attention away from more serious problems. The leading causes of preventable death globally include malnutrition, diarrhoeal diseases, maternal mortality, and chronic diseases, which do not appear on the health security agenda. To the extent that the securitisation of health has focused on national security, it also implies that global health risks are important only when they affect a state's own national population. Thus:

While this link between security and public health has raised the profile of certain diseases, it has also worried some people who work on health policy because the security lens does not arise from, or produce, a commitment to 'health for all'.[69]

McInnes and Lee, for example, have noted that the link between health and security has been disproportionately weighted toward the traditional concerns of security, and that this has tended to narrow the agenda in a way that excludes important public health issues.[70]

In the context of international law, securitisation also has a distinct *legal* dimension, since the Security Council's powers and responsibilities are based on the existence of a threat to peace and security.[71] The prospect of

[67] DL Heymann, 'Evolving Infectious Disease Threats to National and Global Security' in L Chen, J Leaning and V Narasimhan (eds), *Global Health Challenges for Human Security* (Cambridge, Massachusetts, Harvard University Press, 2003), at 117.

[68] See, eg, *ibid*, at 105, 113, 116.

[69] Fidler and Drager, above n 1, at 687.

[70] McInnes and Lee, above n 1. See also A Ingram, 'The New Geopolitics of Disease: Between Global Health and Global Security' (2005) 10 *Geopolitics* 522, at 539.

[71] Under art 39 of the UN Charter the Security Council 'shall determine the existence of any threat to the peace, breach of the peace, or act of aggression and shall make

the Security Council considering HIV/AIDS or other diseases as a threat to international peace and security thus raises particular concerns. In addition to being a significant event in the evolving discourse on health and security, the Security Council's discussion of HIV/AIDS as a security threat represented a 'high-water mark' of broad interpretations of international peace and security in the context of the UN Charter. This is bound to be controversial on both principled and practical grounds. As noted above, the evidence supporting the link between disease and international peace and security in the traditional sense is rather weak, which makes it problematic as the legal foundation for the Security Council's mandate. If, instead, we understand the discussion of HIV/AIDS as a threat to international peace and security to represent a more radical reinterpretation of the Security Council's mandate, this raises its own problems. The Security Council as an institution is not well suited to dealing with a health issue, even one, like the HIV/AIDS pandemic, that is sufficiently serious and widespread to be accepted as a global emergency. Because the Security Council was designed to deal with threats to international peace and security in the traditional sense— understood as inter-state conflict—its powers and responsibilities reflect this orientation. The usual measures employed by the Security Council, such as military action or sanctions, are unlikely to be of much use in this context.[72] The Security Council could attempt to deal with political, economic, and social aspects of the disease, but this would duplicate action that can be more effectively undertaken by other bodies with the appropriate mandate and expertise.[73] The prospect of Security Council action in the case of an immediately 'overwhelming' disease outbreak, especially one that is caused by a deliberate biological attack, seems more plausible. However, even in this context there are concerns that Security Council involvement may not be appropriate,[74] and that cooperation between the WHO and the Security Council could undermine and politicise public health efforts.[75] Finally, any expansion of the Security Council's mandate also means expanding the potential scope of intervention in states' domestic affairs,[76] and this has been criticised as

recommendations, or decide what measures are to be taken in accordance with Articles 41 and 42, to maintain or restore international peace and security'.

[72] M David, 'Rubber Helmets: The Certain Pitfalls of Marshaling Security Council Resources to Combat AIDS in Africa' (2001) 23 *Human Rights Quarterly* 560, at 573.

[73] *Ibid*, at 574–5.

[74] See, eg, DP Fidler, 'From International Sanitary Conventions to Global Health Security: The New International Health Regulations' (2005) 4 *Chinese Journal of International Law* 325 ['International Sanitary Conventions'], at 367, fn 224 (regarding China's opposition to naturally occurring disease events being considered threats to international peace and security).

[75] *Ibid*, at 356–67.

[76] By the terms of the UN Charter, art 2(7), the principle of non-intervention does not apply to enforcement measures taken or authorised by the Security Council under chapter VII.

inappropriate.[77] As will be seen below in the discussion of the IHR, states have jealously guarded their sovereignty in the area of health protection. All of these factors suggest that the securitisation of threats to health is contentious as it relates to the international legal framework, as well as more generally for its impact on public health.

The discourse on health and security has been dominated by traditional conceptions of national security, but there is also a growing body of literature examining health from a human security perspective. The *Human Development Report 1994* included health as one of the seven main categories of human security and referred to leading causes of preventable death such as tuberculosis, diarrhoeal diseases, maternal mortality, and cancer as threats to human security.[78] Others, including the Human Security Network and the UN Secretary-General, have referred to HIV/ AIDS as a threat to human security.[79] Health was also one of the areas examined by the Commission on Human Security. The Commission's report asserts that 'illness, disability and avoidable death are "critical pervasive threats" to human security', and that, furthermore, health is instrumental to human security as a precondition for individual choices and social stability.[80] It identifies and discusses three health challenges that are most closely related to human security: global infectious diseases, poverty-related threats, and violence and crisis.[81] The report suggests that a 'people-centred approach to global health would focus on empowerment and protection'.[82] Empowerment requires strategies to increase individual and community capacity.[83] Protection entails prevention of disease through addressing root causes, developing early warning systems, and increasing capacity to anticipate and mitigate crises affecting health.[84]

A human security approach to health differs from a national security approach in its focus, priorities, and strategies. Chen and Narasimhan suggest that the people-centred perspective of human security better responds to the security needs of people at risk than 'traditional approaches to security and development', since the defence of national

[77] David, above n 72, at 575–6.

[78] UNDP, *Human Development Report 1994* (Oxford, Oxford University Press, 1994), at 27–8.

[79] Human Security Network, 'Statement of Slovenia on Behalf of the Human Security Network at the International AIDS Conference' (13–18 August 2006, Toronto, Canada) <http://www.humansecuritynetwork.org/docs/2006-09-hsn-govor-toronto-ang.pdf> (accessed 19 February 2007); UNGA, Special Session Report, above n 41, at para 23.

[80] CHS, *Human Security Now*, above n 4, at 96.

[81] *Ibid*, at 97–101.

[82] *Ibid*, at 102.

[83] *Ibid*. Community-based health insurance is suggested as one example: *ibid*. See also M Chatterjee and MK Ranson, 'Livelihood Security Through Community-Based Health Insurance' in L Chen, J Leaning and V Narasimhan (eds), *Global Health Challenges for Human Security* (Cambridge, MA, Harvard University Press, 2003).

[84] CHS, *Human Security Now*, above n 4, at 102–3.

borders by military means cannot protect against disease, and traditional approaches to development do not adequately take account of the catastrophic impact that disease may have on individuals.[85] The comprehensive and integrative nature of human security is also thought to be important in the context of health.[86] In order to understand and effectively address threats to health, their complex relationships with a wide range of root causes, determinants, and impacts need to be taken into account. It has therefore been suggested that a human security approach to health 'brings into focus the inter-relatedness of health issues with problems such as poverty, famine, illiteracy, environmental degradation, and others. . . .This characteristic of the human security framework allows for a more comprehensive approach' to health.[87] A human security approach considers health to be one of the core values to be secured,[88] so it treats health as having both intrinsic and instrumental value for security. Priorities would be guided by the severity of health threats and the significance of risk factors from the perspective of individuals, rather than strategic importance or links with pre-determined categories of threats.

This understanding of a human security approach to health assumes a broad definition of human security including a comprehensive range of threats, as opposed to the narrower understanding focusing on conflict and violence, as discussed in chapter two.[89] Even taking the narrower version, though, a human security approach could be concerned with the health impacts of conflict, rather than just the impact of health on military preparedness and the threat of biological attacks, as in the traditional security framework. This is essentially the approach taken by the Human Security Report, which, despite adopting a narrow definition of human security focused on political violence, engages in a useful discussion of the 'indirect costs' of conflict, including effects on health. There is a growing body of public health research examining the health impact of conflict, which can be used in this type of analysis.[90] It has been suggested that:

---

[85] L Chen and V Narasimhan, 'A Human Security Agenda for Global Health' in L Chen, J Leaning and V Narasimhan (eds), *Global Health Challenges for Human Security* (Cambridge, MA, Harvard University Press, 2003), at 11.

[86] *Ibid*, at 11; M Caballero-Anthony, 'Human Security and Primary Health Care in Asia: Realities and Challenges' in L Chen, J Leaning and V Narasimhan (eds), *Global Health Challenges for Human Security* (Cambridge, MA, Harvard University Press, 2003) [*Human Security*], at 240.

[87] Caballero-Anthony, *Human Security*, above n 86, at 251.

[88] *Ibid*, at 240.

[89] See ch 2, nn 12–17, 27–31 and accompanying text.

[90] See, eg, PB Spiegel and P Salama, 'War and Mortality in Kosovo, 1998–99: An Epidemiological Testimony' (2000) 355 *Lancet* 2204; E Depoortere *et al*, 'Violence and Mortality in West Darfur, Sudan (2003–04): Epidemiological Evidence from Four Surveys' (2004) 364 *Lancet* 1315; B Coghlan, 'Mortality in the Democratic Republic of Congo: A Nationwide Survey' (2006) 367 *Lancet* 44.

[90] See, eg, L Roberts *et al*, 'Mortality Before and After the 2003 Invasion of Iraq: Cluster Sample Survey' (2004) 364 *Lancet* 1857; G Burnham *et al*, 'Mortality After the 2003 Invasion of Iraq: A Cross-Sectional Cluster Sample Survey' (2006) 368 *Lancet* 1421.

> [W]hen dealing with war, the health and human security linkage would enable us to analyze both direct and indirect consequences of conflict . . . By linking health and human security, further attention can be drawn to the interrelationship of all of the factors involved in the cause of people's insecurity.[91]

The ways in which the Security Council has addressed risks to health in the years since its historic meeting on HIV/AIDS reflect modest attempts to take into account the health impacts of conflict,[92] which may well be a much more useful way of integrating a human security approach into its work than arguing for the expansion of its mandate through a reinterpretation of threats to international peace and security.

As noted in chapter two, some have raised the concern that discussing issues like health in terms of human security could be problematic because it may carry with it some of the negative effects of securitisation.[93] However, where the link with security has already been made, human security may be useful as a point of reference from which to critique this association and its effects. The scope of concern with health is broader in a human security approach than a traditional national security approach in important respects. It is concerned with disease as a threat in itself, that is, as a primary cause of premature and preventable disability and mortality for individuals, rather than merely as a factor affecting military capacity or national stability. This may be true even in the so-called narrow understanding of human security, to the extent that it pays attention to indirect health impacts of conflict. From a human security perspective, health threats that affect the security of all individuals, as well as those which may have an impact on a particular state and its population, are matters of equal concern. Therefore, a human security approach might address the concerns that have been expressed about the narrow agenda that has resulted from linking health with traditional security perspectives.[94] Assigning priority based on the impact of threats on human security would also provide a way for public health analyses of risks and disease burdens to contribute to the security agenda, rather than having security driving public health priorities.[95]

[91] K Shibuya, 'Health Problems as Security Risks: Global Burden of Disease Assessments' in L Chen, J Leaning and V Narasimhan (eds), *Global Health Challenges for Human Security* (Cambridge, MA, Harvard University Press, 2003), at 210.

[92] See, eg, UNSC Res 1341 (22 February 2001) UN Doc S/RES/1341 (taking account of the effect of conflict in the Congo on rates of HIV/AIDS infection); UNSC Res 1410 (17 May 2002) UN Doc S/RES/1410, at para 3(a) (establishing a 'focal point' for HIV/AIDS as part of UNMISET in East Timor).

[93] K Krause, 'The Key to a Powerful Agenda, if Properly Delimited' (2004) 35 *Security Dialogue* 367, at 368; SN MacFarlane and YF Khong, *Human Security and the UN: A Critical History* (Bloomington, Indiana University Press, 2006), at 242. See ch 2, nn 114–18 and accompanying text.

[94] Ingram, above n 70, at 539–40.

[95] On the use of 'global burden of disease' assessments in guiding a human security approach to health, see Shibuya, above n 91.

So far, very little of the existing analysis has considered the implications of either human security or national security for the developing international legal framework relating to health. The following section examines recent changes to the global regime for disease surveillance and control, which have been undertaken in the midst of this renewed interest in health and security.

Security and Global Disease Control

The risk of a global outbreak of an emerging infectious disease or a highly pathogenic strain of influenza is increasingly discussed as a threat to security. The global spread of SARS in 2003, although its ultimate death toll was relatively low, served to warn the international community how quickly a new disease could spread and how important effective global surveillance and control are in containing an outbreak.[96] Since that time, growing concern about an impending major influenza pandemic has also been discussed as a security threat and has served as an impetus for national and global actions. Unlike the HIV/AIDS pandemic, where the link to security has emphasised links to conflict and impacts on national stability, a serious pandemic of influenza or other acute infectious disease is more often discussed as a threat to national or global security in itself. This difference is likely to be due to the fact that in this context, concern is focused on short- or medium-term emergencies, as opposed to the HIV/AIDS pandemic which, as a 'long-wave' event, does not fit as neatly into the conventional understanding of an emergency.[97] In the words of a recent statement by the WHO Director-General:

> A foreign agent that invades sovereign territory, evades detection, kills civilians, and disrupts the economy is a security threat by most definitions. Not all new diseases are highly lethal, contagious, and able to spread internationally, inciting panic as they do. But those that can are international threats to health security.[98]

The work of the WHO on global infectious disease surveillance and response has focused on the notion of 'global health security' or

[96] WHO, 'Severe Acute Respiratory Syndrome (SARS): Status of the Outbreak and Lessons for the Immediate Future' (20 May 2003) <http://www.who.int/csr/media/sars_wha.pdf> (accessed 25 April 2007), at 1–2; DL Heymann and G Rodier, 'Global Surveillance, National Surveillance, and SARS' (2004) 10 *Emerging Infectious Diseases* 173.

[97] See T Barnett, 'A Long-wave Event. HIV/AIDS, Politics, Governance and 'Security': Sundering the Intergenerational Bond?' (2006) 82 *International Affairs* 297; Ostergard, above n 35.

[98] WHO, 'World Health Day Debate on International Health Security, Statement by Dr Margaret Chan, Director-General of the World Health Organization' (Singapore, 2 April 2007) <http://www.who.int/dg/speeches/2007/020407_whd2007/en/index.html> (accessed 8 April 2007).

'international health security'.[99] The revision of the International Health Regulations (IHR), a major restructuring of international law relating to disease control, was undertaken within this framework.[100] However, it has been noted that the meaning of 'global health security' is not entirely clear.[101] It has also been suggested that traditional conceptions of security are inadequate to deal with this type of threat.[102] Therefore, it may be useful to consider what understanding of security is reflected in the IHR (2005) provisions, and whether human security can usefully serve as a critique of the prevailing approach. Human security has been used in other contexts to draw attention to and question certain common features of the traditional approach to security, in particular the predominant focus on the security of states rather than individuals and the assumption that each state has exclusive responsibility for the security of its population. Issues with respect to both of these can be identified in the IHR (2005) framework.

The IHR essentially establish a collective security framework designed to facilitate cooperation among states for each of them to protect their own territory and population from external threats. The purpose of the IHR (2005), much like that of its predecessor, focuses on preventing the international spread of disease.[103] States take on obligations to prevent disease events from threatening other states, and are permitted to take certain actions to prevent the spread of disease into and within their territories. The concept of a 'public health emergency of international concern' (PHEIC), which is central to the IHR (2005), is defined in article 1 as:

> an extraordinary event which is determined, as provided in these Regulations:
>
> (i) to constitute a public health risk to other States through the international spread of disease; and
>
> (ii) to potentially require a coordinated international response;

---

[99] See, eg, WHO, 'Global Health Security: Epidemic Alert and Response' (21 May 2001) WHA Res 54.14 ['Global Health Security']; O Aginam, 'Globalization of Infectious Diseases, International Law and the World Health Organization: Opportunities for Synergy in Global Governance of Epidemics' (2004) 11(1) *New England Journal of International and Comparative Law* 59; Fidler, 'International Sanitary Conventions', above n 74; WHO, World Health Day 2007, above n 51.

[100] WHO, Global Health Security, above n 98.

[101] P Calain, 'Exploring the International Arena of Global Public Health Surveillance' (2007) 22 *Health Policy and Planning* 2, at 4; McInnes and Lee, above n 1, at 23.

[102] M Curley and N Thomas, 'Human Security and Public Health in Southeast Asia: the SARS Outbreak' (2004) 58 *Australian Journal of International Affairs* 17, at 30.

[103] IHR (2005), above n 13, art 2; IHR (1969), above n 9, foreword. There are some significant differences between the stated purposes of the 1969 and 2005 versions (see B von Tigerstrom, 'The Revised International Health Regulations and Restraint of National Health Measures' (2005) 13 *Health Law Journal* 35, at 69), but this aspect has remained the same. See also art 3(3) of the IHR (2005), which states that the goal of the Regulations is 'the protection of all people of the world from the international spread of disease'.

with annex 2 providing the framework and criteria for determining when an event may constitute a PHEIC. An event that fulfils any two of the following four criteria is potentially a PHEIC: serious impact; unusual or unexpected event; significant risk of international spread; or significant risk of international travel or trade restrictions.[104] The existence of a potential PHEIC gives rise to states' obligations to notify and share information with the WHO[105] and to verify reports upon request by the WHO[106]; the WHO, for its part, will seek verification of reports of a potential PHEIC and offer assistance and collaboration,[107] and has authority to issue temporary recommendations where a PHEIC is found to exist, including measures to be taken by the state in which the event is occurring and/or other states 'to prevent or reduce the international spread of disease and avoid unnecessary interference with international traffic'.[108]

The definitional provisions make clear that 'international concern' in this context focuses on the potential for transboundary impact. In other words, an outbreak of disease in a particular state will be of concern to other states when and if it threatens to affect them. Implicit in this is a presumption that concern is based primarily on self-interest, and security means keeping a disease out of one's own national territory. An outbreak is not necessarily of international concern merely because it has a devastating impact on the local population or dealing with it is beyond the capacity of the affected state. The seriousness of an event or the need for a 'coordinated international response' are not, in themselves, enough to designate an event as a PHEIC; the potential for international impact must also be present. While this does not mean that the WHO or the international community will necessarily be indifferent to other disease events, given that the existence of a PHEIC is the trigger for certain powers and obligations under the IHR (2005), its definition reflects a judgment about when these are justified under international law.

One effect of this definition is to restrict potential intrusions on state sovereignty to those instances where there is a threat to other states, rather than to the affected state's own population. Even where an international threat does exist, encroachments on sovereignty are limited. The protection of state sovereignty was an important issue in the revision of the IHR in several respects.[109] Following earlier suggestions that the WHO

[104] In addition, certain listed diseases such as smallpox or SARS are assumed to fit these criteria and must be notified. See IHR (2005), above n 13, annex 2.

[105] *Ibid*, arts 6, 7.

[106] *Ibid*, art 10(2).

[107] *Ibid*, arts 10(1), 10(3), 13(4).

[108] *Ibid*, art 15(2). The existence of a PHEIC is determined by the Director-General in consultation with the state concerned and the Emergency Committee: *ibid*, art 12.

[109] For discussion, see von Tigerstrom, above n 103, at 54*ff*; Fidler, 'International Sanitary Conventions', above n 74, at 379*ff*.

might have the authority to send teams to verify information and assess the adequacy of control measures, even without the consent of the affected state,[110] many states sought reassurance during the negotiations that WHO teams would enter member states' territories only with their prior consent.[111] The IHR (2005) thus take a more restrained position, allowing the WHO only to offer assistance and to share information about a suspected PHEIC with other states if the affected state does not cooperate. The revisions added a significant new provision allowing the WHO to use information about disease outbreaks from unofficial (non-government) sources; in the event that such information is received, the WHO will seek verification from the state,[112] and, ultimately, may share the information with other states if the affected state does not cooperate with verification and control efforts, 'when justified by the magnitude of the public health risk'.[113] This aspect of the IHR (2005) has been viewed as a significant departure from the traditional, state-centred approach of the previous regime. It is thought to represent a move away from 'Westphalian' public health, based on 'sovereignty, non-intervention, and consent-based international law',[114] towards 'post-Westphalian' global health govern-ance, which recognises the participation of non-state actors and produces 'global public goods for health'.[115] While this is a valid observation, it must also be recognised that the ability for the WHO to use and release information from unofficial sources is a modest intrusion on sovereignty compared to proposals for intervention in other contexts. The IHR do not contemplate any significant intervention in an affected state, whether for the protection of the state's own population or to prevent a potential PHEIC from spreading to other states.[116]

The autonomy of states in choosing and implementing public health measures was also asserted in the revision process and is recognised in the IHR (2005). Among the principles of the IHR (2005) is that: 'States have, in accordance with the Charter of the United Nations and the principles of international law, the sovereign right to legislate and to implement

---

[110] WHO, 'Revision of the International Health Regulations' (28 May 2003) WHA Res 56.28, at para 4. See JG Støre, J Welch and L Chen, 'Health and Security for a Global Century' in L Chen, J Leaning and V Narasimhan (eds), *Global Health Challenges for Human Security* (Cambridge, MA, Harvard University Press, 2003), at 71.

[111] WHO, 'Summary Report of Regional Consultations' (14 September 2004) WHO Doc A/IHR/IGWG/2, at para 8.

[112] IHR (2005), above n 13, art 10(1).

[113] *Ibid*, art 10(4).

[114] Fidler, *SARS*, above n 16, at 47.

[115] *Ibid*, at 50–60.

[116] This does not preclude the possibility of Security Council intervention where a disease outbreak (especially one caused by a deliberate release, although potentially also a serious naturally occurring event) is considered to be a threat to international peace and security: see above nn 59–61 and accompanying text; Fidler, 'International Sanitary Conventions', above n 74, at 366–7.

legislation in pursuance of their health policies'.[117] During the IHR revision process, states asserted, as their sovereign right, the freedom to decide what health protection measures to adopt, rejecting the possibility that measures prescribed by the Regulations or WHO recommendations would be binding. As a result the IHR provisions limiting national health measures were substantially changed, allowing more flexibility.[118] Assertions of sovereignty by a state that is not taking adequate public health measures may present 'substantial risks to both its own citizens and other nations'.[119] Conversely, stringent measures may threaten individuals' physical or economic security. Does this mean that states' sovereignty is protected in the IHR (2005) at the expense of human security?

The IHR (2005) contain more extensive protections for individuals than their predecessor, reflecting the increasing influence of human rights in public health.[120] The IHR (1969) provide that measures should not cause 'undue discomfort' or injury to health, and require the use of less restrictive measures,[121] but the revised Regulations reflect a much more explicit focus on the rights and freedoms of affected individuals. The guiding principles of the IHR (2005) include 'full respect for the dignity, human rights and fundamental freedoms of persons', and a later provision requires that in 'implementing health measures under these Regulations, States Parties shall treat travellers with respect for their dignity, human rights and fundamental freedoms and minimize any discomfort or distress associated with such measures'.[122] All measures are to be applied in a non-discriminatory manner.[123] Health measures to which international travellers are subjected require their 'prior express informed consent', except where 'there is evidence of an imminent public health risk', in which case travellers may be advised or compelled to submit to examination, vaccination or other prophylaxis, or 'additional established health measures' such as isolation, quarantine, or observation, to the extent necessary to control the risk.[124] These provisions aim to minimise interference with individual liberty and physical integrity as a result of measures to prevent the spread of disease.

---

[117] IHR (2005), above n 13, art 3(4).

[118] Compare IHR (1969), above n 9, art 23, and IHR (2005), above n 13, art 43. For discussion of this point, see von Tigerstrom, above n 103. See also Fidler, 'International Sanitary Conventions', above n 74, at 381*ff.*

[119] LO Gostin, 'World Health Law: Toward a New Conception of Global Health Governance for the 21st Century' (2005) 5 *Yale Journal of Health Policy, Law and Ethics* 413, at 417.

[120] See, eg, Fidler and Gostin, above n 16, at 87–8.

[121] IHR (1969), above n 9, art 25; arts 27 and 39(2) require surveillance to be used rather than isolation unless the risk of transmission is 'exceptionally serious'.

[122] IHR (2005), above n 13, arts 3(1), 32.

[123] *Ibid*, art 42.

[124] *Ibid*, arts 23(3), 31(2).

The Regulations do not, however, deal with the effects of disease outbreaks or control measures on human rights or human security in a comprehensive way. The informed consent provisions relate to measures applied to international travellers, not the domestic population. The requirement to use least intrusive measures does not apply to all measures, only medical examinations.[125] Furthermore, apart from the general requirement of non-discriminatory application of measures, they do not address the risk of discrimination or disproportionate impact on vulnerable groups.[126] Although they place some limits on control measures that can be imposed, the IHR (2005) do not directly acknowledge the potentially devastating impacts on individuals' livelihoods and economic security. For example, although there have been less than 300 reported human cases and about 150 deaths from H5N1 avian influenza,[127] countless other individuals have been affected through the loss of poultry stocks. Many of these have been poor smallholders in developing countries, who have lost their primary source of income or food.[128] The economic and social effects of these losses have already been severe,[129] and will continue to grow. The IHR (2005) provisions do not directly address these threats to individuals' security.

It must also be remembered, though, that WHO members have other international law obligations, including human rights obligations, which may also address these risks. Even if these obligations are not specifically incorporated into the IHR provisions, they remain part of the legal framework within which the IHR (2005) will be implemented.[130] The International Covenant on Civil and Political Rights (ICCPR) guarantees relevant rights such as freedom of movement, liberty and security of persons, privacy, and freedom of assembly; it also contains specific provisions governing when rights can be derogated from in emergency

---

[125] *Ibid*, arts 23(2), 31(2). See Fidler, 'International Sanitary Conventions', above n 74, at 369.

[126] Foreign Affairs Canada, 'Pandemics: A Human Security Perspective' (May 2006) <http://geo.international.gc.ca/cip-pic/library/Pandemics%20-%20A%20Human%20Security%20Perspective.pdf> (accessed 25 April 2007), at 17–18.

[127] As of February 2007, there were 276 reported cases and 167 deaths worldwide: WHO, 'Cumulative Number of Confirmed Human Cases of Avian Influenza A/ (H5N1) Reported to WHO' (27 February 2007) <http://www.who.int/csr/disease/avian_influenza/country/cases_table_2007_02_27/en/index.html> (accessed 27 February 2007).

[128] World Bank, 'Avian and Human Influenza: Update on Financing Needs and Framework' (30 November 2006) <http://siteresources.worldbank.org/INTTOPAVIFLU/Resources/AHIFinancing12-06.doc> (accessed 27 February 2007) ['Avian and Human Influenza'], at 3; UN Human Rights Council, 'Human Rights and International Solidarity' (7 February 2007) UN Doc A/HRC/4/8, at para 29.

[129] World Bank, 'Avian and Human Influenza', above n 128, at 3; RR Faden, PS Duggan and R Karron, 'Who Pays to Stop a Pandemic?' (2007) *New York Times*, 9 February.

[130] For discussion of the relationship between the IHR (2005) and human rights obligations, see, eg, von Tigerstrom, above n 103, at 62*ff*; Fidler, 'International Sanitary Conventions', above n 74, at 367–9; Fidler and Gostin, above n 16, at 87–8.

situations and limited for public health purposes.[131] As noted in chapter two, the Siracusa Principles were developed by human rights experts as a guide to the interpretation and application of these limitation and derogation provisions.[132] Although they have been referred to as a 'rudimentary framework', they do directly address the impact on individuals of measures to protect health security at the national or international level. The rights protected in the International Covenant on Economic, Social and Cultural Rights (ICESCR) are also relevant in respect of economic security, for example rights to work, to social security, and to an adequate standard of living including adequate food.[133] The right to health may also provide some protection where states' measures are inadequate rather than excessive, since it requires states to protect their populations from epidemic diseases.[134] Unlike the ICCPR, the ICESCR contains no provisions specifically relating to derogations from rights in emergency situations or to limitations for the purposes of public health, but establishes obligations of progressive realisation[135] and a general provision allowing for limitations on rights 'for the purpose of promoting the general welfare in a democratic society'.[136] Although some gaps remain, compliance with these provisions, along with those in the IHR (2005) themselves, should mitigate the negative impacts of states' health protection strategies on individual security.

A central concern in the implementation of the IHR (2005) framework is that many states will not have the capacity to meet their obligations without significant assistance. This applies both to efforts to alleviate the negative impacts of health measures and to compliance with the expanded surveillance and response obligations imposed by the IHR (2005). For example, with respect to the first, the provision of compensation for direct and indirect losses resulting from the culling of animals as a disease control measure has been common practice in many outbreaks.[137] However, many affected states are developing countries whose capacity to fund and implement compensation schemes is limited. In order to be effective, compensation must approximate the fair market value of the

---

[131] International Covenant on Civil and Political Rights (adopted 16 December 1966, entered into force 23 March 1976) 999 UNTS 171, arts 4, 12(2) 18(3), 19(3)(a), 21, 22.

[132] UN Sub-Commission on the Prevention of Discrimination and Protection of Minorities, 'Siracusa Principles on the Limitation and Derogation Provisions in the International Covenant on Civil and Political Rights' (28 September 1984) UN Doc E/CN.4/1985/4, Annex.

[133] International Covenant on Economic, Social and Cultural Rights (adopted 16 December 1966, entered into force 3 January 1976) 993 UNTS 3 [ICESCR], arts 6, 9, 11.

[134] *Ibid*, art 12.

[135] *Ibid*, art 2(1).

[136] *Ibid*, art 4.

[137] World Bank, 'Enhancing Control of Highly Pathogenic Avian Influenza in Developing Countries through Compensation' (2006) <http://web.worldbank.org/WBSITE/EXTERNAL/TOPICS/EXTARD/0,,contentMDK:21149507~pagePK:210058~piPK:210062~theSitePK:336682,00.html> (25 April 2007) ['Enhancing Control'], at 13–16.

animals lost, and must be predictable and timely.[138] Due to budgetary constraints in developing countries, however, compensation may occur on an ad hoc basis and provide only a low percentage of market value.[139] This not only compromises the effectiveness of public health measures (since inadequate compensation leads farmers to conceal suspected cases or sell diseased birds rather than allowing them to be culled), but threatens human security and, potentially, human rights by putting people's livelihoods at risk.

With respect to the second, the IHR (2005) contain much more extensive commitments relating to member states' domestic capacity for disease surveillance and control. In the IHR (1969), the focus was on minimum standards at entry and exit points.[140] The revised Regulations contain 'core capacity requirements for designated airports, ports and ground crossings', but also 'core capacity requirements for surveillance and response'.[141] The latter include the ability to detect and report disease events throughout the state's territory, to immediately implement preliminary control measures, and to confirm and assess reported events immediately (at the local level) or within 48 hours (at the national level), and the establishment and implementation of national public health emergency response plans to respond to a potential PHEIC.[142] While it is recognised that such core capacities are crucial for effective global surveillance and response, it is also clear that many states will have great difficulty complying with these obligations.[143]

As a result of these capacity concerns, an argument can be made that international assistance to affected states is required for the effective functioning of the global disease control regime. The case for international assistance could rest on several alternative bases. In legal terms, obligations of assistance and cooperation can be found in both the IHR (2005) and the ICESCR. Article 44 of the IHR (2005) provides that states parties 'shall undertake to collaborate with each other, to the extent possible' and 'WHO shall collaborate with States Parties, upon request, to the extent possible' in providing or facilitating technical cooperation and logistical support with respect to public health capacities, and the mobilisation of financial resources for implementation and the development of public health

---

[138] *Ibid*, at 11, 19–26.

[139] *Ibid*, at 19-20. See also S Kanamori and M Jimba, 'Compensation for Avian Influenza Cleanup' (2007) 13(2) *Emerging Infectious Diseases* 341.

[140] IHR (1969), above n 9, pt III.

[141] IHR (2005), above n 13, annex 1.

[142] *Ibid*, pt A.

[143] See, eg, M Caballero-Anthony, 'Combating Infectious Diseases in East Asia: Securitization and Global Public Goods for Health and Human Security' (2006) 59 *Journal of International Affairs* 105, at 117; CW McDougall, 'Paying for Pandemic Preparedness: Equity and Fairness in Global Public Health Surveillance Improvement' (unpublished paper, May 2006), at 5–6.

capacities.[144] However, as in many international agreements, these cooperation and assistance provisions are rather weak. They could be supported by the obligation of states parties to the ICESCR to achieve the realisation of their rights 'individually and through international assistance and co-operation',[145] although the extent of this obligation is not clear.

At the level of underlying principles, international assistance and cooperation in this context could be justified either by the self-interest of states, since each knows that a disease outbreak in another state could spread if not effectively monitored and contained, or, alternatively, by a collective concern with negative impacts on individuals for their own sake. It has been suggested that attention to the impact of influenza control measures on the most vulnerable is required for both practical and ethical reasons.[146] There is likely to be a significant degree of overlap between practical or self-interested reasons, on the one hand, and cosmopolitan ethical reasons, on the other.[147] Given the ease with which diseases spread in a globalised world, mutual vulnerability is more than merely theoretical in this context; the prospect that insecurity in one part of the world could threaten distant populations is more plausible in the case of disease than many other threats. As a result, states attempt to protect their populations not just through border measures—although these still feature prominently in control strategies, despite the truism that infectious agents know no borders—but also through 'forward deployment' of public health capacities,[148] and encouraging and assisting other states to meet the IHR surveillance and control requirements.

Generally, these will benefit the population of those other states as well as protecting the home population. If self-interest and cosmopolitan common responsibility converge here, then does it matter which is the primary foundation for states' actions? Arguably it does, since the overlap between them, while significant, is not complete. First, there will be instances in which the risk to other states is not significant enough to justify action to protect their own populations, or in which they can protect themselves by other means; in such cases they will only provide assistance, if at all, out of a sense of common responsibility. For example, a recent World Bank report suggests that if other effective containment or control measures become available, international support for compensation would no longer be justified.[149] A broader view of states'

[144] IHR (2005), above n 13, art 44.

[145] ICESCR, above n 133, art 2(1).

[146] Berman Institute of Bioethics, 'Bellagio Statement of Principles' (2006) <http://www.hopkinsmedicine.org/bioethics/bellagio/Bellagio_Statement.pdf> (accessed 25 April 2007).

[147] Compare Yach and Bettcher, 'Convergence', above n 2, suggesting that there is a convergence of altruism and self-interest in the context of global health.

[148] DP Fidler, 'A Globalized Theory of Public Health Law' (2002) 30 *Journal of Law, Medicine and Ethics* 150, at 154.

[149] World Bank, 'Enhancing Control', above n 137, at 41.

conduct tends to suggest that where self-interest is not at stake, states show much less concern for the health or economic security of other states' populations.[150]

Second, if states get involved in foreign public health efforts only to protect their own territories and populations, these efforts will be directed towards and measured by their effectiveness in containing the threat, rather than their impact on the local population. This latter concern becomes pressing in the context of the IHR (2005) implementation because of fears that the focus on surveillance and control capacities, and international assistance directed at compliance with those obligations, may divert resources from other important public health needs. There are indications that this is already occurring in some developing countries.[151] If that is the case, the net impact on the population's health could be negative, rather than positive. Also, it would mean that some states (primarily developed states) may in effect be shifting risks onto others (primarily developing states), rather than providing mutual protection. This is a specific example of the concern that securitisation of health may distort priorities in a way that is ultimately harmful to public health, and neglects 'health for all'.[152] If 'global health security' means surveillance and containment to prevent the spread of disease between states, the securitisation of this aspect of public health will assign priority to this goal. This carries the risk of unintended harms to people's health, for example through the 'opportunity costs' of investment in surveillance.[153]

If we instead focused on the security of individuals from critical and pervasive threats to their health, containment of infectious disease would be one goal to be balanced with others, giving equal weight to everyone's security. To be sure, this would not make balancing priorities an easy task, since we still have 'a dilemma: what priority should be given to an unpredictable but potentially catastrophic event, when many existing and urgent health needs remain unmet?'[154] While the Human Development Report stated that human security should focus on the 'worries about daily life' of 'ordinary people' rather than the threat of a 'cataclysmic world event',[155] the two are not necessarily mutually exclusive if the latter is a plausible and serious threat; the Report also said that human security required protection from both chronic and sudden threats.[156] What would

[150] See, eg, *ibid*, at 154–5 (continued promotion of tobacco trade); McDougall, above n 143, at 17–18 (weak support for other health initiatives, such as the Global Fund for HIV, Tuberculosis, and Malaria).

[151] P Calain, 'From the Field Side of the Binoculars: A Different View on Global Public Health Surveillance' (2007) 22 *Health Policy and Planning* 13 ['Different View'].

[152] See, above nn 69–70 and accompanying text.

[153] Calain, 'Different View', above n 151, at 14.

[154] WHO, 'Avian Influenza: Assessing the Pandemic Threat' (2005) <http://www.who.int/csr/disease/influenza/H5N1-9reduit.pdf> (26 February 2007), at 3.

[155] UNDP, above n 78, at 22.

[156] *Ibid*, at 23.

be different about a human security approach to global health security is that it would require explicit attention to unintended negative effects of the global disease control regime. Furthermore, both the potential catastrophe and other urgent needs could be matters of security, rather than one trumping the other. In this respect, a human security approach is a useful complement to an analysis based on the right to health, since the ICESCR provisions provide no more guidance as to balancing priorities, and human security could provide a critique from within security discourse rather than allowing securitisation to dictate priorities.

CONCLUSION

The securitisation of health has tended to focus on the links between health threats and military conflict or terrorist violence, reflecting the traditional concerns of national security, and the protection of states' territories and populations by preventing the transboundary spread of disease. Although this process has resulted in increased attention and resources for public health, it has also given rise to concerns that it may distort priorities and neglect the most pressing threats to public health. An alternative vision of health security based on human security would be comprehensive with reference to both the causes of threats to health and their effects. It takes into account the impact of health threats on the security of individuals, understood as protection from critical and pervasive threats to their lives and essential capacities (the 'vital core' of human life). In keeping with the idea that each person has equal moral value, it would also require concern for the security of all individuals in an interdependent world.

Securitisation has a special significance in the context of the UN, given that the foundation of the Security Council's mandate is the preservation of peace and security. The proposal that the Security Council should address the HIV/AIDS pandemic as a threat to peace and security may have some superficial appeal but on closer examination appears to be quite problematic. The direct link between HIV/AIDS and traditional threats to security remains speculative, and although viewing the human impact of the disease as a security threat in itself seems to reflect a human security approach, it is unlikely to be useful. However, there is another, more promising way of giving effect to a comprehensive view of security at the individual level: the Security Council (and other relevant institutions) can take account of the broader, indirect impacts of conflict including threats to health, and integrate these concerns into existing mandates.

The revision of the IHR has occurred within the context of securitisation, in this case the promotion of 'global health security'. Although the concept of security underlying this initiative is not made explicit, it is revealed in several aspects of the IHR (2005). The IHR regime is designed to allow states a significant degree of freedom in protecting their territories and populations from external disease threats, but potential conflicts between this goal and the security of individuals are mitigated by human rights protections integrated into the IHR (2005) and the broader context of international law. 'International concern' is rather narrowly defined in the IHR (2005) provisions to focus on the potential transboundary spread of disease, but both human security and human rights perspectives would support robust implementation of the cooperation and assistance provisions in the IHR (2005). Human security may have distinct value here in challenging the distortion of priorities that could result from designating disease surveillance and control capacities as matters of security. Difficult questions will remain, however, about how to weigh potential 'catastrophic' and 'everyday' threats to health in setting priorities and implementing control measures.

Conclusion

AS WE SAW in the first chapter, the concept of human security evolved as the product of a convergence of ideas in security and development studies, its articulation prompted by concerns that the security of individuals was often threatened rather than protected by attempts to ensure national military security. It involves making individuals the primary referent objects of security instead of states, meaning that the pursuit of security should focus on protecting individual human beings from threats to their lives, safety, and rights. Various historical factors, especially the end of the Cold War and increasing globalisation, favoured the adoption of this new concept of security by some national governments, UN agencies, and others. It has also been used in the work of several international commissions, as well as being the focus of an extensive report by the Commission on Human Security. Although the concept is now fairly well established, it has remained somewhat marginalised and has enjoyed inconsistent support among states and international organisations.

Some of the hesitance and resistance seen in responses to the concept of human security is likely due to ongoing questions about its meaning and utility. As its use has spread, many different definitions of the concept have been developed, and disagreements about its proper scope have emerged. Typical definitions refer to human security as protection of people from critical or pervasive threats to their lives, safety, rights, and dignity, or as a shift in perspective that puts human beings at the centre of security concerns. Some scholars and national governments favour a narrow definition focusing on conflict and other physical violence, while others prefer a more comprehensive approach that takes into account a range of different threats to human security. It was suggested in chapter two that attempts to define what constitutes a threat to human security by reference to a threshold of seriousness, rather than distinctions between types of threats, seemed more likely to be useful. It has to be acknowledged that the policy agenda required to prevent or mitigate such threats will be unavoidably wide-ranging and ambitious. This is one of the grounds on which some have dismissed the concept, saying that it is too broad or too vague to be useful. There is some justification for this concern, although it is not clear that the breadth or complexity of the human security agenda is necessarily unique to this concept or sufficient in itself to disqualify it as a potentially useful perspective. Another common question, to which we will return below, is whether human security adds anything to other established approaches, especially human rights.

In using human security as a point of reference for setting policy agendas or as a way of framing questions in an alternative or critical way, it was suggested that there are two key components of the concept, both of which must be considered. The first is the human-centred approach, which distinguishes human security from other security concepts by making individual human beings the referent objects, that is, the primary units of analysis and of moral value. From this perspective, the security of all individuals is of equal concern, and a human security approach seeks to take this idea seriously and explore its implications. At the domestic level this means that a security strategy that protects only elites, while making the rest of the population insecure, is unacceptable. It also means that in the global context, the security of all individuals everywhere is the common concern of all, and since each state may not necessarily be able or willing to adequately protect its own people, it must also be a matter of common responsibility. This idea of common responsibility for human security is thus the other key aspect of the concept. It was noted, however, that some understand the need for cooperation to promote human security primarily as a reaction to the global nature of security threats and a sense of interdependence, rather than necessarily as the result of equal concern for everyone's security. As will be discussed further below, the way in which this element of common concern or common responsibility is understood has potentially important implications for how the concept is used.

It was observed in chapter three that writings on human security reveal some ambivalence toward international law, characterising it as both a help and a hindrance in the pursuit of human security. International law has been a useful instrument in addressing many items on the human security agenda, including threats and vulnerable groups of particular concern, and important means of ensuring human security, even if it cannot be presumed that the relevant legal developments have always been effective. This chapter examined the perception that human security is somehow at odds with the prevailing norms and structures of international law and relations, suggesting that the degree of tension depends largely on the interpretation and practical effect of certain key concepts such as sovereignty and non-intervention. Although there are some tensions between the conceptual framework of human security and international law, there are numerous points of affinity as well. The human-centred approach is reflected in most obviously in the development of human rights law, as well as in broader humanitarian principles and, potentially, more inclusive interpretations of threats to peace and security. Notions of common concern and common responsibility resonate with obligations of cooperation, obligations *erga omnes*, principles in international environmental law including those relating to prevention of transboundary harm and the designation of matters of common concern, and the limited extensions of responsibility for the protection of individuals beyond states' territory and jurisdiction. Despite these affinities, there is as yet no single principle or area of law that fully gives expression to the concept of human security in international law. We saw that it is problematic simply to equate a human security approach with certain areas of law that appear to be 'human centred' (such as human rights, humanitarian law, or refugee law); rather, one can find parallels and tensions with the concept throughout international law, and all areas of the law may need to be scrutinised carefully to assess their impacts on human security.

The remaining chapters each examined a particular issue in international law to determine what contribution the concept of human security could make to its analysis, and assess some of the ways in which the concept has already been used in various contexts. All of the areas considered have already been the subject of discussion and debate, from the question of humanitarian intervention, with its long history, to the more recently identified concerns about internally displaced persons (IDPs) or the spread of small arms and light weapons (SALW), and renewed fears of pandemic disease. Each of them has also already been linked to human security, in ways that were found to be more useful in some cases than others. Despite these commonalities, the examples chosen represent different types of legal problems—for example, resolving questions about the legality of certain actions in the case of humanitarian intervention, and developing or reforming legal frameworks to address 'new' threats in the case of SALW or global disease control—and therefore present different challenges and opportunities for the use of a human security approach.

With respect to humanitarian intervention, the concept of human security has sometimes been invoked in support of a right of intervention, giving weight to the argument that the protection of individuals should trump state sovereignty. It was argued in chapter four that this is a misleading characterisation of the issue, since it is not just sovereignty that is violated by military intervention, but also, more crucially, the prohibition on the use of force. Since individuals' security will be threatened by military action, overriding this prohibition does not necessarily advance human security and may in fact do the opposite. Human security could more coherently and productively be used to displace the debate from the unhelpful dichotomy between human rights and sovereignty, and insist on placing the risk of harm to individuals at the centre of the analysis. It was noted that this alternative approach might have broader implications for our understanding of the prohibition on the use of force, but also that it will not itself be able to resolve the question of whether to intervene in specific cases. Next, this chapter examined the emphasis that has been placed on the right of intervention in legal debates, and asked whether a more explicit focus on obligations, such as the 'responsibility to protect' promoted by the International Commission on Intervention and State Sovereignty (ICISS), might better respond to the idea of common responsibility for human security. It was argued that while there are sources of legal obligation that might be relied on, these should not be invoked to claim that there is a duty to undertake military intervention, which would be problematic for human security for the same reasons as a right of intervention. Rather, these potential sources of obligation could form the basis of a broader discussion of states' duties to protect the security of individuals globally, beyond the context of military intervention. The last section of the chapter suggested that the widest possible consideration of such obligations, taking into account the ways in which states may inadvertently contribute to crisis situations in other countries, is essential to respect the need for the use of force to be a last resort.

The legal position of IDPs, discussed in chapter five, is of concern from a human security perspective because displacement is typically associated with insecurity and may be a symptom of a state's failure to protect its population. In this context, international protection is often assumed to be a question of intervention or 'humanitarian access', to which state sovereignty is a barrier. Attempts have therefore been made to reconceptualise sovereignty as responsibility, including a duty to accept assistance for the people in one's territory when it is required for their effective protection, and a corresponding right or obligation of other states to provide such assistance. This idea of sovereignty as responsibility is compatible with a human security approach, provided that the likely effects of any outside intervention are still scrutinised carefully. It was noted that since displaced persons are not the only ones who may be vulnerable, this idea of sovereignty as responsibility may have broader implications. In addition, working by analogy from the idea of burden sharing in refugee protection, it was suggested that common responsibility for human security would imply the need for collective action to protect displaced persons. This would require not just the recognition of 'residual' collective responsibilities in situations of crisis where the home state has failed in its 'default' responsibility of protection, but broader obligations with respect to the full range of actions and policies that contribute to insecurity in other states. Finally, the protection of IDPs as part of a preventive approach to displacement was examined, and here it was suggested that the concept of human security could be a useful point of reference to help to ensure that the primary object of preventive action is the safety of individuals. However, concerns have been expressed that human security has instead been used to promote the perceived security interests of states, and a containment approach to displacement.

The sixth chapter discussed SALW proliferation, an area where the concept of human security has been used explicitly to define and analyse the problem. The campaign against these weapons has attempted to follow the model of the Ottawa process on anti-personnel mines in focusing on direct and indirect humanitarian impacts and privileging human security over considerations of state military security, but the SALW problem is more complex and difficult. The legitimacy of targeting illicit trade in weapons to the exclusion of other issues has been questioned from the point of view of human security and human rights, given that both legal and illegal weapons may have serious effects. The idea that human security favours a broader agenda, while a traditional national security approach favours a narrow focus, was revealed to be something of an oversimplification, however. Not all objections to the broader agenda can usefully be understood in terms of an opposition between national and human security objectives. Resistance to stricter control measures does appear to be the result of the prioritisation of national security in some cases, but the varying positions of states reflect different judgements about what is required to effectively protect either national or human security. A key difference is that a human security or human rights perspective pays greater attention to the potential for legally traded arms to be misused by the state. This means that there is also a need to explore the effects and limits of legal trade.

The next question, then, is what limits are placed by international law on states' freedom to transfer and acquire SALW. Several possible sources of legal restrictions were found, along with recent initiatives to prescribe criteria for regulating arms transfers. Reference to the concept of human security, especially common responsibility for human security, would support these developments. It would, in particular, encourage initiatives proposing mandatory consideration of the impact of arms transfers on human security, even in situations where a transfer would not necessarily be unlawful under current norms. If the obligation to consider such effects were implemented within a decision-making framework that gives priority to human security over other interests (such as the strategic or economic interests of states), this could represent an important concrete application of common responsibility for human security.

The recent trend toward the securitisation of health risks was examined in the final chapter, where it was seen that the higher international profile of public health has been associated with the drawing of links between the spread of infectious disease and national or international security. Disease can be considered a security threat within traditional thinking because of its impact on military preparedness and recent speculation that it may, in extreme circumstances such as the HIV/AIDS pandemic, threaten the stability of some states and therefore increase the risk of conflict. Serious emerging infectious diseases have also been viewed as security threats in broader approaches to national security because of their potentially devastating effect on national populations. Although the securitisation of health has had some positive effects on public health capacity, there are concerns that it may distort priorities and lead to the adoption of strategies that are inappropriate or even harmful. In the context of international law, securitisation carries with it distinct legal implications in the form of potential Security Council action in response to public health threats, which seems unlikely to be helpful. It was suggested that a more useful way of integrating threats to health into the Security Council's mandate would be to increase its awareness of and responsiveness to health risks associated with conflict.

A human security approach, as discussed by the Commission on Human Security and recent academic commentary, would focus on the security of individuals and communities from health threats to which they are most vulnerable, not solely on their impact on national stability or military security, or on the risk of spread to other states. It would also imply that threats to health in one state could be of concern to others due to their severe impact, not only because of the risk of international spread. The promotion of 'global health security' through global disease surveillance and control under the revised International Health Regulations (IHR) seems instead to reflect traditional approaches to security to the extent that they contemplate each national government protecting its own territory from the spread of disease. Although the IHR provide co-operative mechanisms to prevent transmission across borders, they maintain a fairly conservative approach to defining what health threats are of international concern and to respect for state sovereignty. The risk that respect for sovereignty in this context could allow states to threaten individuals through either inadequate or unduly strict health measures is mitigated to a large extent by human rights provisions within and beyond the IHR regime. However, examining the IHR (2005) from a human security perspective reveals some gaps that should be taken into account in their implementation, such as strengthened mechanisms to address impacts on economic security, vigilance to ensure that global surveillance and control efforts do not divert attention and resources away from pressing local health threats, and the need for extensive international assistance and cooperation on these matters. These issues can also be approached from a human rights perspective, but human security could at least function as a useful supplement to challenge some of the risks of securitisation.

HUMAN SECURITY AS A CHALLENGE TO INTERNATIONAL LAW

As noted in chapter three, some have suggested that the concept of human security is fundamentally at odds with existing international law. This view is based on the perception that key concepts and principles of the international legal order, most notably state sovereignty and the related principle of non-intervention, but also the rules governing the use of force, are designed to protect national security as traditionally defined, even at the expense of individuals' security. At the very least, the concept of human security is thought to present a challenge to international law.[1] This challenge can be seen in either a positive or a negative light. Some might welcome an opportunity to reform international law through the use of a concept like human security, and insist that if human security *is* challenging or radical, that is all the more reason to think it is needed. If human security requires fundamental changes to the current structure, though, might it not be utopian and unrealistic to advocate use of the concept, even if it seems appealing? A human security approach may be relegated to the margins in 'an international environment not readily conducive to radical reinterpretations of security'.[2] Alternatively, the concept could be coopted by states seeking to use the term 'human security' without taking on board its political implications.[3] Both of these positions assume that there is an inherent tension between human security and contemporary international law; they differ on what impact this might have on the utility of a human security approach. At the same time, others have suggested that in fact human security does not represent any novel challenge to international law at all, because it is merely a repackaging of familiar ideas. In particular, some see human security as essentially duplicating human rights, and its potential impact on international law redundant given the changes for which human rights are already serving as a catalyst. Although these remain difficult questions, in drawing together some of the themes that emerged in the analysis, we can make at least some preliminary observations.

---

[1] See, in particular, G Oberleitner, 'Human Security: A Challenge to International Law?' (2005) 11 *Global Governance* 185.

[2] WT Tow and R Trood, 'Linkages between Traditional Security and Human Security' in WT Tow, R Thakur and I Hyun (eds), *Asia's Emerging Regional Order: Reconciling Traditional and Human Security* (Tokyo, United Nations University Press, 2000), at 14. In their assessment, the concept of human security is not likely to have a significant impact on foreign policy, which continues to be dominated by national interest and realist approaches: *ibid*, at 16, 25.

[3] See eg M McDonald, 'Human Security and the Construction of Security' (2002) 16 *Global Society* 277, at 281–2; A Burke, 'Caught between National and Human Security: Knowledge and Power in Post-crisis Asia' (2001) 13 *Pacifica Review* 215, at 222.

Human Security and Intervention

It was suggested in chapter three that the nature and extent of the conflict between human security and the international legal order depends on the interpretation of certain key principles. The fundamental concepts and principles at issue, like state sovereignty and the prohibition on the use of force, do not have an absolute or fixed meaning; indeed, quite to the contrary, their interpretation has been the subject of extensive debate and has changed over time. As a result, it seems that they could be interpreted in various ways which may be more or less compatible with the normative and conceptual framework of human security. It further follows that the concept of human security could be used to shape their interpretation or to question their invocation in certain contexts. So, for example, in chapter four we saw that even if the prohibition on the use of force as worded in the UN Charter is commonly understood to emphasise the protection of states (their territorial integrity and political independence), it need not be limited to that function. That is, the role of the prohibition in protecting individuals from the threat of military force need not be only an indirect effect of the protection of states, but could be considered independently. The difference between these views of the prohibition becomes apparent when we consider the possibility of military force against 'failed' states. To disregard the prohibition on the use of force when there is no effective state structure to be protected may be seem plausible, but this does not stand up to scrutiny when we consider that the impact on human security may be equally severe as in the case of an intervention where there is a functioning government in place.

As for state sovereignty, several chapters noted that its legal protection is perceived to be a barrier to efforts to ensure human security. We saw at several points that some states may indeed use arguments based on sovereignty to resist measures that appear to be necessary to ensure human security. States have invoked sovereignty concerns to oppose stricter regulation of arms transfers and to prevent outside intervention in the case of a disease outbreak. In the context of IDPs, one obstacle to international protection has been states' invocation of sovereignty concerns to deny humanitarian access to displaced persons. The concept of 'sovereignty as responsibility' has been proposed as a way of countering this resistance. It reconceptualises state sovereignty in terms of its purpose in protecting the state's people, and implies an element of international responsibility for those people in the event that the state is unable or unwilling to fulfil its protective function. To this extent it is compatible with a human security approach, and the development of this concept demonstrates that it is possible to understand the fundamental principle of respect for sovereignty in a way that is more consistent with human security.

It was also suggested, though, that following through on a human security approach would require several caveats or additions to the idea of sovereignty as responsibility as commonly understood. The first is that it is not enough to justify intervention on the basis that the state has failed in its responsibilities and has thus ceased to 'deserve' the protection of its sovereignty. As noted in chapter two, that is a view of sovereignty promoted by some liberal theorists, but it is not quite satisfactory from the point of view of protecting human security. From a human security perspective, the central consideration is not what a state is entitled to, but what the impact of intervention is likely to be on the security of its people. The second point is that the way that the responsibilities of states are categorised—'default' or 'primary' responsibilities of people's own state as opposed to 'residual' responsibilities of other states—is inadequate to capture the complex relationships of interdependence that affect human security in today's world, and the nature and extent of responsibilities that will be required to provide effective protection.

The common assumption that sovereignty may need to be limited or overridden for the protection of human security has raised concerns that human security will be invoked as a pretext for intervention by powerful states. In chapter four, the invocation of human security to support a right of forcible humanitarian intervention was examined, and criticised for the way it glosses over the threat of harm from the intervention itself. Since it is not only the sovereignty of the state but also the safety of individuals that is threatened by the prospect of military action, saying that intervention should be permitted because human security should trump the sovereignty of states is unhelpful and even dangerous. Even in the case of non-forcible intervention, for example to protect IDPs, it was suggested that any proposed intervention must be scrutinised as to its impact on human security. Critics have also alerted us to the risk that human security may be used as a cover for interventionist containment strategies in the home states of IDPs, which aim primarily to advance the security interests of potential states of asylum. It seems clear, though, that human security would more coherently be used to critique such strategies.

Furthermore, as we saw in all of the later chapters, assuming that intervention is the primary means of operationalising the notion of common responsibility for human security is unduly limiting. Instead of seeing other states only as would-be rescuers, we can also consider the ways in which their actions and policies may have contributed to the threats to people's security in the potential 'target' state. Shared responsibility for preventing or minimising threats requires that we pay attention to this aspect and consider what obligations have been or could be imposed on states to address this reality. In chapters four and five a broader consideration of states' obligations was encouraged, and in chapter six the implications of transnational responsibilities were more fully explored in the context of limitations on arms transfers. The discussion of HIV/AIDS and security in chapter seven highlighted another facet of this question by suggesting that a human security approach could more usefully be given effect by integrating health concerns into existing Security Council actions than by arguing that pandemic disease should be a new basis for Security Council intervention. Furthermore, effective protection of human security from threats to health would be better achieved through global cooperation and assistance for public health capacities and mitigation strategies, rather than crisis intervention. In the analysis of several different issues it therefore appeared that the view emphasising intervention as a means of promoting human security is not the only possible or even the best view.

Human Security and Common Responsibility

If a broader range of responsibilities shared by all states is required to protect human security, what challenges does this present for international law? The cosmopolitan dimension of human security is sometimes said to be the most radical aspect of the concept. What was described as the 'weak' version of common concern for human security is less challenging, because it implies that states are concerned with insecurity abroad only to the extent that it threatens their own populations. This approach is more closely aligned with the current international legal framework, which continues to attach substantial rights and responsibilities to the special relationship between a sovereign state and the people within its jurisdiction. A significant shift in this division of responsibility would, indeed, be a radical change, although there are already examples of transnational or global responsibilities, some of which have been examined in the chapters above. A stronger version of common responsibility for human security seems likely to face considerable resistance from national governments, which see protecting their own people as their primary task and may be unwilling to accept the political cost associated with any increased risk to their people's security for the benefit of vulnerable populations elsewhere. This may help to explain why governments have not fully committed to a human security approach. For example, examining Canadian foreign policy, Hataley and Nossal have observed:

> Canada's response to the Timor crisis . . . suggests an important limit of the human security agenda: it is easier to embrace the rhetoric of human security than it is to transform the human security agenda into concrete policy initiatives. When a government must choose between safety for other people and safety for its own people, it is more likely to put other people at risk than its own.[4]

[4] TS Hataley and KR Nossal, 'The Limits of the Human Security Agenda: The Case of Canada's Response to the Timor Crisis' (2004) 16 *Global Change, Peace & Security* 5, at 17.

Hataley and Nossal are undoubtedly correct in suggesting that it would be a challenge in political as well as legal terms to expect national governments to put the security of foreigners above that of their nationals. However, it is important to appreciate that giving effect to common responsibility for human security will not always amount to asking governments to risk their own people's security. The assumption seems often to be that protecting human security abroad will mean sending military forces. However, one of the key arguments in the chapters above is that this is an unduly narrow and distorted view of the proposed responsibility to protect. Much more emphasis should be placed, instead, on upstream preventive measures such as attention to the impact of economic policies or the regulation of arms transfers. Not only do such measures better protect human security by preventing crises or mitigating their impacts, but they are also less likely to require governments to trade off the security of their own people against that of others.

This approach remains challenging in another respect: it would entail expansive obligations on states to prevent harm outside their jurisdictions, beyond those which currently exist in international law. Existing legal obligations include a limited set of transnational human rights obligations, obligations to ensure respect for humanitarian law, and the duty to prevent genocide, even outside the state's territory or jurisdiction. While these are significant, it must be acknowledged that they are still limited in scope. The current legal framework does not require states to take account of the global impacts of their conduct on human security in any comprehensive way. If we look at international environmental law by way of comparison, as seen in chapter three there is a general obligation to prevent environmental harm beyond one's borders. The concept of transboundary harm in international law has so far been reserved 'almost exclusively for environmental issues' where there is 'a relatively direct line of causation from activity to physical consequences'.[5] Some scholars have explored the possibility of extending this concept to address other types of harm with direct impacts on human security (such as terrorism or drug trafficking).[6] The analogy works better in some contexts than others, but it seems clear that the obligations in each of them do not amount to an equivalent general obligation for the prevention of transboundary harm. In fact, some relevant areas of international law seem designed to limit rather than extend the scope of responsibility.[7] We could conceive of a framework that recognises obligations on all states to prevent harm to

[5] RM Bratspies and RA Miller, 'Introduction' in RM Bratspies and RA Miller, *Transboundary Harm in International Law: Lessons from the* Trail Smelter Arbitration (Cambridge, Cambridge University Press, 2006), at 7.

[6] See the chapters in part three of Bratspies and Miller, *ibid.*

[7] See N Vennemann, 'Application of International Human Rights Conventions to Transboundary State Acts' in Bratspies and Miller, *ibid*, and the discussion below.

individuals' security, the content of which would vary in nature and scope according to each state's influence on the source of harm.[8] In order for these obligations to be comprehensive enough to encompass prevailing threats to human security, though, they would need to be extended considerably beyond those currently existing in international law. Such a proposal would be likely to face some resistance, not only because it would create additional constraints on states, but also because assessing the relationships of causation linking state conduct and global threats to human security would be very complex and challenging.

Human Security and Human Rights

The relationship between human security and human rights is of particular interest from the perspective of international law. If, as some suggest, a human security approach would merely duplicate familiar arguments from human rights, it would be at best an additional source of support for human rights, and at worst an alternative and weaker framework that could actually undermine progress already made in the protection of human rights. As noted in chapter two, human rights and human security are widely viewed as overlapping and mutually support-ive, sharing a common normative foundation, but there seems to be little clear agreement on what their respective roles might be, if indeed they are distinct.

The increasing influence of human rights was undoubtedly part of the impetus to shift the referent object of security from states to human beings. Human security has been located within a tradition in international law that includes the rise of human rights as well as humanitarian and refugee law, said to reflect a growing 'recognition that people's rights are at least as important as those of states'.[9] We saw in the third chapter that there are important parallels between these areas of law and the conceptual frame-work of human security. It was also noted that human rights have been credited by some with transforming traditional state-centred international law in ways that are similar to the challenge of human security. As a result, human rights provide part of the legal foundation for the pursuit of human security and have already shaped international law in a direction

---

[8] See, for example, the recent decision of the International Court of Justice considering what is required of a state to comply with its obligation to prevent genocide, focusing on the influence the state has over the perpetrators of the genocide: *Application of the Convention on the Prevention and Punishment of the Crime of Genocide (Bosnia and Herzegovina v Serbia and Montenegro)*, Judgment of 26 February 2007, at paras 430, 434. We might also make an analogy to the concept of common but differentiated responsibilities in international environmental law: see ch 3, nn 106–10 and accompanying text.

[9] L Axworthy, 'Human Security and Global Governance: Putting People First' (2001) 7 *Global Governance* 19, at 19. See also ch 3, n 21*ff* and accompanying text.

that is consistent with a human security approach. It was also suggested in that chapter, however, that a human security approach to international law could not simply be equated with human rights as an area of international law, or even with the sum of 'human-centred' international law including human rights, humanitarian law, and refugee law, since the distinction between 'state-centred' and 'human-centred' international law is not as simple as it might appear.

There are several instances in which human rights and human security perspectives seemed to overlap in the analysis of issues in subsequent chapters. Chapter four made reference to human rights as part of the notional opposition between the protection of human rights or human security, on one hand, and the protection of state sovereignty, on the other, that is sometimes assumed to underlie the humanitarian intervention debate. Human security was used as the principal reference point in the critique of this debate, but it is likely that we could arrive at the same conclusion on this point by focusing on human rights; the opposition between human rights and sovereignty is equally problematic.[10] In this context it therefore seemed to be important to assess the role of human security in the debate because others have attempted to use it to support certain positions, rather than because it necessarily had a unique contribution to make. Human rights have also played an important role in the debate surrounding protection for IDPs; in particular, human rights obligations are the main foundation for the argument that states should not unreasonably deny humanitarian access to displaced populations. This is part of the underlying basis of the idea of sovereignty as responsibility, although it speaks more to the responsibilities of the sovereign state toward its population than the responsibilities of other states to provide protection if it fails. In the sixth chapter the potential for states using SALW to be either protectors or abusers of their populations was seen to be important to the issue of limits on legal transfers. The recognition of this ambivalent role and its importance can be attributed equally to a human rights or human security perspective. Finally, in chapter seven it was seen that growing awareness of human rights in public health influenced the revision of the IHR and the context in which it will be implemented, in ways that would help to protect human security.

There is clearly a significant degree of overlap between human rights and human security perspectives, as we can see from these examples. In particular, human rights law contains a well-developed body of norms to address the potential for states to threaten or fail to protect individuals within their jurisdiction, and the legal framework even includes specific

---

[10] Indeed, as noted in chapter four, a few other authors have made similar arguments with respect to human rights and sovereignty: see, eg, K Bennoune, '"Sovereignty vs. Suffering"? Re-Examining Sovereignty and Human Rights through the Lens of Iraq' (2002) 13 *EJIL* 243; CM Chinkin, 'Kosovo: A "Good" or "Bad" War?' (1999) 93 *AJIL* 841, at 845.

principles dealing with limits on individuals' rights for national security reasons.[11] Human security still has a role in drawing attention to ways in which states and the pursuit of national security may negatively affect individuals' security in ways that do not amount to human rights violations. It may also be useful because of the way it works within security discourse to remind us of this risk, which tends to be glossed over in some discussions of security. It is also, therefore, well positioned to serve as a corrective to the tendency to prioritise issues that become labelled as security threats. However, it seems clear that human security has a relatively modest function here as a supplement to human rights.

We can also, however, find examples illustrating that human security might play a distinct role in some respects, beyond what might already be derived from human rights. The common responsibility dimension of human security is important to the notion of a 'responsibility to protect' as formulated by the ICISS, and the internationally shared responsibilities associated with the sovereignty as responsibility framework. In chapter six it was argued that while some limits on SALW transfers could be derived from human rights obligations, more extensive obligations to consider the human security impacts of transfers in particular situations would be required to provide more effective protection. It would be difficult to attach the full range of these to recognised human rights obligations. In the context of global disease surveillance and control, it is unclear whether the full extent of international assistance and cooperation required to ensure adequate public health capacity and mitigate the human impact of disease outbreaks and control measures could be derived from existing human rights obligations, although if obligations of cooperation with respect to economic, social, and cultural rights were broadly interpreted, they would provide an important basis for these efforts.

An important question, of course, is whether the role that human security has played in these examples as a supplement to a more limited scope of human rights arguments or obligations is due to inherent differences between them, or merely contingent on the ways in which each happens to have been used in different contexts. Unfortunately, however, it is extremely difficult to make sound generalisations in answer to this question, because so much depends on how human security and human rights, respectively, are defined and used. The discussion in chapter two highlighted the lack of agreement on the proper scope and definition of

---

[11] See, eg, International Covenant on Civil and Political Rights (adopted 16 December 1966, entered into force 23 March 1976) 999 UNTS 171, arts 4, 12(3), 13, 14(1), 19(3)(b), 21, 22(2); UN Sub-Commission on the Prevention of Discrimination and Protection of Minorities, 'Siracusa Principles on the Limitation and Derogation Provisions in the International Covenant on Civil and Political Rights' (28 September 1984) UN Doc E/CN.4/1985/4, Annex.

human security; meanwhile, the extent of international human rights obligations remains the subject of ongoing discussion and development. Among the examples just cited, some are likely to point to important differences between human rights and human security, while others do not. Take, for example, the fact that human rights-influenced provisions in the IHR (2005) focus on physical integrity, discriminatory application of public health measures, and protection of privacy, while having little to say about protection of livelihoods and food security, or potential health impacts that might result from the distortion of public health priorities toward global surveillance. This may well reflect historical divisions between civil and political rights, on one hand, and economic, social, and cultural rights, on the other, but since the current international framework includes both, there does not seem to be any obvious reason why human rights-based concerns in global disease surveillance and control should neglect impacts on individuals' standard of living or health.

Where consistent differences in the respective roles of human rights and human security are apparent, they seem to have most to do with the limitations on transnational duties in human rights as compared to the more extensive obligations that might be derived from common responsibility for human security. As outlined in chapter three, there are some transnational dimensions to states' obligations under international human rights law, and there appears to be increasing interest in exploring the limits of these among scholars, activists, and human rights institutions. However, it remains the case that most obligations under human rights treaties are owed to individuals within the territory or jurisdiction of a state, and this has been interpreted quite narrowly in recent cases, extending only to individuals or territory under the effective control of the state. Broader transnational obligations of cooperation and assistance exist with respect to economic, social, and cultural rights, but the scope of these obligations is uncertain and enforcement mechanisms are weak. Human rights and associated obligations are still, by and large, treated as flowing between a state and the individuals with whom it has the special relationship of jurisdiction. Notwithstanding increasing interdependence and globalisation, this relationship still has important legal significance. The notion of common responsibility for human security, by contrast, would extend beyond this to include a range of situations in which a state does not have jurisdiction or control over individuals but its acts or omissions may create, contribute to, mitigate, or prevent threats to their security. This broader understanding of global responsibility for individuals' security played an important role in each of the chapters, which would be difficult to duplicate using a human rights framework.

If the main difference between human rights and human security is the extent of global or transnational obligations that attach to each of them, this points to at least two possible ways in which we could conceive of the relationship between these concepts. Especially given that there is already some interest in exploring and extending the boundaries of transnational human rights obligations, human security could be invoked as a support and catalyst for carrying forward such developments. In essence, the aim might be to gradually expand the scope of human rights obligations to match the cosmopolitan dimensions of common responsibility for human security. Given that many already believe human rights to have a cosmopolitan basis, this does not seem such a far-fetched idea. However, there is an alternative approach which may be preferable. Rather than trying to stretch the limits of human rights obligations, we could recognise a distinct and supplementary role for human security as a way of thinking about, and advocating for, broader responsibilities. Not every responsibility recognised in international law that relates to the protection of individuals must be based on a corresponding legal right of individuals to receive that protection. There may be good reasons (both practical and theoretical) for continuing to focus on the relationship of jurisdiction as the primary site of human rights obligations, recognising that there is something special about that relationship, even in a globalised world. This would not, however, preclude the development and recognition of more extensive responsibilities on states where their conduct affects human security beyond their jurisdiction.

Some may yet remain to be convinced that human security has a sufficiently distinct role in comparison to human rights or other frameworks. The criticism that human security is redundant and adds nothing to existing concepts is perhaps the most difficult to address because it is far from clear what criteria and threshold are to be used in deciding whether a 'new' concept is sufficiently novel and useful to be worth talking about. Its novelty and utility also clearly depend on the ways in which the concept is defined and used, which remain the subject of debate.

ASSESSING THE UTILITY OF HUMAN SECURITY

Different Understandings of Human Security

The contributions of a human security approach to analysis and policy debates, especially as distinct from human rights, seem to depend to a significant degree on the element of common responsibility for human security. It was argued in chapter two that this notion of common responsibility or common concern is most coherent in a formulation that treats the security of each individual as a matter of equal worth and concern, echoing certain versions of moral cosmopolitanism. However, it was also noted that scholars and, in particular, policy-makers were not consistent in adopting this 'strong' version of common responsibility for human security, sometimes emphasising instead a 'weak' version of common concern which treats insecurity of distant populations as a matter of concern only because of its potential impacts on security at home. In a globalised world of interdependence and 'mutual vulnerability', insecurity anywhere is thought to potentially threaten security everywhere. This approach does not necessarily treat the security of individuals in foreign countries as being of equal importance to the security of a state's own nationals, however. It has been suggested that if a human security agenda is taken seriously, 'the state embracing it should organize itself in a way to be able to implement its commitment to the safety of ordinary people in other places'.[12] This implementation will be complex and challenging, and therefore will require a high level of support. That support may be lacking, especially if it appears that the government will have to risk the security of its own people to give effect to this commitment. Although it was suggested above that common responsibility will not always require this, it will certainly be a political concern.

This could mean that states will merely pay lip service to human security and fail to give effect to it through their policies, at least when they cannot also justify action based on potential domestic impacts due to mutual vulnerability. Without the cosmopolitan dimension, a human security approach loses part of its distinctive value as compared to national security. It can function as a corrective when the pursuit of national security fails to provide security for individuals, but remains focused on national interests. If this approach is adopted, states may use the language of human security to justify policies that protect their own populations while actually increasing risks for foreigners. This seems essentially to be the criticism of human security discourse in the context of prevention and containment of displacement, as we saw in chapter five. It was suggested there that invoking human security to support such policies was a misuse of the concept. However, this is based on the understanding that it includes the strong, cosmopolitan version of common responsibility for human security. To the extent that this dimension is lost or rejected, this will influence the distinctive value that the concept has in analysis, and the range of policy positions it might be used to support.

Another source of uncertainty as to the meaning of human security is the debate over its scope. As we saw in chapter two, one of the definitional questions that has been most contentious is whether human security, or a human security agenda, should include protection from a broad range of serious and pervasive threats or a narrower set of threats from conflict or other systematic physical violence. It was suggested that it would be

---

[12] Hataley and Nossal, above n 4, at 7.

preferable to define the scope of threats to human security by reference to a threshold of severity rather than categorisations of sources or types of threats. Although testing this point was not a major objective of the present work, analysis of the issues examined did seem to suggest that drawing distinctions between different types of threats was not useful, or even feasible in some cases. For example, the threats against which displaced persons require protection and the root causes of displacement include both violence and economic, health, or environmental factors. Although the primary concern with respect to SALW is the direct impact of their use in armed violence, other significant concerns include indirect impacts on livelihoods and economic development. Given that there are links between conflict and other threats like disease as contributing causes or 'indirect costs' of conflict, any attempt to limit the agenda to a narrow focus on conflict seems to be no more than a convenient starting point which quickly breaks down in practice.[13] A broad definition of human security encompassing any serious risk to health seemed, in the analysis of global disease surveillance and control, to be not only workable but important as a critique of some of the negative effects that might otherwise result from securitisation.

The ongoing debate about the concept of human security, including these two questions, means that there will continue to be some variation in the ways in which it is used. Does this mean that human security is useless because its content is so unclear that it can be used to justify contradictory positions?[14] This criticism seems unduly harsh, for two reasons. First, we need to remember that any concept of security could be invoked to support different and even contradictory policies, since policy choices are based not only on the framework provided by a concept of security but also empirical evaluations and difficult predictions in the face of uncertainty and complexity. We should not, therefore, be surprised if the same is the case for human security. Secondly, it may be difficult or impossible to prevent individuals or governments from attaching the label 'human security' to arguments that seem inconsistent with its conceptual basis. However, if we can distinguish between uses of the concept which are or are not consistent with a commonly understood meaning, as we have at several points of this analysis, this suggests that it does indeed have some stable content against which those uses can be evaluated.

---

[13] For example, the Human Security Report, although expressly adopting the narrower approach, includes a very useful analysis of 'indirect costs', in particular health impacts: Human Security Centre, *Human Security Report 2005: War and Peace in the 21st Century* (New York, Oxford University Press, 2005), at pt IV.

[14] See H Owens and B Arneil, 'Human Security Paradigm Shift: A New Lens on Canadian Foreign Policy?' (1999) 7(1) *Canadian Foreign Policy* 1, at 2 (noting concerns that the concept could lead to incompatible policy prescriptions).

Potential and Limits

There are important limits to the functions that human security can serve; however, these are not just a result of the breadth or vagueness of the concept, but are, to a large extent, inherent in a concept of this nature. It will be more useful in some functions and some contexts than others, and if we understand these limits we can more realistically assess its potential. Just as it was difficult to make valid generalisations about the distinctive role of human security as distinct from human rights, it is also challenging to summarise the concept's potential on the basis of a few selected examples. However, the analysis has permitted some insights into the ways in which human security may or may not be useful as a way of approaching questions and problems in international law. Its potential seems to be greater than admitted by its harshest critics, yet more modest than claimed by some of its proponents. It also seems to vary depending on the context in which it is used and the functions we expect it to fulfil.

Despite the common threads running through the examples discussed in chapters four to seven, there are significant differences between them which affect the ways in which we might use the concept of human security. Humanitarian intervention involves a long-running legal contro-versy about the legality of the use of force under particular circumstances. In this context it seemed that human security could be most useful as a way of critiquing and redefining the terms of the debate. It served this function to some extent in relation to IDPs as well, by questioning the ways in which states' roles in international protection for IDPs have been framed. In both cases human security also served as a potential point of reference from which to critique policy choices, especially in evaluating whether the ways in which states implement a preventive approach actually serve to protect human security. Chapters six and seven involve areas in which the international legal framework is being developed and reformed in response to recently perceived threats, from SALW proliferation and emerging infectious diseases, respectively. Here human security had a role to play in defining the problem, serving as a guide to law reform, and critiquing the formation and implementation of new normative frameworks.

The last two examples also illustrate the different roles that human security may have depending on whether and how issues have already been part of a broader security agenda. In the case of SALW, arms are clearly part of the traditional sphere of national security. However, the problem was identified primarily as a matter of human security, since it was one that had been neglected in national security agendas; the shift in focus to impacts on individuals revealed a 'new' security concern. Identifying SALW proliferation as a problem was therefore the result of shifting the focus of security. Health issues, especially emerging and pandemic diseases, have been subject to a process of securitisation in recent years as they have been linked with traditional security concerns like armed conflict, military preparedness, and terrorism. In this context, human security functions as an alternative approach and a critique of some of the potentially negative effects of securitisation. Since, as we have seen, securitisation always carries with it some risks, human security may be especially important in this role as a critique of securitisation and its aftermath. Even where the human security agenda itself is central to identifying security issues as in the case of SALW, this critical function needs to be kept in play to prevent the issue from being absorbed into a traditional security approach, as was alleged to have happened in the UN conferences on small arms.

Finally, in all of these examples, a recurring theme of the analysis has highlighted a significant limit on the role that we can expect human security to play. Put very simply, human security seems to offer a better way of asking questions, but does not provide us with many answers. For example, shifting to a human security approach does not tell us whether a right of humanitarian intervention exists or should exist. In fact, it was suggested that attempting to use the concept of human security to resolve this debate was misleading and unhelpful, and that we would be better off using the concept to shift the debate and encourage us to focus on different questions: what could or should be done to avoid having to ask this question at all? When a crisis does arise, human security does not and cannot tell us whether, in a particular factual context, military intervention is more likely to protect or threaten human security. It guides us to the criteria we should use in making this decision—impacts on individual security, rather than respect for sovereignty or the lack thereof—but will not provide a clear formula for finding the answer. The analysis of international protection for IDPs, regulation of SALW transfers, and global responses to infectious disease all led to similar conclusions: that human security can provide a framework for analysing issues, a range of permissible answers and, more importantly, the criteria by which to decide on a course of action. However, decisions in each context will ultimately depend on determinations which are highly fact-specific and must take into account complex networks of causation.

Whether we are developing legal norms to address a new threat, or applying existing norms, reference to human security helps in identifying questions to ask rather than revealing answers. Those who are expecting the concept to provide clear guidance to policy-makers will be frustrated by this limitation. We need to remember, though, that other security concepts have not provided clear answers to policy dilemmas either, so it would be unrealistic to expect this of human security. Accepting these limits on the concept's function will help to avoid inflated expectations of the assistance it can provide, and to reduce the risk of its being misused or trivialised as an easy solution to difficult problems. A human security approach may instead represent a more challenging yet productive opportunity to rethink debates and developments in international law.

Bibliography

Acharya A, 'Debating Human Security: East Versus West' (2001) 56 *International Journal* 442.

Acharya A and A Acharya, 'Human Security in Asia Pacific: Puzzle, Panacea or Peril?' (2000) 27 *CANCAPS Bulletin/Bulletin du CONCSAP* 1 <http://www.cancaps.ca/cbul27.pdf> (accessed 6 March 2007).

Acharya A and DB Dewitt, 'Fiscal Burden Sharing' in JC Hathaway (ed), *Reconceiving International Refugee Law* (The Hague, Martinus Nijhoff, 1997).

Adelman H, 'From Refugees to Forced Migration: The UNHCR and Human Security' (2001) 35(1) *The International Migration Review* 7.

Agathangelou AM and LHM Ling, 'Power, Borders, Security, Wealth: Lessons of Violence and Desire from September 11' (2004) 48 *International Studies Quarterly* 517.

Aginam O, 'Globalization of Infectious Diseases, International Law and the World Health Organization: Opportunities for Synergy in Global Governance of Epidemics' (2004) 11(1) *New England Journal of International and Comparative Law* 59.

Akehurst M, 'Humanitarian Intervention' in H Bull (ed), *Intervention in World Politics* (Oxford, Clarendon Press, 1984).

Aleinikoff TA, 'State-centred Refugee Law: From Resettlement to Containment' (1992) 14 *Michigan Journal of International Law* 120.

Alkire S, 'Conceptual Framework for Human Security (Excerpt: Working Definition and Executive Summary)' (16 February 2002) <http://www.humansecurity-chs.org/activities/outreach/frame.pdf> (accessed 27 February 2007).

Allott P, *Eunomia: New Order for a New World* (Oxford, Oxford University Press, 1990).

Altman D, 'Understanding HIV/AIDS as a Global Security Issue' in K Lee (ed), *Health Impacts of Globalization: Towards Global Governance* (Houndmills, Palgrave Macmillan, 2003).

Amnesty International and Human Rights Watch, 'Address to the United Nations Conference on the Illicit Trade in Small Arms and Light Weapons in All Its Aspects' (New York, 16 July 2001) <http://disarmament.un.org/cab/smallarms/statements/Ngo/aisl.html> (accessed 13 March 2007).

Annan K, 'The Quiet Revolution' (1998) 4 *Global Governance* 123.

Archibugi D, 'Cosmopolitan Guidelines for Humanitarian Intervention' (2004) 29 *Alternatives* 1.

Arya A, 'Confronting the Small Arms Pandemic' (2002) 324 *British Medical Journal* 990.

Australia, Department of Foreign Affairs and Trade, 'Future Directions for the United Nations,' (Inaugural Sir Kenneth Bailey Memorial Lecture, University of Melbourne, 29 April 1995) <http://www.dfat.gov.au/archive/speeches_old/minfor/gexi.html> (accessed 26 February 2007).

Axworthy L, 'Human Security: An Opening for UN Reform' in RM Price and MW Zacher, *The United Nations and Global Security* (New York, Palgrave MacMillan, 2004).

—— 'Human Security and Global Governance: Putting People First' (2001) 7 *Global Governance* 19.

—— 'Introduction' in R McRae and D Hubert (eds), *Human Security and the New Diplomacy: Protecting People, Promoting Peace* (Montreal and Kingston, McGill-Queen's University Press, 2001).

—— 'Towards a New Multilateralism' in MA Cameron, RJ Lawson and BW Tomlin (eds), *To Walk Without Fear: The Global Movement to Ban Landmines* (Toronto, Oxford University Press, 1998).

Axworthy L and S Taylor, 'A Ban for All Seasons: The Landmines Convention and Its Implications for Canadian Diplomacy' (1998) 53 *International Journal* 189.

Ayoob M, 'Defining Security: A Subaltern Realist Perspective' in K Krause and MC Williams (eds), *Critical Security Studies: Concepts and Cases* (Minneapolis, University of Minnesota Press, 1997).

—— 'Humanitarian Intervention and State Sovereignty' (2002) 6 *International Journal of Human Rights* 81.

Azzam F, 'The Duty of Third States to Implement and Enforce International Humanitarian Law' (1997) *Nordic Journal of International Law* 55.

Babovič B, 'The Duty of States to Cooperate with One Another in Accordance with the Charter' in M Šahovič (ed), *Principles of International Law Concerning Friendly Relations and Cooperation* (Dobbs Ferry, NY, Oceana Publications, 1972).

Bain WW, 'Against Crusading: the Ethic of Human Security and Canadian Foreign Policy' (1999) 6(3) *Canadian Foreign Policy* 85.

—— 'The Tyranny of Benevolence: National Security, Human Security, and the Practice of Statecraft' (2001) 15 *Global Society* 277.

Bajpai K, 'Human Security: Concept and Measurement' (Kroc Institute Occasional Paper 19:OP:1, August 2000).

Baldwin DA, 'The Concept of Security' (1997) 23 *Review of International Studies* 5.

Barnett T, 'A Long-wave Event. HIV/AIDS, Politics, Governance and 'Security': Sundering the Intergenerational Bond?' (2006) 82 *International Affairs* 297.

Barnett T and G Prins, 'HIV/AIDS and Security: Fact, Fiction and Evidence—A Report to UNAIDS' (2006) 82 *International Affairs* 359.

Barry B, 'International Society from a Cosmopolitan Perspective' in DR Mapel and T Nardin (eds), *International Society: Diverse Ethical Perspectives* (Princeton, Princeton University Press, 1998).

Barutciski M, 'Tensions Between the Refugee Concept and the IDP Debate' (1998) 3 *Forced Migration Review* 11.

Barutciski M and A Suhrke, 'Lessons from the Kosovo Refugee Crisis: Innovations in Protection and Burden-sharing' (2001) 14 *Journal of Refugee Studies* 95.

Batchelor P and G McDonald, 'Too Close for Comfort: An Analysis of the UN Tracing Negotiations' (2005–06) 2005(4)/2006(1) *Disarmament Forum* 39.

Beeson M and AJ Bellamy, 'Globalisation, Security and International Order After 11 September' (2003) 49 *Australian Journal of Politics and History* 339.

Beier JM and AD Crosby, 'Harnessing Change for Continuity: The Play of Political and Economic Forces Behind the Ottawa Process' in MA Cameron, RJ Lawson and BW Tomlin (eds), *To Walk Without Fear: The Global Movement to Ban Landmines* (Toronto, Oxford University Press, 1998).

Bell D and M Renner, 'A New Marshall Plan? Advancing Human Security and Controlling Terrorism' (8 October 2001) <http://www.worldwatch.org/node/1706> (accessed 26 February 2007).

Bellamy AJ, 'Responsibility to Protect or Trojan Horse? The Crisis in Darfur and Humanitarian Intervention after Iraq' (2005) 19 *Ethics and International Affairs* 31.

Bellamy AJ and M McDonald, '"The Utility of Human Security": Which Humans? What Security? A Reply to Thomas and Tow' (2002) 33 *Security Dialogue* 373.

Bennett J, 'Rights and Borders' (1999) 4 *Forced Migration Review* 33.

Bennoune K, '"Sovereignty vs. Suffering"? Re-examining Sovereignty and Human Rights through the Lens of Iraq' (2002) 13 *EJIL* 243.

Bergen P and A Reynolds, 'Blowback Revisited' (2005) 84(6) *Foreign Affairs* 2.

Berman Institute of Bioethics, 'Bellagio Statement of Principles' (2006) <http://www.hopkinsmedicine.org/bioethics/bellagio/Bellagio_Statement.pdf> (accessed 25 April 2007).

Bettati M, 'Un droit d'ingérence?' (1991) 3 *Revue générale de droit international public* 639.

Birnie P and A Boyle, *International Law and the Environment*, 2nd edn (Oxford, Oxford University Press, 2002).

Bloche MG, 'WTO Deference To National Health Policy: Toward an Interpretive Principle' (2002) 5 *Journal of International Economic Law* 825.

Boisson de Chazournes L and L Condorelli, 'Common Article 1 of the Geneva Conventions Revisited: Protecting Collective Interests' (2000) 837 *IRRC* 67.

Booth K, 'Security and Emancipation' (1991) 17 *Review of International Studies* 313.

Bowring B, 'The "droit et devoir d'ingérence": A Timely New Remedy for Africa?' (1995) 7 *Revue africaine de droit international et comparé* 493.

Boyle AE, 'International Law and the Protection of the Global Atmosphere: Concepts, Categories and Principles' in R Churchill and D Freestone (eds), *International Law and Global Climate Change* (London, Graham and Trotman, 1991).

—— 'The Principle of Co-operation: The Environment' in V Lowe and C Warbrick (eds), *The United Nations and the Principles of International Law: Essays in memory of Michael Akehurst* (London, Routledge, 1994).

Boyle K and S Simonsen, 'Human Security, Human Rights and Disarmament' (2004) 3 *Disarmament Forum* 5.

Bratspies RM and RA Miller, 'Introduction' in RM Bratspies and RA Miller, *Transboundary Harm in International Law: Lessons from the* Trail Smelter Arbitration (Cambridge, Cambridge University Press, 2006).

Bratt D, 'Blue Condoms: The Use of International Peacekeepers in the Fight Against AIDS' (2002) 9(3) *International Peacekeeping* 67.

Brem S and K Rutherford, 'Walking Together or Divided Agenda? Comparing Landmines and Small-Arms Campaigns' (2001) 32 *Security Dialogue* 169.

Brownlie I, *International Law and the Use of Force by States* (Oxford, Clarendon Press, 1963).

—— *Principles of Public International Law*, 6th edn (Oxford, Oxford University Press, 2003).

Brownlie I and CJ Apperley, 'Kosovo Crisis Inquiry: Memorandum on the International Law Aspects' (2000) 49 *ICLQ* 878.

Brownlie I and CJ Apperley, 'Kosovo Crisis Inquiry: Further Memorandum on the International Law Aspects' (2000) 49 *ICLQ* 905.

Bruderlein C, 'People's Security as a New Measure of Global Stability' (2001) 842 *IRRC* 353.

Brunnee J and SJ Toope, 'Environmental Security and Freshwater Resources: Ecosystem Regime Building' (1997) 91 *AJIL* 26.

Bruntland GH, 'Global Health and International Security' (2003) 9 *Global Governance* 417.

Bunch C, 'A Feminist Human Rights Lens' (2004) 16 *Peace Review* 29.

Burchill S, 'Liberal Internationalism' in S Burchill and A Linklater (eds), *Theories of International Relations* (New York, St Martin's Press, 1995).

—— 'Realism and Neo-realism' in S Burchill and A Linklater (eds), *Theories of International Relations* (New York, St Martin's Press, 1995).

Burke A, 'Caught between National and Human Security: Knowledge and Power in Post-crisis Asia' (2001) 13 *Pacifica Review* 215.

Burnham G *et al*, 'Mortality after the 2003 Invasion of Iraq: A Cross-Sectional Cluster Sample Survey' (2006) 368 *Lancet* 1421.

Button C, *The Power to Protect: Trade, Health and Uncertainty in the WTO* (Oxford, Hart, 2004).

Buzan B, *People, States and Fear: An Agenda for International Security Studies in the Post-Cold War Era*, 2nd edn (New York, Harvester Wheatsheaf, 1991).

—— 'A Reductionist, Idealistic Notion that Adds Little Analytical Value' (2004) 35 *Security Dialogue* 369.

—— 'Rethinking Security after the Cold War' (1997) 32 *Cooperation and Conflict* 5.

—— 'The Timeless Wisdom of Realism?' in S Smith, K Booth and M Zalewski (eds), *International Theory: Positivism and Beyond* (Cambridge, Cambridge University Press, 1996).

Buzan B, O Wæver and J de Wilde, *Security: A New Framework for Analysis* (Boulder, CO, Lynne Rienner, 1998).

Caballero-Anthony M, 'Combating Infectious Diseases in East Asia: Securitization and Global Public Goods for Health and Human Security' (2006) 59 *Journal of International Affairs* 105.

—— 'Human Security and Primary Health Care in Asia: Realities and Challenges' in L Chen, J Leaning and V Narasimhan (eds), *Global Health Challenges for Human Security* (Cambridge, MA, Harvard University Press, 2003).

Calain P, 'Exploring the International Arena of Global Public Health Surveillance' (2007) 22 *Health Policy and Planning* 2.

—— 'From the Field Side of the Binoculars: A Different View on Global Public Health Surveillance' (2007) 22 *Health Policy and Planning* 13.

Canada, DFAIT, 'Axworthy Outlines Canada's United Nations Security Council Presidency Agenda', News Release No 64 (6 April 2000) <http://w01.international.gc.ca/minpub> (accessed 26 February 2007).

—— 'Canada and Human Security', Statement No 2000/8 (17 February 2000) <http://w01.international.gc.ca/minpub> (accessed 26 March 2007).

—— 'Canada and Norway Form New Partnership on Human Security', News Release No 117 (11 May 1998) <http://w01.international.gc.ca/minpub> (accessed 26 February 2007).

—— *Freedom from Fear: Canada's Foreign Policy for Human Security* (Ottawa, DFAIT,

2000) <http://www.humansecurity.gc.ca/pdf/freedom_from_fear-en.pdf> (accessed 27 February 2007).

—— *Human Security: Safety for People in a Changing World* (Ottawa, DFAIT, 1999).

—— 'Informal, Intersessional Programme of Work: Announcement by Canada' (7 July 2006) <http://www.fac-aec.gc.ca/department/can_announcement-en. asp> (accessed 13 March 2007).

—— 'Notes for an Address by the Honourable Lloyd Axworthy Minister of Foreign Affairs to the Empire Club', Statement 99/43 (28 June 1999) <http:// w01.international.gc.ca/minpub> (accessed 26 February 2007).

—— 'Notes for an Address by the Honourable Lloyd Axworthy, Minister of Foreign Affairs, to the G-8 Foreign Ministers' Meeting', Statement 99/40 (9 June 1999) <http://w01.international.gc.ca/minpub> (accessed 26 February 2007).

—— 'Notes for an Address by the Honourable Lloyd Axworthy Minister of Foreign Affairs to the 51st General Assembly of the United Nations', Statement 96/37 (24 September 1996) <http://w01.international.gc.ca/minpub> (accessed 26 February 2007).

—— 'Notes for an Address by the Honourable Lloyd Axworthy, Minister of Foreign Affairs, to the 55th UN General Assembly', Statement 2000/31 (14 September 2000) <http://w01.international.gc.ca/minpub> (accessed 26 February 2007).

Cassese A, '*Ex iniuiria ius oritur*: Are we Moving towards International Legitimation of Forcible Humanitarian Countermeasures in the World Community?' (1999) 10 *EJIL* 23.

—— 'A Follow-up: Forcible Humanitarian Countermeasures and *Opinio Necessitatis*' (1999) 10 *EJIL* 791.

—— *International Law* (Oxford, Oxford University Press, 2001).

—— *International Law in a Divided World* (Oxford, Clarendon Press, 1986).

Centre for Humanitarian Dialogue, *Putting People First: Human Security Perspectives on Small Arms Availability and Misuse* (Geneva, Centre for Humanitarian Dialogue, 2003) <http://www.hdcentre.org/datastore/PPFeng.pdf> (accessed 29 March 2007).

Charlesworth H and C Chinkin, *The Boundaries of International Law: A Feminist Analysis* (Manchester, Manchester University Press, 2000).

Charney JI, 'Anticipatory Humanitarian Intervention in Kosovo' (1999) 93 *AJIL* 834.

Chatterjee M and MK Ranson, 'Livelihood Security Through Community-Based Health Insurance' in L Chen, J Leaning and V Narasimhan (eds), *Global Health Challenges for Human Security* (Cambridge, MA, Harvard University Press, 2003).

Chen L, J Leaning and V Narasimhan (eds), *Global Health Challenges for Human Security* (Cambridge, MA, Harvard University Press, 2003).

Chen L and V Narasimhan, 'A Human Security Agenda for Global Health' in L Chen, J Leaning and V Narasimhan (eds), *Global Health Challenges for Human Security* (Cambridge, MA, Harvard University Press, 2003).

Chesterman S, *Just War or Just Peace? International Law and Humanitarian Intervention* (Oxford, Oxford University Press, 2001).

Chimni BS, 'The Principle of Burden-Sharing' in BS Chimni (ed), *International Refugee Law: A Reader* (London, Sage Publications, 1999).

Chinkin C, 'The Legality of NATO's Action in the Former Republic of Yugoslavia (FRY) Under International Law' (2000) 49 *ICLQ* 910.

Chinkin CM, 'Kosovo: A "Good" or "Bad" War?' (1999) 93 *AJIL* 841.

Chyba CF, 'Biological Security' (Paper commissioned by the United Nations and Global Security initiative of the United Nations Foundation) <http://www.un-globalsecurity.org/pdf/chyba.pdf> (accessed 28 January 2007).

Coghlan B, 'Mortality in the Democratic Republic of Congo: A Nationwide Survey' (2006) 367 *Lancet* 44.

Cohen R, 'Developing a System for Internally Displaced Persons' (2006) 7 *International Studies Perspectives* 87.

—— 'The Guiding Principles on Internal Displacement: An Innovation in International Standard Setting' (2004) 10 *Global Governance* 459.

Cohen R and FM Deng, *Masses in Flight: The Global Crisis of Internal Displacement* (Washington, DC, Brookings Institution, 1998).

Commission on Global Governance, *Our Global Neighborhood: The Report of the Commission on Global Governance* (Oxford, Oxford University Press, 1995).

Commission on Human Security, 'Declaration on Human Rights as an Essential Component of Human Security' (Workshop on Relationship Between Human Rights and Human Security, San Jose, Costa Rica, 2 December 2001) <http://www.humansecurity-chs.org/activities/outreach/sanjosedec.pdf> (accessed 27 February 2007).

—— *Human Security Now: Protecting and Empowering People* (New York, Commission on Human Security, 2003) <http://www.humansecurity-chs.org/finalreport/index.html> (accessed 26 February 2007).

—— 'Plan for the Establishment of the Commission on Human Security', Press Release (24 January 2001) <http://www.humansecurity-chs.org/activities/outreach/pressrelease.pdf> (accessed 26 February 2007).

—— 'Relación entre Derechos Humanos y Seguridad Humana' (Documento de trabajo) (Comisión sobre Seguridad Humana—Universidad para la Paz—Instituto Interamericano de Derechos Humanos, Reunión de Expertos, San José, Costa Rica, 1 December 2001) <http://www.humansecurity-chs.org/activities/outreach/sanjosedoc.pdf> (accessed 27 February 2007).

—— 'Report: Meeting of the Commission on Human Security' (8–10 June 2001) <http://www.humansecurity-chs.org/activities/meetings/first/report.pdf> (accessed 9 March 2007).

— 'Report: Second Meeting of the Commission on Human Security' (16–17 December 2001) <http://www.humansecurity-chs.org/activities/meetings/second/report.pdf> (accessed 27 February 2007).

Conlon J, 'Sovereignty vs. Human Rights or Sovereignty and Human Rights?' (2004) 46 *Race and Class* 75.

Coupland R, 'Humanity: What is it and How does it Influence International law' (2001) 83 *IRRC* 969.

Coursen-Neff Z, 'Preventive Measures Pertaining to Unconventional Threats to the Peace such as Natural and Humanitarian Disasters' (1998) *New York University Journal of International Law and Politics* 645.

Craven M, 'Humanitarianism and the Quest for Smarter Sanctions' (2002) 13 *EJIL* 43.

Crawford J, *The International Law Commission's Articles on State Responsibility:*

Introduction, Text and Commentaries (Cambridge, Cambridge University Press, 2002).

Crisp J, 'Refugees and International Security: An Introduction to Some Key Issues and Policy Challenges,' (Geneva, 4th International Security Forum, 15–17 November 2000) <http://www.isn.ethz.ch/4isf/4/Papers/ISF_WS_II-4_Crisp. pdf> (accessed 10 March 2007).

Crosby AD, 'Myths of Canada's Human Security Pursuits: Tales of Tool Boxes, Toy Chests, and Tickle Trunks' in CT Sjolander, H Smith and D Steinstra (eds), *Feminist Perspectives on Canadian Foreign Policy* (Don Mills, Ontario, Oxford University Press, 2003).

Cukier W, A Chapdelaine and C Collins, 'Globalization and Small/Firearms: A Public Health Perspective' (1999) 42(4) *Development* 40.

Cukier W and S Shropshire, 'Domestic Gun Markets: The Licit–Illicit Links' in L Lumpe (ed), *Running Guns: The Global Black Market in Small Arms* (London, Zed Books, 2000).

Curley M and N Thomas, 'Human Security and Public Health in Southeast Asia: the SARS Outbreak' (2004) 58 *Australian Journal of International Affairs* 17.

D'Amato A, 'The Invasion of Panama Was a Lawful Response to Tyranny' (1990) 84 *AJIL* 516.

David M, 'Rubber Helmets: The Certain Pitfalls of Marshaling Security Council Resources to Combat AIDS in Africa' (2001) 23 *Human Rights Quarterly* 560.

de Larrinaga M and C Turenne Sjolander, '(Re)presenting Landmines from Protector to Enemy: The Discursive Framing of a New Multilateralism' in MA Cameron, RJ Lawson and BW Tomlin (eds), *To Walk Without Fear: The Global Movement to Ban Landmines* (Toronto, Oxford University Press, 1998).

de Waal A, 'HIV/AIDS: The Security Issue of a Lifetime' in L Chen, J Leaning and V Narasimhan (eds), *Global Health Challenges for Human Security* (Cambridge, MA, Harvard University Press, 2003).

Deng FM *et al*, *Sovereignty as Responsibility: Conflict Management in Africa* (Washington, DC, Brookings Institution, 1996).

Denters EMG, 'IMF Conditionality: Economic, Social and Cultural Rights, and the Evolving Principle of Solidarity' in PJIM de Waart, P Peters and E Denters (eds), *International Law and Development* (Dordrecht, Martinus Nijhoff, 1988).

Department of Homeland Security, *Department Six-point Agenda* <http://www. dhs.gov/xabout/history/editorial_0646.shtm> (accessed 7 March 2007).

Depoortere E *et al*, 'Violence and Mortality in West Darfur, Sudan (2003–04): Epidemiological Evidence from Four Surveys' (2004) 364 *Lancet* 1315.

Deudney D, 'The Case Against Linking Environmental Degradation and National Security' (1990) 19 *Millennium: Journal of International Studies* 461.

Donnelly J, *Realism and International Relations* (Cambridge, Cambridge University Press, 2000).

—— 'The Social Construction of International Human Rights' in T Dunne and NJ Wheeler (eds), *Human Rights in Global Politics* (Cambridge University Press, Cambridge, 1999).

—— 'State Sovereignty and International Intervention: The Case of Human Rights' in GM Lyons and M Mastanduno (eds), *Beyond Westphalia?: State Sovereignty and International Intervention* (Baltimore, Johns Hopkins University Press, 1995).

Downing TE, 'Creating Poverty: the Flawed Economic Logic of the World Bank's Revised Involuntary Resettlement Policy' (2002) 12 *Forced Migration Review* 13.

Duxbury N, 'Human Security and the Basic Norm' (1990) 76 *Archiv fur Rechts- und Sozialphilosophie* 184.

ECOWAS (Economic Community of West African States), Declaration of a Moratorium on Importation, Exportation and Manufacture of Light Weapons in West Africa (31 October 1998) <http://www.iss.co.za/AF/RegOrg/unity_ to_union/pdfs/ecowas/1ECOWASFirearms.pdf> (accessed 25 April 2007).

Edström B, 'Japan's Foreign Policy and Human Security' (2003) 15 *Japan Forum* 209.

Egeland J, 'Arms Availability and Violations of International Humanitarian Law' (1999) 81 *IRRC* 673.

Eskeland L and P Herby, 'United Nations Conference on the Illicit Trade in Small Arms and Light Weapons in All Its Aspects' (2001) 843 *IRRC* 864, at 865.

EU, EU Code of Conduct on Arms Exports (8 June 1998) Council Doc 8675/2/98, Rev. 2, 8.6.1998.

Evans PM, 'Human Security and East Asia: In the Beginning' (2004) 4 *Journal of East Asian Studies* 263.

Faden RR, PS Duggan and R Karron, 'Who Pays to Stop a Pandemic?' (2007) *New York Times*, 9 February.

Falk RA, 'Kosovo, World Order, and the Future of International Law' (1999) 93 *AJIL* 847.

Fassbender B and A Bleckmann, 'Article 2(1)' in B Simma (ed), *The Charter of the United Nations: A Commentary*, 2nd edn (Oxford, Oxford University Press, 2002) vol I.

Feldbaum H, K Lee and P Patel, 'The National Security Implications of HIV/AIDS' (2006) 3 *PLoS Medicine* e171.

Fidler DP, 'Bioterrorism, Public Health and International Law' (2002) 3 *Chicago Journal of International Law* 7.

—— 'From International Sanitary Conventions to Global Health Security: The New International Health Regulations' (2005) 4 *Chinese Journal of International Law* 325.

—— 'A Globalized Theory of Public Health Law' (2002) 30 *Journal of Law, Medicine and Ethics* 150.

—— *SARS, Governance and the Globalization of Disease* (Houndmills, Palgrave Macmillan, 2004).

Fidler DP and N Drager, 'Health and Foreign Policy' (2006) 84 *Bulletin of the World Health Organization* 687.

Fidler DP and LO Gostin, 'The New International Health Regulations: An Historic Development for International Law and Public Health' (2006) 34 *Journal of Law Medicine and Ethics* 85.

Fischer D, *Nonmilitary Aspects of Security: A Systems Approach* (Aldershot, Dartmouth, 1993).

Fitzpatrick J, 'The Human Rights of Refugees, Asylum-Seekers, and Internally Displaced Persons: A Basic Introduction' in J Fitzpatrick (ed), *Human Rights Protection for Refugees, Asylum seekers, and Internally Displaced Persons: A Guide to International Mechanisms and Procedures* (Ardsley, NY, Transnational Publishers, 2002).

Flynn MJ, 'Political Minefield' in RA Matthew, B McDonald and KR Rutherford (eds), *Landmines and Human Security: International Politics and War's Hidden Legacy* (Albany, State University of New York Press, 2004).

Foreign Affairs Canada, 'Pandemics: A Human Security Perspective' (May 2006) <http://geo.international.gc.ca/cip-pic/library/Pandemics%20-%20A%20 Human%20Security%20Perspective.pdf> (accessed 25 April 2007).

Fossum JE, '*Gidsland* and Human Security' (2006) 61 *International Journal* 813.

Foster M, 'Kosovo and the 1997 Landmines Treaty' (September 1999) *Ploughshares Monitor* <http://www.ploughshares.ca/libraries/monitor/mons99c.html> (accessed 29 March 2007).

Franck TM, 'Lessons of Kosovo' (1999) 93 *AJIL* 857.

Franck TM and NS Rodley, 'After Bangladesh: The Law of Humanitarian Intervention by Military Force' (1973) 67 *AJIL* 275.

Freitas R, 'Human Security and Refugee Protection after September 11: A Reassessment' (2002) 20(4) *Refuge* 34.

Frowein J and N Krisch, 'Article 39' in B Simma (ed), *The Charter of the United Nations: A Commentary*, 2nd edn (Oxford, Oxford University Press, 2002) vol I.

Fujioka M, 'Japan's Human Rights Policy at Domestic and International Levels: Disconnecting Human Rights from Human Security?' (2003) 15 *Japan Forum* 287.

Furtado X, 'Human Security and Asia's Financial Crisis: A Critique of Canadian Policy' (2000) 55 *International Journal* 355.

Galtung J, 'Twenty-five Years of Peace Research: Ten Challenges and Some Responses' (1985) 22 *Journal of Peace Research* 141.

Gamba V, 'Problems and Linkages in Controlling the Proliferation of Light Weapons' in J Dhanapala *et al* (eds), *Small Arms Control: Old Weapons, New Issues* (Aldershot, Ashgate, 1999).

Garrett L, 'The Return of Infectious Disease' (1996) 75 *Foreign Affairs* 66.

Gaulin T, 'A Necessary Evil? Reexamining the Military Utility of Antipersonnel Landmines' in RA Matthew, B McDonald and KR Rutherford (eds), *Landmines and Human Security: International Politics and War's Hidden Legacy* (Albany, State University of New York Press, 2004).

Geissler N, 'The International Protection of Internally Displaced Persons' (1999) 11 *International Journal of Refugee Law* 451.

Ghatak S, *Introduction to Development Economics*, 3rd edn (London, Routledge, 1995).

Gibney M, K Tomaševski and J Vedsted-Hansen, 'Transnational State Responsibility for Violations of Human Rights' (1999) 12 *Harvard Human Rights Journal* 267.

Giesecke J, 'International Health Regulations and Epidemic Control' in RD Smith *et al*, *Global Public Goods for Health: Health Economic and Public Health Perspectives* (Oxford, Oxford University Press, 2003).

Gillard E, 'What is Legal? What is Illegal? Limitations on Transfers of Small Arms under International Law' <http://www.armstradetreaty.com/att/what.is. legal.what.is.illegal.pdf> (accessed 29 March 2007).

—— 'What's Legal? What's Illegal?' in L Lumpe (ed), *Running Guns: The Global Black Market in Small Arms* (London, Zed Books, 2000).

Gilson J and P Purvis, 'Japan's Pursuit of Human Security: Humanitarian Agenda or Political Pragmatism?' (2003) 15 *Japan Forum* 193.

Glasius M and M Kaldor, 'Individuals First: A Human Security Strategy for the European Union' (2005) 1 *Internationale Politik und Gesellschaft* 62.

Goodwin-Gill GS, 'After the Cold War: Asylum and the Refugee Concept Move On' (2001) 10 *Forced Migration Review* 14.

—— 'Refugees and Security' (1999) 11 *International Journal of Refugee Law* 1.

Goose SD and F Smyth, 'Arming Genocide in Rwanda' (1994) 73(5) *Foreign Affairs* 86.

Gostin LO, 'International Infectious Disease Law: Revision of the World Health Organization's International Health Regulations' (2004) 291 *Journal of the American Medical Association* 2623.

—— 'World Health Law: Toward a New Conception of Global Health Governance for the 21st Century' (2005) 5 *Yale Journal of Health Policy, Law and Ethics* 413.

Graham K, '"We Have Come to a Fork in the Road . . . Now We Must Decide": Human Security in Context' (Opening Address at the 17th Annual Meeting of the Academic Council of the United Nations System, 30 June–2 July 2004; UN-CRIS Occasional Paper 0-2004/17) <http://www.cris.unu.edu/admin/documents/OP%20KENNEDY%20GRAHAM%20Geneva%203%20Short.pdf> (accessed 27 February 2007).

Gray C, *International Law and the Use of Force* (Oxford, Oxford University Press, 2000).

Green LC, *The Contemporary Law of Armed Conflict*, 2nd edn (Manchester, Manchester University Press, 2000).

Greene O, 'Examining International Responses to Illicit Arms Trafficking' (2000) 33 *Crime, Law and Social Change* 151.

Greenwood C, 'International Law and the NATO Intervention in Kosovo' (2000) 49 *ICLQ* 926.

Grossman C and DD Bradlow, 'Are We Being Propelled Towards a People-Centered Transnational Legal Order?' (1993) 9 *American University Journal of International Law and Policy* 1.

Gruskin S, J Mann and MA Grodin (eds), *Health and Human Rights: A Reader* (New York, Routledge, 1999).

Gwozdecky M and J Sinclair, 'Case Study: Landmines and Human Security' in R McRae and D Hubert (eds), *Human Security and the New Diplomacy: Protecting People, Promoting Peace* (Montreal and Kingston, McGill-Queen's University Press, 2001).

Hammerstad A, 'Whose Security? UNHCR, Refugee Protection and State Security After the Cold War' (2000) 31 *Security Dialogue* 391.

Hampson FO, *Madness in the Multitude: Human Security and World Disorder* (Don Mills, Ontario, Oxford University Press, 2002).

Hampson FO and DF Oliver, 'Pulpit Diplomacy: A Critical Assessment of the Axworthy Doctrine' (1998) 53 *International Journal* 383.

Hans A and A Suhrke, 'Responsibility Sharing' in JC Hathaway (ed), *Reconceiving International Refugee Law* (The Hague, Martinus Nijhoff, 1997).

Hartley K, 'The Economics of the Peace Dividend' (1997) 24 *International Journal of Social Economics* 28.

Hataley TS and KR Nossal, 'The Limits of the Human Security Agenda: The Case of Canada's Response to the Timor Crisis' (2004) 16 *Global Change, Peace & Security* 5.

Hathaway JC, 'Reconceiving Refugee Law as Human Rights Protection' (1991) 4 *Journal of Refugee Studies* 113.

—— 'Reconsideration of the Underlying Premise of Refugee Law' (1990) 31 *Harvard International Law Journal* 129.

Hayden P, 'Constraining War: Human Security and the Human Right to Peace' (2004) 6(1) *Human Rights Review* 35.

—— *Cosmopolitan Global Politics* (Aldershot, Ashgate, 2005).

Heinbecker P and R McRae, 'Case Study: The Kosovo Air Campaign' in R McRae and D Hubert (eds), *Human Security and the New Diplomacy: Protecting People, Promoting Peace* (Montreal, McGill-Queen's University Press, 2001).

Henckaerts J-M and L Doswald-Beck, *Customary International Humanitarian Law* (Cambridge, Cambridge University Press, 2005).

Henk D, 'Human Security: Relevance and Implications' (2005) 35 *Parameters* 91.

Henkin L, 'Kosovo and the Law of "Humanitarian Intervention"' (1999) 93 *AJIL* 824.

Herby P, 'Arms Transfers, Humanitarian Assistance and International Humanitarian Law' (1998) 325 *IRRC* 685.

Heymann DL, 'Evolving Infectious Disease Threats to National and Global Security' in L Chen, J Leaning and V Narasimhan (eds), *Global Health Challenges for Human Security* (Cambridge, MA, Harvard University Press, 2003).

Heymann DL and G Rodier, 'Global Surveillance, National Surveillance, and SARS' (2004) 10 *Emerging Infectious Diseases* 173.

Higgins R, 'Intervention and International Law' in H Bull (ed), *Intervention in World Politics* (Oxford, Clarendon Press, 1984).

—— *Problems and Process: International Law and How We Use It* (Oxford, Clarendon Press, 1994).

Hollis R, 'The U.S. Role: Helpful or Harmful?' in LG Potter and GG Sick (eds), *Iran, Iraq, and the Legacies of War* (New York, Palgrave Macmillan, 2004).

Holmes RL, 'Can War Be Morally Justified? The Just War Theory' in JB Elshtain (ed), *Just War Theory* (Oxford, Blackwell, 1992).

Homer-Dixon T, 'Environmental Scarcity and Intergroup Conflict' in MT Klare and DC Thomas (eds), *World Security: Challenges for a New Century*, 2nd edn (New York, St Martin's Press, 1994).

Hoogensen G and SV Rottem, 'Gender Identity and the Subject of Security' (2004) 35 *Security Dialogue* 155.

Hubert D, 'An Idea that Works in Practice' (2004) 35 *Security Dialogue* 351.

—— 'Small Arms Demand Reduction and Human Security: Towards a People-Centred Approach to Small Arms' (Ploughshares Briefing 01/5, 2001) <http://www.ploughshares.ca/libraries/Briefings/brf015.html> (accessed 13 March 2007).

Hubert D and M Bonser, 'Humanitarian Military Intervention' in R McRae and D Hubert (eds), *Human Security and the New Diplomacy: Protecting People, Promoting Peace* (Montreal and Kingston, McGill-Queen's University Press, 2001).

Hudson H, '"Doing" Security As Though Humans Matter: A Feminist Perspective on Gender and the Politics of Human Security' (2005) 36(2) *Security Dialogue* 155.

Human Rights Watch, 'Civilian Deaths in the NATO Air Campaign' (February 2000), Volume 12, Number 1(D) <http://www.hrw.org/reports/2000/nato> (accessed 9 March 2007).

—— 'Press Statement: UN Conference on Small Arms Trafficking' (9 July 2001) <http://www.hrw.org/campaigns/mines/2001/arms-press-0710.htm> (accessed 25 April 2007).

Human Security Centre, *Human Security Report 2005: War and Peace in the 21st Century* (New York, Oxford University Press, 2005).

—— *Human Security Brief 2006* <http://www.humansecuritybrief.info/> (accessed 7 March 2007).

Human Security Network, 'The Human Security Network' (2006) <http://www.humansecuritynetwork.org/network-e.php> (accessed 25 April 2007).

—— 'A Perspective on Human Security: Chairman's Summary' (Lysøen, Norway, 20 May 1999) <http://www.humansecuritynetwork.org/docs/Chairman_summaryMay99-e.php> (accessed 6 March 2007).

—— 'Report on the Status of the Human Security Network's Main Action Areas' (2002) <http://www.humansecuritynetwork.org/docs/santiago_annex2-e.php> (accessed 27 February 2007).

—— 'Second Ministerial Meeting: Chairman's Summary' (Lucerne, 11–12 May 2000) <http://www.humansecuritynetwork.org/docs/Chairman_summary-e.php> (accessed 25 April 2007).

—— 'Statement of the Human Security Network to the United Nations Conference on the Illicit Trade in Small Arms and Light Weapons in All its Aspects' (2001) <http://www.humansecuritynetwork.org/docs/SALW_Statement-e.php> (accessed 25 April 2007).

—— 'Statement of Slovenia on Behalf of the Human Security Network at the International AIDS Conference' (13–18 August 2006, Toronto, Canada) <http://www.humansecuritynetwork.org/docs/2006-09-hsn-govor-toronto-ang.pdf> (accessed 19 February 2007).

—— 'The Vision of the Human Security Network' <http://www.humansecuritynetwork.org/menu-e.php> (accessed 27 February 2007).

Human Security Unit, 'Human Security Unit: Overview and Objectives' <http://ochaonline.un.org/DocView.asp?DocID=3293> (accessed 26 February 2007).

Hutchinson DN, 'Solidarity and Breaches of Multilateral Treaties' (1988) 59 *BYBIL* 151.

ICISS (International Commission on Intervention and State Sovereignty), *Responsibility to Protect: Report of the International Commission on Intervention and State Sovereignty* (Ottawa, International Development Research Centre, 2001) <http://www.iciss.ca/pdf/Commission-Report.pdf> (accessed 26 February 2007).

ICRC (International Committee of the Red Cross), *Arms Availability and the Situation of Civilians in Armed Conflict* (Geneva, ICRC, 1999) <http://www.icrc.org> (accessed 13 March 2007).

—— 'Arms Transfers, Humanitarian Assistance and International Humanitarian Law' (19 February 1998) <http://www.icrc.org> (accessed 13 March 2007).

—— 'Internally Displaced Persons: The Mandate and Role of the International Committee of the Red Cross' (2000) 82 *IRRC* 491.

—— 'UN Conference on Illicit trade in Small Arms: ICRC Statement' (New York, 12 July 2001) <http://www.icrc.org> (accessed 13 March 2007).

Independent Commission on Disarmament and Security Issues, *Common Security: A Programme for Disarmament* (London, Pan Books, 1982).

Independent International Commission on Kosovo, *The Kosovo Report: Conflict, International Response, Lessons Learned* (Oxford, Oxford University Press, 2000).

Ingram A, 'The New Geopolitics of Disease: Between Global Health and Global Security' (2005) 10 *Geopolitics* 522.

International Crisis Group, 'HIV/AIDS As a Security Issue' (ICG Report June 2001) <http://www.crisisgroup.org/home/index.cfm?action=login&ref_id=1831> (accessed 25 April 2007).

International Law Association, 'London Declaration of International Law Principles on Internally Displaced Persons' (July 2000), reprinted in (2001) 12 *International Journal of Refugee Law* 672.

International Law Commission, 'Commentaries to the Draft Articles on Prevention of Transboundary Harm from Hazardous Activities', UNGA, Report of the International Law Commission, Fifty-third session (2001) GAOR 56th Session Supp 10, 377.

—— 'Draft Articles on Prevention of Transboundary Harm from Hazardous Activities', UNGA, Report of the International Law Commission, Fifty-third session (2001) GAOR 56th Session Supp 10, 370.

—— 'Draft Articles on State Responsibility', UNGA Res 56/83 (28 January 2002) UN Doc A/RES/56/83, Annex.

Islam MR, 'The Sudanese Darfur Crisis and Internally Displaced Persons in International Law: The Least Protection for the Most Vulnerable' (2006) 18 *International Journal of Refugee Law* 354.

Islamic Republic of Iran, Permanent Mission to the United Nations, 'Statement by H.E. Mr. Manouchehr Mottaki, Foreign Minister of the Islamic Republic of Iran, Before the UN Conference to Review Progress made in the Implementation of the Programme of Action to Prevent, Combat and Eradicate the Illicit Trade in Small Arms and Light Weapons' (28 June 2006) <http://www.un.org/events/smallarms2006/pdf/arms060628iraneng.pdf> (accessed 3 August 2006).

Israel, 'Statement by Ambassador Miriam Ziv, Deputy Director General for Strategic Affairs, Ministry of Foreign Affairs, Jerusalem, UN Conference to Review Progress made in the Implementation of the Programme of Action to Prevent, Combat and Eradicate the Illicit Trade in Small Arms and Light Weapons' (27 June 2006) <http://www.un.org/events/smallarms2006/pdf/arms060627israel-eng.pdf> (accessed 25 April 2007).

Japan, MOFA, *Diplomatic Bluebook 2000: Toward the 21st Century—Foreign Policy for a Better Future* (Tokyo, MOFA, 2000).

—— *Diplomatic Bluebook 2002* (MOFA, Tokyo, 2002) <http://www.mofa.go.jp/policy/other/bluebook/2002/index.html> (accessed 6 March 2007).

—— 'Statement by Director-General Yukio Takasu at the International Conference on Human Security in a Globalized World' (Ulan-Bator, 8 May 2000) <http://www.mofa.go.jp/policy/human_secu/speech0005.html> (accessed 27 February 2007).

—— 'Statement by HE Mr Shigeo Uetake, Senior Vice Minister for Foreign Affairs of Japan at the International Conference on Financing for Development' (22 March 2002) <http://www.mofa.go.jp/announce/svm/uetake0203.html> (accessed 27 February 2007).

—— 'Toward Effective Cross-sectorial Partnership to Ensure Human Security in a Globalized World' (Statement by Mr Yukio Takasu, Director-General of Multilateral Cooperation Department, at the Third Intellectual Dialogue on Building Asia's Tomorrow, Bangkok, 19 June 2000) <http://www.mofa.go.jp/policy/human_secu/speech0006.html> (accessed 6 March 2007).

—— *The Trust Fund for Human Security: For the 'Human-centered' 21st Century*

(Tokyo, MOFA, 2006) <http://www.mofa.go.jp/mofaj/press/pr/pub/pamph/pdfs/t_fund21.pdf> (accessed 27 February 2007).

Jockel J and J Sokolsky, 'Lloyd Axworthy's Legacy: Human Security and the Rescue of Canadian Defence Policy' (2000–2001) 56 *International Journal* 1.

Johnson C, *Blowback: The Costs and Consequences of American Empire* (New York, Henry Holt, 2004).

Jones C, *Global Justice: Defending Cosmopolitanism* (Oxford, Oxford University Press, 1999).

Joyner CC, 'Legal Implications of the Concept of the Common Heritage of Mankind' (1986) 35 *ICLQ* 190.

Kälin W, 'The *Guiding Principles* on Internal Displacement—An Introduction' (1998) 10 *International Journal of Refugee Law* 557.

Kanamori S and M Jimba, 'Compensation for Avian Influenza Cleanup' (2007) 13(2) *Emerging Infectious Diseases* 341.

Kaplan A, 'Homeland Insecurities: Reflections on Language and Space' (2003) 85 *Radical History Review* 82.

Karp A, 'Negotiating Small Arms Restraint: The Boldest Frontier for Disarmament?' (2000) 2000(2) *Disarmament Forum* 5.

Kennedy D, 'The International Human Rights Movement: Part of the Problem?' [2001] *European Human Rights Law Review* 245.

Khong YF, 'Human Security: A Shotgun Approach to Alleviating Human Misery?' (2001) 7 *Global Governance* 231.

Kim W and I Hyun, 'Toward a New Concept of Security: Human Security in World Politics' in WT Tow, R Thakur and I Hyun (eds), *Asia's Emerging Regional Order: Reconciling Traditional and Human Security* (Tokyo, United Nations University Press, 2000).

King G and CJL Murray, 'Rethinking Human Security' (2001–2002) 116 *Political Science Quarterly* 585.

Kingsley-Nyinah M, 'What May Be Borrowed; What Is New?' (1999) 4 *Forced Migration Review* 32.

Kirgis, Jr FL, 'Standing to Challenge Human Endeavours that could Change the Climate' (1990) 84 *AJIL* 525.

King NB, 'Security, Disease, Commerce: Ideologies of Postcolonial Global Health' (2002) 32 *Social Studies of Science* 763.

Klare M, 'An Overview of the Global Trade in Small Arms and Light Weapons' in J Dhanapala *et al* (eds), *Small Arms Control: Old Weapons, New Issues* (Aldershot, Ashgate, 1999).

Kourula P, *Broadening the Edges: Refugee Definition and International Protection Revisited* (The Hague, Martinus Nijhoff, 1997).

Krause K, 'Facing the Challenge of Small Arms: The UN and Global Security Governance' in RM Price and MW Zacher (eds), *The United Nations and Global Security* (New York, Palgrave MacMillan, 2004).

—— 'The Key to a Powerful Agenda, if Properly Delimited' (2004) 35 *Security Dialogue* 367.

—— 'Lucerne Presentation, Lysoen Network' (11 May 2000, Lucerne, Lysoen Network Second Ministerial Meeting) <http://humansecuritynetwork.org/docs/report_may2000_1-e.php> (accessed 13 March 2007).

—— 'Multilateral Diplomacy, Norm Building, and UN Conferences: The Case of Small Arms and Light Weapons' (2002) 8 *Global Governance* 247.

Kytömäki E, 'Regional Approaches to Small Arms Control: Vital to Implementing the UN Programme of Action' (2005–06) 2005(4)/2006(1) *Disarmament Forum* 55.

Lammers E, *Refugees, Gender and Human Security: A Theoretical Introduction and Annotated Bibliography* (Utrecht, International Books, 1999).

Latham A, 'Light Weapons and Human Security—A Conceptual Overview' in J Dhanapala *et al* (eds), *Small Arms Control: Old Weapons, New Issues* (Aldershot, Ashgate, 1999).

—— 'Taking the Lead? Light Weapons and International Security' (1997) 52 *International Journal* 316.

Lauterpacht H, *International Law and Human Rights* (London, Stevens and Sons, 1950).

Lavoyer J-P, 'Guiding Principles on Internal Displacement' (1998) 324 *IRRC* 463.

Leaning J, 'Psychosocial Well-Being over Time' (2004) 35 *Security Dialogue* 354.

Lee K and R Dodgson, 'Globalization and Cholera: Implications for Global Governance' in K Lee (ed), *Health Impacts of Globalization: Towards Global Governance* (Houndmills, Palgrave Macmillan, 2003).

Lee K, S Fustukian and K Buse, 'An Introduction to Global Health Policy' in K Lee, K Buse and S Fustukian (eds), *Health Policy in a Globalising World* (Cambridge, Cambridge University Press, 2002).

Lee LT, 'Internally Displaced Persons and Refugees: Toward a Legal Synthesis?' (1996) 9 *Journal of Refugee Studies* 27.

Liotta PH, 'Through the Looking Glass: Creeping Vulnerabilities and the Reordering of Security' (2005) 36 *Security Dialogue* 49.

—— 'Boomerang Effect: The Convergence of National and Human Security' (2002) 33 *Security Dialogue* 473.

Liotta PH and T Owen, 'Sense and Symbolism: Europe Takes On Human Security' (2006) 36(3) *Parameters* 85.

Lodgaard S, 'Human Security: Concept and Operationalisation' (Expert Seminar on Human Rights and Peace) (15 November 2000) UN Doc PD/HR/11.1 <http://www.upeace.org/documents/resources/report_lodgaard.doc> (accessed 7 March 2007).

Loescher G, 'Refugee Protection and State Security: Towards a Greater Convergence' in RM Price and MW Zacher (eds), *The United Nations and Global Security* (New York, Palgrave MacMillan, 2004).

Lonergan S, K Gustavson and B Carter, 'The Index of Human Insecurity' (January 2000) 6 *Aviso* <http://www.gechs.org/aviso/06/index.html> (accessed 9 March 2007).

Loten J, 'Case Study: The Challenge of Microdisarmament' in R McRae and D Hubert (eds), *Human Security and the New Diplomacy: Protecting People, Promoting Peace* (Montreal and Kingston, McGill-Queen's University Press, 2001).

Lowe V, 'International Legal Issues Arising in the Kosovo Crisis' (2000) 49 *ICLQ* 934.

Lumpe L, S Meek and RT Naylor, 'Introduction to Gun-running' in L Lumpe (ed.), *Running Guns: The Global Black Market in Small Arms* (London, Zed Books, 2000).

Luoparjärvi K, 'Is there an Obligation on States to Accept International Humanitarian Assistance to Internally Displaced Persons under International Law' (2003) 15 *International Journal of Refugee Law* 678.

MacFarlane SN and YF Khong, *Human Security and the UN: A Critical History* (Bloomington, Indiana University Press, 2006).

MacFarlane SN, CJ Thielking and TG Weiss, '*The Responsibility to Protect*: Is Anyone Interested in Humanitarian Intervention?' (2004) 25 *Third World Quarterly* 977.

MacFarlane SN and TG Weiss, 'The United Nations, Regional Organisations and Human Security: Building Theory in Central America' (1994) 15 *Third World Quarterly* 277.

MacLean G, 'The Changing Perception of Human Security: Coordinating National and Multilateral Responses' (1998) <http://www.unac.org/en/link_learn/canada/security/perception.asp> (accessed 7 March 2007).

—— 'Instituting and Projecting Human Security: A Canadian Perspective' (2000) 54 *Australian Journal of International Affairs* 269.

Marks S, *The Riddle of all Constitutions: International Law, Democracy, and the Critique of Ideology* (Oxford, Oxford University Press, 2000).

Martin G, 'International Solidarity and Co-operation in Assistance to African Refugees: Burden-Sharing or Burden-Shifting?' (1995, Special Issue) *International Journal of Refugee Law* 250.

Mathews JT, 'Redefining Security' (1989) 68(2) *Foreign Affairs* 162.

—— 'The Environment and International Security' in MT Klare and DC Thomas (eds), *World Security: Challenges for a New Century*, 2nd edn (New York, St Martin's Press, 1994).

Mathews RJ and TLH McCormack, 'The Influence of Humanitarian Principles in the Negotiation of Arms Control Treaties' (1999) 834 *IRRC* 331.

McCarthy P, 'Scratching the Surface of a Global Scourge: The First Five Years of the UN Programme of Action on Small Arms' (2005–06) 2005(4)/2006(1) *Disarmament Forum* 5.

McCoubrey H, *International Humanitarian Law* (Aldershot, Dartmouth, 1998).

McCoubrey H and ND White, *International Law and Armed Conflict* (Aldershot, Dartmouth, 1992).

McDonald M, 'Human Security and the Construction of Security' (2002) 16 *Global Society* 277.

McDougall CW, 'Paying for Pandemic Preparedness: Equity and Fairness in Global Public Health Surveillance Improvement' (unpublished paper, May 2006).

McGoldrick D, 'The Principle of Non-intervention: Human Rights' in V Lowe and C Warbrick (eds), *The United Nations and the Principles of International Law: Essays in memory of Michael Akehurst* (London, Routledge, 1994).

McInnes C, 'HIV/AIDS and Security' (2006) 82 *International Affairs* 315.

McInnes C and K Lee, 'Health, Security and Foreign Policy' (2006) 32 *Review of International Studies* 5.

McRae R, 'Human Security in a Globalized World' in R McRae and D Hubert (eds), *Human Security and the New Diplomacy: Protecting People, Promoting Peace* (Montreal and Kingston, McGill-Queen's University Press, 2001).

McRae R and D Hubert (eds), *Human Security and the New Diplomacy: Protecting People, Promoting Peace* (Montreal and Kingston, McGill-Queen's University Press, 2001).

McSweeney B, *Security, Identity and Interests: A Sociology of International Relations* (Cambridge, Cambridge University Press, 1999).

Melvern LM, *A People Betrayed: The Role of the West in Rwanda's Genocide* (London, Zed Books, 2000).

Mendes E, 'Human Security, International Organizations and International Law: The Kosovo Crisis Exposes the "Tragic Flaw" in the UN Charter' (1999) 38 *Human Rights Research and Education Centre Bulletin* <http://www.cdp-hrc.uottawa.ca/publicat/bull38.html> (accessed 9 March 2007).

Meron T, 'The Humanization of Humanitarian Law' (2000) 94 *AJIL* 239.

—— 'The Martens Clause, Principles of Humanity, and Dictates of Public Conscience' (2000) 94 *AJIL* 78.

Mgbeoji I, 'Beyond Rhetoric: State Sovereignty, Common Concern, and the Inapplicability of the Common Heritage Concept to Plant Genetic Resources' (2003) 16 *Leiden Journal of International Law* 821.

Miller D, 'The Limits of Cosmopolitan Justice' in DR Mapel and T Nardin (eds), *International Society: Diverse Ethical Perspectives* (Princeton, Princeton University Press, 1998).

Mooney ED, 'In-country Protection: Out of Bounds for UNHCR?' in F Nicholson and P Twomey (eds), *Refugee Rights and Realities: Evolving International Concepts and Regimes* (Cambridge, Cambridge University Press, 1999).

Murphy SD (ed), 'Contemporary Practice of the United States Relating to International Law' (2001) 95 *AJIL* 873.

—— *Humanitarian Intervention: The United Nations in an Evolving World Order* (Philadelphia, University of Pennsylvania Press, 1996).

National Intelligence Council, *The Global Infectious Disease Threat and Its Implications for the United States* (National Intelligence Estimate NIE 99-17D, January 2000).

Nef J, *Human Security and Mutual Vulnerability* 2nd edn (Ottawa, IDRC, 1999).

Nelles W, 'Canada's Human Security Agenda in Kosovo and Beyond' (2002) 57 *International Journal* 459.

Newman D, 'A Human Security Council? Applying a "Human Security" Agenda to Security Council Reform' (1999–2000) 31 *Ottawa Law Review* 213.

Newman E, 'A Normatively Attractive but Analytically Weak Concept' (2004) 35 *Security Dialogue* 358.

Nojumi N, *The Rise of the Taliban in Afghanistan: Mass Mobilization, Civil War, and the Future of the Region* (New York, Palgrave, 2002).

Norton-Taylor R, 'Two-thirds of Teenagers Too Fat to Be Soldiers' (1996) *The Guardian*, 3 November, <http://www.guardian.co.uk/frontpage/story/0,,1938441,00.html> (accessed 29 March 2007).

Nossal KR, 'Seeing Things? The Adornment of "Security" in Australia and Canada' (1995) 49 *Australian Journal of International Affairs* 33.

OAS (Organization of American States), General Assembly, 'Human Security in the Americas' (Document presented by the Delegation of Canada, 30th Regular Session) (26 April 2000) OEA/SER.P, AG/doc.3851/00.

Oberleitner G, 'Human Security: A Challenge to International Law?' (2005) 11 *Global Governance* 185.

Odello M, 'Commentary on the United Nations' High-Level Panel on Threats, Challenges and Change' (2005) 10 *Journal of Conflict and Security Law* 231.

OECD (Organisation for Economic Co-operation and Development), 'The OECD Guidelines for Multinational Enterprises: Text, Commentary and Clarifications' (31 October 2001) OECD Doc DAFFE/IME/WPG(2000)15/FINAL.

Office of Homeland Security, *National Strategy for Homeland Security* (July 2002) <http://www.dhs.gov/xlibrary/assets/nat_strat_hls.pdf> (accessed 7 March 2007).

Ogata S, 'International Security and Refugee Problems after the Cold War, Assuring the Security of People: the Humanitarian Challenge of the 21st Century' (Olof Palme Memorial Lecture, Stockholm, 14 June 1995) <http://www2.sipri.se/sipri/Lectures/Ogata.html> (accessed 26 February 2007).

Orford A, 'Locating the International: Military and Monetary Interventions after the Cold War' (1997) 38 *Harvard International Law Journal* 443.

OSCE (Organization for Security and Co-operation in Europe), 'OSCE Document on Small Arms and Light Weapons' (24 November 2000) FSC.DOC/1/00.

—— 'OSCE Principles on the Control of Brokering in Small Arms and Light Weapons' (24 November 2004) Decision No 8/04, FSC.DEC/8/04.

Ostergard RL, 'Politics in the Hot Zone: AIDS and National Security in Africa' (2002) 23 *Third World Quarterly* 333.

Owen T, 'Challenges and Opportunities for Defining and Measuring Human Security' (2004) 3 *Disarmament Forum* 15.

—— 'Human Security—Conflict, Critique and Consensus: Colloquium Remarks and a Proposal for a Threshold-Based Definition' (2004) 35(3) *Security Dialogue* 373.

Owens H and B Arneil, 'Human Security Paradigm Shift: A New Lens on Canadian Foreign Policy?' (1999) 7(1) *Canadian Foreign Policy* 1.

Pakistan, Permanent Mission to the United Nations, 'Statement by Brigadier Javed Iqbal Cheema, Director General, Ministry of the Interior at the UN Conference to Review Progress Made in the Implementation of the Programme of Action to Prevent, Combat and Eradicate the Illicit Trade in Small Arms and Light Weapons in all its Aspects' (28 June 2006) <http://www.un.org/events/smallarms2006/pdf/arms060628pakist-eng.pdf> (accessed 25 April 2007).

Palwankar U, 'Measures Available to States for Fulfilling Their Obligation to Ensure Respect for International Humanitarian Law' (1994) 298 *IRRC* 9.

Paris R, 'Human Security: Paradigm Shift or Hot Air?' (2001) 26 *International Security* 87.

—— 'Still an Inscrutable Concept' (2004) 35 *Security Dialogue* 370.

Permanent Mission of Canada to the United Nations, 'Statement by Ambassador Gilbert Laurin, Deputy Permanent Representative of Canada to the United Nations, to the Opening of the UN Conference to Review Progress Made in the Implementation of the Programme of Action to Prevent, Combat and Eradicate the Illicit Trade in Small Arms and Light Weapons in all its Aspects' (26 June 2006) <http://www.un.org/events/smallarms2006/pdf/arms060626can-eng.pdf> (accessed 13 March 2007).

Permanent Mission of India to the United Nations, 'Statement by Mr. Hamid Ali Rao, Joint Secretary (Disarmament and International Security Affairs) Ministry of External Affairs at the United Nations Conference to Review Progress Made in the Implementation of the Programme of Action to Prevent, Combat and Eradicate the Illicit Trade in Small Arms and Light Weapons in all its Aspects'

(26 June 2006) <http://www.un.org/events/smallarms2006/pdf/arms060627 Ind-eng.pdf> (accessed 13 March 2007).

Permanent Mission of the Republic of Cuba to the United Nations, 'Statement by the Head of the Delegation of Cuba, H.E. Manuel Aguilera de la Paz, Deputy Minister of Foreign Affairs' (3 July 2006) <http://www.un.org/events/smallarms2006/pdf/arms060703cuba-eng.pdf> (accessed 13 March 2007).

Permanent Mission of the Russian Federation to the United Nations, 'Statement by Mr Petr G Litavrin, Deputy Head of the Delegation of the Russian Federation at the Conference to Review Progress Made in the Implementation of the Programme of Action to Prevent, Combat and Eradicate the Illicit Trade in Small Arms and Light Weapons (SALW) in All its Aspects' (27 June 2006) <http://www.un.org/events/smallarms2006/pdf/arms060627rus-eng.pdf> (accessed 13 March 2007).

Perrez FX, *Cooperative Sovereignty: From Independence to Interdependence in the Structure of International Environmental Law* (The Hague, Kluwer, 2000).

Peters R, 'RevCon IANSA presentations: Vision for 2012' (30 June 2006) <http://www.un.org/events/smallarms2006/pdf/arms060630iansa-rebecca.pdf> (accessed 13 March 2007).

Peterson VS, 'Security and Sovereign States: What Is at Stake in Taking Feminism Seriously?' in VS Peterson (ed), *Gendered States: Feminist (Re)Visions of International Relations Theory* (Boulder and London, Lynne Rienner, 1992).

Petrasek D, 'Human Rights "Lite"? Thoughts on Human Security' (2004) 3 *Disarmament Forum* 59.

Pettersson B, 'Development-induced displacement: internal affair or international human rights issue?' (2002) 12 *Forced Migration Review* 16.

Phuong C, *International Protection of Internally Displaced Persons* (Cambridge, Cambridge University Press, 2004).

Plender R, 'The Legal Basis of International Jurisdiction to Act with Regard to the Internally Displaced' (1994) 6 *International Journal of Refugee Law* 345.

Pogge T, 'Cosmopolitanism and Sovereignty' (1992) 103 *Ethics* 48.

Price-Smith AT, *The Health of Nations: Infectious Disease, Environmental Change, and Their Effects on National Security and Development* (Cambridge, MA, MIT Press, 2002).

Provost R, *International Human Rights and Humanitarian Law* (Cambridge, Cambridge University Press, 2002).

Ragazzi M, *The Concept of International Obligations Erga Omnes* (Oxford, Clarendon Press, 1997).

Ramcharan BG, *Human Rights and Human Security* (The Hague, Martinus Nijhoff, 2002).

Randelzhofer A, 'Article 2(4)' in B Simma (ed), *The Charter of the United Nations: A Commentary*, 2nd edn (Oxford, Oxford University Press, 2002) vol I.

Randelzhofer A, 'General Introduction to Article 2' in B Simma (ed), *The Charter of the United Nations: A Commentary*, 2nd edn (Oxford, Oxford University Press, 2002) vol I.

Regehr E, 'Reshaping the Security Envelope' (2005) 60 *International Journal* 1033.

—— 'Small Arms and Light Weapons: A Global Humanitarian Challenge' (Working Paper No 01-4, June 2001) <http://www.ploughshares.ca/libraries/WorkingPapers/wp014.html> (accessed 29 March 2007).

Regional Human Security Centre, 'Pan-Arab Brainstorming Session, August 31, 2000: Narrative Report' (2000) <http://www.id.gov.jo/human/activities2000/report6.html> (accessed 9 March 2007).

Reisman WM, 'Coercion and Self-Determination: Construing Charter Article 2(4)' (1984) 78 *AJIL* 642.

—— 'Humanitarian Intervention to Protect the Ibos' in R Lillich (ed), *Humanitarian Intervention and the United Nations* (Charlottesville, University of Virginia Press, 1973).

—— 'Kosovo's Antinomies' (1999) 93 *AJIL* 860.

—— 'Sovereignty and Human Rights in Contemporary International Law' (1990) 84 *AJIL* 866.

Reynolds P, 'Multiple Failures Caused Relief Crisis', BBC News 7 September 2005, <http://news.bbc.co.uk/2/hi/americas/4216508.stm> (accessed 27 February 2007).

Riedel E, 'Article 55(c)' in B Simma (ed), *The Charter of the United Nations: A Commentary*, 2nd edn (Oxford, Oxford University Press, 2002) vol II.

Rist G, *The History of Development: from Western Origins to Global Faith*, P Camiller (trans) (London, Zed Books, 1997).

Roberts D, 'Human Security or Human Insecurity? Moving the Debate Forward' (2006) 37 *Security Dialogue* 249.

Roberts L *et al*, 'Mortality Before and After the 2003 Invasion of Iraq: Cluster Sample Survey' (2004) 364 *Lancet* 1857.

Rogers A, 'Humanitarian Intervention and International Law' (2004) 27 *Harvard Journal of Law and Public Policy* 725.

Rothschild E, 'What is Security?' (1995) 124(3) *Daedalus* 53.

Ruddick EE, 'The Continuing Constraint of Sovereignty: International Law, International Protection, and the Internally Displaced' (1997) 77 *Boston University Law Review* 429.

Rutinwa B, 'How Tense is the Tension between the Refugee Concept and the IDP Debate?' (1999) 4 *Forced Migration Review* 29.

Samuels JW, 'Organized Responses to Natural Disasters' in R St John Macdonald, DM Johnston and GL Morris (eds), *The International Law and Policy of Human Welfare* (Alphen aan den Rijn, Netherlands, Sijthoff and Noordhoff, 1978).

Sandoz Y, '"Droit" or "devoir d'ingérence" and the right to assistance: the issues involved' (1992) 228 *IRRC* 215.

Sands P, *Principles of International Environmental Law, Vol 1: Frameworks, Standards and Implementation* (Manchester, Manchester University Press, 1995).

Schabas WA, *Genocide in International Law: The Crime of Crimes* (Cambridge, Cambridge University Press, 2000).

Scheper-Hughes N, 'Katrina: The Disaster and its Doubles' (2005) 21(6) *Anthropology Today* 2.

Schmeidl S, 'The Early Warning of Forced Migration: State or Human Security?' in E Newman and J van Selm, *Refugees and Forced Displacement: International Security, Human Vulnerability, and the State* (Tokyo, United Nations University Press, 2003).

Seidensticker E, 'Human Security, Human Rights, and Human Development' (5 February 2002) <http://www.humansecurity-chs.org/activities/outreach/0206harvard.pdf> (accessed 6 March 2007).

Sheehan M, *International Security: An Analytical Survey* (Boulder, CO, Lynne Rienner, 2005).

Shibuya K, 'Health Problems as Security Risks: Global Burden of Disease Assessments' in L Chen, J Leaning and V Narasimhan (eds), *Global Health Challenges for Human Security* (Cambridge, MA, Harvard University Press, 2003).

Shue H, *Basic Rights: Subsistence, Affluence, and U.S. Foreign Policy*, 2nd edn (Princeton, NJ, Princeton University Press, 1996).

Shusterman J, 'An Interview with the Human Security Unit' (2006) 2 *Revue de sécurité humaine/Journal of Human Security* 97.

Simma B, 'NATO, the UN and the Use of Force: Legal Aspects' (1999) 10 *EJIL* 1.

Skogly SI and M Gibney, 'Transnational Human Rights Obligations' (2002) 24 *Human Rights Quarterly* 781.

Slaughter A-M, 'International Law in a World of Liberal States' (1995) 6 *EJIL* 503.

—— 'A Liberal Theory of International Law' (2000) 94 *American Society of International Law Proceedings* 240.

Small Arms Survey, *Small Arms Survey 2001: Profiling the Problem* (Oxford, Oxford University Press, 2001).

—— *Small Arms Survey 2002: Counting the Human Cost* (Oxford, Oxford University Press, 2002).

—— *Small Arms Survey 2003: Development Denied* (Oxford, Oxford University Press, 2003).

—— *Small Arms Survey 2004: Rights at Risk* (Oxford, Oxford University Press, 2004).

—— *Small Arms Survey 2005: Weapons at War* (Oxford, Oxford University Press, 2005).

Sohn LB, 'The New International Law: Protection of the Rights of Individuals Rather than States' (1982) 32 *American University Law Review* 1.

Soroos MS, 'Global Change, Environmental Security, and the Prisoner's Dilemma' (1994) 31(3) *Journal of Peace Research* 317.

Spiegel PB and P Salama, 'War and Mortality in Kosovo, 1998–99: An Epidemiological Testimony' (2000) 355 *Lancet* 2204.

Stairs D, 'Canada and the Security Problem' (1999) 54 *International Journal* 386.

Steans J, *Gender and International Relations: An Introduction* (Cambridge, Polity Press, 1998).

Steiner HJ and P Alston, *International Human Rights in Context: Law, Politics, Morals*, 2nd edn (Oxford, Oxford University Press, 2000).

Støre JG, J Welch and L Chen, 'Health and Security for a Global Century' in L Chen, J Leaning and V Narasimhan (eds), *Global Health Challenges for Human Security* (Cambridge, MA, Harvard University Press, 2003).

Study Group on Europe's Security, *A Human Security Doctrine for Europe: The Barcelona Report of the Study Group on Europe's Security Capabilities* (15 September 2004) <http://www.lse.ac.uk/Depts/global/Publications/HumanSecurity Doctrine.pdf> (accessed 7 March 2007).

Suhrke A, 'Burden-sharing During Refugee Emergencies: The Logic of Collective Versus National Action' (1998) 11 *Journal of Refugee Studies* 396.

—— 'Human Security and the Protection of Refugees' in E Newman and J van Selm, *Refugees and Forced Displacement: International Security, Human Vulnerability, and the State* (Tokyo, United Nations University Press, 2003).

Suhrke A, 'A Stalled Initiative' (2004) 35 *Security Dialogue* 365.

Tesón FR, *Humanitarian Intervention: An Inquiry into Law and Morality*, 2nd edn (Irvington-on-Hudson, NY, Transnational Publishers, 1997).

—— 'The Liberal Case for Humanitarian Intervention' in JL Holzgrefe and RO Keohane, *Humanitarian Intervention: Ethical, Legal, and Political Dilemmas* (Cambridge, Cambridge University Press, 2003).

—— *A Philosophy of International Law* (London, Westview Press, 1998).

Thakur R, 'Developing Countries and the Intervention-Sovereignty Debate' in RM Price and MW Zacher (eds), *The United Nations and Global Security* (New York, Palgrave MacMillan, 2004).

—— 'A Political Worldview' (2004) 35 *Security Dialogue* 347.

Thirlway H, 'The Law and Procedure of the International Court of Justice 1960–1989: Part Two' (1990) 61 *BYBIL* 3.

Thomas C, 'A Bridge Between the Interconnected Challenges Confronting the World' (2004) 35 *Security Dialogue* 353.

Tickner JA, *Gender in International Relations: Feminist Perspectives on Achieving Global Security* (New York, Columbia University Press, 1992).

Timothy K, 'Human Security Discourse at the United Nations' (2004) 16 *Peace Review* 19.

Tomuschat C, 'Human Rights between Idealism and Realism' (Academy of European Law, 13th Session, Florence, Italy, 18 June 2003).

Toope SJ, 'Does International Law Impose a Duty Upon the United Nations to Prevent Genocide' (2000) 46 *McGill Law Journal* 187.

Tow WT and R Trood, 'Linkages between Traditional Security and Human Security' in WT Tow, R Thakur and I Hyun (eds), *Asia's Emerging Regional Order: Reconciling Traditional and Human Security* (Tokyo, United Nations University Press, 2000).

ul Haq M, *Reflections on Human Development*, 2nd edn (Delhi, Oxford University Press, 1999).

Ullman RH, 'Redefining Security' (1983) 8(1) *International Security* 129.

Ungerer CJ, 'Approaching Human Security as "Middle Powers": Australian and Canadian Disarmament Diplomacy after the Cold War' in WT Tow, R Thakur and I Hyun (eds), *Asia's Emerging Regional Order: Reconciling Traditional and Human Security* (Tokyo, United Nations University Press, 2000).

United Kingdom, Foreign and Commonwealth Office, 'Guiding Humanitarian Intervention' (Speech by the Foreign Secretary, Robin Cook, American Bar Association Lunch, QEII Conference Centre, London, 19 July 2000) <http://www.fco.gov.uk> (accessed 9 March 2007).

United States, 'Statement by Robert G. Joseph, Undersecretary of State for Arms Control and International Security, at the United Nations Conference to Review Progress made in the Implementation of the Programme of Action to Prevent, Combat and Eradicate the Illicit Trade in Small Arms and Light Weapons in All Its Aspects' USUN Press Release #137(06) (27 June 2006) <http://www.un.org/events/smallarms2006/pdf/arms060627usa-eng.pdf> (accessed 25 April 2007).

United States, Mission to the United Nations, 'Statement by Ambassador Richard C Holbrooke, United States Permanent Representative to the United Nations' USUN Press Release #44(00) (28 March 2000) <http://www.un.int/usa/00_044.htm> (accessed 10 March 2007).

Upadhyaya P, 'Human Security, Humanitarian Intervention, and Third World Concerns' (2004) 33 *Denver Journal of International Law and Policy* 71.

Van Bueren G, 'Deconstructing the Mythologies of International Human Rights Law' in C Gearty and A Tomkins (eds), *Understanding Human Rights* (London, Pinter, 1996).

Vander Zwaag D, 'The Concept and Principles of Sustainable Development: 'Rio-Formulating' Common Law Doctrines and Environmental Laws' (1993) 13 *Windsor Yearbook of Access to Justice* 39.

Väyryen R, 'Multilateral Security: Common, Cooperative or Collective?' in MG Schechter (ed), *Future Multilateralism: The Political and Social Framework* (Tokyo, United Nations University Press, 1999).

Vennemann N, 'Application of International Human Rights Conventions to Transboundary State Acts' in RM Bratspies and RA Miller, *Transboundary Harm in International Law: Lessons from the* Trail Smelter Arbitration (Cambridge, Cambridge University Press, 2006).

Vessey J, 'The Principle of Prevention in International Law' (1998) 3 *Austrian Review of International and European Law* 181.

Vignard K, 'Editor's Note' (2004) 3 *Disarmament Forum* 1.

Vincent M, 'IDPs: Rights and Status' (2000) 8 *Forced Migration Review* 29.

—— 'Protection and Assistance to IDPs' (1999) 4 *Forced Migration Review* 34.

Vines A, 'Combating Light Weapons Proliferation in West Africa' (2005) 81 *International Affairs* 341.

von Tigerstrom B, 'International Law and the Concept of Human Security' in T Dolgopol and J Gardam (eds), *The Challenge of Conflict: International Law Responds* (Leiden, Brill, 2006).

—— 'The Revised International Health Regulations and Restraint of National Health Measures' (2005) 13 *Health Law Journal* 35.

Wæver O, 'Securitization and Desecuritization' in RD Lipschutz, *On Security* (New York, Columbia University Press, 1995).

Walker RBJ, 'The Subject of Security' in K Krause and MC Williams (eds), *Critical Security Studies: Concepts and Cases* (Minneapolis, University of Minnesota Press, 1997).

Walt SM, 'The Renaissance of Security Studies' (1991) 35 *International Studies Quarterly* 211.

Wassenaar Arrangement, 'Elements for Effective Legislation on Arms Brokering' (12 December 2003) <http://www.wassenaar.org/publicdocuments/2003_effectivelegislation.html> (25 April 2007).

—— 'Statement of Understanding on Arms Brokerage' (11–12 December 2002) <http://www.wassenaar.org/publicdocuments/2002_statementofunderstanding.html> (accessed 25 April 2007).

Wedgwood R, 'NATO's Campaign in Yugoslavia' (1999) 93 *AJIL* 828.

Weiss TG, 'The Sunset of Humanitarian Intervention? The Responsibility to Protect in a Unipolar Era' (2004) 35 *Security Dialogue* 135.

Wellman C, 'Solidarity, the Individual and Human Rights' (2000) 22 *Human Rights Quarterly* 639.

Wheeler NJ, *Saving Strangers: Humanitarian Intervention in International Society* (Oxford, Oxford University Press, 2000).

WHO (World Health Organization), 'Application of the International Health Regulations (2005)' (26 May 2006) WHA Res 59.2.

—— 'Avian Influenza: Assessing the Pandemic Threat' (2005) <http://www.who.int/csr/disease/influenza/H5N1-9reduit.pdf> (accessed 26 February 2007).

—— 'Cumulative Number of Confirmed Human Cases of Avian Influenza A/ (H5N1) Reported to WHO' (27 February 2007) <http://www.who.int/csr/disease/avian_influenza/country/cases_table_2007_02_27/en/index.html> (accessed 27 February 2007).

—— 'Global Crises—Global Solutions: Managing Public Health Emergencies of International Concern through the Revised International Health Regulations' (2002) <http://www.who.int/csr/resources/publications/ihr/en/whocdsgar 20024.pdf> (accessed 25 April 2007).

—— 'Global Health Security: Epidemic Alert and Response' (21 May 2001) WHA Res 54.14.

—— 'Revision and Updating of the International Health Regulations' (12 May 1995) WHA Res 48.7.

—— 'Revision of the International Health Regulations' (28 May 2003) WHA Res 56.28.

—— 'Revision of the International Health Regulations' (23 May 2005) WHA Res 58.3.

—— 'Severe Acute Respiratory Syndrome (SARS): Status of the Outbreak and Lessons for the Immediate Future' (20 May 2003) <http://www.who.int/csr/media/sars_wha.pdf> (accessed 25 April 2007).

—— 'Small Arms and Global Health: WHO Contribution to the UN Conference on Illicit Trade in Small Arms and Light Weapons July 9–20, 2001' (August 2001) UN Doc WHO/NMH/VIP/01.1.

—— 'Summary Report of Regional Consultations' (14 September 2004) WHO Doc A/IHR/IGWG/2.

—— 'World Health Day 2007: International Health Security: Invest in Health, Build a Safer Future' (Issues Paper, 2007) <http://www.who.int/world-health-day/2007/en/index.html> (accessed 8 April 2007).

— 'World Health Day Debate on International Health Security, Statement by Dr Margaret Chan, Director-General of the World Health Organization' (Singapore, 2 April 2007) <http://www.who.int/dg/speeches/2007/020407_whd2007/en/index.html> (accessed 8 April 2007).

Wiebe V, 'The Prevention of Civil War through the Use of the Human Rights System' (1995) 27 *New York University Journal of International Law and Politics* 409.

Willerman R, 'Victim Assistance: Landmine Survivors' Perspectives' in RA Matthew, B McDonald and KR Rutherford (eds), *Landmines and Human Security: International Politics and War's Hidden Legacy* (Albany, State University of New York Press, 2004).

Wilson ME, 'Health and Security: Globalization of Infectious Diseases' in L Chen, J Leaning and V Narasimhan (eds), *Global Health Challenges for Human Security* (Cambridge, MA, Harvard University Press, 2003).

Wolfers A, 'National Security as an Ambiguous Symbol' in A Wolfers, *Discord and Collaboration: Essays on International Politics* (Baltimore, Johns Hopkins Press, 1962).

Wolfrum R, 'Article 1' in B Simma (ed), *The Charter of the United Nations: A Commentary*, 2nd edn (Oxford, Oxford University Press, 2002) vol I.
—— 'Article 56' in B Simma (ed), *The Charter of the United Nations: A Commentary*, 2nd edn (Oxford, Oxford University Press, 2002) vol II.
Woodward D *et al*, 'Globalization and Health: A Framework for Analysis and Action' (2001) 79 *Bulletin of the World Health Organization* 875.
Woodward SL, 'Should We Think Before We Leap? A Rejoinder' (1999) 30 *Security Dialogue* 277.
World Bank, 'Avian and Human Influenza: Update on Financing Needs and Framework' (30 November 2006) <http://siteresources.worldbank.org/INT TOPAVIFLU/Resources/AHIFinancing12-06.doc> (accessed 27 February 2007).
—— 'Enhancing Control of Highly Pathogenic Avian Influenza in Developing Countries through Compensation' (2006) <http://web.worldbank.org/ WBSITE/EXTERNAL/TOPICS/EXTARD/0,,contentMDK:21149507~pagePK:2 10058~piPK:210062~theSitePK:336682,00.html> (accessed 25 April 2007).
—— *World Development Report 1979* (Washington, DC,World Bank, 1979).
WTO (World Trade Organisation), 'Amendment of the TRIPS Agreement: Decision of 6 December 2005' (8 December 2005) WTO Doc WT/L/641.
—— 'Declaration on the TRIPS Agreement and Public Health' (20 November 2001) WTO Doc WT/MIN(01)/DEC/2.
Wyatt C, 'The Forgotten Victims of Small Arms' (2002) 22 *SAIS Review* 223.
Yach D and D Bettcher, 'The Globalization of Public Health, I: Threats and Opportunities' (1998) 88 *American Journal of Public Health* 735.
—— 'The Globalization of Public Health II: The Convergence of Self-Interest and Altruism' (1998) 88 *American Journal of Public Health* 738.
Yankey-Wayne V, 'The Human Dimension of the United Nations Programme of Action on Small Arms: The Key Role of Africa' (2005–06) 2005(4)/2006(1) *Disarmament Forum* 83.
Zambelli M, 'Putting People at the Centre of the International Agenda: The Human Security Approach' <http://hei.unige.ch/ped/docs/Human-security.doc> (accessed 27 February 2007).
—— 'Draft Framework Convention on International Arms Transfers' (Working Draft of 24 May 2004) <http://www.iansa.org/documents/2004/att_0504.pdf> (accessed 13 March 2007).
—— 'Limburg Principles on the Implementation of the International Covenant on Economic, Social and Cultural Rights', reprinted in (1987) 9 *Human Rights Quarterly* 122.
—— 'Timeline: Human Security in Canadian Foreign Policy' in R McRae and D Hubert (eds), *Human Security and the New Diplomacy: Protecting People, Promoting Peace* (Montreal and Kingston, McGill-Queen's University Press, 2001).

UN DOCUMENTS

UN, 'Copenhagen Declaration on Social Development', 'Report of the World Summit for Social Development' (19 April 1995) UN Doc A/CONF.166/9, Resolution 1, Annex I.

UN, *A More Secure World: Our Shared Responsibility* (Report of the Secretary-General's High-Level Panel on Threats, Challenges and Change) (New York, UN Department of Public Information, 2004).

—— 'Programme of Action to Prevent, Combat and Eradicate the Illicit Trade in Small Arms and Light Weapons in All Its Aspects', Report of the Conference on the Illicit Trade in Small Arms and Light Weapons in All Its Aspects (2001) UN Doc A/CONF.192/15, 7.

—— 'Report of the Conference on the Illicit Trade in Small Arms and Light Weapons in All Its Aspects' (2001) UN Doc A/CONF.192/15.

—— 'Report of the Group of Governmental Experts on Small Arms' (19 August 1999) UN Doc A/54/258.

—— 'Report of the Panel of Governmental Experts on Small Arms' (27 August 1997) UN Doc A/52/298, Annex.

—— 'Suggested Common Guidelines for National Controls Governing Transfers of Small Arms and Light Weapons, Working Paper Submitted by Kenya' (22 June 2006) UN Doc A/CONF.192/2006/RC/WP.2.

—— *'We the Peoples' The Role of the United Nations in the 21st Century: Millennium Report of the Secretary-General of the United Nations* (New York, United Nations, 2000).

UN Committee on Economic, Social and Cultural Rights, 'General Comment 3: The Nature of States Parties Obligations' (14 December 1990) UN Doc E/1991/23.

—— 'General Comment 8: The Relationship Between Economic Sanctions and Respect for Economic, Social and Cultural Rights' (12 December 1997) UN Doc E/CN.12/1997/8.

—— 'General Comment 14: The Right to the Highest Attainable Standard of Health' (11 August 2000) UN Doc E/C.12/2000/4.

—— 'Poverty and the International Covenant on Economic, Social and Cultural Rights, Statement of the Committee on Economic, Social and Cultural Rights to the Third United Nations Conference on the Least Developed Countries' (4 May 2001) UN Doc E/C.12/2001/17, Annex VII.

UN DDA (Department of Disarmament Affairs), 'About the Conference' (2001) <http://disarmament.un.org/cab/smallarms/about.htm> (accessed 13 March 2007).

—— 'Disarmament Issues' (no date) <http://disarmament.un.org/issue.htm> (accessed 13 March 2007).

—— Multilateral Arms Regulation and Disarmament Agreements (no date) <http://disarmament.un.org/TreatyStatus.nsf> (accessed 13 March 2007).

UN Human Rights Committee, 'General Comment No 31: The Nature of the General Legal Obligation Imposed on States Parties' (26 May 2004) UN Doc CCPR/C/21/Rev.1/Add.13.

—— 'United States of America: Concluding Observations' (27 July 2006) UN Doc CCPR/C/USA/Q/3/CRP.4.

UN Human Rights Council, 'Human Rights and International Solidarity' (7 February 2007) UN Doc A/HRC/4/8.

UN IASC (Inter-Agency Standing Committee), *Implementing the Collaborative Response to Situations of Internal Displacement: Guidance for United Nations*

Humanitarian and/or Resident Coordinators and Country Teams (Geneva, United Nations, 2005).

UN Institute for Disarmament Research, 'Human Security' <http://www.unidir.ch/html/en/human_security.html> (accessed 26 February 2007).

UN OCHA (Office for the Coordination of Humanitarian Affairs), 'Inter-Agency Internal Displacement Division' <http://www.reliefweb.int/idp/> (accessed 10 March 2007).

—— 'Terms of Reference for an IDP Unit within OCHA' (2002) <http://www.relief web.int/IDP/docs/references/IDPUnitTORFinal.pdf> (accessed 10 March 2007).

UN Secretary-General, 'Secretary-General Disappointed Small Arms Conference Ended Without Agreement, but Says Global Community Committed to Action Plan to Curb Illicit Trade' Press Release SG/SM/10558 (10 July 2006).

—— 'Statement of the United Nations Secretary-General to the General Assembly on Presenting his Millennium Report' (3 April 2000) <http://www.un.org/millennium/sg/report/state.htm> (accessed 12 March 2007).

—— 'Supplement to an Agenda for Peace: Position Paper of the Secretary-General on the Occasion of the Fiftieth Anniversary of the United Nations' (25 January 1995) UN Doc S/1995/1.

UN Sub-commission on the Prevention of Discrimination and Protection of Minorities, 'Siracusa Principles on the Limitation and Derogation Provisions in the International Covenant on Civil and Political Rights' (28 September 1984) UN Doc E/CN.4/1985/4, Annex.

UN Sub-commission on the Protection and Promotion of Human Rights, 'Norms on the Responsibilities for Transnational Corporations and Other Business Enterprises With Regard to Human Rights' (26 August 2003) UN Doc E/CN.4/Sub.2/2003/12/Rev.2.

—— 'The Question of the Trade, Carrying and Use of Small Arms and Light Weapons in the Context of Human Rights and Humanitarian Norms' (30 May 2002) UN Doc E/CN.4/Sub.2/2002/39.

UN University, 'Advancing Knowledge for Human Security and Development: UNU Strategic Directions 2005–2008' <http://www.unu.edu/strategic directions05-08.pdf> (accessed 26 February 2007).

UNAIDS (United Nations Programme on HIV/AIDS), *On the Front Line: A Review of Policies and Programmes to Address AIDS Among Peacekeepers and Uniformed Services* (New York, UNAIDS, 2005).

UNCHR (United Nations Commission on Human Rights), 'Compilation and Analysis of Legal Norms, Report of the Representative of the Secretary-General' (5 December 1995) UN Doc E/CN.4/1996/52/Add.2.

—— 'Compilation and Analysis of Legal Norms, Part II: Legal Aspects Relating to Protection from Arbitrary Displacement, Report of the Representative of the Secretary-General' (11 February 1998) UN Doc E/CN.4/1998/53/Add.1.

—— 'Guiding Principles on Internal Displacement, Report of the Representative of the Secretary-General, Mr. Francis Deng, submitted pursuant to Commission resolution 1997/39: Addendum' (11 February 1998) UN Doc E/CN.4/1998/53/Add.2, Annex.

—— 'Internally displaced persons: Report of the Representative of the Secretary-General' (25 January 1994) UN Doc E/CN.4/1994/44.

UNCHR 'Internally Displaced Persons: Report of the Representative of the Secretary-General' (2 February 1995) UN Doc E/CN.4/1995/50.

—— 'Internally displaced persons: Report of the Representative of the Secretary-General' (22 February 1996) UN Doc E/CN.4/1996/52.

—— 'Summary Record of the 45th Meeting' 56th Sess (1 May 2000) UN Doc E/CN.4/2000/SR.45.

—— Res 2002/31 (22 April 2002) UN Doc E/CN.4/2002/200.

UNDP (United Nations Development Programme), *Human Development Report 1990* (Oxford, Oxford University Press, 1990).

—— *Human Development Report 1993* (Oxford, Oxford University Press, 1993).

—— *Human Development Report 1994* (Oxford, Oxford University Press, 1994).

—— *Human Development Report 1995* (Oxford, Oxford University Press, 1995).

UNECOSOC Res 1994/24 (26 July 1994) UN Doc E/1994/L.18/Rev.1.

UNESCO (United Nations Educational Scientific and Cultural Organisation), 'SecuriPax Forum: The International Network for the Promotion of Human Security and Peace' <http://www.unesco.org/securipax> (accessed 26 February 2007).

—— *What Agenda for Human Security in the Twenty-first Century?* (First International Meeting of Directors of Peace Research and Training Institutions, UNESCO, Paris, 27–28, November 2000) <http://unesdoc.unesco.org/images/0012/001238/123834e.pdf> (accessed 26 February 2007).

UNGA (United Nations General Assembly), 'Convening of an International Conference on the Illicit Arms Trade in All Its Aspects: Report of the Secretary General' (20 August 1999) UN Doc A/54/260.

—— 'Declaration of Commitment on HIV/AIDS', UNGA Res S-26/2 (20 August 2001) UN Doc A/RES/S-26/2.

—— 'Declaration on Principles of International Law Concerning Friendly Relations and Co-operation among States in accordance with the Charter of the United Nations', UNGA Res 2625 (XXV) (24 October 1970) UN Doc A/8028.

—— 'Declaration on Protection of the Global Climate for Present and Future Generations of Mankind', UNGA Res 43/53 (6 December 1988) UN Doc A/RES/43/53.

—— 'Guiding Principles on Humanitarian Assistance', UNGA Res 46/182 (19 December 1991) UN Doc A/RES/46/182, Annex.

—— 'In Larger Freedom: Toward Development, Security and Human Rights for All, Report of the Secretary-General' (21 March 2005) UN Doc A/59/2005

—— 'Political Declaration on HIV/AIDS', UNGA Res 60/262 (15 June 2006) UN Doc A/RES/60/262.

—— 'Special Session of the General Assembly on HIV/AIDS: Report of the Secretary-General' (16 February 2001) UN Doc A/55/779.

—— 'United Nations Millennium Declaration', UNGA Res 55/2 (18 September 2000) UN Doc A/RES/55/2.

—— 'Vienna Declaration and Programme of Action' (12 July 1993) UN Doc A/CONF.157/23.

—— 'World Summit Outcome', UNGA Res 60/1 (12 September 2005) UN Doc A/RES/60/1.

UNGA Res 2956(XXVII) (12 December 1972).

UNGA Res 43/131 (8 December 1988) UN Doc A/RES/43/131.

UNGA Res 45/100 (14 December 1990) UN Doc A/RES/45/100.

UNGA Res 47/105 (26 April 1993) UN Doc A/RES/47/105.

UNGA Res 48/116 (24 March 1994) UN Doc A/RES/48/116.

UNGA Res 49/169 (24 February 1995) UN Doc A/RES/49/169

UNGA Res 60/1 (24 October 2005) UN Doc A/RES/60/1.

UNGA Res 61/89 (18 December 2006) UN Doc A/RES/61/89.

UNHCR (United Nations High Commissioner for Refugees), 'Agenda for Protection' (26 June 2002) UN Doc AC/AC.96/965/Add.1.

UNHCR, 'Human Security: A Refugee Perspective' (Keynote Speech by Mrs Sadako Ogata, United Nations High Commissioner for Refugees, at the Ministerial Meeting on Human Security Issues of the 'Lysoen Process' Group of Governments, Bergen, Norway, 19 May 1999) <http://www.unhcr.org/admin/ADMIN/3ae68fc00.html> (accessed 25 April 2007).

—— 'Internally Displaced Persons: The Role of the United Nations High Commissioner for Refugees' (20 June 2000) UN Doc EC/50/SC/INF.2.

—— 'International Solidarity and Burden-Sharing in All Its Aspects: National, Regional and International Responsibilities for Refugees' (7 September 1998) UN Doc A/AC.96/904.

—— 'Mechanisms of International Cooperation to Share Responsibilities and Burdens in Mass Influx Situations' (19 February 2001) UN Doc EC/GC/01/7.

—— 'Note on International Protection' (13 September 2001) UN Doc A/AC.96/951.

—— 'Protection Aspects of UNHCR Activities on Behalf of Internally Displaced Persons' (17 August1994) UN Doc EC/SCP/87.

—— *The State of the World's Refugees: A Humanitarian Agenda* (Oxford, Oxford University Press, 1997).

—— *The State of the World's Refugees 2000: Fifty Years of Humanitarian Action* (Oxford, Oxford University Press, 2000).

—— *The State of the World's Refugees 2006: Human Displacement in the New Millennium* (Oxford, Oxford University Press, 2006).

—— *Statistical Yearbook 2001* (UNHCR, Geneva, 2002).

—— 'UNHCR's Operational Experience with Internally Displaced Persons' (1 September 1994) <http://www.unhcr.org/publ/PUBL/3d4f95964.pdf> (accessed 25 April 2007).

—— 'UNHCR's Role with Internally Displaced Persons' (23 April 1993) UN Doc IOM-FOM/33/93.

UNSC (United Nations Security Council), 'The Impact of AIDS on Peace and Security in Africa' (10 January 2000) UN Doc S/PV.4087.

—— 'Note by the President of the Security Council' (31 January 1992) UN Doc S/23500.

—— 'Report of the Secretary-General to the Security Council on the Protection of Civilians in Armed Conflict' (8 September 1999) UN Doc S/1999/957.

—— 'Statement by the President of the Security Council' (4 September 2001) UN Doc S/PRST/2001/21.

UNSC Res 134 (1 April 1960) UN Doc S/4300.

UNSC Res 181 (7 August 1963) UN Doc S/5386.

UNSC Res 182 (4 December 1963) UN Doc S/5471.

UNSC Res 688 (5 April 1991) UN Doc S/RES/688.

UNSC Res 794 (3 December 1992) UN Doc S/RES/794.
UNSC Res 1067 (26 July 1996) UN Doc S/RES/1067.
UNSC Res 1078 (9 November 1996) UN Doc S/RES/1078.
UNSC Res 1080 (15 November 1996) UN Doc S/RES/1080.
UNSC Res 1296 (19 April 2000) UN Doc S/RES/1296.
UNSC Res 1308 (17 July 2000) UN Doc S/RES/1308.
UN SC Res 1314 (11 August 2000) UN Doc S/RES/1314.
UNSC Res 1318 (7 September 2000) UN Doc S/RES/1318.
UNSC Res 1341 (22 February 2001) UN Doc S/RES/1341.
UNSC Res 1357 (21 June 2001) UN Doc S/RES/1357.
UNSC Res 1373 (28 September 2001) UN Doc S/RES/1373.
UNSC Res 1410 (17 May 2002) UN Doc S/RES/1410.
UNSC Res 1460 (30 January 2003) UN Doc S/RES/1460.
UNSC Res 1484 (19 May 2003) UN Doc S/RES/1484.
UNSC Res 1528 (27 February 2004) UN Doc S/RES/1528.
UNSC Res 1539 (22 April 2004) UN Doc S/RES/1539.
UNSC Res 1542 (30 April 2004) UN Doc S/RES/1542.
UNSC Res 1556 (30 June 2004) UN Doc S/RES/1556.
UNSC Res 1564 (18 September 2004) UN Doc S/RES/1564.
UNSC Res 1593 (31 March 2005) UN Doc S/RES/1593.
UNSC Res 1679 (16 May 2006) UN Doc S/RES/1679.

INTERNATIONAL INSTRUMENTS

Agreement Governing the Activities of States on the Moon and Other Celestial Bodies (adopted 5 December 1979, entered into force 11 July 1984) 1363 UNTS 3.
American Convention on Human Rights (22 November 1969) OASTS No 36.
American Declaration of the Rights and Duties of Man, OAS Res XXX adopted by the Ninth International Conference of American States (1948), reprinted in Basic Documents Pertaining to Human Rights in the Inter-American System, OEA/Ser L V/II.82 Doc 6 Rev 1 at 17 (1992).
Cartagena Declaration on Refugees (22 November 1984) Annual Report of the Inter-American Commission on Human Rights, OAS Doc OEA/Ser.L/V/II.66/doc.10, Rev 1 at 190.
Charter of the Organization of American States, (signed 30 April 1948, entered into force 13 December 1951) OASTS No 1-C, 61; 119 UNTS 48 (as amended).
Code of Conduct of Central American States on the Transfer of Arms, Ammunition, Explosives and Other Related Materiel (adopted and in force 2 December 2005), 'Working Paper Submitted by Nicaragua' (30 June 2006) UN Doc A/CONF.192/2006/RC/WP.6.
Convention Against Torture and Other Cruel, Inhuman or Degrading Treatment or Punishment (adopted 10 December 1984, entered into force 26 June 1987) 1465 UNTS 85.
Convention Governing the Specific Aspects of Refugee Problems in Africa (adopted 10 September 1969, entered into force 20 June 1974) 1001 UNTS 45.
Convention on Biological Diversity (adopted 5 June 1992, entered into force 29 December 1993) 1760 UNTS 79.

Convention on Prohibitions or Restrictions on the Use of Certain Conventional Weapons Which May Be Deemed to Be Excessively Injurious or to Have Indiscriminate Effects (adopted 10 October 1980, entered into force 2 December 1983) 1342 UNTS 137.

Convention on the Prevention and Punishment of Genocide (opened for signature 9 December 1948, entered into force 12 January 1951) 78 UNTS 277.

Convention on the Prohibition of the Use, Stockpiling, Production and Transfer of Anti-personnel Mines and on Their Destruction (opened for signature 18 September 1997, entered into force 1 March 1999) 2056 UNTS 211.

Convention on the Rights of the Child, (adopted 20 November 1989, entered into force 2 September 1990), 1577 UNTS 3.

Convention Relating to the Status of Refugees (adopted 28 July 1951, entered into force 22 April 1954) 189 UNTS 150.

Constitution of the World Health Organization (adopted 22 July 1946, entered into force 7 April 1948) 14 UNTS 185.

Declaration of the United Nations Conference on the Human Environment, Report of the United Nations Conference on the Human Environment, Stockholm, 5–16 June 1972 (UN publication, Sales No E.73.II.A.14 and corrigendum), ch I.

ECOWAS Convention on Small Arms and Light Weapons, Their Ammunition and Other Related Materials (adopted 14 June 2006) <http://www.iansa.org/regions/wafrica/documents/convention-cedeao-english.pdf> (accessed 25 April 2007).

European Convention for the Protection of Human Rights and Fundamental Freedoms (4 November 1950) ETS No 5 (as amended).

Geneva Convention for the Amelioration of the Condition of the Wounded and Sick in Armed Forces in the Field (First Geneva Convention) (signed 12 August 1949, entered into force 21 October 1950) 75 UNTS 31.

Geneva Convention for the Amelioration of the Condition of Wounded, Sick and Shipwrecked Members of Armed Forces at Sea (Second Geneva Convention) (signed 12 August 1949, entered into force 21 October 1950) 75 UNTS 85.

Geneva Convention Relative to the Treatment of Prisoners of War (Third Geneva Convention) (signed 12 August 1949, entered into force 21 October 1950) 75 UNTS 135.

Geneva Convention Relative to the Protection of Civilian Persons in Time of War (Fourth Geneva Convention) (signed 12 August 1949, entered into force 21 October 1950) 75 UNTS 287.

Inter-American Convention Against the Illicit Manufacturing of and Trafficking in Firearms, Ammunition, Explosives, and Other Related Materials (adopted 14 November 1997, entered into force 1 July 1998) OAS 24th Special Sess, AG/doc.7 (XXIV-E/97), rev.1.

International Covenant on Civil and Political Rights (adopted 16 December 1966, entered into force 23 March 1976) 999 UNTS 171.

International Covenant on Economic, Social and Cultural Rights (adopted 16 December 1966, entered into force 3 January 1976) 993 UNTS 3.

International Health Regulations (1969), 3rd edn (Geneva, WHO, 1983).

International Instrument to Enable States to Identify and Trace, in a Timely and Reliable Manner, Illicit Small Arms and Light Weapons, UNGA Res 60/81 (8 December 2005) UN Doc A/RES/60/81.

Nairobi Protocol for the Prevention, Control and Reduction of Small Arms and Light Weapons in the Great Lakes Region and the Horn of Africa (adopted 21 April 2004) <http://www.recsasec.org/pdf/Nairobi%20Protocol.pdf> (accessed 25 April 2007).

Optional Protocol to the Convention on the Elimination of All Forms of Discrimination against Women (opened for signature 6 October 1999, entered into force 22 December 2000) 2131 UNTS 83.

Optional Protocol to the Convention on the Rights of the Child on the Involvement of Children in Armed Conflicts (opened for signature 25 May 2000, entered into force 12 February 2002) UNGA Res 54/263 (16 March 2001), UN Doc A/RES/54/263.

Optional Protocol to the International Covenant on Civil and Political Rights (opened for signature 16 December 1966, entered into force 23 March 1976) 999 UNTS 171.

Protocol Additional to the Geneva Conventions of August 12, 1949, and relating to the Protection of Victims of International Armed Conflicts (Protocol I) (adopted 8 June 1977, entered into force 7 December 1978) 1125 UNTS 3.

Protocol Additional to the Geneva Conventions of August 12, 1949, and relating to the Protection of Victims of Non-International Armed Conflicts (Protocol II) (adopted 8 June 1977, entered into force 7 December 1978) 1125 UNTS 609.

Protocol against the Illicit Manufacturing of and Trafficking in Firearms, Their Parts and Components and Ammunition, supplementing the United Nations Convention against Transnational Organized Crime (adopted 31 May 2001, entered into force 3 July 2005) UN Doc A/55/383/Add.2.

Protocol on Prohibitions or Restrictions on the Use of Mines, Booby-Traps and Other Devices (adopted 10 October 1980, amended 3 May 1996, entered into force 3 December 1998) UN Doc CCW-CONF.I-16 (Part I), Annex B (1996).

Protocol on the Control of Firearms, Ammunition and Other Related Materials (adopted 2001, entered into force 2004) <http://www.sadc.int/english/documents/legal/protocols/firearms.php> (accessed 25 April 2007).

Protocol Relating to the Status of Refugees (adopted 31 January 1967, entered into force 4 October 1967) 606 UNTS 267.

Rio Declaration on Environment and Development, Report of the United Nations Conference on Environment and Development, Rio de Janeiro, 3–14 June 1992, vol I, Resolutions Adopted by the Conference (UN publication, Sales No E.93.I.8 and corrigendum), Resolution 1, Annex I.

Rome Statute of the International Criminal Court (opened for signature 17 July 1998, entered into force 1 July 2002) 2187 UNTS 3.

Statute of the Office of the United Nations High Commissioner for Refugees, UNGA Res 428(V) (14 December 1950), Annex.

Statutes of the International Committee of the Red Cross (8 May 2003) <http://www.icrc.org/Web/Eng/siteeng0.nsf/html/icrc-statutes-080503> (accessed 29 March 2007).

Statutes of the International Red Cross and Red Crescent Movement (1986, as amended 1995) <http://www.icrc.org/Web/eng/siteeng0.nsf/htmlall/ statutes-movement-220506/$File/Mvt-Statutes-ENGLISH.pdf> (accessed 29 March 2007).

UN Convention against Transnational Organized Crime (adopted 15 November 2000, entered into force 29 September 2003) UN Doc A/55/25.

UN Convention on the Law of the Sea (opened for signature 10 December 1982, entered into force 16 November 1994) 1833 UNTS 3.

UN Framework Convention on Climate Change (adopted 9 May 1992, entered into force 21 March 1994) 1771 UNTS 107.

Universal Declaration of Human Rights (adopted 10 December 1948) UN GA Res 217A (III), UN Doc A/810.

Vienna Convention for the Protection of the Ozone Layer (adopted 22 March 1985, entered into force 22 September 1988) 1513 UNTS 293.

WHO Framework Convention on Tobacco Control (adopted 21 May 2003, entered into force 27 February 2005) 2302 UNTS 166.

JURISPRUDENCE

Alejandre v Cuba, American Commission on Human Rights Report No 86/99, OEA/Ser.L/V/II.106 Doc 3 (1999).

Application of the Convention on the Prevention and Punishment of the Crime of Genocide (Bosnia and Herzegovina v Serbia and Montenegro), Judgment of 26 February 2007.

Armed Activities on the Territory of the Congo (Democratic Republic of the Congo v Uganda), Judgment of 19 December 2005.

Banković et al v Belgium et al, Admissibility Decision, 12 December 2001 (Application No 52207/99).

Barcelona Traction, Light and Power Company, Limited, Second Phase, [1970] ICJ Rep 3.

Corfu Channel, Merits [1949] ICJ Rep 4.

East Timor (Portugal v Australia), [1995] ICJ Rep 90.

Gabcíkovo-Nagymaros Project (Hungary /Slovakia), [1997] ICJ Rep 7.

Lac Lanoux Arbitration (Spain v France) (1957) 12 RIAA 281.

Legal Consequences of the Construction of a Wall in the Occupied Palestinian Territory (Advisory Opinion), Advisory Opinion of 9 July 2004.

Legality of the Threat or Use of Nuclear Weapons [1996] ICJ Rep 226.

Legality of the Use of Force (Yugoslavia v Belgium), Request for the Indication of Provisional Measures, Verbatim Record, CR 99/15, 10 May 1999.

Loizidou v Turkey (Preliminary Objections), Series A No 310 (1995).

Lopez Burgos v Uruguay (29 July 1981) UN Doc CCPR/C/13/D/52/1979.

Military and Paramilitary Activities in and against Nicaragua (Nicaragua v United States of America), Merits [1986] ICJ Rep 14.

Nationality Decrees in Tunis and Morocco (1923) PCIJ Ser B, No 4.

Öcalan v Turkey, Judgment, 12 May 2005 (Application No 46221/99).

Prosecutor v Tadić (Interlocutory Appeal) ICTY-94-1 (2 October 1995).

Prosecutor v Tadić (Opinion and Judgment) ICTY-94-1 (7 May 1997).

South West Africa, Second Phase [1966] ICJ Rep 6.

Trail Smelter Case (United States v Canada) (1941) 3 RIAA 1905.

Index